THE LONG LIFE

THE LONG LIFE

HELEN SMALL

OXFORD
UNIVERSITY PRESS

OXFORD
UNIVERSITY PRESS

Great Clarendon Street, Oxford OX2 6DP

Oxford University Press is a department of the University of Oxford.
It furthers the University's objective of excellence in research, scholarship,
and education by publishing worldwide in

Oxford New York

Auckland Cape Town Dar es Salaam Hong Kong Karachi
Kuala Lumpur Madrid Melbourne Mexico City Nairobi
New Delhi Shanghai Taipei Toronto

With offices in

Argentina Austria Brazil Chile Czech Republic France Greece
Guatemala Hungary Italy Japan Poland Portugal Singapore
South Korea Switzerland Thailand Turkey Ukraine Vietnam

Oxford is a registered trade mark of Oxford University Press
in the UK and in certain other countries

Published in the United States
by Oxford University Press Inc., New York

British Library Cataloguing in Publication Data

Data available

Library of Congress Cataloging in Publication Data

Data available

Typeset by Laserwords Private Limited, Chennai, India
Printed in Great Britain
on acid-free paper by
Biddles Ltd., King's Lynn, Norfolk

ISBN 978-0-19-922993-2

1 3 5 7 9 10 8 6 4 2

In memory of Sheila Stern

Preface

The Long Life is an examination of old age in Western philosophy and literature. It explores the implications for old age of certain ways of thinking about what it is to be a person, to have a life, to have (or lead) a *good* life, to be part of a just society. It also investigates the largely hidden role that ideas about old age have played in thinking on these questions and others to which its relevance is less immediately obvious—including thinking about thinking itself.

Given such a broad remit, it is necessary to say what the book is not. Despite the impression that may be given by ordering the chapters quasi-chronologically from Plato to contemporary evolutionary theory, and (more circuitously) Shakespeare to contemporary fiction, *The Long Life* is not a history of philosophical or literary thinking about old age. It addresses a series of distinct questions about old age's place within different kinds of thinking about lives and persons. Each of the chapters begins from a philosophical perspective—Platonic epistemology, Aristotelian and neo-Aristotelian virtue ethics, narrative theories of lives, rational arguments about life-planning and distributive justice, Parfit's 'Reductionist View' of persons, one (far from standard) account of metaphysics, and recent scientific theories of evolved senescence—then extends or challenges the arguments through a consideration of literary texts (*Death in Venice, King Lear, Le Père Goriot, The Old Curiosity Shop, Endgame*, poems by Philip Larkin and Stevie Smith, more recent novels by Saul Bellow, Philip Roth, J. M. Coetzee, Margaret Drabble, Michael Ignatieff). I have not attempted to explain what happened to the Platonic view of old age after Plato, or how some literary representations of old age (Shakespeare's and Mann's particularly) have struck deeper roots than others in Western culture.

The book I initially envisaged would have made reference to a much wider range of literary texts, but it gradually became apparent that detailed exploration of ideas necessitated focusing on a small group of (in the main) well-known works. I have tried to avoid the dictionary-of-quotations prose that writing about old age often attracts: a style that seeks to demonstrate the richness of the subject, and the pervasiveness of some intuitions and dispositions towards it, by marshalling as many voices as possible. The casualty of that decision is that some philosophical texts and a great many more novels, plays, and poems have not found room here. Montaigne and Bacon and Schopenhauer are not treated in any detail; neither are Sophocles, Yeats, Woolf, Dylan Thomas, or (to mention just one contemporary writer) Jane Smiley. A more extensive focus on poetic writing and its complexities of prosody and voice would have produced a better literary book, but it would also, I think, have produced a book less accessible to readers whose interest in the subject lies beyond literary criticism—including, perhaps, most philosophers.

Other writers may want to take the questions raised here into theology and the history of religion, fields I have treated (somewhat artificially) as separate from philosophy. Chapter 5's discussion of metaphysics may suggest one point of departure. I hope the book will also attract those whose interest in old age is more directly socio-political. *The Long Life* was written against a background of pressing social and political concern about 'the greying of Western societies'. Some of what I say, especially in the Introduction and Chapters 4 and 7, has a clear connection to public policy, but I have deliberately kept the arguments for the most part general. Of course, writing a book about longevity may in and of itself be seen as an attempt to give old age more importance in our sociological thinking. That was not, or not quite, my intention. Much recent sociology and political writing about the 'greying of society' asks old age to do more than its fair share of the explanatory work about our collective prospects. How we respond as societies to the growing numbers of people living to be old is now regularly said to be key to the future economic prosperity of developed and developing nations and their capacity to deliver social justice. Like others before me, I see this as a misplacing of the problem. Rather than isolate the old as the difficulty, we need to think in terms of (for example) the deeper causes of a gross disparity in national life expectancies around the world; rather than thinking about the 'burden of retirees', we should think more broadly about the wider nature and purpose of work.

It is conventional if not quite mandatory for those who write about old age to state their own age. I am doubtful of the value of doing so if it is taken as establishing one's right to talk about the subject. A basic assumption of this book is that we all of us have an interest in old age, and that the intensity of our interest is not just, and not simply, related to how long we have lived. But, given that much of what I say here has to do with questions of subjectivity, of self-interest, or what it means to be a person, and what it means to live through time, I will follow the convention and disclose that I wrote *The Long Life* between the ages of 34 and 42.

I am indebted to many friends and colleagues, but most of all to the four people who read the complete manuscript and commented in detail (more than once): Stefan Collini, John Kerrigan, Bruce Robbins, and Peter Wright. Also to George Levine, Teresa Mangum, and one anonymous reader for the press. They have saved me from errors, and often prompted me to rethink. My undisclosed philosophical reader was especially helpful. To John Kerrigan I owe a particular debt for encouraging my interest in the topic at the very beginning. I am also grateful to Malcolm Schofield for his exacting attention to the Plato and Aristotle sections; to Amélie Rorty, who read the Aristotle section and helped me to see several of the questions in the book more clearly; also to Jeffrey Wainwright who was an acute respondent on Aristotle and *Lear*. Michael R. Rose, George C. Williams, and Ian Collins lent their much-needed scientific expertise to Chapter 8. Gillian Beer, Kate Flint, Hermione Lee, and Sally Shuttleworth gave *The Long Life* intellectual and practical support from the start. Mary Poovey pressed me to be more explicit about history, and gave me a sharper eye for trans-Atlantic differences in potential readership. Ruth Morse generously allowed me the use of her apartment in Paris for three Septembers and an April, and with it the quiet needed to bring the book to completion. Tim and Immy Gardam gave indispensable support, and much happiness, in the later stages of writing and revision.

My greatest debt is to the Leverhulme Trust for awarding me a Leverhulme Major Research Fellowship (2001–4). Without the complete break from teaching and administration it provided I could not have attempted a book of this scope. I spent much of my Leverhulme tenure as a Visiting Scholar at New York University. My thanks go to John Guillory, and to Cathy Monseur, Daniel Javitch, Nigel Smith, Anne Humphreys, Gerhard Joseph, Carolyn Williams, Nancy Henry, David Sider, Patricia Okoh-Esene, Lisa Vogel, and Nyieta Charlot for their hospitality and assistance during my time in New York. I am also grateful to the University of Oxford (Faculty of English) and Pembroke College, Oxford, for grants allowing me to travel between Britain and the United States. Chapters of *The Long Life* benefited from being tested on audiences at the universities of Chicago, Exeter, Kent, Manchester Metropolitan, Oxford, MIT (Boston, Calif.), Pennsylvania (Philadelphia), and Tufts (Medford, Mass.), and at the Annual Conferences of the Modern Languages Association of America 2001 and 2003. I am grateful to the following people for their invitations, questions, and suggestions: Étienne Balibar, Wilfred Beckerman, Dinah Birch, the late Wayne Booth, Colin Bundy, John Carey, Karen Chase, Rita Copeland, Margreta de Grazia, Rod Edmond, Elizabeth Falaize, Tim Farrant, John Fyler, Reginia Gagnier, Simon Gaunt, Philip Gibbon, Heather Glen, Claire Harman, Mary Jacobus, Adrian Johns, Jeri Johnson, Mark Kilfoyle, Michael Levenson, Teresa Mangum, Sharon Marcus, Lisa Niles, Deborah Epstein Nord, Angelique Richardson, Harriet Ritvo, Modhumita Roy, Hilary Schor, Nick Shrimpton, Peter Stallybrass, Robert Stevens, Barry Supple, Mark Treharne, David Wallace, William C. Wimsatt, Sarah White, Alison Winter, Kathleen Woodward, and Blair Worden. April Warman was an exemplary research assistant in the late stages, photocopying research materials for the final chapter, proofreading the final draft, and putting together the bibliography. Stephen Wall kindly cast an exacting eye over the final draft, and pointed out several infelicities of expression. Not least, I have been wonderfully lucky in my editor, Andrew McNeillie, who has been encouraging and goading in just the right measure.

Sheila Stern gave me, on many occasions, warm hospitality, absorbing conversation, and the perfect home for writing. She was one of my best practical examples of how to live a long life well. Her death, while this book was in the final stages of revision, turns what would have been a dedication into a gesture of love and thanks *in memoriam*. This is also the place to record, again, my love and gratitude for my parents. Both were older than the parents of most of my contemporaries (my father was 56 when I was born, my mother twenty years his junior). They died well before I began work on this book, but they helped to shape my interest in the subject from early on.

An earlier version of Chapter 5 (the Adorno and Dickens sections only) appeared as 'The Bounded Life: Adorno, Dickens, and Metaphysics', in

Victorian Literature and Culture 32/2 (2004), 547–63. The paragraphs on late style, from the same chapter, appear in abbreviated and somewhat modified guise in 'Tennyson and Late Style', *Tennyson Research Bulletin* 8/4 (2005), 226–50. The rest of this book is published here for the first time.

'The Old Fools' is reprinted by kind permission of Faber and Faber (UK) and Farrar, Straus, and Giroux, New York (USA). 'Exeat' is reprinted by kind permission of Hamish MacGibbon (UK) and New Directions (USA).

Contents

Introduction

The old are expected to be philosophical. This is commonly little more than a wish that a life nearing the end of its possible biological span should be reconciled to the proximity and inevitability of death—a wish that has its famous refuseniks ('Do not go gentle', 'I stood in rage'[1]). But having a philosophy of death, or feeling the desirability of such a philosophy in others, is not the same thing as having a philosophy of old age. When Socrates claimed that it was the task of philosophy to teach us how to die, he gave it, one writer has suggested, an 'easier' remit than teaching us what it means to be old.[2] The questions raised by death are familiar, readily framed if not readily answered: is death just the ceasing of biological functions? (if so, what *counts* as the ceasing of biological functions?) what does it mean for our experience of life that we know it to be lived towards death? is there a sphere of transcendence beyond our being in the here and now? Old age offers less well-established terrain: isn't it just more of the same? 'what we've been doing all along only with more decades added on'.[3]

There have, of course, been philosophers of old age. Plato, Aristotle, Cicero, Montaigne, Bacon, Beauvoir are the names most often thought of. But, in the main, philosophy—leaving aside medical ethics, for the moment—has been far more interested in 'mortal questions'.[4] Living to be old has historically been seen as exceptional, the questions it raises supererogatory to the main arguments to be had about lives, and goods, and values. In keeping with that perception, the bibliography of philosophical writing about old age is weighted far more heavily towards essays, letters, paragraphs, aphorisms, than towards books. And yet this literature might still be expected to have had greater influence than it has had on how interested people (we are all, in theory, interested) have thought about age and ageing. Beauvoir's *La Vieillesse* (1970) is the exemplary as well as extreme case.[5] Its view of old age as a major constraint on the freedom of the subject marked an important redirection of her thinking, in *Le*

Deuxième Sexe (1949), about the extent to which human beings can confer meaning on their own lives. But references to *La Vieillesse* in subsequent writing about old age have been far fewer than one would expect.[6] When her name does appear, Beauvoir is characteristically treated as a political agitator on behalf of the old (a problematic one, given her emphasis on decline) and as a memoirist and social commentator on old age, but not as a philosopher, with a specific conception of what a life is, of how lives accrue and sustain meaning, and of philosophy's relationship to politics.[7]

This book is an attempt to show what might be required if we are to become more seriously philosophical about old age. My main premise is that, when we think about old age, our thinking rests on larger, but usually tacit, assumptions about what a life is, what a person is, what a *good* life is, what social justice is, and much else besides. Though there have been important philosophies of old age, for the most part philosophy has treated the last phase of life as of minor importance. If we want to think deeply about old age, we therefore, I argue, do better to look to broader claims about lives and persons and values, and even about thinking itself (what it is, what it is for, when in our lives we do it best). In other words, while this is a book about thinking *about* old age, it is as fundamentally a book about thinking *with* old age.

One difficulty in the way of doing this well, at once an obstacle and a potential stimulus, is that what philosophers and non-philosophers have had to say about old age has, in essence, changed very little since classical antiquity. Thinking about old age has always tended towards extremes of optimism and pessimism, often in close conjunction. For every conventional negative association of 'old age' there is an equally recognizable counter-association: rage/serenity; nostalgia/detachment; folly/wisdom; fear/courage; loss of sexual powers and/or opportunities/liberation from sex; loss of the capacity or right to labour/release from a long life of labour. To grow old may be, in Montaigne's phrase, a 'privilege' and 'special favour'; it may also be (Montaigne again), a 'withering' and 'languishing'.[8] If we are fortunate, personally, socially, culturally, we will have cause to value it for bringing us wider experiences (more rewarding leisure, new friendships and family relationships); we may believe, and others may even confirm, that it has brought us greater wisdom; on the other hand, it may seem to erode much or all that has defined a good life—the 'alacrity', as Flaubert called it,[9] our health, the social and professional roles that in the past have brought respect and authority, the friendships and family relationships that are dependent upon the health and longevity of others as well as ourselves.

One of the questions that the philosophy and literature of old age therefore require us to ask is how far conventional attitudes are rooted in reality, how far in prejudice and fear. Their relative weighting has been responsive to historical pressure and to acts of individual will, but the terms themselves, and the structures of expectation they express, can seem exceptionally *un*responsive. They are not definitions of old age, but they are stubborn attendants on it. They have the irritant persistence of banalities, the plausibility as well as the reductiveness of cliché. The negatives have been more often in the ascendancy than the positives, and most difficult to budge when they have involved the perception of bodily and mental decline. They offend most recent writers about ageing, especially when they start to look like biological essentialism,[10] but, given their historical and psychological persistence, and the degree to which many of them are subjects of common observation and experience, they are not dismissible as mere stereotypes.

'Old age' is defined here as the later years of a long life, when there is an inevitable and irreversible deterioration in the organism as a consequence of its age. The traditional and still common locution is 'past one's prime'. I assume familiarity with the fact that, in common usage, 'old' is a highly flexible term—that it has been applied at various historical periods and in various contexts across the age range from early adulthood to the furthest limit, real and imagined, of the human lifespan. That flexibility is in many respects unhelpful: 'old' embraces too large a portion of the human lifespan, and is semantically overweighted towards 'old old age'. Indeed, 'age' is commonly synonymous with 'old age'.[11] Refinements of terminology, such as 'old old age', 'late age', 'late life', and, in earlier periods, 'green old age', are sometimes resorted to, but they betray the basic poverty of our vocabulary here, and they are often impediments rather than aids to social and political reform. Our sense of who is old to a degree shifts back as we ourselves age: a 76-year-old may look old to a 56-year-old, but relatively young to a 96-year-old. And our relation to our own age is particularly complex. It is often described as bifurcated: unless life has severely strained a person's emotional or physical resources, most people report that they feel younger than they 'actually are'. 'Multiply split or layered' would be more accurate than 'complex'. The age we feel is not necessarily the same as our calendrical age, nor is it the same as how we are perceived, or how we register ourselves being perceived by others.

But to say that our perceptions of age are to a degree age-dependent, to a degree subjective, and to a degree culturally conditioned, is not to say that they are only those things. Much of what makes old age interesting and problematic as a subject for philosophy and literature stems from the fact that it is a necessity, and that—very roughly speaking—we recognize age-related deterioration when we see it, both in others and in ourselves. Unless we die first, it is in the nature of time and our condition as biological creatures that we shall grow old. Something can be done to slow or conceal the signs of ageing, and politically we can, and should, contest the ill effects of being labelled 'old' in advance of any serious decline in capacity, but the consequences of ageing chromosomes, and the 'wear and tear' of being alive, are ineluctable.[12] This is why, for Aristotle, old age was separately a subject for ethics and for physics: the behaviour and treatment of the old were ethical problems but ageing itself was a non-ethical question of the human mechanism—as he put it in the *Nicomachean Ethics*, 'an act neither voluntary nor involuntary' (*EN* 1135b1). And yet, old age is also not simply a necessity. Not everyone lives to be old, and not everyone who does so experiences the physical or social effects of ageing in the same ways or to the same degree. In that sense, we may view old age as a contingency, though of a rather impure sort. It is not just a matter of circumstances coming to the agent from outside him or herself; nor is it just a matter of subjectivity, psychology, and feelings. It involves both, but is, strictly, neither.

The questions prompted by old age's oddly indeterminate status in our lives (at once inevitable, and not at all inevitable) and by the intuitive character of many of our responses to it, are fundamental to how we think about the meaning and value of lives generally, but in recent writing about ageing they are often brushed aside in favour of demonstrating the perniciousness of ageism. I take that perniciousness as read, and it is not my subject. The problems I am interested in are more fundamental: they have to do with what we think is the relation between a long life and a good life; with what we think it means to be a person; with whether and for how long identity persists; and with how our sense of all these things inheres in our conceptual structures for defining goods and values and justice and knowledge. The definition of 'old age' given above is, it should be clear, non-moral, but it raises a number of questions for moral philosophy: does length of life have implications for the formal or psychological integrity of a life? does it alter the capacity for virtue? does it alter the value of a life? if so, to and for whom, and under what circumstances? It also raises questions for other kinds of philosophy: does old age have any implications for rational, as opposed to moral, thinking about lives? are thinking about metaphysics and thinking about old age at all connected in the history of philosophy and/or literature, and if so why? And what happens when questions like these run up against scepticism about the prior assumptions they involve: about, for example, the validity of the notion of life stages, about the integrity of personhood, about comparability between or within lives, and about metaphysics itself?

Given the ongoing need to challenge negatively prejudicial perceptions of old age, some may think it an unhelpful, even retrograde move to make philosophy and literature the focus of this book. Neither philosophy nor literature is especially rich in positive responses to age. Even in very recent years, representations of old age in fiction, drama, and poetry have been symptomatic of a culture (in Kathleen Woodward's phrase) 'profoundly ambivalent, and primarily negative, about old age'.[13] It is noticeable how often black comedy has been the mode of choice, at once mocking and confirming long-standing prejudices. Deborah Moggach's *These Foolish Things* (2004), imagining the outsourcing of care of the British aged to Bangalore, participates in a long tradition of comedy and satire running back from Kingsley Amis's *Ending Up* (1974) with its septuagenarian commune, 'Tupenny Hapenny Cottage', and Muriel Spark's *Memento Mori* (1959), in which Death makes a civil phone call to his elderly victims shortly before he strikes ('Remember, you must die'), to the drama and verse satires and epigrams of classical antiquity.[14]

Literature at least has a prominent and ongoing tradition of engagement with old age. Unlike much of the writing that has been re-examined, over many decades now, with a focus on the implicit representation of gender or race or class, the literary works on old age discussed in this book are mainly and explicitly about being or growing old. It should not, in theory, be necessary to bring the subject out from the shadows. It is therefore the more surprising that so few critics have read these works *for* what they have to say about old age. Remarkably little of the vast literature on *King Lear*, for example, says much or anything about old age. Critics have tended to think of that play, and most of the works discussed in this book, as being about more general subjects (the human condition, man's relation with nature) or more specific ones (anger, love, kingship, English history). Similarly, they have often, and not without justification, seen literary depictions of old age as metaphors or symbols for other things: the status of art, the promise or otherwise of immortality (late Yeats, raging against the impermanence of the flesh and seeking the eternity of art; not-quite-so-late T. S. Eliot, rejecting the supposed 'wisdom of age' in favour of the mystic involutions of time in Christian theology[15]). Old age in literature is rarely if ever only about itself—but as far as criticism has been concerned, it has oddly rarely been much about itself at all.

In philosophy, the case is different. The tradition of writing about old age, though distinguished, is not as rich—in recent centuries nowhere near so. Direct and sustained consideration of old age has been unusual even in those philosophical contexts where one might expect to find it: arguments about lives, persons, morals, reasons, and (less to be expected) metaphysics. It flickers in and out of these debates, occasionally recognized as a significant contingency, but far more often treated as marginal, if treated at all. This apparent dearth of interest in old age is especially striking, once remarked, in texts that are principally about temporality. Take, for example, Heidegger's *Being and Time*. Although the subject of *Being and Time* is the relationship between consciousness and temporality, and although it contains extensive discussion of being's 'horizon of temporality', of death as a limit of being, of existential finitude, it makes not a single reference to age or ageing. In one sense, this should not be surprising: the question of ontology is logically prior to that of ageing, and, for Heidegger, one assumes, age could not be introduced without an unwelcome taint of psychology. Even so, the unstated and unexplained exclusion of human temporality is a problem with the Heideggerian philosophical model.[16] We do not simply persist in time: we age, and our perception of being-towards-death is situated and quantified and scrutinized as well as psychologized in the language of ageing (which is not to say that this is *all* the language of ageing does).[17]

In saying this, I am not seeking to 'expose' philosophy's 'neglect' of old age, or to reprimand philosophers, individually or collectively, for time-of-life bias. There seem to me good reasons why academic philosophy has not been more attentive to old age. Many branches of philosophy have to assume a normative view of persons, and the exceptionalism, until the twentieth century, of living long allows old age, even now, to be treated as non-normative. An additional, more speculative reason has to do with the historically recent emergence of specialist disciplines for the study of old age. Geriatric medicine and gerontology have, since the late nineteenth century and the late 1940s respectively, claimed an expertise in the subject that has helped to push philosophy away from the forefront of debate. Writing within both these disciplines tends to relegate philosophy to history, its insights assumed to have been incorporated into and superseded by science.[18] That relegation is confirmed by most cultural and social histories of old age, where philosophy typically features only in its classical and early modern guises, with Bacon as a late transitional figure to modern science, and Beauvoir the sole post-Enlightenment representative.[19] It is more surprisingly the case also in the relatively new and self-consciously interdisciplinary fields of 'age studies' (the study of ageing across the life course)[20] and 'critical gerontology' (that strand within gerontology which has especially advocated stronger ties to the humanities).[21]

But if the philosophical tradition of reflection about old age has been less copious than one might have expected, it has, as I have already remarked, been fairly consistent in its presentation of old age. From the very beginnings of philosophy, old age has been seen as cause for special optimism and for particular pessimism (often for both). The most extended exposition of those two extremes of response to late life, and therefore in many ways the best illustration of it, is be found in the contrast between Cicero's *De Senectute* and Beauvoir's *La Vieillesse*. As exemplary statements (much quoted by other writers) of why we should, and why we should not, wish to grow old they deserve closer attention here.

De Senectute is the most famous attempt by a philosopher to tell us why we should want to grow old. This short essay on old age, one of several works written in Cicero's early sixties in his search for consolation after the death of his daughter Tullia, is stoicism in its most invigorating guise. It presents reasons (many have thought them to be the best reasons we have) to reject the view that old age is an evil, and to welcome late life as the zenith of a person's capacities.

De Senectute takes the form of a conversation between the 84-year-old Cato the Elder and two much younger men, 35-year-old Scipio Aemilianus and his friend Gaius Laelius, whom Cato seeks to persuade of the virtues and pleasures of age. (Like most philosophers of classical antiquity, Cicero addresses himself exclusively to educated free men.) 'I regard nature as the best guide', Cato says early on: 'I follow and obey her as a divine being. Now since she has planned all the earlier divisions of our lives excellently, she is not likely to make a bad playwright's mistake of skimping the last act. And a last act was inevitable.'[22] In the sentence which follows, and which has become almost proverbial, he takes another classic metaphor, in which the virtuous life is likened to the flourishing of a plant, and draws it on to its 'natural' conclusion. We are like plants which grow and flourish—and which must in time also ripen, wither and fall. 'There had to be a time of withering, of readiness to fall, like the ripeness which comes to the fruits of the trees and of the earth' (215). And again: 'death comes […] to old people when the time is ripe' (241). *De Senectute*'s quarrel is not with nature, then, but with the unthinking prejudice that has mistaken the failings of individuals for definitive characteristics of old age. Cato freely admits that he has known many embittered old men. They lost the taste or the ability for pleasure, and without pleasure life was not life. They complained of neglect, they were bad tempered and churlish. But this was not the inevitable consequence of their years: 'the trouble [was] due to character, not age' (216). There are no vices associated with old age, Cato argues, which cannot also be found among the young, and none (apparently) which cannot be extirpated by a sound early training in the virtues. We lay the foundations for our own old age: if we live badly in our youth and prime we may come to be morally reprehensible and physically dependent in late life; but if we live well early on, we can look forward to an active old age, with all the external and internal goods longevity entails: authority, honour, wisdom, serenity.

Cato acknowledges four common reasons why most men do not anticipate old age with enthusiasm: 'it takes us away from active work', 'it weakens the body', 'it deprives us of practically all physical pleasures', and 'it is not far from death' (219). He counters each in turn. We misunderstand activity if we define it in terms of the physical capacities of the young. One might as well say that 'the pilot has nothing to do with sailing a ship because he leaves others to climb the masts and run along the gangways and work the pumps' (220). Our power to act nobly and our right to authority increase rather than diminish with age, because '[g]reat deeds […] are the products of thought, and character, and judgement', all of which grow stronger with experience (220), and (this, clearly, is the philosopher's prejudice speaking) we should all prefer to be Pythagoras than Milo, revered more for powers of mind than of body (226). Cato marshals numerous examples of men who have retained their mental strength into late life, Democritus, Plato, and Zeno most prominent among the philosophers. He also cites others who have retained undiminished physical vigour—the elderly farmers of his Sabine country, still out in the fields sowing and reaping (222).

Cato is reluctant to concede any necessary diminution of physical strength in late life, holding that any failure of the body in old age is a consequence of 'youthful dissipations' (224). But he also finds other grounds for resisting the association between age and enfeeblement: weakness is, essentially, poor health, and the young may suffer from that as well as the old. And if our physical powers should decline with age, there are strong consolations in the life of the mind. Cato himself is spending his eighties learning Greek and writing a history of Rome. As for the loss of sensual pleasures, nothing is more to be welcomed. Remember Sophocles, who rejoiced in his old age to be no longer a slave of passion (232). Cicero is not as inflexible as some Stoic writers on the greater dignity of a life without sensual gratification: he holds that, contrary to popular prejudice, old age is not without sensual appetites, but possesses and responds to them in moderation, without threat to decency or dignity. Finally, *De Senectute* finds nothing to fear in age's proximity to death. We are at risk of death all our lives, and in old age we have the great advantage of being able to look back on a long life already achieved, during which we have had time to prepare ourselves philosophically for the end. So long as one can fulfil one's obligations, Cicero claims, one has the right to go on living indefinitely—but the longer we live the greater should be our courage in the face of mortality (241–2). The Athenian democrat Solon was exemplary: asked by the Spartan tyrant, Pisistratus, where he found strength for continued opposition, Solon answered, 'Old age' (242).

'He gives one an appetite for growing old', Montaigne commented of Cicero. It is certainly an encouraging philosophy. Much of its appeal stems from the refusal to accept that limitations placed on the powers and rights of individuals on grounds of age have any basis beyond ignorance and irrational prejudice. In this way the essay is continuous with Cicero's characteristic emphasis, and that of the Roman and Greek Stoics generally, on the rights and freedoms of the individual. Aristotle, to whom Cicero was indebted, thought that living on into old age tends to demoralize us (see Ch. 2). *De Senectute* aims to restore our faith in the robustness of our own virtue, and to put moral character within every individual's own control. Its blunt moral causalism (live well, age well; live badly, age badly) has been a staple in writing about old age, both optimistic and pessimistic, ever since. Even in the age of genetics, it retains significant currency in popular thinking about physical health and mental vitality.

Yet it is difficult to shake off the sense that *De Senectute* has to work very hard to resist the tide not just of popular prejudice but of common intuition. There is a standard objection to stoicism which says that, welcome its defence of our dignity though we may, we don't really believe it 'in our hearts'.[23] That criticism seems especially pertinent here. Moreover, as a defence of old age, *De Senectute* is in conflict with itself. There is an evident tension between Cicero's desire to set up old age as a special category and his wish to deny it validity as a category. He wants to claim high privileges and powers for old age, but he also wants to take age out of consideration. People say 'age' when really they mean to speak of 'ill-health and enfeeblement'. Some of the sense of an argument pulling in two directions no doubt arises from the occasion of writing: Cicero was attempting to prove his ongoing political serviceability to Rome at a point when the Republic was under Caesar's dictatorship and enmired in corruption.[24] Ventriloquized through Cato, the defence of old age is not only a protest against Cicero's own exclusion from political influence but an apology for the whole senatorial system. 'I am old but I am not old', he is saying; and 'this whole class of men like me, currently without political influence, should be recognized as the polity's best resource.'

Both claims raise the question of whether authority in old age is not, in reality, authority on sufferance—a caution perhaps confirmed by the manner of Cicero's death. Though he helped to bring about the downfall of Caesar, he was murdered at the age of 63 by Caesar's successor, Antony, whom Cicero had publicly criticized for refusing to recognize the authority of the Senate. Unlike a younger man, who might have fled successfully or fought for his life, Cicero did not resist. Plutarch records that he ordered his servants to 'set the litter down'. Then, 'clasping his chin with his left hand, as was his wont, [he] looked steadfastly at his slayers, his head all squalid and unkempt, and his face wasted with anxiety, so that most of those that stood by covered their faces'. His head was cut off; also 'his hands—the hands with which he wrote [...] his speeches against Antony'.[25] At least one modern biographer sees Cicero's end as a sign of how anachronistic his support for the Republican ideal had become: 'The Republic had died old and sick and tired, but in his eyes it remained green and fair. New concepts were needed, new methods, new approaches, new assumptions; yet all he could offer were the old discredited ones, as he strove to hold back the advance of history'.[26]

Cicero himself was ready to concede that his arguments in favour of old age would be counter-experiential for many of his readers. In the preamble to *De Senectute*, he refers to old age not as a gift but as 'a burden' which he and Atticus, his 65-year-old addressee, are both now forced to carry. He appears to find it something of a miracle that the composition of this essay has banished his own disgruntlement with old age, and 'even made the condition seem agreeable and attractive'. *De Senectute* is, then, a triumph of mind over circumstance—a true Stoic achievement. 'No praise is too great for philosophy!', Cicero enthuses (214). But in grounding the defence of old age primarily in our capacities, Cicero is closing his eyes to the observable truth that ageing weakens those capacities. He holds implacably, and with no concessions to time or biology, that the 'virtuous use' of moral purpose (*prohairesis*, as it was expressed by the later Stoic, Epictetus), will be 'always within our power, no matter what the world does'.[27] And in appealing over our bodies to our intellects—and (many have felt) over our intellects to our hopes—he is open to the charge that he has wilfully overlooked what is truthful, as well as what is prejudicial, in the common association of old age with vulnerability. *De Senectute* seeks to show us that there is no rational basis to fears and emotions which, after all Cato's arguments have been heard, we may nevertheless feel justified in thinking reasonable. We may, for example, hold to the view that the approach of death is not made more agreeable by our possession of a long past; similarly, we may persist in feeling that our desires and intentions are as strong as they have ever been, and that they are seriously damaged, if not rendered invalid, by the shortening of our future.

These objections to Cicero are germane to Simone de Beauvoir's view of old age, which takes, in many respects, a polarly opposed view of the subject. For her, the problems with *De Senectute* were multiple. It was a philosophy addressed to the conditions of a male social elite and not to women or to those lower in the social order; it was insufficiently responsive to the real losses of capacity that come with age; it was a prime instance of the coercive idealization of the old ('They are required to be a standing example of all the virtues' (3)); and—as I read between her lines—it was, in the end, no more than pessimism in disguise. Being stoical about old age is gritting one's teeth in the face of dire circumstances (and gritting one's teeth effectively concedes that this is so). What offends Beauvoir most is Cicero's apparent confidence that we determine the quality of our own old age: that it is the coming to fruition, in Cicero's own metaphor, of the life that we have nurtured for ourselves from youth onwards. Beauvoir has an acid reply, taken from Sainte-Beuve: 'We harden in some places and rot in others. We never ripen' (380). She is not, or not just, fencing with metaphors. The fundamental error in stoicism, as she sees it, is that it tells us we can be independent of the world, instead of recognizing that our life, our being, is conducted in dialectical relation with the world. We are subjects, with desires, capacities, hopes, but we are also objects of other people's perceptions and of our societies' cultural mores and political and ideological structures.

Beauvoir's account of her existentialism was phenomenological: she held that our existence is situated, our freedoms subject to the constraints of embodiment and of historical and social circumstance. The fundamental difference between *La Vieillesse* and her earlier, more celebrated work, *Le Deuxième Sexe*, is that in old age 'no challenge' to the world's judgement is deemed 'permissible' (284).[28] 'Whether we like it or not,' Beauvoir argues, 'in the end we submit to the outsider's point of view' (290). *Le Deuxième Sexe* was concerned to alert its readers to the injustice and non-necessity of existing social, cultural, and political constraints on the freedom of the female subject; the later work is about constraints that are seen to be in large measure inevitable, so that the extent of the injustice in society's maltreatment of the old is much harder to separate out and contest. A representative anecdote from *La Vieillesse* concerns travelling with Sartre before the war and being 'utterly taken aback' to hear a friend described, by a fellow traveller, as 'an old lady'. The 'alien eye', not able to recognize the younger woman in the older, 'had transformed her into another being' (289). The alien eye, precisely because it *is* alien, seems to Beauvoir to register the truth. There is a 'universal law' of ageing (295), and unless we die first it will come to apply to us all.

Because she sees the self in old age as to such a large degree defined by the world, Beauvoir finds truth in cliché almost as much as she discovers in it myth-making and distortion. Commonplaces about old age are not commonplaces for nothing. They may offend us, but offence is not rational ground for doubting them: 'The great number of clichés and set phrases about old age that we have come across show that it is a reality which runs clean through history' (279; also 436). Beauvoir does not deny that the state of the aged has varied through different places and times, but she insists that there are 'constants', and that they make it possible to bring together the testimony of people from very different cultures and historical moments and to treat them as cumulative evidence. The mind grows rigid and conservative; the body fails, and loses its physical attractiveness ('no one ever speaks of "a beautiful old woman"; the most one might say would be "a charming old woman" ' (297)). There are exceptions (quite a few in the course of the book), but what interests her is the rule.

And—this is where *La Vieillesse* becomes most interesting—submission to the rule is not easy:

> We must assume a reality that is certainly ourselves although it reaches us from the outside and although we cannot grasp it. There is an insoluble contradiction between the obvious clarity of the inward feeling that guarantees our unchanging quality and the objective certainty of our transformation. All we can do is waver from the one to the other, never managing to hold them both firmly together.   (290)

This 'contradiction' between inward and outward being is of a different order from anything we have faced in earlier life. The much greater difficulty it presents is a consequence of how we experience our lives in time. Our relation to futurity, Sartre had argued in *L'Être et le néant* (1943), sets us up for ontological disappointment. One never inhabits the future as present in the same way one inhabited it (formerly) as expectation. Beauvoir explains: 'Even if the present conforms to my expectations [in the past], it could not bring me what I expected—that fullness of being at which life so vainly aims. [...] no man can say, "I have had a fine life" because a life is something that one does not *have*, that one does not possess' (368).

There is much that Beauvoir fears about old age, and a good deal more that makes her angry. But as *La Vieillesse* draws towards its conclusion, it becomes clear that there is one deprivation more fundamental than all the others. The shrinking of our future (a phrase Beauvoir takes from Freud (524)) makes it almost impossible to hold on to the 'projects' which for her, as for Sartre, are our way of giving our lives meaning. Authentic projects, as Sartre argued in *L'Être et le néant*, are those that acknowledge the limitations of our facticity, and Beauvoir recognizes that as we grow old those limitations increase, physically and, often, intellectually. Ontological disappointment is not so bad, it turns out, as this reduction of the scope in which we can *be* disappointed. She is terrified of the possibility (one she finds amply documented by history) that in old age our minds may 'unravel' and we shall betray ourselves, reneging on projects and sympathies that have hitherto defined our life.

There is, she claims, 'only one solution if old age is not to be an absurd parody of our former life, and that is to go on pursuing ends that give our existence a meaning—devotion to individuals, to groups or to causes, social, political, intellectual or creative work' (540). The projects we choose will almost certainly be less and less grand, and, should our loss of capacity be very serious, we may not be in a position to choose at all. If she is right, we should not try too hard to resist this reduction in our field of activity. To persist in a view of ourselves as 'not yet really old' will be bad faith (the cardinal error for existentialists): going on believing in something about ourselves in the face of clear counter-evidence. But in the case of femininity there was an advantage to *not* being in bad faith: the woman who lives in bad faith is the one who lives in denial of her own intellectual and moral and even physical capacities, which are stronger than she is prepared to admit. To acknowledge these capacities is to take up a fuller life. The old person who lives in bad faith is, by contrast, one who claims capability, and attractiveness, and a relation to the future which she or he does not any longer really possess. And yet it is apparent that for Beauvoir it is almost impossible for the old person *not* to live in bad faith. Bad faith is the only way to keep going. 'It is far better not to think about it too much' (541), the philosopher (of all people) concludes.

In the series of individual case studies that make up the last chapter of *La Vieillesse*, Beauvoir demonstrates that there is 'no inherent justice' in the old age people get. And yet, the desire for something very like justice—for a principle of causality that is, finally, moral—keeps showing through, and to such an extent that Beauvoir, for all her hostility to the Stoic view of old age, ends up sounding oddly like a Ciceronian Stoic. Châteaubriand was a narcissist all his life, and his melancholic old age, in Beauvoir's view, befitted that life (525–33); Lamartine's vanity, want of foresight, and political hypocrisy brought him to an 'appalling old age' (533–8 (537)); for ourselves, the best we can do is 'live a fairly committed, fairly justified life so that one may go on in the same path even when all illusions have vanished and one's zeal for life has died away' (541). Those who manage this will be the 'handful of privileged people' (541). There is a politics of outrage in *La Vieillesse*, but it is not, in the end, a politics with much hope attached. At the very end of the book, Beauvoir returns to the large question with which she began: is the suffering of the old necessary, and if so, in what measure? Much, she concludes, is unavoidable: 'it is an empiric and universal truth that after a certain number of years the human organism undergoes a decline. The process is inescapable. [...] it results in a reduction in the individual's activities: very often it also brings a diminution in his [or her] mental faculties and an alteration in his [or her] attitude towards the world' (539). But she also lays a large measure of blame at the doors of society. It is society's fault that old age happens too early to too many people, that its physical effects are more rapid and worse than they need be, and that it is so often 'morally atrocious' (542). Her wish would be for an end to the degradation of the old, but she does not foresee, even in the 'ideal society', an end to their suffering (543).[29]

Beauvoir concludes—and this may be another reason why *La Vieillesse* has found so few followers—by refusing, or at best giving lukewarm support to, political activism on behalf of the old. To pursue better old age policies (better pensions, housing, leisure provision), she argues, may alleviate the ills of the old, but it is not the answer we need. Such efforts intervene too late in a systemic problem. The situation of the old is the outcome of fundamental failures in our social relations, above all of an economic system that deprives everyone but the Ciceronian elite of the means (intellectual, financial, social) to define projects for themselves which would give their lives value. 'Our claim cannot be otherwise than radical—change life itself' (543).

'Literature is born when something in life goes slightly adrift', Beauvoir wrote in *The Prime of Life* (the second volume of her autobiographical trilogy): 'the first essential condition is that *reality should no longer be taken for granted*; only then can one both perceive it, and make others do so'.[30] Like Sartre, she had high expectations of literature. She thought that it should be 'committed': that it should not only 'give a name to oppression, to stupidity, to injustice', but encourage and assist the desire for change—without of course 'exaggerating the possibilities of literary action'.[31] But for the most part, literature in *La Vieillesse* fails to meet that demand. In keeping with Beauvoir's retreat from her earlier accent on the freedom of the subject, it shrinks to being the social and practical record of constraint, distinguished from philosophy by its honesty but not by any transformative power. 'The poets', she writes, 'were much more sincere than the moralists, because they did not expect to gain anything from their poetry' (121). So, in contradistinction to Cicero's moralistic optimism, Horace and Ovid and Juvenal recorded the 'bitterness' of personal experience. *King Lear* she reads as absurdist theatre *avant la lettre*: it shows us 'the old man's outlook upon humanity, the outlook of one cut off from the future and reduced to the mere passiveness of his immediate being' (167), and so reveals to us the ultimate meaninglessness of our projects. Villon, Corneille, Molière, Proust, Yeats, Ionesco, Beckett are all there, too—though by the twentieth century the evidence provided by literature seemed to Beauvoir of secondary interest to the larger documentary record. Even the novelists have tended to represent the old only from the outside, and literature as a whole has failed to recognize the need for commitment, continuing to peddle the same jaded stereotypes (210).

Beauvoir was, for reasons already mentioned, exceptional in the range and extent of her attention to the literary. But even philosophers who do not adopt a phenomenological approach have regularly found literature a prompt and a support to their thinking about what it means to be old. The literary models of old age that have most often captured attention have, as for Beauvoir, been tragic and male. When Aristotle wants to demonstrate the vulnerability of *eudaimonia* to the contingencies of age, the example he reaches for is Homer's Priam;[32] when Adorno wants evidence of the loss of a metaphysical 'beyond' and (he argues) the correlative reduction of the old to mere objects, rubbish, he turns to Dickens's *The Old Curiosity Shop* and Beckett's *Endgame*;[33] when Amartya Sen wants to demonstrate how the well-being of societies and individuals can vary not just among individuals but for one individual over time, he advances King Lear;[34] when Bernard Williams wants an instance of the tedium of immortality, he goes to Karel Čapek's *The Makropulos Case* and the Janáček opera derived from it;[35] when James Griffin, considering well-being and its measurement, wants an illustration of how the distinction between selfish and selfless action can crumble in the presence of desire he cites Père Goriot.[36]

Familiarity is one reason why these philosophers have deferred to literature on old age. For better and worse, Priam, Lear, Goriot, and a few others are still reference points most of us hold in common, even if only with second- or third-hand familiarity. Specificity is another reason: the particular instance, complex enough in its representations, motivations, and consequences, and gripping enough its imaginative realization, to serve as an illustration of real situations or dilemmas. For a literary critic there are, of course, serious problems with this use of literature as 'evidence', often little if at all differentiated from ethnological data, the historical record, or personal testimony. As a discipline, literary criticism characteristically emphasizes the aesthetic; and the aesthetic, whether understood as creativity, non-instrumental imagination, form for form's sake, or defamiliarization, is often defined by its distance from the ordinary functioning of society. In this vein, a frequent reproach from literary critics to philosophers is that they want literature to operate too illustratively, naively, and are therefore drawn to a very narrow band of literary genres and modes: primarily classical drama and realistic fiction. Martha Nussbaum's early work on philosophy and literature attracted this complaint: treating literary texts too exclusively in terms of 'their subject matter and their social function',[37] taking them as far-more-transparent-than-not representations of life, which allowed her to deepen and refine philosophy's claims about the contingency of happiness, or the requirements for justice.

Nussbaum has been one of the most sympathetic mediators between philosophy and literary criticism. I am conscious both that this book owes a debt to her (in Ch. 2) and that it may be assumed to be closer to her work than, in my own mind, it is, so some distinguishing claims are in order. For Nussbaum, the relationship between literature and philosophy is primarily an ethical 'alliance'.[38] In *The Fragility of Goodness* she argues specifically for literature's ability to advance 'each citizen's moral education' beyond what philosophy can do, while remaining in keeping with philosophy's aims (the philosophy in question being Aristotelian virtue ethics). Literature lends complexity, 'sheer difficulty', even 'indeterminacy' to the problems of ethical deliberation that philosophy aims to guide us through. It also presents them in such a way that they simultaneously engage our emotions but leave them 'sufficiently distant from each reader's experience not to bring to the fore bias and divisive self-interest'. It can count, in short, as 'a shared extension of all readers' experience'.[39] In *Poetic Justice* (1995) and *Upheavals of Thought* (2001) Nussbaum repeats and refines these claims: literature is an extension of our ethical education. Where particular texts have taken strongest hold in our collective imagination they provide ways by which we may recognize ourselves as a society, a civic body.

In many ways I am sympathetic to this, as I suspect most literary critics are in some degree. It is hard to turn down a legitimation of what we do that offers us such flattering terms: ethical, rational, educative, and capable of improving the good functioning of society. (On the other hand, put like that, who would not want to rebel?) Nussbaum is not offering to legitimate literary criticism per se; she is providing a rationale for reading literature with philosophy—so some of my literary-critical twitches (the desire to preserve less responsible possibilities and more aesthetic scope for literature, a higher prioritization of language, form, genre) are, perhaps, beside the point. But as an account of why we might want to read philosophy and literature together her emphasis on its potential to make us better citizens is narrowing as well as expansive. Ethical deliberation, including deliberation with and through emotional response, is one of the things that philosophy and literature can do together, but not the only one. I assume Nussbaum herself would agree with this. In pairing philosophy and literature in this book I have wanted to test out several of the other ways in which they might invite us to think about persons, lives, time, ends, form.

This description, and indeed much of this Introduction, evidently give a structural priority to philosophy. After all, exploring how we think about and through old age means more for philosophy, often defined as 'thinking about thinking', than for literature, which is only sometimes 'about thinking' and often not best described as 'about' anything at all. Approaching the subject of old age through philosophy in the first instance is therefore likely to be discomfiting to some—even many—literary-critical readers. What I see as reason to look harder at philosophy (its focus on the foundations of thinking) will seem to them reason to steer clear. In so far as I see an 'alliance' between literature and philosophy, it is only in the most general terms, and it is avowedly a product of my interests as a reader, rather than (in most cases) being acknowledged or even capable of being acknowledged by the writers I am concerned with. The specific relation between philosophy and literature in each of the chapters that follow is a product of the particular ways in which each of the writers has thought about old age in relation to wider questions about lives, persons, goods, values; also of how the philosophers concerned thought about the work of philosophy, and how the literary writers concerned thought about the work of the imagination.

The book is deliberately essayistic. It begins with Plato's repeated claim that philosophy is best practised in old age, and explores, first, the grounds of that endorsement of age (its foundation in certain ways of thinking about lives, desire, knowledge, metaphysics), and, second, the exploitation of old age as a rhetorical trope in the course of defining Platonic philosophy. It then considers the way in which Plato's thinking about old age was reworked by Thomas Mann, in the early twentieth century, to support a particular definition of the life and work of the literary artist. The second chapter examines the place of old age within Aristotle's virtue ethics. Aristotle's negative characterization of the old in the *Rhetoric* is well known, but the place of old age in his ethical thought has been little considered. In the *Nicomachean Ethics*, living on into old age with failing capacities is seen to increase one's vulnerability to tragedy—yet Aristotle makes surprisingly little allowance for loss of capability in the final judgement to be made on a life, such as that of Homer's Priam, which ends tragically in old age. I read Shakespeare's *King Lear* in conjunction with Aristotle, treating it not as an Aristotelian text but as one that dramatizes many of the same questions, deepening and further complicating them as it puts Lear's tragedy (unlike Priam's) centre stage.

Chapter 3 presses harder at what I see as the major area of difficulty in Aristotle's legacy for moral thinking about old age: the (necessarily) incomplete separation of teleology from chronology. It examines that legacy as it appears in the writing of Alasdair MacIntyre and others who, like him, have leant heavily on the analogy between lives and narratives; it also considers the most distinctive, and counter-intuitive, classical alternative to thinking about lives as being temporally shaped, Epicurean/Lucretian hedonism. These two strands are brought together through a discussion of Saul Bellow's last novel, *Ravelstein*, written when he was in his mid-eighties and published five years before his death in 2004. *Ravelstein* sets up an argument between two close friends and ideological allies, both of whom resist seeing their lives as self-contained narratives. One (Ravelstein) favours a large historical view, seeking to live out his life against the grand canvas of Western intellectual history. The other (the narrator) favours something much closer to the Epicurean model: a life lived against the background of 'eternity'. Strenuously, but also comically, he declines to think of his old age as the last stage in a linear narrative with only one possible end.

Chapter 4 continues, despite the reservations of the previous chapter, to work with the assumption that lives are unified and, for some purposes, may (reductively) be described in narrative terms. It shifts the focus, however, from moral and ethical accounts of lives to recent, competing theories of rational life-planning aimed at producing a fair distribution of social resources between the old and the young. I discuss prudential life planning, as advocated by Norman Daniels, and the welfarist objections made to Daniels's model by Dennis McKerlie, who fears that prudence alone would not sufficiently protect those who experience serious loss of autonomy in old age (for example through dementia). Justice, if McKerlie is right, requires that such cases be given priority on the grounds of absolute need. I examine the refinements that might need to be made to McKerlie's prioritarian view in the light of Angieszka Jaworska's call for a prudential outlook on old age which respects what agency remains to people, even in advanced cases of Alzheimer's and other dementias. I then pursue this discussion into a close reading of two poems concerned with the question of what it means to choose for our own old age, and the first of which is specifically invoked by McKerlie as an illustration of the bad old age a just society should be prepared to extend care to: Philip Larkin's 'The Old Fools' and Stevie Smith's 'Exeat'.

Chapter 5 extends the previous chapter's interest in rational (as distinct from moral) approaches to lives and persons. Its comparative reading of Derek Parfit's *Reasons and Persons* and Balzac's *Le Père Goriot* explores Parfit's criticisms of the temporal bias towards the near future that operates in the classic theory of self-interest, and his claim that, if we were neutral with respect to time, we would be less worried by ageing and death. It also takes up his 'Reductionist View' of persons, which has much less sanguine implications for old age, and which requires (Parfit argues) an extension of the principle of paternalism in order to guard us from grave imprudence. I extend the discussion through a close reading of *Le Père Goriot* which chimes with Parfit's thinking in several important respects, including the awareness of common temporal bias, and the advocacy (though not on such principled terms) of a less unifying view of lives and persons.

Chapter 6 takes a fresh look at the subject of metaphysics, first raised in the reading of Plato. It starts from a consideration of Theodor Adorno's late lectures on metaphysics, in which old age is seen as a window onto the whole problem of metaphysical thought in the twentieth century. By way of exploring more deeply Adorno's claims about old age, I read these late lectures against two literary works whose treatment of old age was particularly important to him: Dickens's *The Old Curiosity Shop* and Beckett's *Endgame*.

Chapter 7 examines Bernard Williams's brief remarks on old age, made in the course of larger arguments about why we should not want to live forever ('The Makropulos Case: Reflections on the Tedium of Immortality' (1973)). Others have found these arguments troublesome. I agree with Williams's claim that, given that we are mortal, old age and decline may be the one set of conditions under which many (most?) of us, if we are lucky, will come to think of our own mortality as a tolerable fact. But I suggest that there are other reasons than boredom (the principal reason Williams gives) why we should not want to live forever; and I argue—through close readings of J. M. Coetzee's *Disgrace* and Philip Roth's *The Dying Animal* (both 1999), that old age and decline are not simply biological facts, as Williams treats them, but highly responsive to a person's perception of their ability to go on possessing certain goods crucial to their sense of themselves as themselves—including favourable historical, political, and intellectual environments.

The final chapter explores contemporary evolutionary theory as the major reason we have to dispense with, or substantially revise, ethical naturalism about old age. (Ethical naturalists take the view that there is, innate in all natural beings, an appropriate, and appropriately moral, way for those beings to act.) Examining recent developments in the evolutionary theory of senescence, it considers the challenges science poses to the other ways of seeing old age discussed in this book. It ends with a reading of Michael Ignatieff's *Scar Tissue* (1992)—a novel explicitly concerned with what our new knowledge of the science of ageing may mean for the way in which we think both about our individual futures, and about the relationship between the arts, the sciences, and philosophy.

The schools of philosophical thought and the kinds of literature pursued in this book are, as will be amply clear from this summary, eclectic. They have been chosen solely because they were where I found ideas about old age most interestingly at work. My primary aim is to demonstrate the degree to which intuitions and assumptions and ways of reasoning about old age have helped to condition our thinking about much larger and more fundamental questions (and vice versa): what it means to live a life; what it means to live a *good* life; what it means to be a person; what it means for a society to be just; what the limits are, not only to experience but to thought; what is entailed in living in time; what difference a knowledge of contemporary science may make to the ways in which we think about several of these matters. In many respects I am starting where Simone de Beauvoir left off: with the recognition that, if we want to think differently about old age, we need to think differently about 'life itself'—and (I would add) about thinking itself. 'The whole system', as she put it, 'is at issue.'[40]

I

The Platonic Threshold

And a delightful vision came to him, spun from the sea's murmur and the glittering sunlight. It was the old plane tree not far from the walls of Athens—that place of sacred shade, fragrant with chaste-tree blossoms, adorned with sacred statues and pious gifts in honour of the nymphs and of Acheloüs. The stream trickled crystal-clear over smooth pebbles at the foot of the great spreading tree; the crickets made their music. But on the grass, which sloped down gently so that one could hold up one's head as one lay, there reclined two men, sheltered here from the heat of the noonday: one elderly and one young, one ugly and one beautiful, the wise beside the desirable. And Socrates, wooing him with witty compliments and jests, was instructing Phaedrus on desire and virtue.

Thomas Mann, *Death in Venice*, 1912[1]

It is one of the founding scenes of philosophy: the old man wooing and instructing the young man. And right at the start of Plato's *Phaedrus*, Socrates makes a joke about it. Hearing the young Phaedrus wax lyrical about a speech he has just heard Lysias give, arguing that a handsome boy is better advised to surrender to a man not in love with him than to one who loves him, Socrates quips: 'Splendid! I wish he would add that it should be to a poor man rather than a rich one, an elderly man (*presbyteros*[2]) rather than a young one (*neoteros*), and, in general, to ordinary folk like myself' (227c).[3] Lysias' claim invites scepticism from the outset—so a more attentive or experienced listener to Socrates might deduce; but Phaedrus, eager to prove his own eloquence by repeating what he has heard, misses the warning note and falls in happily with the old philosopher's avowal that he is eager to know more. So, the two sit beneath the plane tree, and the dialogue on beauty and virtue begins.

The difference between age and youth shapes their talk in several ways. Most obviously it structures their interactions as teacher and pupil and, rhetorically at least, potential lover and beloved. 'The elderly' and 'the young', 'the wise' and 'the desirable', as Mann put it—though Mann's 'elderly' (*Ältlicher* (390)) overpitches matters somewhat. In the pederastic culture of Plato's Athens, the lover/teacher was expected to be a mature man,[4] but if Socrates is older than most such relations would presume (past his prime), it is clear that he has not yet reached advanced old age.[5] On the other hand, Socrates himself seems to want to bring a more emphatic sense of old age into the discussion. The joke about the likelihood of a handsome boy surrendering to an old man is not the last such example. Having listened to Phaedrus' reading of the speech in favour of the non-lover, Socrates is persuaded to offer his own impromptu disquisition on the same theme, and improve upon Lysias if he can. Among the more plausible reasons he offers for arguing that the non-lover is a better choice than the lover, is an appeal to proverbial wisdom: 'There's an old saying about "not matching May with December," based, I suppose, on the idea that similarity of age tends to similarity of pleasures and consequently makes a couple good friends' (240c). An 'old' man (*presbyteros* again) is bound to be jealous, 'goaded' by the beauty of the boy to want to see, hear, touch, and otherwise take pleasure in him. 'But what pleasure or what solace will he have to offer to the beloved? How will he save him from experiencing the extremity of discomfort in those long hours at his lover's side, as he looks upon a face which years have robbed of its beauty, together with other consequences which it is unpleasant even to hear mentioned, let alone to have continually to cope with in stark reality' (240d–e). And when 'wisdom and temperance' at last reassert their command over the older lover, and he recants on promises and vows which, he now sees, were absurd and demeaning—what is the boy to do then? ' "As wolf to lamb, so lover to his lad," ' Socrates concludes: 'There, I knew I should [break out into verse], Phaedrus' (241a–d).

   Once again, irony is wasted on Phaedrus. Convinced that he has heard the first half of a 'good' speech on love, with the second part (in favour of the non-lover) still to come, he presses Socrates to continue, but has the chagrin of hearing instead a thorough recantation. 'That was a terrible theory, Phaedrus, a terrible theory that you introduced and compelled me to expound' (242d). And by patient question and argument Socrates leads Phaedrus to see the enormity of the error. Love is not the evil thing that Lysias' speech made him out to be. Love is a god—and when he inspires the relation between a man and a beautiful boy that relation becomes a possible route to immortality. 'All soul is immortal' (245c), but some souls have fallen to earth and been tied to mortal beings. Their existence is like that of a chariot drawn by a pair of winged steeds—one good, the other wayward and troublesome (246a–b). Wings, by their very nature, will try to soar upwards to the heavens, where the soul will be nourished on the 'Plain of truth' (248b), Socrates tells his young listener, but a soul that has fallen to earth cannot normally return to the sphere of the immortals for ten thousand years. It will 'speed' back to the gods sooner only if its mortal bearers bring the wayward steed into subjection, dedicating themselves to the pursuit of wisdom and choosing three times, in three revolutions of a thousand years, the life of philosophy (248e–249a).

As the focus of the *Phaedrus* shifts from erotic desire to the desire for truth, the disparity between youth and old age quietly slips out of the forefront of the discussion, to be replaced by a more mutually enabling and more generalized (non-age-specific) account of the lover, now drawn within the protective fold of the first-person plural. Beauty, as personified in young men, is the gods' great gift to mortals, Socrates explains, because it is in the perception of beauty that we may come closest to apprehending a true image of the ultimate good. The physical perfection of the beloved boy fills with 'awe and reverence' the soul of the true lover (the one who knows how to keep 'the wanton horse' subdued) (254e, 254b), and the effect of his own beauty begins to be reflected back to the boy himself. As his 'ripening age' and 'destiny' lead him to see past the bad counsel of those who have told him that it is shameful to have converse with a lover, he will learn to take pleasure in conversation with him and discover 'with amazement' the depths of his kindness (255a–b). And, if lover and beloved can resist the temptation to physical expression of their desire,

> the victory [will] be won by the higher elements of mind guiding them into the ordered rule of the philosophical life, their days on earth will be blessed with happiness and concord, for the power of evil in the soul has been subjected, and the power of goodness liberated; they have won self-mastery and inward peace. And when life is over, with burden shed and wings recovered they stand victorious in the first of the three rounds in that truly Olympic struggle. (256a–b)

For those couples who do not achieve full mastery over their physical desires, the end is not disaster. They will be good and loyal friends, elevated by love, and when death comes they will quit the body wingless 'yet eager to be winged, and therefore they carry off no mean reward for their lovers' madness' (256d).

By this stage in Socrates' argument, the opening jests about old lovers have been all but forgotten: any prejudice the boy may have imbibed against the older man has been overcome through his own growth towards a more mature understanding, and the association of love with physical desire has in any case been elevated into a vision of the attainment of immortality. This sublimation of the lover in the philosopher/teacher makes it possible to discern, retrospectively, Socrates' motive for twice introducing old age at the start of his dialogue with Phaedrus. The apparently supererogatory attention to old age was a rhetorical ploy—a way of leading Phaedrus to think of the lover as an older man who, by virtue of his age, can then more readily be imagined capable of forgoing the pleasures of the flesh and choosing the path of philosophy. As Phaedrus reports him, Lysias did not imagine the lover as an old man, nor was he guilty of cheap humour at the expense of the old. Socrates introduced the subject, and lowered the tone, in order to get Phaedrus thinking about the lover's desire in terms more adaptable than they would otherwise be to metaphysics.

This strategic use of old age as a means to wrongfooting one's philosophical opponents, and redirecting the terms of the debate thereafter, is a common feature of the Socratic dialogues. In the *Euthydemus* it provides a structure for satire: Crito, hearing that Socrates intends taking lessons in disputation from the eristic teachers, Euthydemus and Dionysodorus, asks bluntly 'I say, Socrates! Aren't you afraid, at your time of life, that you are too old?' (272b).[6] 'Not the least' Socrates replies, his only anxiety has been that he will bring mockery on his tutors—though, of course, he goes on to trounce them. In this case, the acceptance of the role of old man is not just a (false) modesty topos, but a way for Socrates to expose the eristics' disdain for philosophy and prevent them from misleading his impressionable 'fellow pupil', the young Clinias. In the *Protagoras* Plato plays comically on this same trope. Socrates, badgered by the young Hippocrates to introduce him to the great teacher Protagoras, in his turn assumes the role of young man in need of the older Protagoras's wisdom—and is treated as such by Protagoras. As Socrates proves himself far the more capable philosopher of the two, the lashings of irony become unmistakable (see esp. 316c, 317c, 318b, 342e). Elsewhere, Socrates more openly appeals to his own old age as a means of clearing the rhetorical ground and asserting his credibility. When he is put on trial for corrupting the young, he rests his claim to speak the truth on his age: 'from me you shall hear the whole truth', he tells the jury at the start of his defence '—not [...] in flowery language like [that of my accusers], decked out with fine words and phrases. No, what you will hear will be a straightforward speech [...]. It would hardly be suitable, gentlemen, for a man of my age to address you in the artificial language of a schoolboy orator' (17c).[7]

There is, then, an awareness on Socrates' part of rhetorical and philosophical advantage to be gained from (though not automatically due to) a man who speaks from the position of 'old age'. This association between philosophy and age holds more generally true in Plato. Almost without exception those who philosophize well in the Platonic writings are old.[8] This is not to say that the philosopher is by definition old; rather, that the requirements of the philosophical life are set in such a way that only the old will be eligible to fulfil them. Book 6 of the *Republic* stipulates that concentration on philosophy is appropriate to that time in a man's life when his physical powers are on the wane and he has fulfilled the civic obligations of maturity:

> lads and boys [...] should occupy themselves with an education and a culture suitable to youth, and while their bodies are growing to manhood take right good care of them, thus securing a basis and a support for the intellectual life. But with the advance of age, when the soul begins to attain its maturity, they should make its exercises more severe, and when the bodily strength declines and they are past the age of political and military service, then at last they should be given free range of the pasture and do nothing but philosophize, except incidentally, if they are to live happily, and, when the end has come, crown the life they have lived with a consonant destiny in that other world.   (498b–c)[9]

In book 7 of the *Republic*, the age for philosophizing is said to start at 50 (540a–b).[10] In the *Laws*—written, if Plutarch was correct, in Plato's old age[11]—it is put a little later, at 60 (785b).[12] It is in the *Laws*, too, that Plato links the capacity for wisdom most explicitly with length of experience, though insisting, all the while, that good philosophers are rare: 'For wisdom and assured true conviction, a man is fortunate if he acquires them even on the verge of old age' (653a). 'Senior men', defined variously as 'quinquagenarians' and 'sexagenarians' (670a, 812b), are the makers and guardians of the Platonic legal system, the censors of its music and literature, and supervisors of physical training (770a, 802b, 812b–c, 813c–d, 965a), drawing as necessary on the quicker energies of younger men (964e–965a). Throughout the *Laws*, old men are held to be the best protectors of the polity, embodying, in so far as anyone can, its wisdom and intelligence.

That said, the *Laws* is, as Malcolm Schofield has put it, 'an idiosyncratic text', not least in its explicit handling of the limitations of age.[13] It is presented as a conversation between three men, two of whom are elderly and not practised in philosophy (Megillus the Spartan and Cleinias the Cretan), the other of whom, the Athenian Stranger, is a philosopher, and may conceivably be Socrates. Megillus and Cleinias, who have grown up under the restrictive regimes of their respective countries, have neither the intellectual training nor the range of experience the Athenian possesses. Schofield suggests that, by placing the Athenian in dialogue with them, Plato deliberately frames the conversation as 'intellectually limited and limiting'.[14] Its 'gerontocratic religious rhetoric' is overtly controlling, and tied to a view of law as 'a rational principle superior to human capacity to exercise rule'—but the rhetorical framework also enables the educated reader to recognize that Plato has consciously eschewed free enquiry in favour of a discourse which can express a 'transcendent moral framework for political and social existence' while remaining persuasive to the whole of a population, and not just its philosophers.[15]

Something of the same reasoning can be seen at work in the opening of Plato's great statement of political theory, the *Republic*, which begins with a visit by Socrates to the father of Lysias. Cephalus provides the only direct testimony in Plato's writings to the experience of advanced old age. '[A]s the satisfactions of the body decay,' he tells Socrates, 'in the same measure my desire for the pleasures of good talk and my delight in them increase' (328d).[16] Socrates, in his turn, welcomes the opportunity to question the older man. 'I enjoy talking with the aged' (*presbytais*[17]), he tells Cephalus, 'For to my thinking we have to learn of them as it were from wayfarers who have preceded us on a road on which we too, it may be, must sometime fare […]. I would fain learn of you what you think of this thing, now that your time has come to it, the thing that the poets call "the threshold of old age" (*geraos oudoi*) [… W]hat report have you to make of it?' (328e). Like Sophocles before him, Cephalus declares himself glad to have escaped the 'raging and savage beast' of sexual desire and to have attained a state of tranquillity (329c). He concedes, readily enough, that the comforts he has found in old age have much to do with his wealth—with the proviso that a man's experience of ageing will always reflect his disposition. The most reasonable of men will not find old age and poverty easy to endure, while wealth alone will not make an unreasonable man content in his declining years (330a).

The exchange anticipates many of the keynotes of Cicero's *De Senectute*, three centuries later,[18] with the major difference that Cephalus' testimony is not the main matter of the *Republic*. It has the tone and function of a ceremonial opening to the argument: an acknowledgement of honour due to old age, linked, narratively, to the homage Socrates pays to the goddess Bendis. (He encounters Cephalus because he has gone to the temple near the old man's home to make his devotions.) Cephalus himself is not presented as a philosopher of any great merit. What authority he has in conversation with Socrates rests on his age and his place in society: his ability to speak from the perspective of a long and prosperous life. So, Cephalus remarks that old age is the point at which even unreflective men become conscious that they must soon pay the price for whatever good and ill they have done in their lives (330d–331b)—but when the conversation moves towards a more discriminating definition of justice, he makes his apologies and goes to watch the sacrifices, quitting the field in favour of the younger men who are eager to debate with Socrates.[19] Even here, in Plato's most considered portrait of old age, attention to age for its own sake is plainly subservient to the wider work of philosophy. The association of old age and philosophy is mutually supportive, and partially rather than absolutely definitive. It is contingent on the gender, social status, education, and capacities of the individual, and it involves a distinction between the old and the very old. Old age will enhance an educated man's opportunity and his inclination for philosophy, but it will not, in itself, make him a good philosopher. Once he enters advanced old age it is understood that his acuity of mind and his energy will begin to fail. Indeed, Xenophon reports that Socrates accepted death at his trial because he knew his mental powers were declining.[20] As Thomas Hurka notes, commentators often dismiss this story but it is in keeping with other remarks about death in the Platonic dialogues, including the famous claim that death is not an evil for a good person.[21]

All this is background support for the rhetorical rather than intrinsic importance of old age in the *Phaedrus*. Unlike the *Republic* and the *Laws*, the *Phaedrus* is not concerned with laying down a specific plan for the philosophical life or for the governance of the state, but it rests on the same assumptions about the value of a long life. So: the older lover/philosopher is presumed to be far more likely than a younger man to possess the

understanding and the self-control that Socrates describes as the right response to the boy's beauty. He will also have reached a stage when he is
free to devote himself to the pursuit of wisdom. There are no guarantees
here, only an ideal to be aspired to, but the largely tacit privileging of age
and experience is continually underwritten by Socrates himself, whose use
of flirtation as a pedagogic technique enacts, for Phaedrus' benefit, the absorption of the ostensibly undesirable old lover into the role of desirable old
philosopher. 'Where is that boy I was talking to?' Socrates teases Phaedrus,
before beginning the true defence of love: 'He must listen to me once more,
and not rush off to yield to his nonlover before he hears what I have to say.'
'Here he is', Phaedrus replies—flirting in greater earnest, it would seem,
than Socrates—'quite close beside you, whenever you want him' (243e).

Just once more in that dialogue, Socrates broaches the subject of old
age openly. When he comes to instruct his young companion on the
superiority of the spoken over the written word, he asks Phaedrus to reflect
upon why a man might seek to 'sow his seed in literary gardens'. Such
a man, Socrates himself speculates, is 'collecting a store of refreshment
both for his own memory, against the day "when age oblivious comes
(*lethes geras*)," and for all such as tread in his footsteps' (276d). To commit
knowledge to writing is not the most important aspect or stage of the
philosopher's endeavours—it will be much better to have 'planted and
sown' spoken words, 'words which can defend both themselves and him
who planted them, words which instead of remaining barren contain a seed
whence new words grow up in new characters' (277a)—but neither is it
negligible. Indeed, it is in line with Plato's prioritization of speech that he
makes the preservation of one's own ideas in old age the first reason to
value the written word, above the hope of preserving one's achievements
for futurity.

This recognition of what will happen if 'age oblivious comes' might
be thought to constitute a serious threat to philosophy: what good is a
philosopher without command of memory? Is age, after all, the period of
our lives when we are best equipped to pursue wisdom? But a potential
reason for scepticism about Platonic philosophy's association with old age is
not allowed to register as such. Rather, writing appears to serve the very old
much as it serves the young Phaedrus, who claimed to be ready to impress
Socrates with his reconstruction of Lysias' speech, but whom Socrates
quickly rumbled as practising from a script, concealed inside his cloak
(228d–e). Phaedrus needs or believes he needs assistance from a text because

he has not yet learned the skill of memorial retention. An older philosopher may need the support of writing on the not dissimilar grounds that his memory has exceeded or exhausted its mature capacity. Such a philosopher will find pleasure, Socrates tells Phaedrus, in watching the intellectual progress of the young, assisted as may be by his own writings, while other men in old age 'regal[e] themselves with drinking parties' (276d).

It sounds like a stepping back from some of the larger claims Socrates has been making for old age. In reality it is anything but. By acknowledging this physiological and temporal constraint on what the philosopher can hope to achieve, Plato is defining a limit within which—and only within which—philosophy can legitimately be pursued. He is also following up on the *Symposium*'s interest in age as a means to defining not 'just' the pedagogic contexts and the metaphysical aims of philosophy, but its most fundamental mechanisms.[22]

Like the *Phaedrus*, the *Symposium* follows a process of reasoning from a starting point in unthinking disparagement of age to a conclusion which endorses, not age per se, but a dedication to philosophy and a depth of understanding that are seen to be achievable only with age (if at all). Socrates himself is, once again, exemplary and, as ever, exceptional. But, unlike the *Phaedrus*, the *Symposium* also makes use of old age in the service of a detailed account of how we accrue knowledge, and what it means for a mortal to seek immortal wisdom. It is Agathon, and not Socrates this time, who gives voice early on to a commonplace prejudice against age. Love, he tells the company (taking dispute with Phaedrus' opening characterization of *Eros* as the first, and in that sense the oldest, of all the gods), is 'the most beautiful and best' because he is 'the youngest of the gods' (195a).[23] (It is a sign of how platitudinous both compliments are that they might as well be interchangeable: Eros is oldest, Eros is youngest—'you rake up everything you can think to say and attribute it to Love', Socrates will protest (198e).) The youth of Eros, Agathon continues, is proved by his 'flitting as he does in flight from old age [...]. Love [...] by his nature hates old age and does not come anywhere near it. It is with the young that he always is, and he *is* young; the old saying has it right, that like always draws near to like' (195b).

As in the *Phaedrus*, it is Socrates' task to extricate the assembled company from the philosophical error entailed in this unthinking dismissal of old age. Once again, he sets about demonstrating what a good speech in praise of Love should sound like.[24] At the core of Socrates' speech on love is his recollection of another pedagogic scenario, long in the past, when he was the one in need of tuition. He himself had no good grasp of the philosophy of love, he tells his audience, until he was instructed by the Mantinean wise woman, Diotima (201d).[25] Diotima's account of love, as reconstructed, or constructed, by Socrates (it is not clear whether this is supposed to be true history or a useful fiction), rests on a belief that all that is good in mortal souls strains towards immortality. Such yearning is the reason human beings are 'so powerfully affected by love', she claims (207c). She then outlines a double homology between the processes of human biology and, first, psychology, secondly, the manner in which human beings acquire knowledge.

The basic division between the mortal and the divine, Diotima explains, is that the mortal cannot remain unchanged by time—it cannot remain 'always the same' (208a). The closest a human being can come to perpetuating him or herself, then, is through a continual 'coming-into-being' (208).[26] Mortal nature

> always leaves behind something else that is new in place of the old, since even during the time in which each living creature is said to be alive and to be the same individual—as for example someone is said to be the same person from when he is a child until he comes to be an old man, and yet, if he's called the same, that's despite the fact that he's never made up from the same things, but is always being renewed, and losing what he had before, whether it's hair, or flesh, or bones, or blood, in fact the whole body. And don't suppose that this is just true in the case of the body; in the case of the soul, too, its traits, habits, opinions, desires, pleasures, pains, fears—none of these things is ever the same in any individual, but some are coming into existence, others passing away. It's much stranger even than this with the pieces of knowledge we have: not only are some of them coming into existence and others passing away, so that we are never the same even in respect to the things we know, but in fact each individual piece of knowledge is subject to the same process. For what we call 'going over' things exists because knowledge goes out of us; forgetting is the departure of knowledge, and going over something creates in us again a new memory in place of the one that is leaving us, and so preserves our knowledge in such a way as to make it seem the same. In this way everything mortal is preserved, not by always being absolutely the same, as the divine is, but by virtue of the fact that what is departing and decaying with age leaves behind in us something else new, of the same sort that it was. (207d–208b)

Just as the human species must continually be replacing itself, so the individual body must constantly repair itself as component materials fall away, and in the soul (*psyche*) new desires or attitudes continually emerge and grow while others are diminishing or disappearing. The same principle (this is the point of Diotima's exposition) is at work in our attempts to acquire knowledge, which are not a cumulative, progressive achievement but a matter of constant loss and replenishment. (There is a tacit allusion, perhaps, to the Danaides, perpetually refilling leaking water jugs.)

This is not the gestural recognition of the *Phaedrus* that age will in all probability bring a limit to our mental powers. For a start, it matters that Diotima is speaking not of old age but of the ageing process (the difference between what a man is as a child and as an old man). Even more clearly than in the *Phaedrus*, old age is of significance not in its own right but as a means to thinking about philosophy—and in this case, not about its aims or its content but about the process by which it takes place. By contemplating first the continual 'departing and decaying' that is the ageing of our bodies and psyches, then the continual 'departing and decaying' of memory and knowledge, Diotima teaches, we can be brought to understand that philosophizing occurs within the defining parameters of our condition as mortal beings. We live, feel, and learn by a combined process of addition and subtraction, growth and attrition, and this fact constitutes not the end limit so much as the mechanism—the active, temporal quality—of our living, feeling, thinking.

When Plato brings memory into conjunction with biology, Derrida observes, his aim is to establish the finitude of memory: 'Memory is finite by nature. Plato recognizes this by attributing life to it. As in the case of all living organisms, he assigns it [...] certain limits. A limitless memory would in any event be not memory but infinite self-presence.'[27] But if one looks closely at the homology (it is more than an analogy) between biology and the acquisition of knowledge in the *Symposium*, it is apparent that Plato is constraining the terms on which we are invited to think about what it means to be a living organism. In both the *Phaedrus* and the *Symposium* Plato has almost nothing to say about mortality as death-relatedness (which is what most interested Derrida[28]). His concern is rather with mortal life as the determining structure within which we exist and think. So, when Diotima describes the continual 'ebbing away' of life and of knowledge she is not (or not primarily) saying that all men must die and all knowledge is limited: she is saying that all organisms and all memories continually decay and must continually be repairing themselves. To learn and to seek to retain knowledge is, according to Diotima, a state of resistance to the natural and inevitable depletion of what we are, and what we know, at any given moment.

Ageing is an obvious, perhaps an inevitable, resource for Plato's philo-sophical purposes here. But it is also worth noting how underspecified the equation between the workings of the mind and the workings of the body remains in the *Symposium*. Is this state of resistance active or passive? Is not our ability to accumulate learning subject to choice, to education, to effort? If it is, does it respond to these things more than, or no more than, or less than, our ageing? Plato does not say. Moreover, the perceived homology easily—too easily—admits a misreading of the kind of limit biology involves.[29] In looking at the difference between infancy and old age we can readily perceive the constant process of change through which a human being is sustained over time. There is a substantial risk, however, that the reader will move too quickly (as Derrida does) from the idea of ageing to that of dying, from recognition of waste to an assumption of absolute loss. Substantial risk, that is, that the rhetorical exploitation of old age as an explanatory figure for knowledge will lead us to place the wrong kind of limit (distinct from life, and opposed to it, rather than of the very nature of life) on what Platonic philosophy can achieve.

Hence (I take it) Plato's care to keep old age under control, even as he makes use of it rhetorically. In the *Phaedrus*, the reference to old age helped to put a case for philosophy as our human endeavour to approach closer to the divine, enabling Socrates to establish the philosopher as a lover of wisdom more than a lover of men. In the *Symposium* ageing works much more specifically to describe the activity of acquiring knowledge. It makes visible to us the built-in inefficiency of our existence as living, feeling, and thinking beings; but it is none the less strongly yoked to a metaphysical view of philosophy. Once we recognize our mortal condition for what it is, Diotima argues, we will be spurred to reach beyond it towards the permanence of the divine. Philosophy is not bound by mortality, it is defined by it, and defined in such a way that philosophy is understood to be continually reaching beyond the conditions of its own existence but necessarily contained within its limits. At which point the argument of the *Symposium* becomes essentially the same as that of the *Phaedrus*: some men will be content with physical procreation, but the truly wise and virtuous man will recognize, through the loveliness of a beautiful boy, the 'loveliness of form' (210b). From there he may come to perceive the beauty of non-bodily things, beginning with 'laws and institutions' then proceeding to 'every kind of knowledge' (210c),[30] and ending with that ultimate 'wondrous vision which is the

very soul of the beauty he has toiled so long for […] an everlasting
loveliness which neither comes nor goes, which neither flowers nor
fades' (562).[31]

By the close of this long and supple argument to define the best kind
of love as the love of wisdom, *eros* has been established as man's path to
immortality—and the oldest speaker at the symposium is triumphant. Or
would be, one presumes (Aristophanes still wants to argue with Socrates)
were it not for the reappearance of Alcibiades. Alcibiades' arrival, drunk
and determined to see Agathon and his guests drink and be merry, puts
an end to the philosophical debate and brings the pleasures of the body
back into the symposium. Declaring his love for Socrates before them all,
and confessing the abject failure of his most shameless efforts to seduce
the philosopher, Alcibiades flagrantly makes the mistake of loving the
wisdom-lover more than wisdom. In doing so he reminds the symposium
of what 'a volatile force *eros* is to tap': 'the saga of Alcibiades' disastrous
political ambitions waits in the wings of this dialogue', G. R. F. Ferrari
notes.[32] But there is more to be said for Alcibiades' interruption than this.
In the course of making Socrates himself, and not his teachings, the focus
of attention, Alcibiades pulls old age back to the forefront of the dialogue,
enlisting it, once again, in the service of flirtation, and this time without
even a pretence of interest in sublimation. 'When we listen to you', he
tells Socrates, 'we're absolutely staggered and bewitched' (215d).[33] Then
(offering his fellow guests the benefit of his own sorry experience): 'I just
refuse to listen to him—as if he were one of those Sirens, you know—and
get out of earshot as quick as I can, for fear he keep me sitting listening till
I grow old (*catageraso*)' (216a).[34]

Old age, if prepared for well, may make a man a philosopher, Socrates
has taught, but Alcibiades reinstates the more immediate priorities of youth:
love is here and now, and too much philosophy may make you old before
your time, before you have enjoyed your youth. The old Socrates, he
warns, has the uncanny power of a youthful siren to lure young men
towards his own old age: getting out of earshot is the only way to save
yourself. The effect may be to underline just how difficult a challenge
the philosopher faces if he wishes to bring the young on board. But if
Alcibiades is a recalcitrant pupil he is not an imperceptive one. His joke
sabotages one of Socrates' most characteristic pedagogic and philosophic
techniques: the exploitation of the rhetorical standpoint, the unexamined
assumptions, the biological verities of old age in the service of practising

and defining philosophy. And Alcibiades reminds us (and Socrates), at a moment when it would otherwise be easy to forget, that what we have been listening to was no old man's lecture *ex cathedra* but a conversation of the old with the young. If philosophy is best fitted, in Plato's view, to the old, it is nevertheless always the product of a dialectical process of reasoning between the old and the young, and between the virtue associated with old age and the desire ascribed to youth.

Alcibiades briefly puts a spotlight on what might otherwise remain the very discreet work done by old age in Socratic teaching. Age comes close to being a vanishing figure in the Platonic dialogues: not, in and of itself, of much moment to Plato, and yet a crucial component in the description of the philosopher. It is the principal structuring factor in the pedagogic scenario of the *Phaedrus*, and Socrates' explicit identification of himself with the role of 'the old man' helps set the initial terms of the debate on love. But the more serious philosophical work happens when old age goes under-ground. It makes subtly persuasive the sublimation of physical desire into metaphysical ardour. It also (at the end of the *Phaedrus*) establishes a limit on what can be expected from human philosophy—a limit much more closely expounded in Diotima's claim that knowledge is governed by the same prin-ciples of growth, change, and obsolescence that define our mortal condition.

None of which means that philosophy's objective, or even its promise, according to Plato is to rescue us from the 'miseries of old age'.[35] What Platonic philosophy does for old age is rather (and it is no small thing) to establish thinking about the 'declining' years of life as the best possible position—actual and rhetorical, experiential and imagined—from which to do philosophy.

In *Death in Venice*, Gustav von Aschenbach, besotted with the Polish boy Tadzio, finds himself recalling his boyhood reading of Plato:

> the ageing artist welcomed [his emotional intoxication] unhesitatingly, even greedily. His mind was in labour, its store of culture was in ferment, his memory threw up thoughts from ancient tradition which he had been taught as a boy, but which had never yet come alive in his own fire. Had he not read [...] that only with the help of a bodily form is the soul [...] able to exalt itself to a higher vision[? ... T]he Love-god, in order to make spiritual things visible, loves to use the shapes and colours of young men, turning them into instruments of Recollection by adorning them with all the reflected splendour of Beauty, so that the sight of them truly sets us on fire with pain and hope.   (237–8)

The rudiments of the Platonic story are all there, laid down in Aschenbach's schooldays and waiting to be brought back to memory: the idealization of the homoerotic love relation, the belief that beauty is a way of making 'spiritual things visible', the notion that attraction to a physical form may be a route to the apprehension of 'higher' things. And Tadzio, at 14 or so (Aschenbach guesses), seems willing enough to play Phaedrus to Aschenbach's Socrates: 'returning his glance, [...] no less serious than himself, just as if he were regulating his attitude and expression by those of the older man, and as if the general mood had no power over him while Aschenbach kept aloof from it' (255). Entranced by the boy's loveliness, the 'ageing artist' produces one brief essay—just 'a page and a half of exquisite prose' inspired by Eros (239).[36] 'Tak[ing] the boy's physique for a model as he wrote, [he] let his style follow the lineaments of this body which he saw as divine, and [...] carry its beauty on high into the spiritual world, as the eagle once carried the Trojan shepherd boy up into the ether' (239).

But there is something skew about Aschenbach's recapitulation of Platonism, and it is not a question of Mann having misremembered Plato from his school texts: he reread both the *Phaedrus* and the *Symposium* in preparation for *Death in Venice*, marking up his copy of the *Symposium* heavily and taking extensive notes from both works.[37] Even in the first stages of Aschenbach's captivation by Tadzio's beauty, this is too febrile a love to match the Socratic ideal. It is a darker, more irrational but at the same time more anxiously self-scrutinizing passion, indebted as much to German Romanticism,[38] to Nietzsche's theory of tragedy, and to nineteenth- and early twentieth-century psychology as to Plato.[39] It is also an account which, for all its pleasure in recollecting the *Phaedrus*, is wary of giving too explicit endorsement to pederasty. The only 'boy' (*Jugend*) mentioned in that first long passage is not Tadzio but Aschenbach himself in youth (*SE* 390). 'Boys' proper have been upgraded to 'young men' (or, 'manly youths') (*menschlicher Jugend*). And while caution curbs the frankness of Plato's eroticism in one direction, the undertow of unsublimated desire distorts the philosophy in others. Socrates did not teach Phaedrus that the lineaments of the body were themselves divine: rather, that they were a means to glimpsing the divine. The Platonic lover participates in the 'flood of passion' that Zeus experienced for Ganymede (255c), but if passion is to assist the mortal soul's restoration to its original divine state it is explicit in the *Phaedrus* that men cannot be permitted the licence of the gods: physical desire must be brought into line with 'the ordered rule of the philosophical life' (256a). In Mann, by comparison, simile deviously sabotages Platonic sublimation, presenting Aschenbach's moment of 'inspiration' as a sexual abduction of the boy under cover of art.[40]

Death in Venice's metaphorical compounding of homoerotic desire with the cholera plague sweeping into Europe from Asia recalls the *Phaedrus*'s description of the early stages of passion. The 'shuddering', and the 'strange sweating and fever' that seize Plato's lover, his soul 'throb[bing] like a fevered pulse' (251a, 251d), are repeated in the symptoms of love that are also the signs of Aschenbach's disease: the 'shiver [...] down the spine', the 'sticky sweat', and 'feverish' excitement (247–8, 264, 258). But all the work of the Socratic dialogue thereafter goes into sublimation. In *Death in Venice* there is no effort at resistance. Aschenbach is unable and unwilling to elevate himself above this humiliating, absorbing access of physical desire. He sinks into its 'voluptuous' embrace, much as he sinks into the comfort of the unlicensed, coffin-like gondola that transports him to the Lido. ('La lugubre gondola', Liszt called it.) Beauty does not always 'incite to thought', James Snead remarks (of Visconti's 1979 film of *Death in Venice* as well as the novella): sometimes it 'relaxes, seduces, narcoticizes'.[41]

By the close of *Death in Venice* Aschenbach knows his own failure to match up to the classical ideal. At the end of a long hot afternoon pursuing Tadzio through the narrow streets and passageways of Venice, he loses the trail and sinks down beside a well in a litter-strewn square (a debased descendant of the stream of Acheloüs). With the stench of carbolic disinfectant in his nostrils, he acknowledges how far he is from the wisdom of the philosopher:

> Beauty [...] is indeed the sensuous lover's path, little Phaedrus, it is the artist's path to the spirit. But do you believe, dear boy, that the man whose path to the spiritual passes through the senses can ever achieve wisdom and true manly dignity? Or do you think rather (I leave it to you to decide) that this is a path of dangerous charm, very much an errant and sinful path which must of necessity lead us astray? [...] Do you see now perhaps why we writers can be neither wise nor dignified? That we necessarily go astray, necessarily remain dissolute emotional adventurers? The magisterial poise of our style is a lie and a farce, our fame and social position are an absurdity, the public's faith in us is altogether ridiculous, the use of art to educate the nation and its youth is a reprehensible undertaking which should be forbidden by law. (264–5)

Magisterial even when denouncing the magisterial, Aschenbach is incapable of the Socratic mode. He is a novelist, not a philosopher, and therefore, one might argue, necessarily on terms of bad faith with Plato; but he is also constitutionally out of sympathy. His concept of wisdom is never uncoupled from a Kantian preoccupation with 'dignity' (*Würde*), nor from a concern with manliness as a hallmark of private and public worth.[42] In lieu of Socrates' wit Aschenbach musters only 'rueful' self-mockery (264). He is not even in dialogue with his Phaedrus, who is present only to the imagination as Aschenbach's 'drooping, cosmetically brightened lips shap[e] the occasional word' of an internal monologue (264). And by the end of it Aschenbach has pre-scripted his own death scene with an egoism Socrates would have abjured:[43] 'now I shall go, Phaedrus, and you shall stay here; and leave this place only when you no longer see me' (265).

It is the abandonment of dialogue that does most damage to the Socratic model. Tadzio may be receiving an education in desire, but his responsiveness is always potentially a projection of Aschenbach's wishes. Up until the point where cholera is known to be spreading through the city the lover's silence is merely feeble (and a condition of proximity to the boy[44]), but his failure to inform Tadzio's mother of the danger of remaining in Venice makes him culpable. Fear of Tadzio's removal from the scene overrules a basic moral obligation and feeds into the death-dealing strain in Aschenbach's desire: that pulse of satisfaction when he sees the boy's 'brittle teeth, and surmises that 'he'll probably not live to grow old' (228; also 251). The implication that a short life-expectancy for Tadzio establishes a kind of parity with Aschenbach's own age, that there is pleasure in thinking that the boy will not outlive his own beauty, or that, if Aschenbach cannot have him, perhaps no one else shall—none of this is redeemed by any compensatory suggestion that Tadzio will never suffer as Aschenbach suffers. '[D]isgust at his own ageing body' (261), and exhilaration at what little power he may have to command his beloved's presence, contribute to the portrait of a man who resembles the butt of the joke in Socrates' 'false' model of love more than he resembles Socrates.

And yet Aschenbach's insistence on his own age is no less rhetorical a pose than Socrates' jesting about old lovers; and the work it does is no less serious or complex. For a start, it is not hard to detect in Aschenbach's reflections on the ineligibility of old age a displacement of the less negotiable illegitimacy of homosexual desire. When Socrates quips about the undesirability of an old lover, the joke is itself evidence that the pederastic relation is not a problem in Plato (the difficulty is with age not with gender). Age has a more defensive relation to desire in a historical and cultural context much less receptive to homoerotic love.[45] Aschenbach, watching the boy Jashu link arms with Tadzio, kiss him, and, at the end, wrestle brutally with him as if 'bent on revenge for […] long servitude' (266), feels, like so many of Mann's heroes, exiled from the expressive freedoms of youth, but to be 'old' is, in the situation, the less revealing of two reasons for deeming himself barred from a nearer relation with the boy.[46] It is also, whether consciously or unconsciously on Aschenbach's and Mann's part, the less absolute impediment. There is no changing the gendering of Aschenbach's desire, but age is in some measure a matter of perception. Perhaps the boy will not be put off; perhaps he will agree to see Aschenbach's interest as a form of 'paternal fondness' (227) or a flattering attention from a 'cultured' 'older man' (243). This is why Aschenbach is vulnerable to the hotel barber with his hair dyes and his rouge and his eyeliner and his slick patter: 'After all, we are only as old as we feel in our minds and hearts […] permit me simply to give your colour back to you' (262).

The accent in *Death in Venice* is not on 'old', as in the *Phaedrus* and the *Symposium*, but on 'ageing': becoming elderly, growing old. Aschenbach is 53, but prematurely aged by years of too-disciplined artistic labour. (The age is given in Mann's working notes, though not in the text itself, which indicates only that he is over 50.[47]) Mann was 35 when he encountered the 10-year-old Count Wladyslaw Moes, the original of Tadzio, on holiday in Venice; just 36 when he began writing the novella.[48] Fifty-three may have suggested itself as a simple numerical inversion. At what should be the height of Aschenbach's career, he has begun to experience a 'growing weariness which no one must be allowed to suspect nor his finished work betray by any tell-tale sign of debility or lassitude' (201). The signs are nevertheless there to be read in his work. Beneath the '[e]legant self-control' of his fiction, a discerning critic will discover 'a state of inner disintegration and biological decay' (205).

That this 'ageing artist' finds himself so often in the presence of those whom he unhesitatingly identifies as old—the 'dandified old man' on the steamer (213), the 'old man with a boat-hook' who receives him at the Lido (217), Tadzio's 'old nanny' (224), the 'amusing old man' who sells the children sweets (225), the 'barefooted, white-bearded old man' who prepares his place on the beach (236 and 223)—only intensifies

the sense that he himself is nearing that threshold but not yet definitively there.[49] It is no accident that these people are all poor, servants,
or, in the case of the ageing roué, servile, and that they remain name-
less. They personify Aschenbach's recognition that to become old will
be to lose social (and sexual) visibility. The old in this novella have no
imagined interiority, whereas 'ageing' is in significant measure subjective. Free indirect style, and a pointed scrupling over what Aschenbach
may and may not feel and intend, are vehicles for doubt—at once saving and depleting—over just how far he has progressed towards the
excluded status of old age. The distanced, objectivizing view of the third-
person narration merges continually with his own anxious self-regard:
'Too late! he thought [...] Too late! But was it too late? [...] the fact
now seemed to be that the ageing lover no longer wished to be disenchanted' (240); or, 'the joy of an intoxication of feeling that had come
to him so late (*späten* (400)[50]) and affected him so profoundly—all this
encouraged and persuaded him to indulge himself in the most astonishing
ways' (248–9).

In David Luke's English translation, 'ageing' (*alternd*) is consistently
rendered as an adjective: 'the ageing Aschenbach' (231), 'the ageing artist'
(237), 'the ageing lover' (240). The German original has 'der alternde
Künstler' (390), but in the other instances it is an adjectival noun. Not
'the ageing Aschenbach' or 'the ageing lover'; just 'dem Alternden' (384),
'der Alternde' (392), 'the Ageing' (English can only render it adjectivally
as 'the ageing one'). The effect is bleakly reifying, depersonalizing, while
at the same time suggesting another 'ironic citation'[51] of Aschenbach's
manner—humiliated but looking to shore up his dignity. English, requiring
a name or an identity, loses the German language's compaction of concept
and individual, neutrality and involvement, and runs the risk of hardening
irony into parody.

The ability of the word *alternd* to discredit and defend Aschenbach's love
for Tadzio in roughly equal measure marks a shift away from Plato's (and
Socrates') externalizing reflections on old age towards a more ambiguously
internalized account of ageing. But it also signals a fundamental difference
in the momentum and the temporal trajectory of desire—a difference
vital to Mann's use of age to define, not the life and work of the
philosopher, but the life and work of the artist. Where Plato wrote of the
lover/philosopher's desire, Mann writes of the lover/artist's *Sehnsucht*: not
'desire' in the urgent future-directed sense that word implies in English

so much as 'longing'. In the German it 'connotes an experience both metaphysical and visceral', suitable equally to 'a mystic or a voyeur'.[52] In *Death in Venice* it tends more exactly to proleptic regret. Aschenbach's desire looks ahead to a time when what is longed for will already be over: 'in his mind's eye he was watching Hyacinthus, doomed to perish. [...] H]e saw the discus, steered by cruel jealousy, strike the lovely head; he himself, turning pale too, caught the broken body in his arms, and the flower that sprang from that sweet blood bore the inscription of his undying lament…' (242).[53]

Aschenbach's desire for Tadzio is a state of anticipatory bereavement. He can imagine catching that body in his arms only by first imagining it broken and himself left to mourn a love whose fulfilment is, in the present, still possible, but which he knows will never happen. To reconfigure Socrates' description of love as 'longing' after this fashion subverts the Platonic model, and not just through the deathly fantasy of possession. *Death in Venice* emotionally and intellectually thwarts Platonic sublimation, mimicking its self-suppression but preventing love from going forward beyond the tragic end it predicts for itself. The object of sublimated desire is no longer in the sphere of transcendent truths; instead the image of the beautiful boy remains, framed in a future scene of death which borrows the colours of myth but evokes at most an aesthetic transcendence (an 'undying lament'). In effect Aschenbach takes Socrates' statement about how the 'Love-god' uses young men as 'instruments of Recollection' (*DV* 238, 249c−e), and makes it his guide, reconstructing desire as a loop-back effect: desire which can only perceive itself retrospectively from the point when all hope of fulfilment will be over. When Aschenbach says 'hope' he really means a luxury of despair. When he looks at the future what he sees is himself looking back in 'pain' (238).

As in the *Phaedrus*, old age has disappeared from the surface of the Hyacinthus passage, but it has set the groundwork for the structure of desire described. In place of Socrates' use of old age to assist the sublimation of erotic desire into the search for truth, Mann offers ageing as the defensive face of a failure of erotic sublimation. And in place of Plato's view of ageing as a progression, he presents ageing as an elliptical figure: the as yet only projected stage of life at which one will look back and see one's current desires and hopes as definitively over. It matters that ageing is understood to be distinct from (even, in this case, opposed to) death, but not in the same way it mattered for Diotima. Ageing helps to isolate not the quasi-physiological mechanism of mortal knowledge but the psychological mechanism by which the lover-artist perceives the object of desire as ungraspable, and defines his own relation to it as necessarily and self-consciously tragic. When the idea of transcendence returns in the final paragraphs of *Death in Venice*, it is evoked purely as mood or atmosphere. The dying man rests his eyes on the sculptural form of Tadzio, this 'pale and lovely soul-summoner' who stands in shallow water at the edge of the sea and appears to point his lover towards the 'nebulous vastness [...] an immensity rich with unutterable expectation. And as so often, he set out to follow him' (267). Platonic metaphysics has become a 'metaphysics of tragedy' (the phrase would soon be made current by one of Mann's great admirers, Georg Lukács[54]). Or as Mann put it in his working notes for the novella: 'Dignity is rescued only by death (this is the "tragedy", the "sea")'.[55]

Just as the process of Platonic epistemology resembles the structure of Platonic desire (future-directed, continually working to replace what is being lost) the understanding of artistic representation in *Death in Venice* mimics Mannian *Sehnsucht*. For this extension, and diversion, of the Platonic model towards art, especially literature, Mann was indebted to his reading in 1911, or early in 1912, of Lukács's collection of neo-Platonic essays *Soul and Form* (*Die Seele und die Formen*) (1911).[56] At least one of the essays, 'Longing and Form' ('Sehnsucht und Form'), was already familiar to Mann, a shorter version having appeared in *Die Neue Rundschau*, the house journal of his German publisher, S. Fischer Verlag, in February 1911.[57]

Lukács took the Platonic account of sublimation as the conceptual basis for a series of critical reflections on the problem of form, in which he attempted to arbitrate between the Platonic sense of that word and what he took it to mean for art. His reworking of Plato was filtered through the German Romantic philosophical tradition, especially Hegel, G. E. Lessing, Schlegel, Nietzsche:[58] anti-modernist, committed to the Hegelian historical dialectic (or a version of it), and wedded to a belief in the mystical excess of life and experience over representation. Lukács's 'poet', in which term he includes all creative artists (21), attempts to impose a strict series of laws on what the Platonist knows to be 'a thousand hazards and vagaries of freedom' (20). On both sides there is profound longing (*Sehnsucht* again) for an end to the opposition between freedom and artistic form. In the essay on 'Platonism, Poetry and Form', the longing is primarily on the part of the Platonist, who craves the poet's 'certainty' (23). In 'Longing and Form' it is the poet who longs to be allowed to relax his struggle to impose the laws of art upon the 'infinite waves of relativity' (20). Many artists have been worn out in the attempt, Lukács claims, in a sentence evocative of Aschenbach: 'as soon as they started on the weary road towards universal, model-creating life (these are only different words for the concept of form), they disintegrated, flattened out, committed suicide or decayed inwardly' (22).

For Lukács, Plato's *Symposium* was the great attempt to formulate a philosophy of longing. 'Socrates turned his longing into a philosophy whose peak was unattainable, the highest goal of all human longing: intellectual contemplation. By advancing thus towards the ultimate, insoluble conflict, his longing became free from conflict in terms of real life […] Eros ceased to be the god of love and became a cosmic principle. […] But it will always be denied to men and poets to soar as high as this. The object of their longing has its own gravity and its own self-demanding life' (94). For Lukács, the longing of art is always tragic. The best testimony he finds to it among contemporary forms of writing is the 'lyrical novel', which is capable of being at one and the same time 'matter-of-fact' and 'sensual'. A lyrical novel represents the soul in the only way it can be made visible: in 'small', 'arbitrary' outward manifestations in the midst of a 'harshly indifferent reality' (105). It cannot be accused of 'dissolv[ing] everything into mere mood', because it understands that atmosphere, handled correctly, is an aspect of form, 'a principle of modelling' (195).

When Mann takes the Platonic description of the old lover/philosopher and adapts it to an account of the ageing artist, unable to sublimate his desires equivalently into art, he is clearly thinking along Lukácsian lines—not least in choosing the form of the lyrical novel (or novella). But in its attention to the rhetorical possibilities of old age, *Death in Venice* goes back to the original terms of debate in the *Phaedrus* and the *Symposium*. The only point at which Lukács comes near to employing age as a structuring figure in *Soul and Form*, beyond the reference to the inward decay of the poet, is a brief passage in which he asserts the impossibility of anything being 'completely fulfilled in life. […] Everything flows, everything merges into another thing, and the mixture is controlled and impure', he writes: 'To live is to live something through to the end: but *life* means that nothing is ever fully and completely lived through to the end' (152–3).

For Mann this incompleteness—even, or especially, as a life nears its end—finds its most potent expression via the thought of ageing. Aschenbach, until he sees Tadzio, has held to the view that an artist realizes his powers most fully when he is old. '[H]e dearly longed to grow old', we are told, 'for it had always been his view that an artist's gift can only be called truly great and wide-ranging, or indeed truly admirable, if it has been fortunate enough to bear characteristic fruit at all the stages of human life' (204).[59] Having been 'young and raw with the times' (206), he has steadily purged the 'excesses' of his youth and achieved a dignified 'purity' of voice. Eschewing 'direct audacities, new and subtle nuances', he has honed his later style toward 'the exemplary and definitive, the fastidiously conventional, the conservative and formal and even formulaic' (208). But when he gazes at Tadzio and sees the 'discipline' and 'precision of thought [...] expressed in that outstretched, youthfully perfect physique' (237) he relinquishes unnatural forcing of the energies and shape of his life. He wants, suddenly, what Lukács's poet wants: to be allowed to give up the arduous striving of the artist and be permitted simply to take pleasure in the 'uncontrolled and impure' (153).[60] The association of age with the fullest exercise of powers developed over a long life gives way to a sharply contrasting view of age: one in which the accomplished artist sits back before the revelation of another, 'pure[r] will', a 'divine' will (for Aschenbach a pretty fiction) that has 'lightly and graciously' set up a human image of pure perfection 'for him to worship' (237).

The seduction lies in the notion of ease. Until this point age has been about work—a continuation and rounding out of his life's commitment to the labour of art—but from the moment he arrives in Venice and gazes 'on Beauty itself' (237), ageing becomes a licence to abandon the struggle with the forms of art. Returning to the Lido after a half-hearted attempt to leave Venice, Aschenbach feels his will 'bewitched' and 'relaxed' (235).[61] Dreaming away the late morning by the sea, it is as if he has been 'snatched away now to the Elysian land, to the ends of the earth, where lightest of living is granted to mortals, [...] and the days flow past in blessed idleness, with no labour or strife' (235). The sea may appear to represent death at the close of the novella, but it also stands also more subtly and much more consistently for indefinition   the freedom from art's formal constraint for which Aschenbach increasingly longs, and whose seductive power he has always, at some level, felt. 'There were profound reasons for [Aschenbach's] attachment to the sea', *Death in Venice* observes:

he loved it because as a hard-working artist he needed rest, needed to escape from the demanding complexity of phenomena and lie hidden on the bosom of the simple and tremendous; because of a forbidden longing deep within him that ran quite contrary to his life's task and was for that very reason seductive, a longing for the unarticulated and immeasurable, for eternity, for nothingness. (224)

This attraction towards the obliterative power of nothingness, inarticulacy, simplicity, and, especially, sleep is one of Mann's hallmarks.[62] It can be seen in his characteristic reliance on the terminal dash or ellipsis, as if the prose is drawn more towards sustaining atmosphere than towards expression. Tonio Kröger feels it (in the short story of that name), describing that 'melancholy northern mood' of 'long[ing]': 'To sleep … To long to be able to live simply for one's feelings alone, to rest idly in sweet self-sufficient emotion, uncompelled to translate it into activity, unconstrained to dance'.[63] Hans Castorp succumbs to it for years on the Magic Mountain. Mann himself testified to its lure. Sleep overpowers 'cold, calculated resolve', he asserted in the short sketch 'Sleep, Sweet Sleep' written three years before *Death in Venice*. What 'a metaphysical piece of furniture' is a bed! It releases one from 'egoistic concentration, the will to form, to limit, to shape, to embody'.[64]

In *Death in Venice* this cast of mind turns Socrates' philosophically energized 'resistance' into a luxury of resignation. Platonic *ethos* becomes Mannian *pathos*. But while that seduction is marked in the novella as a sign of 'ageing' (the relaxing will of a 53-year-old writer who has worked too hard for too long), Mann himself understood it to be a symptom of his own age at the time of writing. In a letter to his brother Heinrich in January 1904, he observed his predilection for exactly this sentimental relaxation of philosophy, linking it, explicitly, to age. 'We are both on either side of thirty,' he wrote (he was 28, Heinrich 32), 'an age when one easily takes for *ethos* what is simply *pathos*'.[65] Others would think of 30 as young, but for Mann it was the age around which youth becomes conscious of its own passing, and therefore of the limits of what the artist can achieve (this was before he had read Lukács).[66] In an essay on Theodor Fontane, published in 1910, he drew attention to Fontane's nervous, weepily morbid temperament at the same age: 'at the age of thirty he finds himself in a condition where he sits down to weep for fifteen minutes at a time; he is afraid he may die before he finishes *Tannhäuser*'.[67]

In the same month as the letter to Heinrich, Mann wrote a newspaper article in which this preference of the *c.*30-year old for *pathos* over *ethos* was

given another philosophical context (entirely compatible with his subsequent taste for Lukács). One of the attractions of Nietzsche for him was the
respect for 'the atmosphere of ethics, the Faustian flavour, the cross, death,
and the grave'.[68] *Death in Venice*'s debt to the Dionysiac vitalism of *The Birth
of Tragedy* has been much commented upon: that surging up of primitive,
sexual energy that issues most explicitly in Aschenbach's 'obscene' dream
of 'an orgy of limitless coupling, in homage to the [Stranger-god]' (260–1).
But the Dionysiac and Freudian models distract to some extent from where
the structuring of art and ideas and emotion happens most persistently in
Death in Venice: not vertically (what was repressed welling up) but hori-
zontally (the anticipation of a longed-for release). Mann had in fact little
sympathy with those aspects of Nietzsche's rhetoric that involved repeatedly
declared antipathy to the Platonic association of philosophy with old age.[69]

When Nietzsche decries Socrates' hostility to the Dionysiac principle,
in *The Birth of Tragedy*, he portrays Socratic rationalism as an intellectual
and moral betrayal of youth and art by age and philosophy (a deliberate
provocation to the rationalist tradition, on his part—condemning Socrates
again on the charge for which he was put to death). Socrates' opposition
to tragedy 'required of his disciples abstinence and strict separation from
[the] unphilosophical attractions [of the tragic arts]', Nietzsche writes
disparagingly, '—with such success that the youthful tragic poet Plato first
burned his poems that he might become a student of Socrates'.[70] '*The
dying Socrates* became the new ideal never seen before, of noble Greek
youths: above all the typical Hellenic youth, Plato, prostrated himself
before this image with all the ardent devotion of his enthusiastic soul'
(89). This opposition to Socrates' appropriation of philosophy for old age
(its experience, its sobriety, its perceived proximity to the metaphysical)
is a recurrent note in Nietzsche's writings—and, in its direct inversion of
Plato's weighting of age above youth, a sign of how close he is to Plato even
when most confrontational[71]—but it is never stronger than in *Untimely
Meditations* (1873–6), where he rails against the suppression of the 'genius'
and 'energy' and 'life' of youth in the grey-beard scientific and historicist
philosophy of the day. '[Y]outh still possesses that instinct of nature which
remains intact until artificially and forcibly shattered by [...] education'.
We need, he declares, a new philosophic 'empire of youth'.[72]

On the question of age Mann pits himself directly against Nietzsche.
However much he shares Nietzsche's sense of youth's innate understanding
of the tragic arts, however much he indulges a taste for 'Nietzschean'

atmospherics, and however closely indebted *Death in Venice* is at certain points to *The Birth of Tragedy*, Mann's conviction was that 'genius', 'energy', and 'life' show themselves most freely in old age. On this point he was entirely on the side of Plato (and, by implication, saw Nietzsche's resentment of age as itself a symptom of youth). The essay on Theodor Fontane indicates just how consciously Mann identified old age as a means to defining the best possibilities for a writer's life and work. He describes Fontane as having urged himself towards old age, even as a young man, in order to embrace 'the ideal qualities of that last stage of life: benignity, kindness, justice, humour, and shrewd wisdom—in short a recrudescence on a higher plane of childhood's artless unrestraint' (287). Unlike Aschenbach, Fontane lived to justify his own hopes for age. The prose of his late years is an 'expansive prose, easy-going, lucid', Mann observes: 'despite its apparent artlessness and lack of effort it has a certain elevation, a roundness and fullness, a kind of inner determination which is evidently possible only after long practice with poetic forms' (298). Looking at a portrait of Fontane in old age, Mann sees a 'splendid, virile head' and 'kindly, merry, penetrating eye', not the 'pale, sickly, sentimental' figure he was in youth: 'on his toothless mouth under the bushy white beard [there is] a smile of understanding gaiety' (287–8). 'Life is behind [him]' (289), and that thought seems to relieve him of the fear of not living and not producing: he now finds himself 'at the consummation of his individual powers' and he goes on to 'give the world a mere eighteen volumes, each one up to *Effi Briest* better than the one before' (288).

At times old age assumed a totemic authority in Mann's critical thinking. A 1922 essay, for example, argues for an 'aristocracy of nature' exemplified in the old age of Goethe and Tolstoy, before which a 'moral "sentimentalist"' such as Schiller or Dostoyevsky, both of whom died comparatively young, must bow.[73] But a far more persistent note is the association of old age with release from the constraints on the artist. Old age stands as a promise of liberation at the end of a long life of labour: coming into one's own powers, with the burden of a life's work behind one and the skills and techniques of art now so practised that whatever one produces hereafter will have the ease and authority of long experience. He offers a late variation on the same theme in an essay on 'Michelangelo's Erotic Poetry', composed in 1950, when Mann was 75. There he presents Michelangelo as an example of old age triumphing over youth through its visual apprehension of beauty. Michelangelo's old body is, like Aschenbach's, a source of shame to him, but he takes refuge in the Platonic view that 'the god is in the loving and not in being loved—being loved is only the vehicle of divine enthusiasm'—and makes his love for the young Tommaso Cavalieri the inspiration for St Peter's Basilica.[74]

Aschenbach's longing to give up the labour of writing is a decadent version of this same way of thinking about the structure of an artist's life. The allure of Venice is the allure of early retirement. It is the unburdening that Fontane enjoys in his eighties, but it comes, for Aschenbach, pathologically too soon. Old age, as Mann wrote in 'Old Fontane', is a time when 'no "resilience" is required of a man, either by others or by himself—a time in which the question: "What is the good of it all?" ha[s] become natural, socially acceptable, and therefore a sympathetic attitude of mind' (288). By implication, such an attitude in a younger man will be a sign of moral laxity—as Aschenbach (some twenty years younger than Fontane) knows it to be in himself. To be released from discipline by age in this way is to be released also from the idea that the limits of representation define the artist's work and his life as necessarily tragic. To age 'tragically', as Aschenbach does (the distancing quotation marks are Mann's[75]), is a sign that the legitimate shape of a life has been betrayed.

'It seems that he had been aware of it', Mann writes of Fontane's longing for old age (287). The statement rings as true of Mann himself. Numerous letters and essays testify to his conviction from the beginning of his career onwards that the struggles of the artist would be both eased and vindicated if he could only live long enough. A 'prolific old age', he wrote to Heinrich Mann while still in his twenties, would make up for a 'barren youth'[76] (though his was hardly that). But the use of old age to define the possibilities for art is nowhere more elaborately dramatized than when, in his mid-thirties, he makes the 'ageing' Aschenbach's story a means to reflecting upon his own literary development. One of the reasons *Death in Venice* is often taken as an even more confessional novel than it is, is that it makes Aschenbach the established author of works that Mann had projected but not yet written (and never completed): a 'lucid and massive prose-epic about the life of Frederic of Prussia', a novel on the grand scale entitled *Maya*, the 'powerful tale entitled *A Study in Abjection*', a 'passionate treatise *Intellect and Art*' (202).[77]

For Mann, to think ahead through Aschenbach towards old age was to anticipate the point at which his own struggle to create artistic forms would stop. But it was also to berate the impulse in himself to give up too soon. A 'strange sort of moral self-castigation', Mann called it, when he looked back on *Death in Venice* almost thirty years later.[78] The sentence is usually taken as a reflection on the work's homoeroticism, but it is also a wry observation on his youthful taste for *pathos* and the relationship to his own writing expressed through the 'ageing Aschenbach'. For Mann, at 35, to imagine his own unwritten works as the achieved output of an artist much nearer the end of his career, was to indulge in a fantasy of art bypassing, or overstepping, the burden of labour—a fantasy that, in a man not yet old, must be dubiously legitimate. But writing about Aschenbach giving up before his time on writing was also, of course, a way of keeping himself at work, and taking the measure of how much remained to be done. Mann was kinder to himself, both in 1911 and in 1940, than his novella is to Aschenbach. He could afford to preserve a more generously ironizing view of his own ageing than his protagonist's anxious self-scrutiny admits: a kind of double consciousness whereby he watches his 30-something-year-old self, and leaves room for an older, healthier, saner, self to emerge.

The most surprising aspect of Mann's attitude to ageing is how consistent he remained in it. In 'What I Believe' (1938) he looked back on himself as he had been in his late twenties and thirties:

> When I was young I was infatuated with that pessimistic and romantic conception of the universe which set off against each other life and spirit, sensuality and redemption, and from which are derived some most compelling effects—compelling and yet, humanly speaking, not quite legitimate, not quite genuine. In short I was a Wagnerite. But it is very likely in consequence of riper years that my love and my attention have more and more fixed upon a happier and saner model—the figure of Goethe.[79]

The typical cast of mind of youth is, in the eyes of the 63-year-old Mann, 'not quite legitimate, not quite genuine' by comparison with that of age. But that sense of something inauthentic about the philosophical outlook of youth had been there from the start. It is what puts the tragedy of *Death in Venice* in quotation marks for Mann, even at the point of planning the story, marking its pathos as something which belongs to the young man's cast of mind, along with his taste for Nietzsche and for the early Lukács, and which his older self, he knows in advance, will reject as immature.

Throughout Mann's life, the labour of art seemed to be made possible, its object graspable, only through the sustaining idea that there would be an end to labour. Time and again in his writing he uses old age to establish a structure of proleptic retrospection. Looking at his life from the anticipated vantage point of age allowed Mann to take seriously Lukács's dictum that '*life* means that nothing is ever fully and completely lived through to the end', and yet decline to commit art too absolutely to a Lukácsian metaphysics of tragedy. Life and art, for Mann, though not for Aschenbach or Lukács, have as their joint safeguard the notion of a timely old age: a space before the end in which the writer/artist will already have lived and produced his art, and will be free to submit to sensory experience without forcing it to obey the laws of artistic form. Then, if he is lucky, life and art will come, as Fontane's did, 'easily' (298).

According to his daughter Erika, Mann aged very much as he hoped to. In mid-life he had seemed to her 'distant', 'stiff', 'conventional', but in his seventies and eighties he became 'relaxed', 'tender', and remarkably open—willing even to joke about his homosexual desires.[80] There are contradictory testimonies to his old age, including his own diary remarks about periods of depression, and about a still tormenting capacity for desire which he now, even more emphatically, considered beyond hope of fulfilment. But that, too, had been part of what he looked for from old age all along: old age as both the loss of the possibility of fulfilling desire and (connectedly) a freeing up of the possibility of expressing desire. On one point only, he felt his own ideal for old age had failed to materialize. At 78 he found himself more like Wagner than like Fontane, Michelangelo, or Goethe: 'Approaching 70 Wagner wrote his final work, the Parsifal, and died not long afterward. At about the same age I wrote my work of last significance, the Faustus, [...] but kept on living... What I lead now is an afterlife that struggles in vain for sustenance'.[81] If there is any more truth in this statement than in the happier statements from his seventies and eighties that rival it, it has to be said that Mann's predicament was to an unusual degree of his own making. That old age would be an 'afterlife' had been the idea all along.

The debt to Plato in *Death in Venice* goes much deeper than the retelling of the story of Socrates and Phaedrus alone suggests. Both Plato and Mann take the idea of an older man's love for a boy and make it the basis for an account of love which is, ultimately, an account of their own respective disciplines: philosophy and art. For both, writing in what most would think of as their prime, the imagined perspective of old age offers a vantage point from which to think—about the nature of wisdom, in the *Phaedrus* and the

Symposium, about the nature of artistic representation for Mann. In both cases the model of old age is inseparable from a model of a whole life. The philosophical life has old age as its apogee; the artist's life has old age as its promised release from the burden of art—and as such also its authenticating moment. In each case there is a deeper perception that ageing, understood as a process, rather than a mere adjunct of or preliminary for death, may be a means to apprehending the terms on which we acquire knowledge in this world (for Plato) or on which we subdue it to the forms of writing (for Mann). In the Socratic dialogues, thinking about ageing assists a definition of philosophy as the pursuit, by mortal, unstable, constantly changing beings, of the eternal, unchanging truths of the divine sphere. In Mann's novella it enables a characterization of art as the attempt to give utterance to what will always remain unutterable, to give form to what will always remain elusive.

The definition of art via old age in *Death in Venice* is thus a recapitulation of Plato's yoking of old age to a similar kind of definitional work for philosophy, but it is also, as fundamentally, a refusal of the Platonic account. Mann gives us old age as the very opposite of Platonic sublimation: absorption in the commonplace and the accidental and the humanly beautiful. When he employs the idea of transcendence he is looking to define our experience of this world as the domain of art; he does not require our belief in divinity or our commitment to the Platonic notion of ideal forms. His account of the artist's life in that novella is indeed founded on the impossibility of transcendence, and the inevitably tragic outcome of the contest between desire and possibility. For metaphysics he substitutes aesthetics.

On the surface, there are serious losses for old age. *Death in Venice* is not an obvious book to read if one wants to contemplate a 'good' description of ageing. It has been attacked by at least one recent writer on old age as a model we should resist.[82] Plato's use of age rested upon an enabling defence of the capabilities of the old, reserving the notion of decline for advanced old age. Mann seems deliberately to accelerate many of the deprivations of age: the perceived ineligibility of desire, the failing energies. But Mann's other writings, contemporary with and subsequent to *Death in Venice*, frame this approach to art and to life as the characteristic outlook of a 30-something-year-old. They also define it for us as, essentially, rhetorical. The young Mann gives us self-conscious, self-ironizing sentiment, thereby affirming a distinction—polemical, open to dispute—between philosophy as thought and literature as affect, emotion, atmosphere, style, but leaving room for his later self to 'grow out of' *pathos* and into the maturity of *ethos*.

The most important debt to Plato here is the critical awareness that old age is a domain of rhetoric long before it becomes lived experience. It leaves Mann, like Plato, free to take commonplace observations, prejudices, biological facts about old age and put them to work so that these commonplaces and banalities re-emerge as ways of exploring capacity and incapacity, power and impotence in quite other spheres: intellectual, spiritual, aesthetic. Both Plato and Mann certainly offer moral reflection on old age in the course of their claims for philosophy and for art, and the sense that old age is, amongst much else, a moral issue is never entirely out of sight—but neither offers a *primarily* moral account of what it means to live into old age, of what the value of a long life might be, and what the relation is (if any) between a long life and a good life. For that, we need to go to Aristotle.

2

On Seeing the End

At what point in a life can we measure its happiness? For Aristotle, happiness (*eudaimonia*[1]) was indissociable from where a person is in the temporal span of their existence. 'Children cannot be happy', he says in a famous passage of the *Nicomachean Ethics*. 'They are not old enough to be capable of noble acts', so 'when children are spoken of as happy, it is in compliment to their promise for the future'. But neither can those prospering in their maturity be said with confidence to flourish, '[f]or many reverses and vicissitudes of all sorts occur in the course of life, and it is possible that the most prosperous man may encounter great misfortunes in his declining years' (1100a2–8).[2] Witness Priam, once one of the greatest kings of Asia, stabbed or beaten to death (so he foresees, in the *Iliad*), then torn to pieces by 'ravening dogs at [his] own gates—the very dogs that [he himself] fed at table and trained to guard [his] gates'.[3] That such a reversal happens at the very end of a long life does not lessen its tragedy: 'when a person has such misfortunes and ends in a wretched condition, nobody says that he is living well (*oudeis eudaimonisdei*)'.[4]

Before we judge the *eudaimonia* of others, then, Aristotle cautions us to remember the words of the philosopher Solon to Croesus, king of Lydia. Herodotus tells in his history of the Persian wars of how Solon visited Croesus at the height of his prosperity, before his defeat by the Persians, and was given a tour of the king's vast treasuries. The complacent monarch then asked him which of all the men he had encountered he thought most fortunate (*olbiotaton*). Solon named three, all of whom died in their youth or prime,[5] honoured by their families and fellow citizens. When a disgruntled Croesus demanded to know whether his own unparalleled prosperity was to be 'utterly set at nought', Solon replied: 'O Croesus, [...] I see you very rich and the king of many men. But I cannot answer your question until I hear that you have closed your life well. Until a man dies, you may call him 'prosperous' (*olbion*), but you cannot call him 'truly fortunate' (*eutukhea*).[6]

There is a difference between Solon's terminology (*olbion*, used only of worldly goods and *eutuchea*, suggesting broader good fortune) and the ethically richer terms *eudaimonia* (virtuous happiness) and *makariotes* ('supreme happiness' or 'blessedness') preferred by Aristotle. Aristotle explains that Solon did not mean to say that only dead men can be called flourishing (*eudaimon*), which would be a nonsense: rather, only when a man is dead will it 'be safe to call [him] blessed [*makariseien*], on the grounds that he is now beyond the reach of evils and misfortunes' (1100a).[7] In Anthony Kenny's phrase, *makarios* is 'a proleptic predicate',[8] designating a state of complete happiness which will be confirmed only with the end of the life. So: truly 'blessed persons' (*makarioi*) are those not only virtuous and fortunate now but 'destined to live thus and have a death to match [their lives]'; but when someone's life 'is in accordance with complete excellence, sufficiently equipped with external goods, not for some random period but over a complete life', that person should be called *eudaimon* (1101a14–20).

The distinction is, unsurprisingly, disputed[9]—a point of recurrent tension for interpretors of the *Ethics*. How does the requirement that we see a 'complete life' before judging its claim to *eudaimonia* differ, in practice, from *makaria*'s requirement that a life be lived through to a good death? It is clear that Aristotle holds the good life to be a life of virtuous activity in the present and that, in any attempt to lead that life we must be able to make judgements as we go along: we cannot, practically speaking, wait for 'the end' of all. It is tempting, therefore, to finesse the comments on Solon and on Priam away, as being of minor importance.[10] Priam therefore matters, we might want to say, but not especially much: he is a monitory reminder that even a life very near its natural end may, in exceptional circumstances, go badly wrong. But Aristotle is saying more than that: by focusing on the complete life, by drawing our attention to what may happen at the very end of a long life, and by giving us the example of Priam, he is setting a standard for *eudaimonia* not obviously lower than the criteria for *makariotes*.[11] He is not saying that the end matters most, or that what happens to us in old age is intrinsically of more importance than what happens in our prime, but he is saying that how we live in old age may be decisive for whether or not our life as a whole counts as *eudaimon*.

The problem lies in part with the word 'end'. The opening pages of the *Nicomachean Ethics* tell us that we need to know the chief end (*telos*) of human life if we are to succeed in hitting 'the target' (*skopos*) of our final good. A *telos* differs from a *skopos*, in being not a fixed object but an end at which we direct our actions throughout our lives. As Julia Annas explains, it 'suggests an end or goal not in the sense of the thing aimed at but in the sense of the agent's aiming at that end'.[12] But there remains a degree of opacity in Aristotle's thinking about how teleology is then to be read against chronology: how the good life, conceived as direction towards an inward goal, is to be understood temporally. John Cooper goes so far as to claim that Aristotle should not, in fact, be thought of as a teleologist, in the sense encouraged by the common post-Kantian division between 'teleological' and 'deontological' theories of right action.

> Aristotle does not stand with the teleologists, as is generally assumed, but is in certain respects closer to Kant and the deontologists. For if the distinguishing feature of a teleological theory is that in it 'the good is defined independently from the right and then the right is defined as that which maximizes the good', then Aristotle's theory of virtuous action is not a teleological theory. For although he does hold that virtuous action is a means to *eudaimonia*, or human good, *eudaimonia* is not specified independently of virtuous action; on the contrary, *eudaimonia* is conceived as identical with a lifetime of morally virtuous action.[13]

In Cooper's account of Aristotle, there is no separation to be made between having a good life and living a good life (virtue is instantiated in the activity of being virtuous). But a problem remains here over what the 'time' in 'lifetime' then means. The Aristotelian requirement that we see the complete life before we judge, finally, whether a life was *eudaimon* makes it impossible to smooth over the temporal dimension of these claims about the good life entirely by asserting that virtue is immanent in action. For the Aristotelian and neo-Aristotelian, virtue cannot simply be thought of as 'achieved' at the point where virtuous action has become habitual for the mature agent; it is always being tested. The good life therefore remains a temporally articulated concept, and although teleology is definitionally distinct from chronology it must be worked out in, and as, a chronology of education, habituation, choice, and the living through of a sequence of actions that ends only with the agent's death.[14]

These difficulties loom much larger if one goes to Aristotle with a desire to know whether and how we can hope to live well in, and through, old age. If we ask that question of the *Nicomachean Ethics*, Priam's case becomes more worrying than is standardly conceded. A man who suffers blows to his prosperity as fundamental as those which afflict Priam in his late years obviously cannot be called supremely blessed. But can his end not be discounted, in the light of an earlier life generally understood to have been virtuous and prosperous? Should the long good not outweigh the short bad? On a purely additive view, this seems right, even fair. Someone who has lived to be old may have a quantity of good experience which a shorter life cannot possess: does the total sum of well-being accrued over so many years not overrule whatever harms may befall that person in their last years?[15] Must he also forfeit his claim to *eudaimonia*? Despite his wish to assert the priority of virtue, Aristotle's answer in the Priam passage is no. A life which begins badly may become a happy life—early misfortunes may be redeemed by noble acts, benign fortune, and a good end—but, if that good end is missing, active virtue (though primary) will not be enough. *Eudaimonia* will be diminished. In extreme circumstances, such as Priam's, it may be forfeited entirely.

This pressure, after all, on the chronological end is neither exclusively nor (as Herodotus shows) originally Aristotelian. Many would say that it is intuitively how we think about our lives—that we are future-directed creatures—and Aristotle is arguing, as ever, on the basis of generally held wisdom and common experience. But when the demand that we see the end before judging the quality of a life is applied to old age it becomes a deeply troublesome component in the theory of how we best flourish. A life lived into old age is likely to be one that experiences more in the way of contingent harm than a life that ends in the person's prime. Solon yoked old age explicitly to this cumulative view of risk, arguing that we increase our exposure to harm with every day that we go on living. 'Seventy years I regard as the limit of the life of man', he says in the same passage Aristotle refers to. 'In these seventy years are contained […] twenty-five thousand two hundred and fifty [days], whereof not one but will produce events unlike the rest—and not one but may bring disaster.'[16]

Given the perception that old age involves heightened (because ex-tended) risk, it is surprising to find that it receives very little further attention in the *Nicomachean Ethics*: no more than nine or so brief references in addition to the Priam passage.[17] Of these, two are positive, advising us to attend carefully to the opinions of the elderly and those of long experience (1143b10), and asserting the honour due to 'every older person' (1165a28).[18] Three are neutral, upholding care for the old as a function of friendship and a duty of children (1155a14, 1165a22[19]), and offering 'growing old' as an example of a 'natural process' to be considered neither a voluntary nor an involuntary action (1135b1).[20] All the rest are derogatory comments on the diminished virtue of old men: their meanness; their lack of interest in friendship except where a connection is profitable to them; their moroseness and incapacity to please others (1121b14, 1156a25, 1157b14–15, 1158a3–7). These passing, predominantly negative reflections on the moral impact of ageing are rarely noticed by commentators. If they are registered at all they are usually seen as continuous with Aristotle's sensitivity to contingency (*tuche*) generally—a reminder, as Martha Nussbaum puts it, that even those aspects of our lives that are of the 'highest ethical importance and value, can be blighted by bodily changes that we cannot control. We can all look forward to the loss of a high value, if we live long enough'.[21]

Nussbaum is an important voice here because she has done more than anyone to put Aristotle back at the forefront of ethical debate within literary criticism and philosophy. *The Fragility of Goodness* (1986; rev. 2001) is an eloquent defence of Aristotle as the classical philosopher most responsive to the contingency of human flourishing. In Nussbaum's words, Aristotle recognizes that 'certain central human values are available and valuable only within a context of risk and material limitation' (341). Vulnerability is not just an important but an inevitable aspect of the human condition, and the virtue of the *phronimos*, or man of practical wisdom, will be exhibited in the way he meets it. Even in those rare circumstances when a virtuous person is 'dislodged' from *eudaimonia* by 'severe or prolonged' deprivation, we have grounds for valuing what such a life tells us—namely, that 'virtuous condition is not, itself, something hard and invulnerable. Its yielding and open posture towards the world gives it the fragility, as well as the beauty, of a plant' (340).[22]

Fragility is not at odds with 'beauty' in this claim. It is what enables the virtuous disposition towards the world. 'A divine or unlimited life could not have th[e] same virtues and values, [the same] good things, in it' as our human life (341). The sharpness of Nussbaum's passing comment on what 'we can all look forward to' if we 'live long enough' therefore jars. It is the point at which she acknowledges most directly how destructive the processes of ageing may be to Aristotelian *eudaimonia*, and it is unclear how much weight we are expected to give it. When she comes to reflect, briefly, on Aristotle's account of the differences between age and youth (337–9), she makes the important point that age can, in Aristotle's view, 'impede character', putting at risk those many virtues that require 'openness' rather than 'self-defensiveness' (338), but her accent is on the incompatibility of virtue with 'an undue emphasis on self-protection' right through our lives, rather than on old age per se. In the *Rhetoric*, as she notes later, old age is invoked as a 'representative example' of a 'painful and injurious thing' (or, things 'distressing' and 'destructive' in Reese's translation[23]), categorized along with 'death, bodily assault, bodily ill-treatment, [...] illness, lack of food' (1386a7). (It is to be distinguished from 'substantial damages [...] caused by luck', such as 'ugliness, weakness, being crippled, [...] having no good things happen to you' (384).) Like those other pains or injuries, it may impair trust and therefore virtue, bringing about 'a loss in sensitivity and in enjoyment that can lead to the dissolution or at least the diminution of love'. It is a warning to us that *philia* (loving friendship) (which seems the 'greatest of external goods' for Aristotle[24]) is not invulnerable to 'life's changes' (360-1)—but there is no gloss on 'life's changes' here, and nothing to distinguish it from harm in any other form.

Nussbaum treats Priam primarily as an illustration of the contingencies of war (and in this she is entirely representative of past and present conventions of reading this passage). He is 'a good test case for Aristotle's ethical theory', because he is 'a person who ha[s], presumably, developed and maintained a stably virtuous character through life, ha[s] acted well and according to excellence—but who was then deprived by war of family, children, friends, power, resources, freedom' (328).[25] In a six-page discussion of Priam, Nussbaum barely mentions his age (only 'the constraints on him' (328), the loss of his 'sphere of activity' (329), and—adding considerably to Aristotle—his 'having displayed good character in action consistently over the course of a long life' (329)), nor does she place much emphasis on the fact that he is introduced in support of the claim that we must see the end of a life before we judge its *eudaimonia* (though she gives close consideration to the distinction between *eudaimonia* and *makariotes*). Her account of the *Nicomachean Ethics* 1100a1–1101a20 is strongly coloured by her desire to show that devastations of virtuous living by bad luck are extreme cases which, rather than undermining the Aristotelian description of *eudaimonia*, serve to confirm its general validity. '[G]iven a conception of good living that values stable excellences of character and activity [...] such drastic upsets will be rare' (329). As she sees it, Aristotle's account of virtue constrains the definition of risk in such a way that we can cope with most of the contingencies that will beset us, and if some individuals become victims of extreme bad luck or injustice then those are the limit cases, and should be valued as such. In allowing any weight at all to Priam, she argues, Aristotle goes against 'a well-established tradition in moral philosophy, both ancient and modern, according to which moral goodness [...] cannot be harmed or affected by external circumstances' (329) (the allusion is to Plato's Socrates, who claimed that 'a good man cannot be harmed'[26]). Kant, most prominently, held that '*happiness* can be augmented or diminished by fortune; but that which is truly deserving of ethical praise and blame, true moral worth, cannot be' (329).

'It is not surprising', Nussbaum remarks, that interpreters 'under the influence' of the Platonic, Kantian, and other deontological traditions, and 'anxious to make Aristotle look morally respectable', have 'read the Priam passage oddly, so that it no longer says what would be most shocking, namely that ethical praiseworthiness of life, not just happy feeling, can be augmented or diminished by chance reversals' (329). No commentator on the *Nicomachean Ethics* to date, she claims, has recognized the full implications of Aristotle's views on Priam for his theory of the good life—but Nussbaum herself has to be included in this. By taking Priam predominantly as an illustration of the contingencies of war, she too reduces Aristotle's power to shock. Read in context, as a statement about the risks we are exposed to by the fact of growing old, the Priam passage says something more deeply worrying. It tells us that a human life lived to its full (or near its full) biological potential is a life at greater risk of substantial loss of value than a life that ends in its prime.

Every stage of life carries its risks in Aristotle's ethics: children are dependent on the care and the good judgement of others; a man in his prime is likely to be more exposed to the dangers of war and political upheaval than in later years. But old age, as Aristotle describes it, is qualitatively and functionally different from other sources of damage to the good life,[27] and the passage from the *Rhetoric* that categorizes it along with death, bodily assault, illness, and other harms does not adequately convey how destructive its potential is for the theory of *eudaimonia* set out in the *Nicomachean Ethics*. When Aristotle says that our flourishing is at risk from how we are likely to change if we live to a full human lifespan, he is not saying that we may be dislodged from the good life by age *just as we may* be by illness or assault or ill-treatment. He is saying that our well-being is at significant and increasing risk the longer we live on past our prime.

Old age is a peculiar kind of contingency—neither fully a contingency, nor quite a necessity (see Introduction, p. 4). It is a contingency in the sense that it is not certain to be our lot: we may not live to grow old; we may choose not to grow old (we can commit suicide, although for Aristotle suicide was normally forbidden by the law,[28] or there may be conditions, such as war, under which we will virtuously sacrifice our lives for the good of others or the sake of the polis). But old age is also a necessity. Until or unless we die we cannot but continue to age. Aristotle acknowledges as much when he describes the ageing process as an action neither voluntary nor involuntary. What matters more to him is the heightened exposure ageing brings to other contingent harms. It raises the likelihood that we will suffer from serious ill health or enfeeblement. Arguably, it also brings greater because prolonged risk of secondary dishonour through the acts of one's children or grandchildren (or so one might deduce from Aristotle's discussion of whether we can be harmed posthumously by the acts of our descendants (1100a14–1101a22)). Above all, it erodes our capacity for dealing well with contingent ills.

Priam is exceptional in the extreme wretchedness of his end—but he is also, Aristotle tells us, representative: an old man, whose loss of *eudaimonia* has to do with his age rather than with war per se. The reference at this point to the *Iliad* indicates how far Aristotle abided by a Homeric vision of heroic virtue. War was the most testing of circumstances for the adult free man—the ability to take part in battle being essential to the distinction between citizen and slave (a requirement for all owners of property).[29] For Aristotle, as for Homer, the old are at an evident disadvantage under such exacting conditions because they can no longer satisfy the requirements of military action as they could when younger. They cannot compete with the young in physical prowess and they can no longer bear arms, so what respect they retain depends upon voluntary acknowledgements from others, not upon any honour they can actively earn. Hence Achilles' gesture of tact in book 23 of the *Iliad*, when he awards a prize to Nestor at the close of Patroclus' funeral games: 'I give you this prize though you cannot win one. You can now neither wrestle nor fight, and cannot enter for the javelin match nor foot races, for the hand of age has been laid heavily upon you.'[30] Hence also, more starkly, Priam's proleptic elegy for himself a few lines earlier: 'It is fitting for a young man to lie slain in battle,' he tells his son Hector (shortly to die at the hands of Achilles), 'but when it is an old man who is down, and dogs are scavenging on his grey head, grey beard and private parts, we plumb the depths of human degradation.'[31]

Neither Homer nor Aristotle implies that Priam is to blame for what happens to him. But in appealing to Priam, Aristotle appeals to the case of a man who is famously eloquent about the miseries that arise from the frailty of age. Were he Hector, he would still die tragically in the coming battle, we can assume, and his life would not be *eudaimon*, but he, and those who attack him, would not be 'degraded'. If old age is morally due the honour of the young, it is also much more deeply at risk should they choose to dishonour it. In Homer, at least, one has a strong sense of other kinds of virtue in play, including in Priam himself, which remain viable and valuable in old age and are appropriate to its capacities. The old may be unable to meet the physically strenuous criteria applicable to young men in wartime but they can act as virtuous political advisers, friends, heads of their families, and responsible citizens, employing the wisdom and practical experience they have accrued over many years. Nestor is Homer's famous example. The trouble with Aristotle on old age is that, though these virtues are addressed in general terms, they are never presented as virtues characteristic of the old. On the contrary, he portrays the old as, typically, far from virtuous.

In a much cited passage of the *Rhetoric* he gives us this portrait of the typical qualities of the old. I quote it at length (though not in full) because its impact lies partly in its remorselessly cumulative negativity:

Elderly men—men who are past their prime—[…] have lived for many years; they have often been taken in, and often made mistakes; and life on the whole is a bad business. […] They are cynical; that is, they tend to put the worse construction on everything. Further, their experience makes them distrustful and therefore suspicious of evil. Consequently they neither love warmly nor hate bitterly, but following the hint of Bias they love as though they will some day hate and hate as though they will some day love. They are small-minded, because they have been humbled by life: their desires are set upon nothing more exalted or unusual than what will help them to keep alive. They are not generous, because money is one of the things they must have, and at the same time their experience has taught them how hard it is to get and how easy to lose. They are cowardly, and are always anticipating danger; unlike that of the young, who are warm-blooded, their temperament is chilly; old age has paved the way for cowardice […] They are too fond of themselves; this is one form that small-mindedness takes. Because of this, they guide their lives too much by considerations of what is useful and too little by what is noble—for the useful is what is good for oneself, and the noble what is good absolutely. They are not shy, but shameless rather;

[…] they feel contempt for what people may think of them. They lack confidence in the future; partly through experience—for most things go wrong, or anyhow turn out worse than one expects; and partly because of their cowardice. They live by memory rather than by hope; for what is left to them of life is but little as compared with the long past; and hope is of the future, memory of the past. This, again, is the cause of their loquacity; they are continually talking of the past, because they enjoy remembering it. [… T]hey do not feel their passions much, and their actions are inspired less by what they do feel than by the love of gain. Hence men at this time of life are often supposed to have a self-controlled character; the fact is that their passions have slackened, and they are slaves to the love of gain. They guide their lives by reasoning more than by moral feeling; reasoning being directed to utility and moral feeling to moral goodness. […] Old men may feel pity, as well as young men, but not for the same reason. Young men feel it out of kindness; old men out of weakness, imagining that anything that befalls any one else might easily happen to them.[32]

This is in excess of anything in the *Nicomachean Ethics*. As rhetoric, it is of course seeking to do something very different. It is a statement not about the behaviour or even character of individual old men but about 'the linguistic behaviour to be expected' from them as a generalized category of speakers, 'and, specifically, the linguistic norms to be employed by the orator if his speech patterns are to be like theirs'.[33] The identification of psychological 'sources or corollaries' for these speech patterns and 'behavioural characteristics' of the old has to be understood in that context. If any one individual were represented as possessing all the features of Aristotle's linguistic typology he would be a caricature.[34] On the other hand, what is said here is not at odds with the *Nicomachean Ethics*. The larger part of the references to age in the *Ethics* are entirely compatible with the bleakness (and the potential for comedy[35]) of the *Rhetoric*. For Aristotle, old age is typically a state of disabusement with—and by—life. Its governing motivation is neediness; its predominant disposition fear. Experience, instead of lending wisdom, compassion, gravitas, brings—past a certain point—cynicism, narrowness of mind and heart, and a wish (oxymoronically) both to turn away from life and to clutch it ever more nearly, like misers obsessed by the thought of how much may at any moment be taken away. And far from feeling shame at their descent from virtue, the old become so self-concerned and so absorbed by the past that they are immune to the claims of moral principle and future possibility which might lead them back to a good life.

Most demoralizing of all is the perception, here, that the conditions that make for virtue in our prime will, past a certain point, begin to work against us, chilling our affections and corroding our virtues. Aristotle does not say this, but it is a position he must, in the end, be committed to. As we grow still older there will be ever-diminishing possibilities of resistance. Time and life will be running out: if we do ill, there will be less time in which we can make restitution to those we have harmed; if we suffer loss, there will be less time in which it can be compensated for. *Energeia* (unimpeded activity in accordance with excellence) will be reduced, and the very motivation towards virtuous action will be weakened, by age and too-long experience.

There is no identificatory 'we' in Aristotle's characterization of old men. Needy, garrulous, shameless old age is not a state that he acknowledges may one day be his own. Generally he reserves the first person plural for the prosecution of philosophical argument, with illustrative cases couched in the third person—but there is no recognition, however worded, that age is a condition that, other things being equal, he will come to inhabit. The exact composition dates of the *Rhetoric* and the *Nicomachean Ethics* are unknown. The *Ethics* is now thought most likely to date from the period between 335 BCE, when the 49-year-old Aristotle returned to Athens and founded his own philosophical school, and 323 (one year before his death at 62).[36] The *Rhetoric* is often dated to earlier in his life, when he was a student in Plato's Academy.[37] If so, the *Rhetoric*'s harshness represents the thinking of a man whose outlook on old age is as yet remote; the more measured pessimism of the *Nicomachean Ethics* comes from a man reaching the end of his prime or already embarked on old age. Whatever the case, the deduction is there to be made from his comments on ineluctable natural processes: old age cannot be avoided except by dying before we get there. If Aristotle's arguments are taken to their logical conclusion, he himself cannot long resist what ageing will do to his ability to live well.

Aristotelian old age thus attacks the human capacity for *eudaimonia* at its core. It does this by damaging (progressively and ever more irretrievably) the virtuous character.[38] But what makes the description of its effects more damaging than it might otherwise be for virtue ethics is the addition of the requirement, in the *Nicomachean Ethics*, that to make the final judgement on the quality of a life we must wait to see how it concludes. That insistence on seeing the end, coupled with the diminished capabilities associated with age, recalls a familiar complaint against Aristotle. It points up the limits of what virtue can achieve, even with all the Aristotelian supports of a good education and a lifetime's commitment to virtuous practice. But it also adds a difficulty that need not have been there. The effect of Aristotle's acknowledgement that old age is a 'natural process', and therefore neither a voluntary nor an involuntary action, might have been to lift old age out of the debate about good v. bad lives altogether. If ageing is not subject to our volition, we might protest (in Kantian vein), we cannot be held morally responsible for its depletion of our capabilities.

Why does Aristotle not allow old age an equivalent exceptionality to childhood? The logic that leads him to the claim that children are 'not yet' capable of nobility might lead him to say also that the dependent elderly are 'no longer capable' of its most demanding forms. They could then be 'paid the compliment' of respect for their past (their having lived a good life) just as children are 'paid the compliment' of their promise for the future (their potential to go on and live a good life). But he does not say this. A crucial consequence of the long denunciation of the character of the old in the *Rhetoric*, and the briefer criticisms in the *Nicomachean Ethics*, is that the language of vice holds the elderly responsible for their own moral condition. The fact that growing old is a natural and (as long as we are alive) an inevitable process is not seen as enough to remove the old from accountability. Unlike children, the aged are not untrained or ignorant of what virtue requires. On the contrary they are so experienced and so habituated to the bruising ways of the world that they have, it seems, passed through virtue and into another, less amiable and less admirable, moral state.

This is not a description of dementia; it is a description of a moral falling off, and it presents a major problem for anyone who looks to Aristotle's virtue ethics for an account of the good long life. The typical decline in moral character of the old, as Aristotle sees it, involves a reversal in his own basic assumptions about the nature of our engagement with the world, and the cumulative effect of our experience. Until we are old, in Aristotle's writings, time is (implicitly) our ally, bringing us the benefits that come with growth and maturity.[39] But once we enter old age it starts to work against us, threatening to unseat much that we may have achieved by way of living a good life until then. Old age thus operates like an introduction of bad faith into *eudaimonian* ethics, turning factors which have so far been ours to harness to the good (time, experience, habituation) into forces not of our controlling, corrosive of our capacity for virtue and for happiness.

This reading of Aristotle should, needless to say, worry any neo-Aristotelian who holds that on the basis of virtue ethics '(nearly) all of us' can flourish.[40] Unless we are prepared to exempt the old, as Aristotle was not, from the more exacting conditions for virtuous living that obtain in our prime, it is difficult to see how such a statement can hold true once our capacities begin to fail us. Of course, there is an important distinction to be made between the loss of our physical powers and the loss of mental and moral capability. Virtuous character traits do not decline concomitantly with the wasting of the body. But as Aristotle himself conceived of old age, age-related decline does in many cases affect those traits too, even if not in direct parallel, and even if (in many cases) more slowly. On the basis of the *Rhetoric*, and the shorter passages on the character of the old in the *Nicomachean Ethics*, we know that Aristotle had a pessimistic view of our human ability to flourish, almost by definition, much past our prime. This is not to say that he is committed to the view that a person whose virtuous character is impaired in late life by age can no longer be called, in the final judgement, happy. He is, however, committed to the view that such a life would have been significantly happier had nature allowed it to stop sooner. He is also committed to the view that such a life requires, at its end, more in the way of virtue from others: greater compassion, greater magnanimity, more selfless friendship.

How far may the bleakest aspects of this view be dismissed as rhetorical rather than moral? As many critics have noted, there are limited grounds for making critical judgments about the *Nicomachean Ethics* on the basis of its style.[41] These were probably lecture notes or working drafts prepared for publication some time after Aristotle's death, not his own finished texts.[42] The *Rhetoric* is the more stylistically distinctive work, perhaps closer to Aristotle's own voice. But it would be a mistake to read its aggressive cynicism on the subject of the old as just a stylistic exercise: a rhetorical performance piece, for example, in the manner of crabbed age, with its characteristic cynicism, disenchantment, demoralization. This would be to ignore the fact that the general typologization of the speech of the old is also an attempt to summarize a typical or normative psychological and moral state. (Aristotle is equally pejorative about the young, it should be noted, but their prime lies ahead of them, and they can still be educated.) The style of the *Rhetoric* is, moreover, declarative, authoritative, rarely marked by the rhetorical features Aristotle is identifying in the old. Even without the evidence of the *Rhetoric*, there is more than enough in the ethical writings to prompt dismay about the effects of ageing on our ability to lead a good life. The picture is consistent across the *Works*—and to discount the *Rhetoric*'s comments on age would be to understate the seriousness and consistency of Aristotle's sense of old age as a deterioration in the powers and cogencies and, especially, the capacity for virtuous action of one's prime.

One possible response—not likely to find wide support, given contemporary efforts to oust what is fearful, exploitative, or otherwise negatively prejudicial in social attitudes to the old—is to say that Aristotle was substantially right, or at least not wrong. As a broad characterization of the behaviour and cast of mind of those past their mental and physical prime, much of what he says rings true. Taken as prescriptive it would be crass stereotyping, but taken as a profile, a set of features regularly, but by no means definitively, found among the old, it is no more and no less than common observation.[43] There are, to be sure, historical and cultural differences, and an obvious objection to Aristotle's characterization of the old is that it does not recognize clearly enough the external pressures that may shape a person's sense of themselves in old age, as much or more than the internal changes. But then some aspects of Aristotle's characterization of age are even preferable to what a broad typology of the old today would be likely to include. As Michael Silk points out, old men, not just in Aristotle, but across 'extant Greek literature', 'even if beset by personal or familial distress, generally belong to, or are assimilated to, the same privileged, or leisured, or aristocratic, or heroic, or at least socially accepted, strata of their world as most other speakers. They are not usually disadvantaged by isolation [or] by mental decline; and in such respects they differ greatly from many of their unfortunate counterparts in the modern West and its literary representations.'[44]

To note that much of what Aristotle says remains recognizable to us is to raise the very large question of how far attitudes to old age are grounded in factors that have more to do with biology than with history: the decline of physical and mental capacities, the likely psychological consequences of that decline. Aristotle's rhetorical characterization of old age is less important in this context, however, than what he makes of it in a general account of the good life. While his descriptions of old age are broadly representative of his time,[45] the ethical conclusions attached to them are unusually exacting. Plato's view of the old, as we have seen, is sometimes comparable to Aristotle's view in negativity (the 'elderly non-swimmers' of the *Laws*, for example), but he was more sceptical of cliché, more tolerant in the main of the falling away of powers, less ready to admonish the enfeebled; and, unlike Aristotle, he repeatedly identified old age (early old age) as the best time in one's life to practise philosophy.

There are some compensatory strands in Aristotle's thinking. He regards old age as part of a fully lived life, and he counts appropriate preparation for it among the virtues of a man's prime. But he does not prize it. If we accept his statement that we must see the end before we make the final judgement on a life, explicitly linked as it is to a pessimistic account of the impact of old age on virtue, we have no option but to view longevity with extreme wariness. The longer our life, he warns us, the more exposed it will be not just to accident, but to a decline in moral capability that will lead us away from rather than towards the good. Aristotelian old age is not necessarily bad, but a good and flourishing life is defined in such a way that we have cause to wish not to go on past our peak. To do so may be to press our luck. Without absolutely committing us to a tragic view, the *Nicomachean Ethics* thus yokes a commonplace, still persistent view of old age to an account of ethics in which longevity appears less a matter of good fortune than an open door on tragedy in lives which, had they stopped sooner, could have been called happy.

I take King Lear to be the nearest equivalent now to what Priam was for Aristotle: the most familiar artistic representation of old age in European literature. That familiarity allows Lear to function now, as Priam did in classical antiquity, as the obvious example in the literary and dramatic repertoire of a man whose claim to happiness was lost in, and to a significant extent by, old age. Lear, like Priam, is pitiable in that his misfortune is disproportionate; frightening inasmuch as we would not want to share his fate and imaginably could. His life, like Priam's, ends tragically, and that tragedy is in part the consequence of old age's erosion of his capabilities and thence of his character. How *far* it is so is one of the difficulties of interpretation with which the play's directors, audiences, readers have to wrestle.

Shakespeare shared with Aristotle a number of commonplace perceptions of age: there are lines in Shakespeare, as in Aristotle, that uphold the honour and respect due to age; there are also numerous characters reminiscent of the *Rhetoric* (garrulous, nervous, cowardly, selfish, senile). It matters that these *are* commonplaces. The nature and extent of Shakespeare's familiarity with Aristotle remain an open question. The standard view among scholars of Shakespeare's classical learning is that he had limited if any first-hand knowledge of Aristotle's works.[46] The evidence of the plays suggests some knowledge in adulthood of Aristotelian ethics and method, but no absolute proof that Shakespeare read Aristotle directly, rather than mediated through the work of later classical and medieval philosophers (Aristotle's pupil Theophrastus, for example, much imitated in Shakespeare's lifetime), or through more recent writers such as Hooker.[47]

King Lear is not an Aristotelian play, either in form or in its few explicit references to philosophy. On the basis of the *Poetics*, moreover, it is unclear that Aristotle himself would have regarded Lear's case as tragic. One of the questions raised by Aristotle's view of old age in the *Nicomachean Ethics* and the *Rhetoric* is whether a person whose character has been impaired by age can be an appropriate subject for tragedy. Priam might lead us to want to answer yes, but Priam was not impaired in his mental or moral powers (in the *Iliad* he has a painfully acute awareness of his own condition). The *Nicomachean Ethics* indicates that the life of a man such as Lear, mentally and morally impaired by age, will be more vulnerable to tragedy, but it also points us to the conclusion that, if the deterioration is serious, he cannot be a tragic hero. Lear seems to be the agent of his own undoing at the division of the kingdoms, but is he by then already impaired in judgement? His story thereafter continues to disclose more elements of choice than Priam's, but his age and his madness also increasingly put the meaning of choice in doubt.

Shakespeare's formal and ethical assumptions about tragedy are generally much less explicit than Aristotle's and not explicit at all in *Lear*. The earliest published texts of the play categorize it as a history play; and the First Folio's inclusion of it among the tragedies may never have been endorsed by Shakespeare, and was probably due to practical rather than philosophical considerations. What it means to think of the play as a tragedy, and of Lear as a tragic hero (or not), is partly dependent on this textual history, but is also an intractable dilemma arising from the central character's age. There is a basic difficulty for the reader (and performer) of Shakespeare, even more than for the reader of Aristotle, in knowing how much weight we should give to old age in our assessment of a person's—or character's—actions and qualities. Old age was, for Aristotle, one of the circumstances, far from the most prominent, which may jeopardize a good life; in *King Lear* it is prominent, but still only one factor among many. Political wrangling, misjudgement in parental love, and a lack of self-knowledge perhaps not new to Lear with age, all contribute to the disasters that befall him. 'He hath ever but slenderly known himself', Lear's daughter Regan tells us: she is a biased witness, but not necessarily to be discounted.

When compared with Aristotle's ethics, *King Lear* shows broad continuities with some of its assumptions but does not demonstrate direct and close influence of the kind observable between Plato and Mann. Shakespeare's dramatic articulation of vulnerability in old age lends it much greater psychological and contextual specificity than it has in the *Nicomachean Ethics*. It also exposes the subject to new forms of pressure. More openly in *Lear* than in the *Nicomachean Ethics*, being old is the stuff of rhetoric and so of competing ways of thinking about what it means to be old (it is continuous in that respect with the emphasis on rhetoric in Ch. 1). Unlike in the *Nicomachean Ethics*, old age is portrayed as the experience of three, perhaps four, men (just who is old in *Lear* is, as we shall see, a problem), beset by different kinds of harm, and equipped with different capabilities. Because *Lear* is not philosophy but drama, it draws out and gives much greater depth to the main question raised by Aristotle: if age seriously diminishes mental and moral capacity, what part should it play in our judgement of a person's actions and, finally, in our judgement of a person's life? Can we discount the end, or is the end, *in* the end, decisive?

'Is this the promised end?', the loyal baron Kent asks as he witnesses King Lear's final entrance on stage: maddened, howling, bearing Cordelia's body in his arms (5. 3. 237).[48] Editors have often taken Kent's words, and Edgar's choric response, 'Or image of that horror?', to be 'an anachronistic allusion' to the Apocalypse.[49] But anachronism recedes if these men are understood to be saying something less rhetorically high-pitched, more immediate to the scene before them: is this the promised end of our human life? Is this what we risk in the course of time if, like Lear, we live too long?[50] 'The wonder is he hath endured so long,' is Kent's spare elegy when the aged king at last dies: 'He but usurped his life' (5. 3. 292–3). Like much that is said of old age in this play, the vocabulary reaches after expression for what has come to seem a peculiarly intimate act of injustice to the self. 'To appropriate wrongfully to oneself (a right, prerogative, etc.)', is how the *OED* defines 'usurp'. Alternatively, 'to supplant, oust or turn out (a person); to deprive (one) of possessions', 'to seize, intrude or lay hold upon […] without just cause', 'to arrogate to oneself unjustly', or, figuratively, 'to usurp the place of'.[51] To suffer as wretchedly as Lear suffers at 'four score and upward' is, Kent suggests, to do a wrong to one's own life, to expropriate oneself from it by the very act of living on.[52] This is the reverse sentiment to Macbeth's hasty acknowledgement of his wife's end, 'She should have died hereafter' (5. 5. 16):[53] Lear should have died sooner, while his capacity to lead a good life was still of his own commanding.

The final lines of the play recapitulate this elegy with a difference. In the Folio text they are given to Edgar, in the Quarto to Albany:[54]'we that are young | Shall never see so much, nor live so long' (5. 3. 301–2). They have the air of a more formal, though still improvised elegy, a rhetorical bringing down of the curtain on old age; but they may also be spoken as a different kind of wish—a wish to emulate Lear's heroic age, and as such one last obtuseness about the tragedy to which overlong lives are vulnerable. Kent was trying to say something else.[55] The claim that one may outlive one's own life marked a last effort at resistance on his part to the pessimism that Lear's drastic reversal of fortune invites about old age. If Lear 'but usurped his life' his existence can be divided into two: the true life, and the false one in which an 'old', incapable, irrational Lear 'supplanted' the true Lear. The description belies—or tries to belie—Kent's already acknowledged sense of the painful continuity of the whole ('he hath endured so long'),[56] lifting Lear out of the midst of tragedy by having us, *at* the end, *discount* the end, recognizing only the man in his prime and his earlier old age as truly himself.

Kent asks us, in effect, to do the impossible: having reached the tragic conclusion of this unremittingly tragic play, to deny 'the weight of this sad time' (5. 3. 299) and value more what went before it. It matters that we understand him to have failed. For the audience of *Lear* there is no 'before'. Of course, much dramatic writing about age tends to skew our attention towards the end—but this is a play exceptionally short on memory. Even when Lear upbraids his daughters for their failure to return his past care and love for them, there is no specificity to that claim from the past, no memory attached to it. One of the many ways in which Jane Smiley's 1991 rewriting of Lear, *A Thousand Acres*, is acute is that it exploits that gap, making the loss and abuse of memory part of the grounds for the elder daughters' treatment of their father, a contributing factor to, as well as symptom of, his decline. In Shakespeare's play we cannot discount Lear's end, if only because, even in the form of retrospection, we are shown nothing before the point at which he comes before his assembled court, in Act 1 scene 1, and announces the division of the kingdoms.

> 'tis our fast intent
> To shake all cares and business from our age,
> Conferring them on younger strengths, while we
> Unburdened crawl toward death. [...]
>
> Tell me, my daughters,
> Since now we will divest us both of rule,
> Interest of territory, cares of state,
> Which of you shall we say doth love us most,
> That we our largest bounty may extend
> Where nature doth with merit challenge?

(I. I. 37–52)

The Lear of this opening scene does not sound like a man whose end is imminent: his 'divestment' of his responsibilities is undertaken in acknowledgement of old age, but it is not defined by any loss of capability (unless we take the very asking of the love question to be a sign that he is losing his judgement). Until the point where he hands over the coronet, Lear rather amplifies than reduces his power by looking to curb it. 'Younger strengths' is comparative—depletive but not exhausted—and the intention to 'crawl' towards death (recalling Jacques' 'second childishness') is wryly self-dramatizing rather than self-humbling: a mature man's joke. It looks for the laughter of dissent from the courtiers in making light of what is awkwardly apparent. (If there were not some physical decline, would the line work?) The implicit assumption on his part is that he could go on shouldering the state's 'cares and business', but has elected to 'shake' off the 'burden' of kingship. We are told Lear's age (he is in his eighties) so late in the play (4. 6. 55) that our unfolding impression of it is, in practice, highly plastic. Here, Lear speaks and acts as a man whose physical powers remain vigorous (he still rides to the hunt, as we shortly learn), and whose political powers are transferable, or not, at his sovereign will.

His concern to test his daughters' love, rather than their husbands' fitness to rule, implies that in some measure he also knows the risk of formally renouncing power in old age. Once weakness in age is acknowledged, as in the case of Priam or Nestor, whatever authority Lear retains will be authority only as far as it is acknowledged by others. The demand that Goneril, Regan, and Cordelia demonstrate that their love for him meets or exceeds their acknowledged virtues admits an anxiety that goodness anchored only in 'nature' will not be enough to protect old age. In requiring, as Cordelia says, that the heart be heaved into the mouth, Lear is asking (defensively as well as confidently) that nature be turned to rhetoric, and so (ironically) that it be not nature but publicly accountable 'merit' after all.

When Cordelia refuses to comply, Lear's extravagant wrath exposes the vulnerability of the happiness he had expected in old age. Having 'thought to set [his] rest | On her kind nursery' (I. I. 121–2), he must now grasp at a less ideal retirement, in which he will be reliant in turn upon the hospitality of Goneril and Regan. Dividing the kingdom between their husbands, and excluding Cordelia from any part of the inheritance, he looks to impose a saving distinction between power and what he calls 'the name and all th'addition of a king':

> I do invest you jointly with my power,
> Pre-eminence, and all the large effects
> That troop with majesty. […] Only we shall retain
> The name and all th'addition of a king:
> The sway, revenue, execution of the rest,
> Belovèd sons, be yours.
>
> (I. I. 128–36)

What is a king without power, pre-eminence, and large effects? Not negligible, certainly: late sixteenth- and early seventeenth-century political theory held that a powerless king, such as Richard II, was still anointed, divinely appointed, and a danger to any new regime. *Legitimacy*, that is, can still reside in a monarch usurped. The question is rather what *authority* means when it no longer has 'sway, revenue' and 'execution'—hence the force of the analogy (for Shakespeare as for Aristotle), between a disempowered king and any free moral agent in old age.

Kent is the one courtier careless enough of his own interests to challenge Lear. He does so with characteristic bluntness, charging him with abandoning his powers in the name of 'foolish' age:

> What woulds't thou do, old man?
> […] To plainness honour's bound
> When majesty falls to folly. Reserve thy state,
> And in thy best consideration check
> This hideous rashness.
>
> (I. I. 144–9)

'When majesty stoops to folly. Reverse thy doom' is the Quarto reading of that third line.[57] The change to 'falls' is more sharply monitory, conceding more to age (a fall is not usually volitional) even as Kent refuses to accept age as mitigation. In his eyes, Lear needs only to assert his character to keep age's corrosion of character at bay. Moving 'state' from its point of reference in Lear's speech (the affairs of state) to make it reside in Lear himself (your state, status, majesty), the rebuke offers a brace to Lear's judgement: you have a choice, and you are making a bad one. A familiar denigration of 'foolish' age (reminiscent of Aristotle's *Rhetoric*) thus becomes, in intention at least, an instrument of moral correction. Without Kent's intervention, Lear's casting off of Cordelia might simply be attributed to an old man's irrationality. After it, if Kent has succeeded in establishing his moral authority, Lear may be held responsible for himself. If he declines to 'check | This hideous rashness', the old age that he sought to establish as a political choice will be redefined as a culpable departure from his own character, prejudicial to his honour and to his happiness.

This focus on the moral damage taking place within Lear (or, as Kent would have it, done to Lear by himself) is in line with the changes Shakespeare made in adapting the source materials of *King Lear*. In Holinshed's *History of England* (1587), Baldwin, Higgins *et al.*'s *The Mirror for Magistrates* (1574), Spenser's *The Fairie Queene* (1596), and the anonymous *True Chronicle History of King Leir and his Three Daughters* (1605), he found cautionary tales about the surrender of power in old age. Each tells the story of an aged king or prince abused by the one or more children to whom he has abdicated his throne, and rescued through the virtue of his remaining child. In all but the *Chronicle*, 'Leir' is eventually restored to his former powers,[58] and rules for some period before dying a natural death (in the *Chronicle* he is offered his former 'right' to the throne, but willingly cedes it to the French King who has led an army on his behalf[59]). If he does wrong in the initial division of the kingdom it is the fault of 'feeble age', but the consequences are less tragic than in *Lear*. 'Why do I over-live myself, to see | The course of nature quite reverst in me?', the *Chronicle* Leir asks early on.[60] Such self-pity becomes redundant once his enemies are removed. He is affectingly addled by distress early on, but accepts his moral charge to be 'the myrrour of mild patience, | Put[ting] up all wrongs',[61] and once restored to power he is presumed capable of ruling again competently. To be released from injustice is to be released from the moral, and (apparently) the significant physical, deteriorations of age.

Much of the reconceptualization involved in turning the chronicle history tradition into tragedy depends upon Shakespeare's discrediting of the view, represented by Kent, that character can be proof against age. In the long history of *Lear* criticism, Kent has often been taken for the moral hero of the play: 'one of the best-loved characters in Shakespeare', Bradley called him—a judgement that commands less agreement now than it did in 1904.[62] Even before the move to recognize two distinct texts of *Lear*, many critics less admiring of Kent's devotion ('He belongs to Lear, body and soul,' Bradley wrote, 'as a dog does to his master'[63]), expressed puzzlement at the inconsequentiality of his role after Act 1 scene 1. Thereafter, in the Folio text especially, Michael Warren argues, the play seems to have 'no room for Kent's choric utterances or for the maintenance of his functionless disguise'.

Kent's disguise is not, in fact, 'functionless' in relation to age. One of the marks of old age's too easy relegation to the sidelines of interpretation—even when, as in *Lear*, it is the principal subject of the drama—is that critics have rarely noticed the extent to which the age of the fiercest defender of age in the play presents a problem. When Kent 'raze[s his] likeness' (1. 4. 4), he shaves his beard (or, in Peter Brook's film interpretation, cuts his long hair[64]), changes his clothes and adopts the accent of a labourer. But he also assumes (or is it retains?) the appearance of an old man.[65] An 'ancient ruffian', Goneril's steward, Oswald, calls him,[66] 'whose life I have spared at suit of his grey beard' (2. 2. 58–9). This is not just Oswald's insolence. Cornwall confirms it when he sends Kent to the stocks: 'You stubborn, ancient knave, you reverend braggart' (2. 2. 120). 'Sir,' Kent responds, 'I am too old to learn. | Call not your stocks for me' (2. 2. 121–2). The not-uncommon failure to stage this aspect of his disguise may be because he himself contradicts it. When he petitions Lear to take him into his service, he tells the king that he is 'Not so young, sir, to love a woman for singing, nor so old to dote on her for anything. I have years on my back forty-eight' (1. 4. 35–7). This is reason for Lear to trust him: he is old enough to resent any harassment of an old master, young enough to defend him. But, unless spoken within the king's hearing alone, it does not fit easily with how Kent in disguise is perceived by others. A man may be grey at 48, but Oswald and Cornwall's reaction suggests that he looks (and is) significantly more, and pitching his age down to secure employment with Lear.[67]

The only model for Kent in Shakespeare's source texts is Perillus in the *True Chronicle*: a loyal courtier of about the same age as the king, and no more able than Leir to fight off the murderer whom 'Ragan' sends to kill them both—though he can act as the king's friend and encourager. At least one editor has speculated that Shakespeare may have played the part himself in a 1594 performance at the Rose Theatre, when he would have been 29 or 30 (this in line with the myth, or presumed myth, starting in the seventeenth century, that Shakespeare took the role of Old Adam in *As You Like It*, and specialized in parts for old men, owing to an accidental lameness[68]). In adapting the source role, he seems deliberately to have altered an old man's part into that of a man who has the appearance of age but still acts as if in his prime and who claims to be younger than he is in order to protect the old and failing king. The indeterminability of Kent's age is, in other words, an aspect, or may even be taken as a projection, of his belief that the effects of age can be subdued by an actively virtuous character. The obvious gain is in the range of capabilities open to him. Kent, though a grey-bearded 'ancient', can do what Perillus could not: he can trip up an insolent servant, attempt to provoke him to a fight, stand his ground with Regan and Cornwall, and bear a day and a night in the stocks with easy complacency. He can also carry the body of the exhausted Lear. He can try, in short, to act for Lear as he wishes him to act for himself, upholding his right to honour in old age. But capability is not transferable, and as Lear manifestly begins to lose his reason, Kent loses his ability to function as a moral prop. The real effects of age in Lear overtake Kent's exceptional strengths, and with them that remnant of the chronicle tradition's optimism that the moral impact of age is subject to our choice.

The idea, or ideal, of character's resistance to age does not disappear with Kent's relegation to a minor role. It is diverted first into Lear's exchanges with the Fool, and then into the subplot of Gloucester and his sons. In Kent's absence, the Fool labours to make Lear conscious of his 'folly' in ceding his powers to two such daughters. 'There, take my coxcomb. Why, this fellow has banished two on's daughters and did the third a blessing against his will. If thou follow him, thou must needs wear my coxcomb' (1. 4. 96–9). Lear can threaten to have the Fool whipped for overstepping the mark; but the Fool's quick riposte is that Lear has already given his daughters a rod for his own backside. Here, again, is old age as second childhood—but by errant choice, not by necessity:

> thou mad'st thy daughters thy mothers; for when thou gav'st them the rod and putt'st down thine own breeches

> [*Sings*] Then they for sudden joy did weep,
> And I for sorrow sung,
> That such a king should play bo-peep
> And go the fool among.

(1. 4. 146–52)

The one folly is not the same as the other. As this and the following scene progress, the Fool's wit meets more and more with a vacancy of response from Lear, one effect of which is to allow the Fool extreme licence—'I am better than thou art now; I am a fool, thou art nothing' (1. 4. 167–8)—but the final effect of which is to make him redundant. As early as Act I scene 5 King and Fool have become more complementary than antagonistic, so that what look on the page like stichomythic exchanges no longer sound so in performance, but come across as a repeated confluence of upbraiding with a distracted self-upbraiding that shades into raw fear: '*Lear* O, let me not be mad, not mad, sweet heaven! | Keep me in temper; I would not be mad' (1. 5. 40–1).

A fool's sharp-edged folly has no purchase against foolishness like this which is, more accurately, a rapid degeneration of the capacity to reason. 'A shelled peascod' is the Fool's brutal description of Lear to Goneril when she, too, taxes him with waywardness (1. 4. 194–6). The use of wit to goad Lear to self-recognition is at once vindicated and rendered nugatory by his growing inability either to resist the jibes, or fully to fathom them. It is made more subtly redundant by Lear's increasing tendency to speak like a man standing outside himself, disowning the man that he sees himself becoming. 'This is not Lear. | Does Lear walk thus? Speak thus?' (1. 4. 199–200). This is why, when Lear first registers the internal catastrophe befalling him, the Fool's response is suspended tonally between a barbed jest and the beginnings of resignation to a decay which, in so far as its cause lies with age, may be presumed to be irreversible (though its signs may not be steady): '*Lear* Who is it that can tell me who I am? *Fool* Lear's shadow' (1. 4. 203–4).[69]

Does this reading of Kent's and the Fool's interactions with Lear lean too far towards the notion of progressive decline? A large question arises from the play's depiction of old age: whether it presents in Lear a telescoped account of the deterioration that comes with advanced years or whether it deals rather with the ebb and flow of powers during a steady state of being old, in which age is subject to terrible pressures, not all of them generated from within. One could find support for the former view in that very late specification of Lear's age: 'Fourscore and upward' (4. 6. 55)—older than the 70-something an actor might think fit to suggest in the opening scenes. In practice Lear's powers fluctuate, and one effect of the fluctuations is to blur the causes of his downfall. He is at once the victim of his elder daughters' refusal to honour his advanced years, and the victim of his own immoderate anger—a fault consistent with his earlier character (if Goneril and Regan can be believed), but also a mark of age, and (separately) understandable in a man used to exercising monarchic power and for the first time unable to enforce it.[70] Lear oscillates between strength and feebleness, rationality and irrationality, and that very unsteadiness in capacity complicates the presentation of character, making Cordelia's 'I know you what you are' (1. 1. 268) at best optimistic, at worst culpably naive.

There are good grounds, *pace* Kent and the Fool, for saying that when Lear divides the kingdom between his elder daughters he makes the kind of choice in which it is not obvious what a man is choosing or avoiding—a point that seriously complicates any reading of this play as Aristotelian tragedy. This in part for the usual reason: one will never know all that might need to be known, including things about oneself. But that 'usual reason' looms larger in a context where age entails an uneven, not linearly worsening, alienation from what one has been. Lear's choices are in this respect significantly different in kind from the choices that, say, Macbeth or Henry IV makes. It is theatrically significant here that of all Shakespeare's tragic protagonists, Lear is the only one almost entirely deprived of soliloquy as an authoritative mode of self-expression. Old age makes for a different kind of dramatic hero. As E. A. J. Honigmann has argued, it puts Lear's relationships with secondary characters and with his audience at a certain distance ('he never interests us as a husband or lover', only as a father, and one whose primary emotional register is aggression).[71] It is also a factor in the play's diminished sense of a future: Lear 'suffers but hardly initiates action' after the first Act, and his failure 'to fix the audience's attention on a task or plot' reduces the 'forward-looking suspense' characteristic of the other tragedies.[72] One consequence of that reduction, however, is a heightened concentration on the morality of Lear's situation—stronger than in *Macbeth*, or *Othello*, or even *Hamlet*, where the hero's action, however mistaken or dilatory, nevertheless brings the drama to its conclusion.

With the supplanting of the Fool, in his turn, by Edgar, and the redirection from Lear onto Gloucester of Kent's and the Fool's attempts to correct the character of the old, that sense of a more complex morality and subjectivity in Lear starts to have much fuller sway. It is a standard observation in Shakespeare criticism since Schlegel that Lear's tragedy is doubled in the story of Gloucester: also an old man 'with a white beard', who wrongs the child who loves him, 'meets with monstrous ingratitude from the child whom he favours', and is 'driven to death'.[73] Gloucester, however, is never mad or senile as Lear is; he is simply vulnerable to the machinations and brute force of those younger than himself who decline to respect his age. For Bradley, the effect was a broadening out from Lear's individual story into something apparently 'universal', as if cruelty from the young towards the old were a 'constituent' of human nature.[74] But, as more recent criticism has noted, the Gloucester subplot rests on a very different theatrical vocabulary for probing inwardness or interiority. Edmund, Edgar, and Gloucester himself, for all their differences, represent similarly narrowed versions of what a person is and what a person needs[75]—one of their functions being to help define the less simplifying model of agency and need at work in Lear.

For the machiavel Edmund, the powers and ambitions of youth are 'naturally' antipathetic to the diminished capabilities of age. This, at least, is the burden of the letter that he forges to persuade Gloucester that Edgar plots his murder: 'This policy and reverence of age makes the world bitter to the best of our times, keeps our fortunes from us till our oldness cannot relish them. I begin to find an idle and fond bondage in the oppression of aged tyranny, who sways not as it hath power but as it is suffered' (1. 2. 45–50). In a later, one-line soliloquy, he is less concerned to establish motive, more pithily epigrammatic: 'The younger rises when the old doth fall' (3. 3. 23). Such statements seek to bring a state of dramatic opposition into being rather than account accurately for the gradual and mutual whittling away of moral bonds that occurs between Lear and his daughters.

In the context of the machiavel's plot, Gloucester can be Edmund's gull as Lear is never simply his daughters' dupe, and victimized as Lear is never so straightforwardly victimized. It is an easy matter for Edmund to reveal to Regan and Cornwall his father's treachery, corresponding with Cordelia in aid of the French campaign to restore Lear to the throne. Gloucester is also, by dint of his age, an easy target for retribution. And where the ill-treatment of Lear is subtle—the gradually escalating encroachments on his authority, the quiet but morally charged expressions of disrespect—on

Gloucester the attack is sadistically physical. It is not entirely gratuitous (gouging out his eyes is punishment for plotting the reinstatement of Lear) but both torturers and victim understand it as an assault on age by youth: 'Bind fast his corky [withered] arms', Cornwall commands the servants (3. 7. 27),[76] and Regan 'plucks' at his beard: 'So white,' she jeers, 'and such a traitor' (3. 7. 34). Grimly, Gloucester's response when they ask why he has conveyed Lear to Dover seems to suggest the manner of their revenge: 'I would not see thy cruel nails | Pluck out his poor old eyes' (3. 7. 53−4).

The shock of the scene is its gross violation of social conventions rooted in Natural Law.[77] The blinding of Gloucester brutally overturns that 'reverence' towards old age that Aristotle had recognized in the more positive comments of the *Nicomachean Ethics*—a reverence understood as a commonplace virtue throughout Renaissance literature, and one that Shakespeare himself had often invoked in earlier writings.[78] As Cornwall gives the order to the servants to hold Gloucester's chair, Gloucester makes a desperate appeal to these young men to observe the principle of common humanity between youth and age—'He that will think to live till he be old | Give me some help' (3. 7. 66−7). Only one, identified simply as 'First Servant', abandons his office and challenges Cornwall: 'If you did wear a beard upon your chin | I'd shake it on this quarrel' (3. 7. 73−4). He gives Cornwall a mortal wound, but is himself killed by Regan.

The rebellion of the First Servant is an inadequately powerful but important reassertion of Natural Law. In the Quarto version of the play, his intervention is underscored by the actions of the Second and Third Servants, who bring flax and whites of eggs to salve Gloucester's bleeding face. They, too, express a deep intuition that respect for the old is a basic principle in nature. In an unusually strong interpretation of that principle, the Third Servant reflects (warns, perhaps) that Nature should prevent a daughter such as Regan from reaching old age, if all women are not to follow suit: 'If she live long | And in the end meet the old course of death, | Women will all turn monsters' (3. 7. 97−9). But the Second and Third Servants disappear from the Folio text, and, in Quarto and Folio alike, *King Lear* repeatedly shows Natural Law bested by brute, proto-Hobbesian force. The old are especially vulnerable. As a consequence, where for Aristotle old age was a breeding ground of paranoia, any audience of *King Lear* can be expected to tune in more quickly to the justification for paranoia. Easy, conventional perceptions of the incapacity of age breed, all too rapidly, in the Gloucester plot into real and irremediable dishonouring of the old:

neutral observation of old age by the young turns speedily to exploitation of advantage, and then to active cruelty.

When the blinded Gloucester re-enters at the start of Act 4, he is led by one more representative of a better ethos. The 'Old Man' who guides him is a loyal tenant of Gloucester and of his father, somewhat in the mould of the vigorous and virtuous old Adam of *As You Like It*. The fact that he is unnamed, and that he states his age as close to Lear's—'four score' years—lends the scene something of the added abstraction of a morality play. The two figures are watched by Edgar, still in disguise as 'Poor Tom'—Lear's 'noble philosopher', 'learnèd Theban', 'good Athenian' (3. 4. 160, 145, 168; also 142, 164).[79] Immediately before Gloucester and the Old Man appear, Edgar steps out of character as Poor Tom to speak a nine-line soliloquy.

> Yet better thus and known to be contemned
> Than still contemned and flattered. To be worst,
> The lowest and most dejected thing of fortune,
> Stands still in esperance, lives not in fear.
> The lamentable change is from the best,
> The worst returns to laughter. Welcome then,
> Thou unsubstantial air that I embrace:
> The wretch that thou hast blown unto the worst
> Owes nothing to thy blasts.
>
> (4. 1. 1–9)

At this point he sees enter his old father, mutilated, and guided by a man even older than himself. The unavoidable visual awareness an audience has of the difference between their bodies and a young body is enhanced here by Gloucester's blindness and by Edgar's nakedness.[80] Their appearance prompts from Edgar a necessary muting of the youthful arrogance that sustained his optimism seconds earlier—the buoyant assumption in the midst of disaster that there will be time in one's life for Fortune to turn once more her wheel; the confidence that one's body, with all its senses unimpaired, can withstand the blasts of the elements.

Edgar's conduct towards Gloucester recapitulates Kent's towards Lear, repeating also Kent's exile from the court and his recourse to the disguise of a poor commoner; but he botches Kent's moralism as he weakens, too, the Fool's wit. The encouragement he now offers Gloucester resembles Kent's guidance to Lear in its debt to stoicism, but it is a stoicism shorn of Kent's noble anger and reduced merely to the posture of 'patience'. It is also achieved, notoriously, by means of a trick. 'Bear free and patient thoughts' (4. 5. 79), Edgar encourages his father (casting off the role of Poor Tom and assuming the dialect of a local peasant) as Gloucester finds himself miraculously preserved from what should have been a fatal fall. Gloucester seems to have accepted the need for stoicism—'henceforth I'll bear | Affliction till it do cry out itself | "Enough, enough", and die' (4. 5. 76–8)—but it is too thin a philosophy to sustain him. He lives long enough for Edgar to reveal himself as the true son, and ask his blessing, but not to give that blessing.

The only 'fault' Edgar acknowledges in retrospect, when he tells Edmund of this encounter (and that only in the Folio—the Quarto reads 'O father' (5. 3. 186)) is the failure to reveal himself sooner. His last staged interaction with Gloucester should have given him less reason to be self-satisfied. As the battle to restore Lear to his throne is lost, Edgar runs on stage to drag Gloucester from the field:

> Away, old man, give me thy hand, away!
> [...] Give me thy hand. Come on.
> GLOUCESTER No further sir; a man may rot even here.
> EDGAR What, in ill thoughts again? Men must endure
>   Their going hence even as their coming hither.
>   Ripeness is all. Come on.
>
>   (5. 2. 5–11)

In the Folio text, Gloucester is given four flat words of reply, perhaps only to fill out the verse line: 'And that's true too.' Even allowing for the urgency of the situation, Edgar comes out of the exchange sounding crassly formulaic. Cicero's great defence of moral capability in old age—'death comes [...] to old people when the time is ripe' (see above, p. 8)—is no answer to Gloucester's recognition of irreversible damage at the end of his long life, or his implicit appeal to be released from it: 'a man may rot'. Spoken by a blinded old man, without heart or reason to run longer from persecution, those words do serious damage to Edgar's reach-me-down philosophy. After ripeness, rotting. Gloucester knows that in old age there is a limit to resistance, though his son declines to accept it.

If stoicism of Edgar's patly truistic kind has even temporary purchase on Gloucester's situation, its consolations are plainly inadequate to Lear's case. 'Age is unnecessary', he tells Regan, when she starts in earnest to whittle away the entitlements she will allow him (2. 4. 144), and the line puns rawly on want of needs and want of value. Through all Lear's subsequent shifts in temper, however, from rage and fear, through 'patience', to 'fond' foolishness, and finally into the rage of despair, one need does remain fairly constant in him while all others fall away: the need to find out some 'cause in nature' (3. 6. 34) that will explain his daughters' 'hard hearts' and compensate for the lost 'assur[ance]' of his own 'condition' (4. 6. 50–1). But where the subplot rests upon clear oppositions of good and evil, kindness and unkindness, natural and unnatural behaviour, agency and loss of agency, Lear's anguish increasingly confounds them.

Until Act 4 scene 6 at least, he sees his own situation simply: he is 'a man | More sinned against than sinning' (3. 2. 58–9), torn at by 'sharp-toothed unkindness like a vulture' (2. 4. 123–4), driven from reason by the 'filial ingratitude' (3. 4. 14) of those 'unnatural hags', his 'pelican daughters' (2. 4. 267, 3. 4. 71). When he chooses rather to face the raging storm than to continue beneath their roofs, his first claim is that the elements, at least, are outside morality: 'I tax you not, you elements, with unkindness. | I never gave you kingdom, called you children. | You owe me no subscription' (3. 2. 16–18). Yet almost immediately he accuses the wind and the rain, after all, of treachery:

> But yet I call you servile ministers
> That will with two pernicious daughters join
> Your high-engendered battles 'gainst a head
> So old and white as this.

> (3. 2. 21–4)

It is this revised, more troublesome perception, that nature itself conspires in what is (or should be) against nature in human behaviour, which better shows the growing pressure in the play on Natural Law.[81] There is nothing in nature, it suggests, that requires a daughter's kindness to an aged father, or that will prevent the elements from battering a man's head because it is 'old and white'. Worse than that, nature gives the potential cruelty of children its opportunity.

The active injustice of 'pernicious daughters' 'joins' with nature in *King Lear* when it exploits the weakening of Lear's capability by age. Without that weakening they would have, probably, no opportunity, and less claimable provocation, for their behaviour. Goneril recognizes as much when she confers hastily with Regan in the aftermath of the division of the kingdom:

GONERIL You see how full of changes his age is. The observation we have made of it hath been little.[82] He always loved our sister most, and with what poor judgement he hath now cast her off appears too grossly.

REGAN 'Tis the infirmity of his age; yet he hath ever but slenderly known himself.

GONERIL The best and soundest of his time hath been but rash; then must we look from his age to receive not alone the imperfections of long-engraffed condition, but therewithal the unruly waywardness that infirm and choleric years bring with them.   (1. 1. 286–96)

Opportunism is hand in glove here with detached observation. This is why Goneril and Regan's treatment of Lear can take on such momentum: unloving, dishonouring, indefensible though they ultimately are, their treatment of Lear takes root in his departure from his own 'state' at the division of the kingdoms. Goneril does not hesitate to describe his disowning of Cordelia (to her own and Regan's detriment) as 'poor judgement'. Perhaps there is some truth in her claim that age has only added immoderation to habitual waywardness in Lear (even 'the best and soundest thoughts' he has had in his time have 'been but rash'). She seems to have some degree of justice on her side when she protests against the use he makes of his retirement, turning her palace into a common 'tavern or a brothel' (1. 4. 214): a director could decide that the offence is of her own making, but most stage productions take her at her word, and make Act I scene 4 the occasion for some boisterous ensemble acting. There is no equivalent scope in performance for mitigating the harshness of Lear's curse upon her—including its most self-exposing rider: 'If she must teem, | Create her child of spleen […] | Let it stamp wrinkles in her brow of youth' (1. 4. 251–4)—though its very extremity registers Lear's rapidly diminishing ability to transform words into actions ('I will do such things, | What they are, yet I know not; but they shall be | The terrors of the earth' (2. 4. 269–71)).

Kent's and Edgar's answer to Lear would be patience, as the only route back from passion to reason. But patience—in order to be pa-tience—requires a strong and clear mind. It is also, in the Quarto version of *Lear*, a feminine not a manly virtue, let alone one for a king ('Patience and sorrow strove' in Cordelia's face '[w]ho should express her goodliest' (4. 3. 16–17)). Lear prays at first for patience (2. 4. 260, 3. 2. 37–8), and has it wished upon him by Kent (3. 6. 5, 3. 6. 17), but he prays harder, and with greater justice, for the Stoics' 'noble anger' (2. 4. 265): a Senecan rage that will lift him out of feminizing grief and incapable age.[83] Edgar reduces stoicism to mere 'endurance', judging Gloucester incapable of any more active response to injustice; but when Lear, sitting on the ground with weeds in his hair and no boots upon his feet, preaches patience to Gloucester, he does not mean it as an end in itself. He means patience as the revenger's stratagem—'It were a delicate stratagem to shoe | A troop of horse with felt; I'll put't in proof, | And when I have stol'n upon these son-in-laws, | Then kill, kill, kill, kill, kill, kill' (4. 5. 171, 177–80). Even here, when he seems furthest from reason, something in Lear fights the reduction of his capacity for virtuous action in old age. He is capable of smelling out the bad faith that speaks in injunctions to be patient, when what is intended is that one should surrender meekly to injustice. '[B]eing weak, seem so', as Regan says (2. 4. 190).

But what if the injustice is in nature? (The question is a sharper version of Lear's earlier charge against the elements, that they conspired with injustice.) Exposed to the elements in his old age, Lear seems at first to understand the vulnerability of the human body with fresh eyes and to find in his 'exposed' old age a point of connection to the lifelong vulnerability of the poor:

> Poor naked wretches, whereso'er you are,
> That bide the pelting of this pitiless storm,
> How shall your houseless heads and unfed sides,
> Your looped and windowed raggedness, defend you
> From seasons such as these? O, I have ta'en
> Too little care of this. Take physic, pomp,
> Expose thyself to feel what wretches feel,
> That thou may'st shake the superflux to them
> And show the heavens more just.
>
> (3. 4. 28–36)

This is Lear's only soliloquy in the play. It is brief, but enough to register that an old and failing mind may intermittently be capable of lucid reflection upon itself. It is often taken as more than that: as true moral insight born of suffering. At this moment, such a reading would say, Lear is not—as Aristotle's rhetorical portrait of old men had it—made 'small-minded' by age. He is not reduced to 'chilliness', cowardice, or a desire for 'nothing more exalted or unusual than what will help keep [him] alive'. Dependency in old age seems rather to have taken away his self-concerned pomposity, and expanded his sympathies out towards the rest of humanity, registering, for the first time, the unprotectedness of all but the most privileged human lives.

The attraction of that kind of morally compensatory reading of *Lear* over the years has been striking, and brings to mind Beauvoir's caustic remark that one of the subtler forms of oppression the old have to bear is the demand that they be a standing example of the virtues (see p. 11 above). When considered in conjunction with a reading of Aristotle, it seems to overlap with a similarly consoling interpretation of vulnerability in old age that at least one influential neo-Aristotelian has put forward. Alasdair MacIntyre, in his book *Dependent Rational Animals* (1999), makes a case for a revised Aristotelianism that grants more importance to our biological condition. No account of those 'goods, rules and virtues that are definitive of our moral life can be adequate', he urges, if it does not acknowledge 'our initial animal condition', one 'immense[ly] importan[t]' aspect of which is 'the nature and extent of human vulnerability and disability'.[84] MacIntyre's aim is to supplement and correct Aristotle's too robustly capable account of virtue with those aspects of Thomism that acknowledge that we are all, at certain stages of our lives, vulnerable to harm, and dependent upon the charity and kindness of others. Old age is not his primary interest (he has more to say about childhood), but he does acknowledge its relevance: 'We human beings are vulnerable to many kinds of affliction and most of us are at some time afflicted by serious ills. [... Our] dependence on particular others for protection and sustenance is most obvious in early childhood and in old age.'[85]

If MacIntyre is right, old age might, in a revised version of Aristotelian ethics, be a cause not of the closing down of our moral capacities but of our vital opening out to recognize the most fundamental source of contingency in human lives—our existence as embodied creatures. Lear is there before him, using the word 'animal' of the human condition at a point when the word was still relatively strange, predominantly a technical term within natural science, but also cognate with 'anima' ('breath' or 'soul'):[86]'Unaccommodated man' is but 'a poor bare forked animal' (3. 4. 99–100). But even as *King Lear* seems to offer a recognition similar to MacIntyre's, it provokes, or should provoke, moments of scepticism about loss of capability leading to an increase in virtue. Much of the action in Acts 3 and 4 of *Lear* may seem, at first, to lend support to MacIntyre's belief that the diminution of our powers is fully compatible with the expansion of our moral understanding, breaking down some of the assurances ingrained in us by habituation to our own strengths. 'They told me I was everything; 'tis a lie, I am not ague-proof' (4. 5. 102). But the last act of the play demonstrates that those gains are not sustainable and, at this late stage of Lear's life, not sufficiently conscious. The end point is a devastating loss of reason, resilience, and happiness.

Lear's last moment of contentment, led off to prison with Cordelia after the defeat of the French army, yields a celebratedly lyrical account of what happiness in dependent old age might look like:

> Come, let's away to prison.
> We two alone will sing like birds i'th'cage.
> When thou dost ask me blessing, I'll kneel down
> And ask of thee forgiveness; so we'll live,
> And pray, and sing, and tell old tales, and laugh
> At gilded butterflies, and hear poor rogues
> Talk of court news, and we'll talk with them too.
> Who loses and who wins, who's in, who's out,
> And take upon's the mystery of things
> As if we were God's spies; and we'll wear out
> In a walled prison packs and sects of great ones
> That ebb and flow by th'moon.
>
> (5. 3. 8–19)

It is one thing to see old age, as Aristotle did, as a process of demoralization that leaves a life more open than before to tragedy. It is another to see age's vulnerability as a potential force for moral good, and yet without the capability to sustain itself or turn itself towards action, and therefore tending inevitably towards tragedy. Here *Lear* offers a major check on any effort, along the lines suggested by MacIntyre, to redeem the Aristotelian account of old age by revaluing biological vulnerability as a good. This speech is Lear's moment of greatest optimism, voiced when faced with an absolute loss of liberty and power in his old age. It is his 'fond' rebuttal to Cordelia's fear that she has 'with best meaning [...] incurred the worst' for him. 'Myself', she asserts, with her own version of the confidence of youth, 'could else outfrown false fortune's frown' (5. 3. 4, 6). Her 'oppressèd King' and father, she knows, can no longer do the same. Lear would rather beguile the remaining hours with her than deplore his loss of power, accepting his exile to the margins of life, and willingly humbling himself before a loving daughter. With such a philosophy, he would have her believe, one might find a form of happiness more durable than any subject to the 'ebb and flow' of fortune in public life. The speech retains a superficial stoic confidence that the mind can conquer adversity. It is also, of course, proof that adversity can conquer a mind. This is not a vision of a good life defined by reason, but one made possible only by the decay of reason, including the rational awareness of one's own mortality.

Its differences from the Aristotelian view of old age notwithstanding, *King Lear* ends by confirming Aristotle's perception that the loss of capability with advanced years makes a life vulnerable to disaster in ways that are not easily, if at all, recuperable for virtue ethics. Kent's last words try to establish a moral victory on Lear's behalf, crediting him, however counter-intuitively, with being the moral author of his own end, authorizing his own dispossession. But it is a difficult claim to make when a man dies as Lear does, not heroically but in the course of nature, having forfeited so late in a long life everything requisite for happiness. Kent, having tried and failed to arrest that process, is not so blinkered as to fail to understand that any victory achieved by defining age as self-usurpation runs the risk of undervaluing what Lear has suffered. It is he who stops Edgar's effort to keep Lear alive, even now: 'let him pass. He hates him | That would upon the rack of this tough world | Stretch him out longer' (5. 3. 289–91).

A life can end by what Aristotle called 'external cause',[87] or it can end naturally. Increasingly, across Acts 3 to 5 of *King Lear*, old age appears as an excess in nature that nature will not permit to be divested—a stretch of years that may seem to others, and even to oneself, more than one's due, but that cannot be 'shaken off' or given away. This could be a point outside morality and outside history, but for Lear it has intolerable emotional and moral consequences. One cannot wipe the 'stink' of one's own living mortality off one's aged hand, nor can one take upon oneself another's mortality. By making the death that precedes and produces his end not the heroic death of a son like Hector, but the gratuitous death of a loved daughter (the one disaster for which no consolation is enough, Cicero held,[88] and a turn of events that Shakespeare's late seventeenth-century adaptor, Nahum Tate, felt driven to correct), Shakespeare moves towards a different view of old age's relation to tragedy from Aristotle's, even as he brings the end of *Lear* very close to Aristotelian terrain. Priam's tragedy was determined by his inability in old age to meet the criteria for active virtue as Hector does; Lear is physically strong enough to kill the 'slave' he found hanging Cordelia—it is just bad luck that he is too late to save Cordelia herself. Imagining his own end, Priam foresees that he will be thrown out before the gaze of 'all humanity', mere animal flesh, food for dogs; Lear voices a starker and markedly unselfreferential protest against the contiguity of human and animal life: [to Cordelia] 'Why should a dog, a horse, a rat have life, | And thou no breath at all?' (5. 3. 280–1). There is no redistribution possible here from the unvalued to the valued life, nor from the excess of his life to make good the deficit of his daughter's.[89]

Lear himself gives his last breath (as it were) against Aristotle.[90] Though the play ends on Edgar's statement that 'the oldest have borne most', Lear resists that prioritization of his own end, pointing us insistently to this other death beyond his power of prevention. His and Cordelia's ends are not commensurate, he would have us understand, and any tragedy that he has sustained in living 'so long' should have far less weight than the cutting short of her life. 'Look on her, look, her lips, | Look there, look there' (5. 3. 284–5).[91] His efforts are in a theatrical sense almost bound to be unavailing: no staging of the play now is likely to effect or want to effect such a shift of primary attention away from the play's hero to a woman we know far less well. Nevertheless, in that space for thinking which happens after a play finishes, Lear's focus on Cordelia might lead an audience to reflect on the distinction between tragic weight and ethical import—and here Shakespeare remains on the same ground as Aristotle. Lear's sense that the manner of his end in old age matters less than his daughter's premature end is difficult to weigh ethically, in that her premature death is partly a consequence of his own wilfulness and poor judgement. But his wish to weight things in her favour is in keeping with Aristotle's response to age, implicit in the little space the *Nicomachean Ethics* gives to old age by contrast with the prime of life. To give the drastic overturning of Lear's prosperity its due as tragedy does not require us to accept that a disaster experienced in and through old age annuls all that went before. Nor does it oblige us to conclude that the vulnerability of virtue to the processes of time is a death blow to virtue ethics. It might, however, prompt us to reconsider the pressure that Aristotle and *King Lear*, as philosophy and theatre, would have us place upon the chronological end.

3

Narrative Unity of Lives

A succinct way of expressing the problem with Aristotle's account of the good life for thinking about a long life is that it is insufficiently explicit about how we should or shouldn't relate teleology to chronology. The assumption that the two will coincide works for virtue ethics as long as a person is capable and fortunate, but is it not less easy to hold on to in, and for, old age? The *Nicomachean Ethics* gave us one of the most influential philosophical frameworks we have had for understanding the temporality of our lives not just as accumulations of experience in time, but as accruing their meaning over the passage of time. It also left us with a legacy of uncertainty over how and whether we can ever set temporality aside from a more inward-looking definition of the good life.

This chapter seeks to define more clearly the contribution the temporal structure of a life makes to how that life accrues meaning and certain kinds of value for us. I begin by looking briefly at one alternative to Aristotelian teleology, the provocatively anti-teleological view of happiness offered by Epicurean hedonism. Epicurus' views on death and why we should not want to live forever are taken up in Ch. 7. Here I concentrate on his claims about completeness and duration of life, and consider why they have proved unpersuasive, but nevertheless intriguing, to many modern commentators. Unlike Epicurus, most writers, ancient and modern, consider the temporal dimension of our lives extremely important. More specifically, many modern writers hold that our lives make sense to us only in so far as they are seen to possess the temporal logic of a narrative—and they regard this view as implicit in the assumptions of many older authors who would not have used quite this terminology.

Even extended modern accounts of lives as narratives regularly remain very underdefined. I therefore give a detailed account of the 'narrative view', with particular reference to 'completeness' and 'unity' of life, drawing out the differences between how philosophers and literary critics typically construe narrativity. Certain developments of this view are especially relevant to old age. First, I explore some strong intuitive assumptions that many people hold about what a good life narrative entails, and the consequences for how we may think about late life, when a person's physical and/or mental capacity may well be impaired. I agree with Michael Slote's claim, in *Goods and Virtues*, that the likely disposition of some sorts of event in our lives, and the natural change in our capacities as we grow old, requires us to relax the criteria for a good life in old age and (I add) to cease to think in terms of certain kinds of narrative progress. More than that, there may be good reasons for downgrading, or even rejecting altogether, a narrative view of lives as an appropriate structure for thinking about old age. I then turn to a recent work of fiction, Saul Bellow's late novel *Ravelstein*, in which both the Epicurean and the narrative view are represented, and in which both are put under close scrutiny.

Epicurean hedonism poses a major challenge to Aristotle's teleological account of the good life. Epicurus' account of pleasure, chiefly mental pleasure, is well known for its accompanying arguments about the ir-rationality of fearing one's own death. Slightly less familiar is Epicurus' startlingly anti-intuitive redefinition of 'the complete life' so as to detach it altogether from duration of life and release us from the fear of a premature death (as distinct from fear of death per se). Cicero gives a hostile but, it is generally assumed, accurate summary in *De Finibus* (the original Epicurean texts have not survived):

> Epicurus [...] denies that duration of time adds anything to living happily, and says that no less pleasure is experienced in a short period of time than if it were everlasting. This is completely inconsistent. Although he places the final good in pleasure, he denies that pleasure becomes greater in a life lasting an infinite time than in one which is finite and even modest. ... How can someone who thinks that life is rendered happy by pleasure be consistent with himself if he denies that pleasure is increased by duration? If not, then pain is not either. But if the longest pain is the most wretched, does not duration make pleasure more to be desired? ... Remove Jupiter's everlastingness, and he is no happier than Epicurus; both enjoy the final good, that is to say, pleasure.[1]

For Epicurus, if we attain happiness by developing the virtues and reaching a state in which the normal functioning of our natures can take place unimpaired by constraints and impervious to pains or troubles, then we have achieved 'a complete life'.

'Completeness' is here substantially uncoupled from time. As Stephen Rosenbaum explains, in a respectful modern account of Epicureanism, completeness, for Epicurus,

> lies in a certain time-independent quality of one's activities, not in whether the activities produce specific (future) results. If one's natural capacities are engaged by the projects one adopts, and one pursues those projects without desires which can interrupt engagement in those projects, then one has katastematic pleasure [i.e. 'static' pleasure: freedom from pain in the body and disturbance in the soul]. No passage of time is required to bring about such engagement. It is not that the completion of projects in the future is unimportant, but rather that being unimpededly engaged in the activity of completing them is the only essential aspect of their contribution to one's well-being.[2]

And yet, completeness cannot be as entirely detached from time as Rosenbaum's defence of Epicurus suggests. As in the Aristotelian account of *eudaimonia*—and, surely for any model of a good life, that is a model of a *life*—time is required for the agent to recognize and engage with the good, whether that means practising virtue or enjoying pleasure. A perverse reader may entertain the thought here that if lifespans were handed out on the basis of Epicurean achievement, there would be an advantage in being a slow learner. Flippancy aside, what notion of engagement can there be without some notion of duration, however reduced? There is, from that perspective, some sleight of hand involved in the privileging of 'engagement' over 'activity'. What Epicurus has done is to move from a *telos* (the good) to a *skopos* (see pp. 54–5 above) understood as, essentially, a state of being, placing the definition of virtue not in the action, but in the object attained, which is *ataraxia*—a 'condition of static pleasure'[3]—and 'static' pleasure is always 'finished' pleasure, gaining nothing from duration. A necessary consequence of that redescription is a diminishment in the value of the action itself and certainly of its effectiveness, both of which are now considered less significant than the agent's attitude towards action.

'The radical and interesting part of [Epicurus'] theory', Julia Annas concludes, is not the hedonism (which turns out to be 'bland rather than shocking') but the 'internalizing of our final end, so that what we aim at, what we bend our lives towards and monitor our actions to achieve, is something which, once achieved, is altogether indifferent to the temporal shape of a human life.'⁴ 'Altogether indifferent', that is, to what remains thereafter of the individual lifetime. If nothing else, Epicurus has to care about the upward curve of a life from birth to philosophical maturity. (Neither Epicurus nor Lucretius nor Cicero says *when* Epicurean maturity is typically reached—i.e. at what point in our lives we are to be considered capable of right reasoning.) In effect, Epicurean hedonism curtails the temporal shape of the life, end-stopping the good life at the point where the right condition has been attained. Perhaps the most bizarre facet of this philosophical view, then, is its apparent indifference to being tested: it does not seem to require or value demonstrations that such a state, once reached, can withstand the pressure of further experience, contingent ills, and reduction of capacity that are the consequences of living in time. It is, in short, indifferent to large components of what counts for most of us as living a life.

Unsurprisingly, Epicurus has nothing to say about the travails of old age. Instead, he pits himself directly against Plato on the time in life when philosophy will best be done: 'Let no one either delay philosophizing when young, or weary of philosophizing when old', he writes in the 'Letter to Menoeceus',

> [f]or no one is under-age or over-age for health of the soul. To say either that the time is not yet ripe for philosophizing, or that the time for philosophizing has gone by, is like saying that the time for happiness either has not arrived or is no more. [...] both young and old must philosophize—the young man so that as he ages he can be made young by his goods, through his thankfulness for things past, the old man so that he can be at once young and aged, through his fearlessness towards things future.⁵

At no point does Epicurus seem interested by, or even realistic about, incapacity. He makes no allowance at all for the loss of physical and, in many cases, mental power that comes with late age, appearing to assume a consistent competence that is quasi-metaphysical rather than physical in origin ('no one is under-age or over-age for health of the soul').

The objections to Ciceronian stoicism about old age (that it is unrealistic about capacity, and that, though we may want it to be true, we do not really believe it in our hearts—see pp. 10–11 above) are thus equally applicable to Epicurean hedonism. But we can put it more simply, and set aside for a moment the question of how fortunate or unfortunate we may be biologically in our old age. That Epicurus' view seems intuitively wrong about how we live, and Aristotle's view intuitively closer to right, is in the first place because Epicurus flamboyantly disregards what for most people is an irreducible fact about our lives—that they are conducted and experienced over time and alter their significance for us and for others over time. Most of us have a deeply entrenched need to understand our lives and the lives of others not just as instantiated in the moment but as accruing their meaning with the passage of the years.

The notion that, *contra* Epicurus, we intuitively view our lives as accruing meaning over time—and more specifically, that we see our lives as having the form of narratives, plots, or stories—commands considerable assent among philosophers of quite various kinds. Indeed, it is almost pervasive in the humanities and social sciences generally. Alasdair MacIntyre, to take just one prominent example, expresses a common assumption of modern virtue ethics (and not only virtue ethics) when he contends that the basic structural premise of a life is narratological. In *After Virtue* (1981), he observes that Aristotelian virtues are tied to a concept of the 'unity of a human life'—a unity that, for MacIntyre, explicitly includes 'both childhood and old age'.[6] This sense of the unity of a life, he argues, brings with it a 'concomitant concept of selfhood, a concept of a self whose unity resides in the unity of a narrative which links birth to life to death as narrative beginning to middle to end' (205). Without that assumption of the unity of lives over time 'there would not be subjects of whom stories could be told' (218).

MacIntyre goes on to equate 'unity of narrative' more particularly with the ideals of progression and achievement over time. To ask ' "What is the good for me?" ', he writes,

> is to ask how best I might live out that unity and bring it to completion. [...] The unity of a human life is the unity of a narrative quest. Quests sometimes fail, are frustrated, abandoned or dissipated into distractions; and human lives may in all these ways also fail. But the only criteria for success or failure in a human life as a whole are the criteria of success or failure in a narrated or to-be-narrated quest. (218–19)

The burden here, even more than in Aristotle, is on the end—on 'completion', on the bringing to fruition (or the collapse into failure) of the 'quest'. And although, as with Aristotle, this version of what it means to live in time does not *require* old age, it appears (especially in those modern cultures where old age is for the many an expectancy) to pitch life towards old age as its culminatory stage: the point or place at which, if the life in question is a good life, we shall be able to see its achieved unity.

This reading of MacIntyre on age is, I think, a fair account of the implications of his view but it involves quite a lot of extrapolation. For all the emphasis on ends and the need to aim at the 'final *telos*' of our lives (219), old age is not explicitly invoked other than in the one reference to unity requiring old age (no particular length of life is specified). MacIntyre shifts seamlessly from talk of the temporal structure of lives, repeatedly compared with the temporality of a quest narrative beset by 'harms, dangers, temptation and distractions',[7] to a more internal definition of teleology, whose aim has to do with our efforts to form and practise 'a conception of *the* good' (219).

Although he attributes to Aristotle the analogy between lives and narratives (and the move—the slide, indeed—from talk of 'selves' to talk of 'lives'), MacIntyre draws a much stronger connection between the two than Aristotle. What does it mean to say that the unity of a certain concept of the self 'resides in' the unity of a narrative? A soft reading would be that living well requires us to think of our lives, fictitiously, as narratives, and attribute to them certain formal properties that will help us to make them go better (in this context, help us to be more virtuous). The claim 'human lives may *in all these ways* also fail' suggests a more specific version of this option: lives are formally akin to a certain kind of narrative (a quest) and in significant respects are interpretable in terms of the same values (success/failure; progress/frustration, or abandonment, or dissipation). But other sentences in *After Virtue* indicate that MacIntyre holds the stronger position that lives are *comprehensible* only in narrative terms: without narratives we would not have, or be, selves ('there would not be subjects of whom stories could be told').

One could justifiably object, as Galen Strawson does, that the disposition to see one's life in cohesively narrative terms is characteristic only of one kind of psychological make-up, albeit the dominant one at present. This disposition is, he suggests, 'the accepted norm, the "unmarked position" '.[8] Others, Strawson argues, and he includes himself, are much less disposed to think of their lives and their sense of self in terms of unifying stories. (Some plausible reasons, rather than just dispositions, to do so will be considered more closely in Ch. 5.) What matters here is that the narrative view is understood to describe not an inherent property of lives but a way of making sense of lives, whether our own or others. Like most philosophers, and unlike Strawson, MacIntyre assumes that the narrative view either holds true for all of us (it accurately describes how we all think of lives), or that it would be *better* for us if it held true for all of us. (This important difference in how we might interpret his claims is not acknowledged.)

Literary writers and literary critics have a more elaborate vocabulary for narrative and for its interpretation than philosophers. To qualify as 'unified' a literary narrative would have, for example, to satisfy quite complex requirements of aesthetic coherence, including consistency of voice and style within a given narrative perspective (the stated or implied position of the narrator would also be crucial to any literary critical analysis of narrative form). To count as 'complete', it would need to be 'resolved' in any of several, not necessarily compatible, senses: for example, its main problems would need to be answered, or there would need to be a sense of psychological resolution, or (here the analogy with the philosophical interpretation weakens) the ending would need to deliver a strong dramatic impact. These are at once narrower and more flexible terms than philosophy requires. For obvious reasons: very few lives outside literature exhibit the kinds of formal clarity and cogency that come with the aesthetic dimensions of literary storytelling. There are many exceptions and refinements to this account of literary narratives (both conventional and more experimental), and much more could be said about the range of literary techniques and values that may be compatible with a sense of 'narrative unity' or 'narrative completeness',[9] but for the purposes of the philosophical argument those refinements are not necessary.

Within philosophical writing, 'narrative unity' tends to be understood non-literally, and simplifyingly, as a matter of there being significant connections between the different temporal parts or stages of a story and by analogy a life—those connections then requiring further definition (are they psychological, causal, or 'merely' formal; are they morally significant, or endowed with other kinds of value?). 'Narrative completeness' typically refers to the idea that lives 'should exhibit a certain kind of shape, or [...] plot. [...] A life will be complete, on this sort of account, if it exhibits a recognizably finished narrative structure and will be incomplete if it does not.'[10] Completeness does not, however, admit of any exactness about minimum duration, short of which the life will be considered 'in deficit'. As James Warren points out, the notion of a 'complete' life-story must remain computationally somewhat 'indistinct' (without our forfeiting the idea that someone who has died young, say at 18, has died prematurely):

> One preliminary possibility [for defining completeness] is the identification of a number of essential life-stages, the presence of which in a life (in the correct order) would be at least a minimal requirement for that life being complete. Something like this position would fit well with the common and

intuitive presumption that a life which ends at 18, for example, is incomplete. Such a life would lack the essential stages of adulthood and, perhaps, old age which form necessary parts of a complete life.[11]

Warren leaves slightly more doubt than MacIntyre that old age must be experienced if a life is to count as complete. But his 'perhaps' is not sleight of hand. It points, rather, to an inevitable definitional grey area—both with respect to the number of years (or months or days) lived, and with respect to reaching old age, if old age is defined through a strict temporal demarcation of stages. 'There is no need to be concerned', Warren observes,

> about whether 70 years, or 80, should count as the mark of completeness. First, there is something to be said for any expectation of the duration of a complete life to be contingent to an extent on cultural and economic/demographic [one could add biological and psychological] factors. Second, any proposed definite answer to the question of the age at which a life becomes complete would face possible *sorites*-style arguments pointing out the arbitrary nature of a choice of 80 over, say, 81 years.[12]

When we are considering a narrative view of lives, in other words, the question of completeness is better cast as a question about narrative shape than about attaining a specific age, or reaching a final stage called 'old age', on any absolute rule.

What counts, then, as a satisfactory shape for a life? If the standard narrative view is right, narrative unity and completeness, understood as formal connectedness and the satisfying of (still to be specified) kinds of requirement for fulfilment or finishedness, contribute strongly to the perceived quality of a life. MacIntyre, as we have seen, isolates the progress narrative as the best kind of narrative shape for a good life, with attainment of one's goal (wisdom, virtue) constituting fulfilment. His passing gesture towards old age, however, potentially complicates that view in ways he neither explains nor concedes. Given the explicit stipulation that a 'unified life' should extend into old age, one would expect him to ask whether the common characteristics of old age give us any reason to modify his analogy between the good life and the quest narrative. On that possibility he is silent (though the comments on old age in his more recent book *Dependent Rational Animals* suggest that he might agree modification is needed (see Ch. 2, p. 85).

A fuller explanation of why the progress narrative appeals to us, and some indications of why old age may present difficulties for that narrative, can be found in J. David Velleman's essay 'Well-Being and Time'.[13] Unlike *After Virtue*, 'Well-Being and Time' is not primarily concerned with virtue ethics. 'Well-being' is defined as the fulfilment of a person's 'interests', including both self-interest and other, not necessarily self-regarding interests. But Velleman's claims have evident moral implications, and his arguments and examples at several points appeal to moral judgements and values.

Velleman observes that most of us have a very strong preference for the idea of a life which becomes more successful (possesses more fulfilled interests) with the passage of time, over a life which enjoys stable but moderate fulfilment—a preference that holds even if we are told that the first life begins in significant hardship. The preference rests, he claims, on a deep-rooted valuation of improvement as a component in our estimation of a good life. It is not simply an intuitive preference for 'variety and intensity' over 'consistency and moderation', although that preference is also common.[14]

> Consider two different lives that you might live. One life begins in the depths but takes an upward trend: a childhood of deprivation, a troubled youth, struggles and setbacks in early adulthood, followed finally by success and satisfaction in middle age and a peaceful retirement. Another life begins at the heights but slides downhill: a blissful childhood and youth, precocious triumphs and rewards in early adulthood, followed by a midlife strewn with disasters that lead to misery in old age. Surely, we can imagine two such lives as containing equal sums of momentary well-being. [...] Yet even if we were to map each moment in one life onto a moment of equal well-being in the other, we would not have shown these lives to be equally good. For after the tally of good times and bad times had been rung up, the fact would remain that one life gets progressively better while the other gets progressively worse; one is a story of improvement, while the other is a story of deterioration.[15]

Velleman's sense of which life we would intuitively prefer could be amply illustrated by literary examples. The preference for progress is a basic assumption of the *Bildungsroman* and the upward mobility story, and an important component of much comedy, romance, fairy tale. It is also an element in the logic of tragedy: one of the reasons tragedy (certain kinds, at least) is painful is that it affronts the human desire for progress. As with all those genres and modes, Velleman's idea of progress is not simply logical or formal; it is also much of the time implicitly moral. The fact that success follows failure, in the first of his examples, is enabled and explained by the person in question having learned from earlier mistakes or setbacks:

after failing to achieve some goal, he/she tries again, persists, eventually succeeds. Such a pattern has 'instrumental value', Velleman comments. 'An edifying misfortune is not just offset but redeemed, by being given a meaningful place in one's progress through life.' Its meaning for the person concerned and for others has to do with its part in a larger structure—its 'import for the story' of that life.[16]

Is the moral drive behind these narratives a sufficient explanation of our supposed preference for them? Would we respond the same way if Velleman's language did not nudge us towards moralism? What if, instead of hearing of 'struggles and setbacks', 'satisfaction' and 'peacefulness', we were told simply of the changing level of well-being in this person's life (the degree to which their less critical but significant interests are fulfilled—say, their interest in travel, or in reading the whole of Balzac)? The implication, in 'Well-Being and Time', is that, other things being equal, we would still prefer such a life to the more evenly well-off life. Even in the barer context of talk about resources and utilities, we should still prefer the progress narrative to the narrative of stability, though we would probably find it less psychologically engaging. *Why* we prefer the progress narrative even in the morally less inflected case is something Velleman finds hard to explain. 'If asked', he comments, we should be likely simply to respond that 'a life which gets better is, other things being equal, better than a life which gets worse.'[17] This is either tautology—better is better—or a case of two different applications of the word 'better' being unhelpfully brought in to support each other.

Reading David Hume might encourage us to speculate that the answer has to do with our sensory response to being in time: 'We advance, rather than retard our existence', he wrote, 'and following what seems the natural succession of time, proceed from past to present, and from present to future. By which means we conceive the future as flowing every moment nearer us, and the past as retiring'.[18] That we at any moment prefer future goods over past benefits is, in other words, a function of human ontology. A life which gets better, one might then deduce, is bound to be perceived as a better life because it fits our perception that our lives are directed towards the future and away from the past. But this, too, seems inadequate by way of explanation. It tells us that we prefer to go in the direction in which we are, willy nilly, headed. But we don't always prefer this at all. What about mourning, regret, nostalgia, or that state of mind often invoked as desirable in the old, serene indifference to the shortness of one's own future? Few of us are immune to the wish that we could sometimes flout the terms of our existence and move freely back and forth in time so as to experience past pleasures, or rectify or altogether avoid past wrongs.

C. D. Broad finds a similar possible answer in his reading of John M. E. McTaggart's philosophy: the greater inclusiveness of the future. The future has 'all and more than all the content of any state that is prehended as past', and what is more inclusive must be of correspondingly higher value, McTaggart argued.[19] The movement from earlier to later thus corresponds to a progress from less to more inclusive. But this, too, is unsatisfactory, Broad concludes, because it relies upon the suppressed premise that what is later must be of more interest to us—and that, we know from our experience of regret, mourning, etc., to be false. Broad concedes that there may be a psychological fact here that is 'ultimate and incapable of any explanation'.[20]

If the intuitive preference for a life that reads as a progress narrative over a stably fulfilled life, or one that begins well but ends badly, is difficult to explain, it is also, as Velleman too allows, not always true. It is 'a reasonable judgement to entertain', but we can imagine disagreeing with it, he says, and we can imagine conditions or refinements under which it will clearly not be true.[21] On closer scrutiny than Velleman gives it, our preference for a life which gets better can indeed be seen to hold only on quite complex psychological and structural conditions. Look harder at his opposing narratives and numerous caveats are required. The alternative lives he imagines encourage us to think of suffering and pleasure, good and bad fortune, as taking their value from their temporal position in our whole lives, or, in his words, as 'depending on the overall order or structure of events'. But, like MacIntyre, Velleman does not consider the evolving psychological and moral fabric of the self in any more complex sense than that of a broadbrush linear narrative, or 'life story'.[22] If we think more deeply about the psychological impact of the temporal placement of good and bad events in our lives, it is not at all clear that most of us would make the kind of large structural choice he lays out as the better.

For a start, it is likely that we should want to be quite a lot more specific about exactly how early the bad arrives. It would be preferable not to put it in our very earliest years, or much before adulthood. The less formed our psychology, the less trained our intelligence and robust our emotions, the more vulnerable we shall be to the distorting effects of affliction. On the other hand, we might reasonably prefer not to put the burden of suffering too late, when we may not have the stamina to withstand it or a future long enough to compensate for it. Or again, we might consider, as Cicero did, that 'Nature' has got it, roughly, right: the end is the best place to put the worst. We can hope by then to have a good and full enough life behind us and the wisdom to deal with declining capacities and/or well-being; more cynically, we can be confident that death will put an end to any suffering sooner rather than later. In all cases, we would be likely to feel that whether what happens to us is good or bad in itself is less an issue than the degree of responsibility we feel for achieving our 'success' or precipitating our 'disaster'. That and the degree of our luck.

MacIntyre, Velleman, Hume, McTaggart (and many others) may be right, then, about our very broad preference for progress in our lives, but that preference is contingent on a great many factors. The end of a long life complicates it in several ways, and the deficiencies of Velleman's illustration are particularly marked in this respect. His reference to a 'peaceful retirement' asks no serious questions about the desideratum of a good old age. Old age is, in fact, a good example of why many lives are *not* like progress narratives. 'And then she found the Holy Grail' would be a good progress plot ending; 'And then she got hit by a bus' might be just as effective for another kind of plot (depending on what went before). But 'And then she grew old' is not so clear. It describes a change in condition (a gradual one over time), not a terminal event, and (as Ch. 2 showed) it can cause serious difficulty for an account of a good life which invests heavily in the idea of 'bringing to completion'.[23]

A long life, once it reaches old age, brings diminishing returns on one of the most important assumptions of a progress narrative: the potential richness of what lies ahead. To be near (or at, or beyond) the limit of one's life expectancy means having little, and continually lessening, time in which wrongs can be put right, losses recovered from, or rewards enjoyed. Unhappiness at that point is less likely to be compensated for, as the unhappinesses of earlier life may be, by greater prosperity or happiness thereafter. This is not to say that compensation, late in life, may not be all the more valuable or intense *because of* the brevity of time remaining. The issue here is not our attitude to death, although that may greatly affect our capacity for happiness in other ways, but the impact of actions or events that occur late in life upon the structure of that life, and our own or other people's evaluation of it. We may regret the loss of another's life lived well into old age; we ourselves may not wish to die even when we are very old;

we may fear a painful or undignified death; but we do not usually consider the fact of death in old age to be tragic in itself. We do, however, consider failure or grave errors or great suffering in old age to be so: indeed we tend to think it a peculiar loss of dignity that a person should suffer or do wrong after having lived so long, and with physical and perhaps mental resources that are less than they were in maturity.

Are we then bound to see old age as weakening or even imperilling the narrative of a life? Must we view it as depriving us of many important conditions for progress and gradually cutting us off from a way of structuring the good life that we intuitively find appealing and are likely to have looked forward to in earlier life—even though we are not responsible for our loss of capacity? One way out of such a negative response (surely at odds with other intuitions) is to relax our expectations for old age. This is the approach taken by Michael Slote, one of the few philosophers to have written at any length on well-being and late life.[24] In *Goods and Virtues* (1983), Slote puts the case for seeing old age as a stage apart from the rest of our lives (not Cicero's grand 'last act' (see 7 above), nor quite Mann's Lukácsian 'afterlife' (pp. 43–4, 50 above)) but a stage of life in which many of the ethical pressures and expectations relevant in our prime are understood to be no longer appropriate.

If the Aristotelian view is right, and 'what happens late in life is naturally and automatically invested with greater significance and weight in determining the goodness of lives', then we have a problem, he argues, even in the not obviously tragic case.[25] To spend one's last years 'concentrat[ing] on winning senior citizen shuffleboard tournaments' (19) would be to have a lesser claim to have lived a good life than if one spends those years actively 'in harness'. For Slote, a definition of a good life ought to require less of old age: we should look leniently on late years devoted to more modest aims than those that occupied the person's prime. Utilitarian and anti-Utilitarian thinkers alike err, he contends, in treating all time periods within single lives as equivalent. That we speak of many old people as being 'reduced' to such and such activities or capacities is evidence, he thinks, that while we recognize senescence 'may be sad and regrettable', we also instinctively recognize that some of its goods are appropriate to that time of life as they would not be to earlier periods of the life (20).

By this Slote means not that the pleasures of old age or of childhood are without value, nor that, in old age, we should make it a principle to give up our higher aims in favour of playing shuffleboard or watching daytime

TV, but that 'some of the principal goals, disappointments, successes, and satisfactions, characteristic of certain life periods, have value only relative to those periods and make a rather negligible contribution to what seems to matter most in a total human life' (20). The quest narrative and progress narrative may cease to be appropriate models. There is, he argues (in an atypically harsh sentence) 'something ironic about very old people who are still actively engaged in careers, for their undiminished powers seem to mock the second-order inability of those powers long to sustain themselves—compare the pseudo-rejuvenation of those about to die of starvation' (34). By contrast, 'the prime of life', as it is called, is understood to contain the 'goals, strivings, miseries, and satisfactions, that are to be taken most seriously' (21). Our very use of the phrase 'prime of life' implies that 'the failures and successes of other periods are inherently less serious and less determinative of what one's life has, for better or worse, been like' (21).

Slote's argument relies, like Velleman's, on intuition, but it is the intuition which allows us to console ourselves at the deterioration of an old person now inactive or beset by ill-health, with the thought that they 'have had a good run' or 'a good innings', as opposed to the Aristotelian counter-intuition that what happens to one at the end has the weight of a final (even though not a sufficient) statement about one's life. Slote's approach will probably have considerable appeal for anyone dealing with the long-term decline of an elderly relative or friend—a stroke victim, for example, or someone suffering from Alzheimer's, for whom there may be years of sharply diminished quality of existence at the end of a long and otherwise broadly happy life. It will have less attraction for those wanting to argue against ageist practices that deny the old continued access to the full rights and opportunities of those in their 'prime'. Indeed, it is not clear enough in *Goods and Virtues* whether the argument in favour of 'time-period relativity' is a description of a natural order of things or of a culturally and historically contingent one, in which the old have sometimes been systematically denied access to the goals, strivings, satisfactions, and risks open to those in their prime.

There is a related difficulty with Slote's recourse to the notion of life-stages. As he describes it, old age puts in question the force of terms that have played a substantial role in discussions of the conduct of earlier life: 'aim', 'ambition', 'value', 'utility'. But this sense that old age alters the priorities of, and relevant evaluative criteria for, a life is fed from significantly different quarters and Slote is not always explicit about how far he agrees with it. It arises in part because the very old do not have enough of a future in prospect for these terms to seem adequately rich (a view Slote endorses); in part, relatedly, because there is a general and prejudicial belief (not necessarily shared by Slote) that the aims and ambitions of old age are narrowly presentist or pertain only to their own, foreshortened, future; and in part because old age is understood to bring with it an increased risk of diminished mental competence (an objective fact, but in danger of becoming prejudicial given Slote's unmarked shifts between the vocabulary of age and the vocabulary of senility). The term 'prime', as Slote uses it, is unclear for different reasons: does it mean the start of one's maturity (the Spring of one's life, so to speak), or the highpoint of one's effectiveness?

Amélie Rorty puts a succinct case against the vocabulary of life-stages: the idea of life-stages, and developmental theories more broadly, imposes upon lives a form and a logic that bear very little relation to how we actually experience our lives or how we behave. 'What do [these theories] explain?', she asks: 'Some are openly teleological; others are implicitly normative; others characterize the strengths and weaknesses, the virtues and vulnerabilities of what they project as distinguishable life-stages; yet others profess normative neutrality. Even culturally specific, presumptively non-normative theories remain extremely general: they do not purport to explain, let alone predict individual behaviour.'[26] Their real objective, she suggests, is the production of 'ideal types' or normatively neutral empirical descriptions. If we are to have any hope of accounting for actual behaviour we need much more diverse heuristic guidelines, including a willingness to employ the descriptive language of age and ageing more flexibly. 'At any given time, at any given age, we are all ages at once [...] our dialectical relations to fellows impel us to what the world might wrongly call infantilism or sagacity' (217). We are all not only *capable of* but continually *given to* behaving far above and far below the behavioural norms associated with our chronological ages, Rorty observes, and 'at any given time, chance, accidents, contingencies mark our interpretations, our reactions' (251). She concedes that there may well be universal age-related patterns of behaviour—large-scale patterns that can be developmentally traced (as, for example, in Freudian theory)—but the larger they are, the less they explain about the 'improvisatory accident-prone dramas of (what passes for) a person's life' (243).

Slote's argument would be more persuasive if what he terms 'old age' were redescribed not in terms of a life-stage, simply, but in terms of late-life loss of capacity, allowing for widely differing capabilities between people, and within individual lives, right to the end of the human lifespan. With that reservation, his call to apply less demanding criteria for a 'good life' in old age is intuitively appealing—and indeed an obvious way of responding to the fact of diminished capacities in old age. In general, his arguments suggest less strenuous requirements for narrative 'unity' and 'completeness' once a life enters old age. They do not render the narrative view null. The model of narrative progress will retain more validity for some lives than for others. For a minority (those suffering from dementia, most obviously) it will cease to have any meaningful application. In any given life it is likely to remain more appropriate for some areas of activity than for others. The pursuit of professional success, for example, may cease to be a possibility, while the pursuit of meaningful intellectual development, or good care of others, or good conduct of friendships remains.

The major attraction of Slote's approach to old age is that it does not turn an involuntary, biologically caused diminishment of powers and interests into a judgement on the person or the life. It allows for reduced mental and physical strength and stamina, and respects what is there rather than insisting that what was once there is still the relevant standard. Slote's approach to old age offers, then, a way of thinking about the narrative shape taken by many long lives that appeals to some of our strongest intuitions about what it is appropriate to expect from the last years. It gives us morally defensible reasons to make allowances for the effects of time and ageing on human lives, and to incorporate those allowances into our account of a good life. It doesn't give us reasons to value old age especially in its contribution to our sense of the completeness of a life—though such terms could easily be added to it. Time for the development of personal relationships, time for intellectual development, for contemplation, for pleasure, would all be relevant.

Slote's view respects the dignity of the old, and recognizes significant forms of pleasure and occupation in their lives, but rather than seeing the end of life as having special weight, it tells us that it will often be more appropriate to see the end as making a minor contribution to a life story. We can add to this that, if there is severe loss of capacity, we may do better to reject the narrative view altogether. That is, we may find it kinder, and more in keeping with the person's ability to give shape to their own life, to place much less emphasis on narrative, preserving it only weakly, as a dotted line to indicate the fact of an ongoing life, but faded powers of self-direction. In less extreme cases, we may leave considerable room for variation in people's sense of whether the narrative view is a positive resource, enabling them to think of their lives or the lives of others in terms of meaningful continuities and formal integrity, or whether it becomes, after a certain point, oppressive—so that we do better to give the narrative view a less prominent part in our thinking.

It is difficult to think of a literary work about old age that could *not* be taken to illustrate the strengths or the limitations of a narrative view of lives. Perhaps only certain forms of poetry, principally lyric, escape narrative's very broad net. I want to develop the questions raised here about the narrative view of lives through a close reading of a semi-autobiographical novel. This is partly by way of variation from the novella and drama, but principally because the novel, especially the biographical novel, has characteristically provided the most extended and complex articulations of whole lives as stories.

Saul Bellow's *Ravelstein* (1999) is the only literary work considered in this book written by an author over the age of 80. Bellow was 84 when it was published; he had been a Nobel laureate since 1976, and in the view of many of his fellow writers and critics the indisputably dominant figure on the American literary scene for decades. *Ravelstein* is a memoir of the life and the premature death from AIDS of Abe Ravelstein (based on Bellow's good friend, the philosopher and cultural critic Allan Bloom), interwoven with an account of the old age of the narrator, Chick (Bellow himself, or a version of him). It is also a meditation on twentieth-century history, a homage to Chicago, an attack on what Bellow, in sympathy with Bloom, perceived (too pessimistically) as the decline of humanities teaching in the universities of America, and much else. A few of this novel's first reviewers thought that it represented a falling off in Bellow's old age, and found it chiefly of interest as a mildly salacious *roman à clef*.[27] The majority saw it as, on the contrary, a remarkable resurgence of artistic vitality. ('I cashiered him out', the critic Sven Birkerts admitted in *Esquire*, referring to a hostile review he had written three years earlier in the *New York Observer*—but *Ravelstein* proved him wrong.[28])

Centrally concerned with ageing and mortality, *Ravelstein* mounts some serious resistance to a narrative view of lives—specifically, to the idea that 'narrative unity', 'progress', and 'completeness' (understood in terms of a finished narrative shape) are the most appropriate ways of describing a life. Its challenge to the narrative view takes two main forms. The first is familiar from much modern and modernist literature, and consists in repeatedly frustrating narrative chronology and connectedness, plus an explicit commitment to valuing the non-narratable, or only partially narratable, aspects of lives. Priority is instead given to modes of representation that are not narrative in any strong sense—images, scenes, moments, anecdotes, jokes. As a novel, *Ravelstein* possesses formal unity, but of a very sophisticated and non-obvious kind, involving meaningful repetitions, variations on themes, deepening meditations on certain problems. 'Life is not a series of gig lamps symmetrically arranged', as Virginia Woolf famously put it.[29] Bellow has something of her parodying attitude to the conventions of life-writing, and quite a lot of her investment in sometimes nebulously mystical alternatives, but the mysticism is in his case avowedly eccentric, quirkily his own, not (as hers was) a means to expressing supposed general truths.

Secondly, *Ravelstein* implies a number of further criticisms of the narrative view that have less to do with the *narratability* of lives and more to do with the formal integrity accorded to one life by that view. Our life is not singular, Bellow urges, but plural. We have multiple ways of being; we live also not merely as isolated units but caught up in, and in important ways inextricable from, other lives. Both perceptions were given eloquently polemical expression in the speech Bellow made on receipt of the Nobel prize. The novel, he said,

> is a sort of latter-day lean-to, a hovel in which the spirit takes shelter. [...] It tells us that for every human being there is a diversity of existences, that the single existence is itself an illusion in part.

He also quoted at length from Joseph Conrad's claim that the artist appeals to

> the latent feeling of fellowship with all creation—and to the subtle but invincible conviction of solidarity that knits together the loneliness of innumerable hearts ... which binds together all humanity—the dead to the living and the living to the unborn.[30]

Here again he is on familiar terrain. Conrad, with whose uprootedness he claimed to feel a distinctively American affinity, was only one among many modernist writers (Woolf is another prominent example) who held both

that the unity of the single existence is illusory, and that all lives are bound
into the lives of others.

Bellow's novel is not without a sense that Ravelstein's and Chick's lives
could be described as unified, self-contained stories, or that a single life
retains integrity in important respects. Ravelstein's and Chick's backgrounds
both possess elements that could easily be shaped into upward mobility
narratives—'the large outlines of [the] life story', as Chick puts it.[31]
Chick himself has come from fairly humble beginnings as a child of Jewish
immigrant parents to fame and prosperity as a writer; a 'serial marrier' (107),
he has found real happiness late in life with the much younger Rosamund
(a former student of Ravelstein). Ravelstein took the scholarship route to
university out of an unhappy home life in Ohio at the exceptionally young
age of 15; a charismatic and controversial teacher, he has had a relatively
late '*succès fou*' (173) with the publication of a bestselling book on the
decline of the humanities in America, the profits from which keep him in
jetsetting luxury until his death.

The progress narrative aspect of the two men's professional lives is not,
however, what matters to Chick. The writing of Ravelstein's intellectual
biography he leaves, also, to others. The novel's opening pages are in effect
an announcement that it will not pursue a narrative approach to lives, but
will favour what literary critics sometimes refer to as an 'anti-narrative'
approach.[32] A 'piecemeal method' will be best:

> Ravelstein would frequently say to me, 'There's something in the way you
> tell anecdotes that gets to me, Chick. But you need a real subject. I'd like
> you to write me up, after I'm gone … You could do a really fine memoir.
> It's not just a request,' he added. 'I'm laying this on you as an obligation. Do
> it in your after-supper-reminiscence manner, when you've had a few glasses
> of wine and you're laid back and making remarks. I love listening when you
> are freewheeling.' (128–9)

Bellow's novel has the relaxed manner, the intimate tone, and (superficially at least) the unstructured flow of talk between friends. Eschewing
straightforward chronology, it employs numerous techniques which resist the forward movement of plot: disrupted and digressive storylines,
disconnected dramatic encounters, directionless banter, recurrent images
(Ravelstein smoothing his hand over his bald head; Ravelstein enjoying
his state of the art hi-fi system; Ravelstein dressing to go out …). Much
of the novel is verbatim recreation of conversations held over many years.

It doesn't pretend to exactness or to anything like completeness of recall, embracing the selectivity of memory and making a display of its lack of intellectual rigour: facts and quotations are (ostensibly) unchecked, certain parts of the material are gone over twice or even three times, as they weigh on Chick's thoughts. Movement from paragraph to paragraph is typically not by means of logical sequitur but through tacit paths of verbal suggestion or thematic patterning. Stories about unconnected individuals and incidents are interwoven, only retrospectively revealing patterns of moral or emotional significance. Even at the level of syntax, the novel has a tendency to thwart or disperse its own onward flow. This is a hyper-self-reflexive prose, forever revising its own claims, refining, sharpening, justifying, retracting, softening, debunking.

One effect of Bellow's focus on the representative conversation rather than the shape of events across the life is that as readers we are much less tempted than we might otherwise be to see the cutting short of Ravelstein's life as a tragedy. We are invited to see the quality and intensity of the engagement with life, not the duration of the life, as paramount. Relatedly, we are continually aware of Chick's age, but he is (until the very end of the novel) fit, still working, still held in high public esteem, enjoying life. This is not quite the Epicurean disconnection of the good life from temporality, but it shares something of the Epicurean disregard for longevity, and much of the hedonism. What matters is immersion in the present and, to a degree, comic insouciance about the inevitable end point. 'I did not feel myself to be in the threatened category', Chick comments (comparing himself with a contemporary), '[s]o I was not quite ready to deal with the departing contingent' (130). He is also not, or not yet, ready to contemplate a life of shuffleboard or daytime television, preserving a high-cultural disdain for the kind of life Slote asks us to recognize may have a place in old age: 'I like to say, when I am asked about *Finnegan*, that I am saving him for the nursing home. Better to enter eternity with Anna Livia Plurabelle than with the Simpsons jittering on the TV screen' (46).

The jokes are important. One of the things Ravelstein and Chick share is a relish for the guise of Jewish comedian:

> [RAVELSTEIN:] 'How does the furious husband bit go, again? The heartbroken man who tells his buddy "My wife cheats on me." '
> [CHICK:] 'Oh, yes. And the buddy says, "Make love to her every day. Once a day at least. And in a year that will kill her."
> ' "No!" The guy is astonished. "Is that the answer?"

' "Once a day. That often, she'll never survive … "

'Then a sign is brought on stage. … In bold print this sign read[s], "Fifty-one weeks later." And then the husband is pushed onstage in a wheelchair by his wife. He looks very weak. Muffled in blankets like an invalid. The wife is blooming. She is dressed for tennis and has the racket under her arm. She fusses over him, tucks him in, kisses him. His eyes are closed. He looks like death. She says, "Rest, darling, I'll be back after my set—real real soon." As she strides off the feeble husband brings his hand up to his face and behind his hand in a wonderful vaudeville whisper he says confidentially to the audience, "She don't know it, but she's got only a week to live." ' (117–18)

This is comedy as a decoy from the chronological direction of the life narrative—but the punchline is also a behind-the-hand pointer to what comedy is doing: blocking acknowledgement of one's own inevitable movement towards mortality.

'Death', Chick puts it succinctly, 'sharpen[s] the comic sense'. But if he and Ravelstein are both laughing, they are not 'laughing for the same reasons' (14). Ideological allies, both presumptively close to death (one through illness, the other through age), they nevertheless differ fundamentally on certain philosophical basics, including their sense of how we live in time. Chick inclines towards a metaphysical framework of explanation, distinctly, if quixotically, Epicurean in flavour:

> My feeling was that you couldn't be known thoroughly unless you found a way to communicate certain 'incommunicables'—your private metaphysics. My way of approaching this was that before you were born you had never seen the life of this world. To grasp this mystery, the world, was the occult challenge. You came into a fully developed and articulated reality from nowhere, from nonbeing or primal oblivion. You had never seen life before. In the interval of light between the darkness in which you awaited first birth and then the darkness of death that would receive you, you must make what you could of reality, which was in a state of highly advanced development. I had waited for millennia to see this. (95)

A lecture given by Bellow at the University of Chicago when he was 80 provides a specific source for this quaintly individualistic metaphysics in a book called *Solitaria*, by the Russian novelist Vasilii Vasil'evich Rozanov.[33] Bellow records Rozanov's almost identical thought: ' "A million years passed before my soul was let out into the world to enjoy it." ' 'It does seem weirdly mysterious,' Bellow agrees—'our appearance in a world of which we knew nothing beforehand, and from which we quickly learn that we are destined quite soon to disappear', and he quotes, approvingly,

Rozanov's hedonistic conclusion (tempered by a Christian belief in an afterlife): he 'says to his soul, "Have a good time my lovely, my precious one, enjoy yourself. Towards evening you will go to God." '[34] In *Ravelstein* Rozanov is not cited. Instead, Rousseau's *Confessions* and *Reveries of a Solitary Walker* are the implied influences, in so far as Chick suspects that Ravelstein would have dismissed this private metaphysics as 'already covered' by Rousseau.

Rousseau, however, was heavily indebted to Epicurus, as, surely, was Rozanov.[35] One can see traces in Chick's philosophy of the Lucretian materialism behind both writers' thinking, tempered however by a similar rejection of full-blown materialist reductionism; also traces of the Epicurean consolation in the face of mortality, most especially of the Epicurean rejection of teleology. On the other hand, it is a highly idiosyncratic take on the Epicurean view of life and death, mixing materialism with visionary mysticism, claiming a perspective on reality at once remotely impersonal and proximately personal: 'I had waited millennia to see this.' Chick's quality of absorption in the brief 'interval' that is his lifetime is 'childish' (97), he readily admits (it is not for nothing that he is named 'Chick'[36]). The world still has for him the wonder of 'first epistemological impressions' (96). 'For seventy odd years' he has seen reality with the eyes of a small boy (96)—or to put it in Epicurus' terms, age has made no difference to his happy absorption in the present. Ravelstein, he suspects, would tell him it is time to grow up and engage with history (98).

Ravelstein is no Epicurean, however much he plays the hedonist. 'The pleasure of the moment' may often 'consum[e] him' (28), but, intellectually, he is a strong teleologist. Like Bloom he takes Plato as his starting point. 'It is the hardest task of all to face the lack of cosmic support for what we care about,' Bloom wrote in *The Closing of the American Mind*: 'Socrates, therefore, defines the task of philosophy as "learning how to die".'[37] In Ravelstein/Bloom's Neoplatonic rewriting of the Socratic call to transcendence of our temporal condition through the pursuit of wisdom, our temporal condition must and can be brought within the control of the historical intelligence. 'You must not be swallowed up by the history of your own time, Ravelstein would often say.' And, quoting Schiller: ' "Live with your century but do not be its creature" ' (82). The single lifetime accrues weight, in his philosophy, only if its possessor can take command of the historical grand narrative. And having lived happily into his prime, Ravelstein has little care for further duration of life: 'His biological patchiness was a given—faulty, darkened heart and lungs. But to prolong his life was not one of Ravelstein's aims. Risk, limit, death's blackout were present in every living moment' (54). And again: 'He was not going to have a long life. I'm inclined to think he had Homeric ideas about being cut down early. He didn't have to accept confinement in a few dead-end decades, not with his appetite for existence and his exceptional gift for great overviews' (62).

This disregard on Ravelstein's part for greater length of life is unsupported by metaphysics, especially by any religious belief in future immortality. An atheist, he does not ask, ' "Where will you spend eternity?" as religious, the-end-is-near picketers did, but rather, "With what, in this modern democracy, will you meet the demands of your soul?" ' (19). In Chick's eyes, Ravelstein came closer to embodying that credo than any of his contemporaries: 'Ravelstein, who could not be contained in modernity and overflowed all the ages. Oddly enough, he was just like that' (69). The opportunity for cynicism is there. Ravelstein's high condescension to his own limited tenure in history is, after all, supported by enormous wealth. In a memorable image, he is described as standing 'on the observation platform of the Twentieth Century scattering hundred-dollar bills' (68). His appetitiveness (for clothes, for food, for beautiful objects) descends at points to childish greed, 'stuff[ing] himself' with 'kid candy' on the way home from the office (23). And there is a measure of satire, surely, in Chick's account of the pleasure Ravelstein takes in his ongoing connection with a former student, now adviser to the Defence Secretary, who phones with advance notice of press releases. The information is edited, 'you may be sure', Chick comments, but sufficient to allow Ravelstein to go on massaging the whole of political history into one big picture, from Plato and Thucydides to 'up-to-the-minute decisions in the [First] Gulf War' (60). Yet for all that we are clearly invited to see in Ravelstein a great modern example of the examined life.

The potential conflict between Ravelstein's confident grand-narrative perspective on life and Chick's claims, at once more modest and much grander, to an extra-worldly perspective on it all never quite comes to a head. This is largely because the quasi-Epicurean passage and Chick's various musings on the brevity of our mortal existence remain uncommunicated to Ravelstein: Chick does not wish to have 'the metaphysical lenses I was born with' removed 'by critical surgery' (98); besides, Ravelstein is dying, and not 'to be spoken to in such terms' (97). It is too late, mildly indecent, Chick implies, to tell a man in Ravelstein's position that each of us has only one chance to grasp the nature of reality before being subsumed again by the darkness.

There are, of course, significant areas of overlap between their views. Neither places much value on duration of the single life, though neither is as cavalier about time as Epicurus; both have an unusually childlike attitude to life, though they are long past childhood—Ravelstein in his appetitiveness, Chick in his continuing epistemological wonder. But the difference between Ravelstein's belief in the necessity of transcending one's own life through a wider historical engagement and Chick's refusal of that engagement troubles both. Indeed, *Ravelstein* reads increasingly like Bellow's rejection of the task of philosophy as his friend described it—for all his professed admiration of Bloom. 'Maybe an unexamined life is not worth living', Chick quips deflectively to Ravelstein at one point, 'But a man's examined life can make him wish he was dead' (34). And then there is his age: 'I was too old to be a pupil, and Ravelstein didn't believe in adult education. It was far too late for me to Platonize' (180).

His old age makes all the difference from Ravelstein, he contends. '[T]he problem with aging' is the 'speeding up of your end':

> Our way of organising the data which rush by in *gestalt* style—that is, in increasingly abstract forms—speeds up experiences into a dangerously topsy-turvy fast-forward comedy. Our need for rapid disposal eliminates the details that bewitch, hold, or delay the children. Art is one rescue from this chaotic acceleration. Meter in poetry, tempo in music, form and color in painting. But we do feel that we are speeding earthward, crashing into our graves. ' [...] I feel it every day. Powerless thinking itself eats up what is left of life.' (192)

In Chick/Bellow's experience, life in old age is not a progress story, or a quest, or a story of improvement, but a careering plummet through time towards death. And as the pace of existence speeds up, Epicurean disregard for temporality becomes harder to sustain. Up to a point, Bellow seems to be making a specific complaint against narrative as an art form. Aesthetically, our 'one rescue' lies in forms which can exert strict control over the felt acceleration of time, or can give us temporary respite from it: poetry, music, painting. Narrative offers a less sure protection. With narrative we must be canny, or we shall find ourselves overwhelmed by the onward rush of chronology. Bellow is not claiming that narrative *cannot* meet this challenge—one need only think of Sterne, Proust, Joyce, Woolf,

Conrad—but the exclusion of narrative fiction from the list implies that if narrative is to be redemptive it must emulate the other arts' closer control over form and tempo.

The proper mode of old age, if this accelerando goes unresisted, will be farce—the mode of a narrative rushing faster and faster towards chaos. This perception casts a deeper light on Chick's interest in jokes—their importance for him as a means of imposing temporary control on 'chaos'. The first paragraphs of *Ravelstein* are a meditation on the role of the joke in American cultural and political life—prompting a recollection of Chick's one-time collection of scribbled quotations from 'spoofers or self-spoofers'. Throughout the novel, jokes are seen as at once a great resource in the face of our mortality, and potentially a problem. A joke can be a means of keeping the proximity and unavoidability of one's own death at bay, making it psychologically tolerable, but it can also involve turning one's head away from facts that there is an ethical obligation to face.

So Ravelstein at least holds. His great preoccupation as he nears death, and increasingly Chick's preoccupation in writing his life, is that so many deaths in the twentieth century have not been—as Chick's promises to be—natural and timely. He is thinking not of HIV/AIDS (though a partial analogy is hinted at) but of the slaughter of so many Jews like themselves. For Ravelstein, the Holocaust was a pressing reason to turn his attention as he grew older from the classics to modernity, from 'Athens to Jerusalem' in the words of Leo Strauss (here 'Felix Davarr'): 'He said that the Jews had been used to give the entire species a measure of viciousness. [...] "They kill more than half of the European Jews—and you and I, Chick, belong to the remainder"' (174). Sympathetic though he claims to be to Ravelstein's belief that every Jew must therefore confront the great evil of the twentieth century, Chick ducks the confrontation: ' "Why does the century—I don't know how else to put it—underwrite so much destruction? There is a lameness that comes over all of us when we consider these facts"' (169); 'We needn't go into this any further' (179); 'not every problem can be solved' (179); 'if I began to ask questions, I would become involved in self-explanation and I had no stomach for this' (179). Here again, Chick prefers the unexamined life.

That position holds without much difficulty until, a few years after Ravelstein's death, he finds himself suddenly on the brink of death after eating toxic fish on holiday in the Caribbean (a reprise of Bellow's brush with death under the same circumstances in 1994). At that point,

Ravelstein's promptings come back to him with renewed force, and he broods, in his hallucinatory state, on the distinction between a natural and an unnatural, a timely and a premature, end to a life. 'I adjusted myself long ago,' he tells his former wife in one of his visions, 'to dying a natural death, like everybody else' (217), but not everybody dies so fortunately. He has never adjusted himself to the unnatural deaths. Descriptions of cannibalism in the New Guinea rain forest now absorb him (he has been reading up on anthropology while ill); also the death of a young gay man in present-day Chicago. But he is troubled most nearly by the thought of those millions with similar family backgrounds to his and Ravelstein's who died during their same historical period.

Going on averting one's eyes is harder than it might be, in the re-membered light of Ravelstein's determination to press Chick on an uncomfortably close survival of Nazism in their midst. Radu Grielescu (based on the anthropologist of religion, Mircea Eliade) is a lecturer in 'archaic history', connoisseur of fine food and, according to Ravelstein, a former member of the Iron Guard: not, as far as Chick knows, 'a malevolent Jew-hater, but when he was called upon to declare himself, he declared himself' (167). The problem of Grielescu nags at Chick as he is flown home, acutely ill and, though he doesn't know it, very close to heart failure: 'You see, I didn't like Grielescu but I did find him a funny man, and to Ravelstein this was a cop-out, and it was also characteristic of me. To say he was amusing was to give him a pass. But he was suspect—thought to be in league with killers. I can't seem to get a tight grip on the meat-hook peo-ple' (202). That last phrase is characteristic of Bellow's prose—the arresting image that captures the point, but has also the tinge of embarrassment. The meat-hook reference (picking up an earlier line from Ravelstein describing the Iron Guard's butchering of Jews in Bucharest (124)) both says what Chick knows—that way the abattoir lies—and says why he does not want to think about it further. In the context, it's a defensive phrase, but also one uncomfortable with its own cleverness, making a show of ducking.

The easy, and pious, thing for this novel to do would be to tell a story about this friendship which would make it a journey of self-discovery for Chick—a slow process of conversion to Ravelstein's view that one has a moral and intellectual duty to see one's own life as part of a larger historical narrative in which one's relative longevity (even Ravelstein's) must be seen as a privilege not a tragedy. Bellow takes the less sentimental route (one could argue over whether it is more or less 'self-serving') of claiming that there is no way of living one's own life happily into old age and taking on board either one's own mortality or, still more difficult, the premature deaths of so many of one's contemporaries. It's not a repudiation of Bloom's belief in philosophy as our education in how to die, so much as a putting of it to the back of the mind in a manner that justifies Martin Amis's instinctive conjunction of Bloom's Neoplatonism with Bellow's remark, 'Death is the dark backing a mirror needs if we are to see anything.'[38]

Both with and against Ravelstein, then, Chick is persuaded—and apparently hopes to persuade us—of the unproductiveness, even the undesirability, of dwelling too closely on death or on the horrors of twentieth-century history in turn-of-the-twenty-first-century America. He offers two reasons for this choice. The first amounts to a cultural analysis of America: 'I had a Jewish life to lead in the American language, and that's not a language that's helpful with dark thoughts' (167), he says. The second is his sense of the perceptual *accelerando* of ageing: accurate contemplation of history becomes, as if by the very nature of our immersion in temporality, harder and harder to do. The first argument is a concession to Ravelstein, the second a reassertion of his quasi-Epicurean resistance to the narrative view.

In the final pages Chick is dragged back from the brink by two forces: his need to write Ravelstein's memoir, and the extraordinary devotion of his wife. Restored to health with Rosamund's help, in a triumphant reversal of the vaudeville 'old husband' sketch, he muses that the promise to act as Ravelstein's biographer obliged him to stay alive. But he acknowledges, too, the justice of Rosamund's claim that her love would have kept him going, notwithstanding. And at that point he is left, symbolically, with a choice between Ravelstein and Rosamund, between writing and love. He chooses, perhaps surprisingly in the circumstances, Ravelstein. 'Rosamund kept me from dying. I can't represent this without taking it on frontally and I can't take it on frontally while my interests remain centered on Ravelstein. [...] But I would rather see Ravelstein again than to explain matters it doesn't help to explain' (231). With that declaration Chick gives over his closing pages to a lingering recollection of Ravelstein, not in death but at his most fully alive, 'dressing to go out, [...] talking to me' while his favourite music, played on 'authentic period instruments', blares out from the speakers (231–2).

The memoir of Ravelstein's life and death in the first two-thirds of the novel thus comes to look very much like a 'behind the hand' means for Bellow in the final third to acknowledge, and yet refuse to acknowledge, his own likely proximity to death. His resistance to the forward drive of the life-story is, finally, a refusal to accept that proximity to the end must structure how one lives in old age. It would be impossible to live happily on those terms, Bellow suggests. This rejection of chronological progress takes additional support from his refusal to see his own (or Ravelstein's) life as an isolated unit, closed in on its own narrative form.

It makes more sense, in the context of this double challenge to the narrative view of lives, that *Ravelstein* should give reduced priority to what, in other novels, is the great Bellovian theme: the transformation of the world through love. It would have been possible to write *Ravelstein* as a romantic comedy—the healing power of the true wife's love at the end of a comic history of mistakes. That story is there in *Ravelstein*, but it's not the main focus of the novel, and the closing pages thwart any kind of formal closure on the romance note. The choice to turn his attention back to Ravelstein is his last strong anti-narrative gesture. In this novel, declining to describe our lives as unified stories until we absolutely have to (until, that is, we are on the point of dying) is the only way we can hope to live out our time other than as tragedy. There is no claim to public or private virtue here, in leaving one's accountability to death and to history to the very end—only a claim about what might make happiness in old age possible, for some of us.

Partly because Bellow was lucky in the retention of his intellectual powers, and in possessing tolerable health until late age, he could make a good case for not thinking of one's life in conventional narrative terms. But *Ravelstein* does not simply say 'duck acknowledging that you are near the end and you'll be all right'. It is also a riposte, from the perspective of old age, to the widely current belief that we do best to see our lives in narrative terms, and to the idea that doing so will help us to lead happier or more virtuous lives. Its reasons for resistance have something to do with the blackly comic, reductive truth that old age has only one formal end, but they also go beyond it. They involve a commitment (similar to that found in Epicurean hedonism) to living fully in and for the present moment; but they also involve a belief, not found in Epicurus, that our lives are misunderstood if we conceive of them as separate units, or isolated stories, disconnected from the lives of others. And Bellow departs from Epicurus, too, in his strong belief that there is no special virtue or general applicability in a philosophy that suits his particular cast of mind.

Bellow knew very well that people want art to give life form, but they also want quite the opposite. They want 'to hear from fiction what [they do] not hear from theology, philosophy, social theory, and what [they] cannot hear from pure science. [...] a broader, more flexible', but also 'fuller, more coherent, more comprehensive account of what we human beings are, who we are, and what this life is for'.[39] This is a dauntingly elevated prospectus for any one writer to attempt to fulfil (Nobel speeches no doubt carry the risk, perhaps the requirement, of grandeur). But it is, characteristically from Bellow as critic, not a statement about individual lives—rather about 'this life'; so that what it means by 'flexibility' but also 'coherence' and 'comprehensiveness' is not 'unity of a life', but a yet-to-be-described artistic and ethical unity in which all lives may be seen to participate. Our aim, Bellow concluded, should be a novel that gives life 'meaning, harmony and even justice'. This is polemic, of course—the artist defending a role for art specifically distinct from the more 'systematic' forms of thought and more strictly 'rational' forms of inquiry pursued by science and philosophy. Like Mann's theory of art as an impossible attempt to impose form upon experience, it is only one definition of art; but it is a timely reminder that the criteria for a narrative description of lives standardly place a much higher valuation on formal coherence and comprehensiveness than is warranted when we look at real lives, and not theoretical ideals of lives.

The prescriptiveness, or assumed validity, of the narrative view of lives in much current writing in the humanities and further afield (post-structuralist scepticism about the autonomy, coherence, and continuity of the self notwithstanding) is, for all these reasons, a problem. We misrepresent any life when we claim too much authority for formal criteria that we impose from without, and that are, at best, only a frame for defining the goals or achievements of that life. This said, we also misrepresent the sophistication of narrative, when we reduce it to a normative or idealizing template for a life. *Ravelstein* is a good reminder that we can handle very complex narrative structures in our thinking about lives without forfeiting the sense that there *is* a recognizable and sufficiently unified self at their centre. On either count, the narrative view, as generally understood within philosophy, is especially problematic as a framework for thinking about old age. When Michael Slote argues, convincingly, that we should be prepared to apply more lenient criteria for a good life in old age—that we should not require it to meet the standards of progress or utility or value that we have applied earlier in the life—he is isolating one important feature of old age: the 'time-specific' character of many of its activities, pleasures, needs. But he is also pressing us to see where the narrative view, conceived as a means of guiding us towards a good life, may cease to be appropriate. Bellow at 84 was a remarkable instance of the good fortune many writers will have, if their mental powers remain intact, in going on pursuing their profession into late age, enjoying its public and private rewards, and making relatively little concession to time of life. Remarkably, he also became a father again that year, with the birth of a daughter. During the five years remaining to him, however, his powers were gradually eroded by Alzheimer's.[40] If one were to try to estimate the value of those last years, and their contribution to a good whole life, one would want to follow Slote and hold that less exacting criteria should apply.

4

The Power of Choosing

In Margaret Drabble's novel *The Witch of Exmoor* (1996), David D'Angers, Guyanese-born Harvard-educated academic and prospective parliamentary candidate for Middleton, West Yorkshire, thinks to distract his wife and her siblings from the problem of 'what to do' about their ageing mother by introducing them to John Rawls's theory of justice. They should play a game, he suggests, called 'The Veil of Ignorance'. 'It's not a question of imagining a Utopia',

> more a question of unimagining everything that you are, and then working out the kind of society which you would be willing to accept if you didn't in advance know your place in it. If you knew you would have no special privileges or bargaining powers. [...] All you have to imagine is that in the original position of choice you don't know who you are or where you stand—you don't know if you're rich or poor, able or disabled, clever or mentally subnormal, plain or beautiful, male or female, black or white, strong or weak. [...] And from this position you have to examine the first principles of justice, and decide what they are.[1]

They argue, for a while, over what should and should not be assumed in this thought experiment, until David's sister-in-law brings them up short by asking just how serious they are: 'If it were all worked out, according to David's rules—the universal principles of justice and all that—would anyone dare to press the button and make it happen?' A special reason for holding back strikes her (under the circumstances, rather late): 'would you wake up in this new world at the same age as you were when you pressed it? Or might you find yourself a newborn baby, or an old person in a geriatric ward? Does the original position make us all the same age, or not?' But at this question, David draws a line. 'I think you're taking it too literally.'[2]

This chapter is about taking choices for and about old age literally, 'too literally' indeed—moving away from the theoretical considerations of epistemology, virtue ethics, and the narrative unity (or not) of lives that were the subjects of Chs. 1 to 3, to consider more practical deliberations about justice between age groups. What constitutes a fair distribution of limited social resources between the old and the young? Rational life-planning theories, represented in Drabble's novel by John Rawls's classic model, answer that question from various perspectives, including the two with which I am most concerned here, prudentialism (the consequentialist view that aims to maximize benefits for the individual or specific group) and egalitarianism (pursuing the equal distribution of goods between individuals or specific groups). The limitations of rational life-plan modelling should be clear from the outset. Life-planning theories—that is, theories that provide reasons for planning the best (which in most instances means the most prudent) allocation of resources across whole lives—are deliberately normative and to a degree idealizing. They assume things about a life that cannot in practice be assumed by individuals: most obviously, that the individuals whose lives are planned for will live to be old—that they will at least reach the average life expectancy for their age cohort. The concern of these theories is with protecting the needs and interests of old age, not with defining or attempting to respond to wider desires or values.

In other words, we are no longer dealing here with the examined life as it is actively and subjectively lived but with an objectified notion of a life in relation to which we can design the best (that is, fairest) allocation of limited goods or utilities for a just society. There is a clear link between these life-planning models and Velleman and Slote's considerations of well-being and time (see pp. 97–105 above), but in this context I largely exclude the moral implications of the arguments. That said, the distinction between rationalism and moralism is not absolute. Aristotle, for one, thought that prudence was a virtue, and its cultivation a proper subject for ethics: i.e. that making non-moral, ends-driven judgements about how best to use one's resources was an aspect of wisdom. The exercise of temperance would be a simple example. How one plans the allocation of limited financial resources to meet the needs of persons across their lifetimes within the constraints of intergenerational equity is a more complicated matter.

The philosophical section of the chapter begins with Norman Daniels's prudential life-span account of intergenerational justice, which I discuss in conjunction with egalitarian welfarist objections made to it by Dennis McKerlie. I then take the argument on into applied ethics, focusing particularly on the question of choice and autonomy in cases of dementia as discussed (controversially in the first instance) by Ronald Dworkin and (contesting Dworkin's view) Agnieszka Jaworska. The territory of the discussion is necessarily restricted. Prudential and egalitarian life-planning models have been much debated within medical ethics, and the literature on their application to dementia and Alzheimer's patients alone is vast. Some major areas of closely related rational and moral inquiry remain untouched by my argument (euthanasia and the right to die, for example), and many important philosophical contributions to the field are referred to only in passing or in footnotes (including those of Thomas Nagel, Dan W. Brock, Daniel Callahan, and Rebecca Dresser). The issues debated also have obvious relevance for public policy-making, but my treatment of them remains theoretical. It does not appeal to specific facts about the cost of health care or private v. public pensions funding in the UK or US.[3]

The second half of the chapter offers close readings of two poems. Neither Philip Larkin's 'The Old Fools' nor Stevie Smith's 'Exeat' is a direct commentary on prudentialism, but both are explicitly about the meaning of choice in relation to old age, and both pose a number of hard questions for rational life-planning philosophies: what happens when we move from the objective and idealizing notion of choice espoused by many philosophers to recognizing choice as an element in our subjective view of our own futures, vulnerable with us to how we age? Larkin had an intense aversion to prudential life-planning: an often expressed hostility to the idea of a life spent saving for an old age in which one's capacity to hold on to the interests of one's earlier life would (he feared) be seriously compromised. This was emphatically not an Epicurean hostility—rather a cussed conviction that life was not going to offer him much pleasure at any point, and old age would be the worst stage of all. Dennis McKerlie uses 'The Old Fools' to support the claim that people who experience an old age as miserable as the one Larkin imagines should qualify for more than what Daniels's version of prudential planning would offer them: a just society, he argues, will afford them 'egalitarian priority'. This seems to me a misreading of the poem—but, like McKerlie, I see Larkin as an antagonist worth listening to by prudentialists and prioritarian welfarists alike. Smith's more angular take on the long life in 'Exeat' has not, as far as I'm aware, attracted the attention of any philosopher, though it is explicitly a poem about old age and philosophy. Like 'The Old Fools' it has within its sights the potential for conflict between rational arguments and moral arguments about the value of a long life. My reading of it draws out its more oblique moral and emotive perspectives on the question of choice in relation to old age, autonomy, and death, and the challenges it poses to any reasoning about how best we may plan for a long life.

One of the most prominent advocates to date of a prudential approach to distributive equity between the young and the old has been the medical ethicist Norman Daniels. In his book *Am I My Parents' Keeper? An Essay on Justice Between the Young and the Old* (1988) and a number of subsequent essays Daniels observes that disputes about what the young owe to the old (and vice versa) have become more common as the proportion of old to young in our societies has increased. Daniels argues that seeing the problem in those terms, as a competition for resources between different age groups, is an error. Support for old age should not be construed as a question of synchronic distributive justice between distinct parties. The needs and claims of the old differ from those of other social groups because, in the normal course of biology, most of us have the potential to grow old. Rather than ask what a just distribution of public resources would be between the old and the young we should be asking what a prudent allocation would be across a single lifetime. We should then be able to see that each age group in society '*represents* a stage of our lives'.[4]

Rawls's influence on *Am I My Parents' Keeper?* is plain. Daniels's prudential chooser, like the Rawlsian rational calculator,[5] is required to act from behind a veil of ignorance, considering how to budget her resources over her lifetime without knowing her current age, her goals and values, or other particular facts about herself. Because she does not know how long her life will be, her concern for her well-being will be time-neutral across her lifetime. In keeping with Rawls's description of the Original Position, the prudential chooser also cannot assume that she has an equal chance of being anyone, or that her chance of being any particular age is proportional to the number of people in that situation.[6] Rationally, she will want to 'keep [her] options open', allowing herself an adequate opportunity at each stage of life to pursue whatever her plan of life then is (and it is assumed that it will change over time) (58).

Although Daniels's aim is to set out a rational, and morally defensible, basis for choice, and not to make detailed proposals for public health care policy (his main area of concern), he specifically defends age-rationing of resources of the kind practised in the British National Health Service, *c.*1985. (He has a separate chapter on the much more complicated problems of modelling health care in the United States—though it should be said that British health-care provision has, in the intervening years, moved rather closer to the American interlocking-cum-parallelism of public and private schemes.) A prudent chooser, he argues, could justifiably design a lifetime health-care package for herself that rationed available resources on the basis of age-related risk. Special care would be taken to allow for life-preserving intervention in the early years (if she dies young, and the risks of doing so in very early life are higher than in the middle, the rest of her planning is pointless); also for a relatively high level of medical assistance in old age when health problems and deteriorations in capacity are likely to accumulate.[7] She may, however, rationally choose not to budget for life-extending treatment at the expense of protecting herself adequately, or even better than adequately, in earlier life.[8]

The obvious attraction of the lifespan allocation approach to justice between the young and the old is its claim to take the heat out of conflict-of-interest debates. But it is open to objections from several quarters. Some are very general. One has to do with the presentism of prudential planning: societies are not static, and current demographic changes in much of the developed world look set to produce injustices in the course of the next few decades that prudentialism not only has no way of compensating for, but would serve to embed. So, the serious economic difficulties most developed countries now face as they try to budget for the increasingly disadvantageous proportion of young to old are, from one egalitarian perspective, a consequence of having failed to budget prudently for the future pensions and health care of a 'greying' population at the point when the need first became predictable. Younger age cohorts now and in the foreseeable future may consider that they are 'unfairly' paying more for the care of the old than they would have had to pay if those in need of that care had been more heavily taxed in the past. However fair prudentialism's allocations are now, the young may also perceive them as unjustly benefiting earlier generations more than they themselves can expect to be benefited in the future. Daniels's prudentialism would consider these objections misconceived. Prudence, as Daniels interprets it, must be concerned with well-being across complete lives, not with parity of well-being for different age-groups or parity of well-being at specific life stages.

A further limitation has to do with the very narrow definition of interests that obtains when we translate interpersonal well-being into intrapersonal well-being. James Griffin takes issue with such translations per se in his

1986 book *Well-Being*, arguing that there are crucial differences in how they can be measured.[9] The 'global preferences' or 'global desires' a person has for her or his life are inherently maximizing; they embrace and hierarchize that person's experiences of good and bad, and those experiences cannot be meaningfully considered as separate from the global preferences or desires. The same kind of maximization cannot be applied in the many-person case. Where many persons are concerned the values at stake will often necessarily be different from those which pertain to the individual life. There is 'nothing comparable' in this realm to an individual's global preferences (political and social ideals, for example, will always be contested). Moreover, in a group context, one person's gain may be another's loss. This is not equivalently true for an individual's experience of a gain: her conflicts of desire will, by definition, be sufficiently reconciled if she experiences the gain *as* a gain. Perhaps most importantly, collective gains will identify what is better as better, but they cannot identify what is best, as the meeting of an individual's interests or desires can.

Griffin's criticisms put some caveats in the way of applying rational life-planning to how individuals think about their lives. Our ideals for our lives are, in some very basic senses, not generalizable. Conflicting, perhaps irreconcilable, though our intuitions are about old age (Slote v. Velleman, for example), they show up how differently we may think about the desirable shape of our own lives from how we think about what will be good for everyone. As individuals, we may (see Ch. 3) aim (ambitiously) to have our lives yield a narrative of progress right to their end, or, alternatively, we may embrace the counter-intuition that our best, because most capable, years will be our middle years; we may justifiably feel that these views are too individually variable, and too strongly opposed, to command general agreement. This does not invalidate Daniels's prudentialism—he is fully cognizant of the difficulty of finding agreement, given the widely different conceptions of how to live a good life that will coexist in any heterogeneous society[10]—but it tells us not to underestimate the difficulty of finding agreement about what system will be best for all.

A more specific and, for my purposes, more important objection to Daniels's prudentialism arises from a consideration of what its likely consequences would be for the very old and infirm—that is, for those whose quality of life in old age falls well below what we would predict as within the normal range for our society. Prudential planning for old age rattles those who have less faith than Daniels that the provision it deems 'adequate' for old age would be more than barely so. Dennis McKerlie puts a strong version of this objection in 'Justice Between the Young and the Old' (2002). He warns that modelling interpersonal conflicts of interest on intrapersonal interests could be made to justify 'extreme inequality' between the provision made for the young and for the old.[11] As McKerlie sees it, the prudential chooser operating from behind a veil of ignorance would never have enough incentive to look after the interests of her own late life. For two reasons. First, the likelihood of her reaching the most advanced ages is small. She may therefore take the view that there is little point in providing generous resources that she will probably never use. Second, she can reasonably decide that some parts of her life are more important to her than others.

> Some stages in life seem likely to make a greater contribution to the value of our lives as temporal wholes. Suppose we know that we must experience thirty consecutive years of success [and] thirty years of failure, but the location of these two periods inside our lives is up to us. I expect that most of us would choose to succeed between the ages of forty and seventy and to fail between the ages of seventy and one hundred, not the other way around.[12]

The intuition described here is very similar to Michael Slote's and contrary to David Velleman's: it is in our middle years (McKerlie avoids the word 'prime') that we are able to make fullest use of our resources; we are therefore justified in considering those years more important for our lives than our later years, and worth supporting more liberally than the later years. McKerlie thinks that it compounds the likelihood that gravely inadequate provision will be made for a 'bad' old age, beset by serious mental and/or physical illness.

McKerlie's second objection (the likely favouring of the interests of mid-life over those of old age) should not greatly trouble Daniels. To prefer one period of one's life over another is a rationally defensible response to the biological profile of one's capabilities, so long as one does not neglect the other stages of one's life. It is not—as Slote observed—inherently unfair or immoral. Nothing in Daniels's prudential allocation model would lead to the refusal of medical support, certainly not palliative care, on the basis of age to those in need (though problems will surely arise in distinguishing palliative from life-extending measures). Daniels's theory offers a rational justification for distributing resources according to age-specific needs so as to maximize the well-being of the complete life. It does not pretend to cater to deeper interests or desires.

McKerlie's egalitarian concerns about prudential life-planning for old age encourage us to think harder about what a baseline or even relatively generous prudential model of social justice cannot do to provide for the needs of the old—what more may have to come from our public and/or private resources to meet those needs. They also alert us to prudentialism's limited ability to respond to desires as opposed to needs. But they are not fatal to Daniels's case. Daniels's model of justice is not prescriptive. It remains squarely within the Rawlsian tradition of individualist and pluralist liberalism, establishing terms for social cooperation between individuals who remain free to pursue very different plans of life. As in any such liberal model, some interests will not be reconcilable, and many desires will not be met. The aims of the prudential allocation model, Daniels fairly points out, are limited to designing institutions; they do not extend to 'all the egalitarian interventions we might imagine'.[13]

McKerlie's first objection—that prudence, on the basis of a judgement of risks, could tolerate a very inadequate level of provision for the old—does more damage.[14] There does indeed seem to be too little protection for serious debility in late life within Daniels's prudential model. Indeed, the conditions for the veil of ignorance could be seen to *require* a lack of special protection. Daniels's prudential choosers are fully informed about their society's demography, current life expectancy, and health care. They know about its patterns of economic growth, and how and why longevity has been increasing. And they know about 'basic economic and sociological trends' (family support networks, patterns of family stability and mobility, etc.).[15] They also have access to the information (not specified by Daniels, but pertinent) that people who have reached, say, 82 probably have on average a better not worse chance of surviving to 85 than those currently aged 70 have of reaching 85. (Today's octogenarians were fitter than average for their age-cohort ten years ago.[16]) So, the prudent calculator will want to factor this into her planning for her last years, and not taper off her provision for late age sharply in order to favour her prime more heavily—but she will be rationally justified in treating the likelihood of living to 90 as low, and therefore consider provision for that stage in life of minor importance to her.

McKerlie's grounds for disputing the prudential life-planning model are described by Daniels and by McKerlie himself as 'egalitarian'. In fact they are better described as *prioritarian* ('the time-specific priority view' is McKerlie's own revised choice of wording[17]). The priority view breaks with both prudentialism and utilitarianism by requiring that we give the very old and infirm first place in the queue for care. We do this simply because they are badly off, even though a benefit to them may produce a relatively small increase in well-being by comparison with the same level of benefit to someone less badly off.

The implications of the priority view are lucidly set out by Derek Parfit in 'Equality and Priority' (2002).[18] 'Benefiting people matters more the worse off these people are,' Parfit explains—but this means more than thinking it important to benefit the worse off in order to reduce inequality. 'It is irrelevant that these people are worse off *than others*' (214). The Priority View recognizes *absolute* and not just comparative need. So, for example, someone who holds the Priority View will recognize that on average the health of the very old is at a lower *absolute* level than the health of the young. (This is not Parfit's example, but germane.) He concludes: 'on the Priority View, though the better off would lose more, the gains to the worse off count for more. Benefits to the worse off do more to make the outcome better' (221).

This is a helpful clarification of McKerlie's objection to what the prudential lifespan allocation model would find adequate by way of provision for the old. His worry that prudentialism would be satisfied with far too little leads him to press for prioritization of the welfare of the old and infirm above, and in extreme cases, well beyond what prudence would find warranted. This intervention is not about acting in order to reduce inequality or to achieve equality. McKerlie does not hold it bad or unjust that some people are worse off than others (in the case of the old and infirm he appears to grant that this is inevitable); rather, he takes prioritization of the needs of the old and infirm, on the grounds that they are badly off, to be a necessary supplement to what a prudential model of distributive justice would do for them.[19]

The priority view, as applied by McKerlie to the health care of the old and infirm, is in the main rationally persuasive and morally attractive. It is, however, problematically underdefined at the point where priority comes into conflict with the maximizing egalitarian strand in McKerlie's thinking. For most of 'Justice Between the Young and the Old', McKerlie pits himself against the requirement in Daniels that life-planning should aim at the greatest well-being for the complete life, arguing for a prioritarian social concern with the very badly off, even though a benefit to them will have comparatively little impact on the total level of well-being in the society.

But at the very end of the essay McKerlie concedes that maximization will sometimes be the better principle: 'The priority [given] to the badly off is not absolute', he claims: 'it can be outweighed by the consideration of doing the most good. For example, […] we should not conclude that helping the infirm elderly to postpone death trumps all other considerations in distributing health care' (173).

Under what conditions, then, does maximization trump the priority view? McKerlie gives no supporting example at this point, but a case considered earlier in his essay would seem to fill the slot: 'The prudent chooser considers the possibility of suffering from senile dementia in old age. According to Dworkin he would not buy insurance that provided life-extending medical treatment for serious illness while in that state' (162). The senile dementia consideration arises in the context of to a discussion of Ronald Dworkin's treatment of prudential life-planning for old age, which McKerlie sees as close in many respects to Daniels's view but even less palatable in some of its welfare implications.[20] Dworkin treats prudential deliberations about health care in terms of a person using her available resources to purchase insurance which specifies the medical interventions that will be available to her at different stages of her life. Like Daniels, he thinks that this lifespan approach will deliver a fair allocation for old age. But in the case of senile dementia, Dworkin's conclusions about fairness are, as McKerlie puts it, 'controversial'. Dworkin argues that people in the late stages of dementia do not retain the same moral rights—specifically, the same rights to autonomy—as normally competent people (though they do retain the right to dignity). He decides that insurance should not cover life-extending treatment in that state, on the grounds that it can do little for the quality of the complete life compared with the medical interventions that might be needed earlier in the life.

McKerlie does not go so far as to call this conclusion 'morally vicious', as Richard Posner has;[21] he does, however, think that 'we should find it troubling' (162). But, in the extreme cases, is it not the conclusion implied by his own concession that the priority argument will sometimes be outweighed by the consideration of what will do the most good? On the basis of the examples and information offered in his own essay, I take it that McKerlie would have to answer yes. That is certainly the implication of the illustration he offers for the additional claim that priority competes also with concerns based on complete lifetimes: given a choice between offering life-extending care to an 80-year-old who will die in a month, and a 20-year-old who will die in five years, he argues, the greater gain to the 20-year-old's complete lifetime outweighs the urgency of the benefit to the 80-year-old. It is not obvious why the case of an 80-year-old with severe dementia, but whose life could be extended significantly beyond a month, would be treated more generously.

There are, however, good reasons why McKerlie might want to hold to the priority view in such a case, and not give in to the maximization view except if the dementia is very severe indeed. In an exemplary essay in applied ethics,[22] Agnieszka Jaworska also takes issue with Ronald Dworkin's conclusions about what a just health-care system based on prudence would offer the old—but she does so not by way of an argument against prudent calculation itself, rather by rethinking the criteria prudence would use to judge quality of life in cases of dementia. As she sees it, Dworkin applies unduly exacting criteria for well-being and autonomy in the cases he considers. According to Dworkin, we should discriminate between two types of prudential interest a patient may have: 'experiential interests' and 'critical interests'.[23] Experiential interests are the interests espoused in the present; they involve time-specific wishes and feelings, and they lapse with a person's death. Critical interests are generated in relation to a person's core values: fulfilling them matters for that person, even if the person is unaware of their being fulfilled, because it means bringing about the state of affairs that the person judged good. Jaworska gives the example of a person having a critical interest in protecting the well-being of his family which extends after his death and will be met if the family is provided for according to the terms of his will (111).

Dworkin does not dispute that Alzheimer's patients retain experiential interests, even in the very late stages of their illness. He does, however, deny, in the cases he addresses, that the demented patients are capable of affirming critical interests, although they may still possess them (critical interests can survive the capacity to affirm them, and may extend beyond the holder's death—as in the instance of care for one's family). In some cases, the patients' experiential interests run counter to critical interests that were deeply important to them before the illness took hold. So (this example is close to but not identical with one Jaworska discusses), a patient may all her life have expressed a deep desire not to receive life-extending measures were she to become seriously demented, but when that happens she may, on the contrary, express pleasure in her experiences and a strong desire to go on living. Dworkin argues that once she loses the capacity to make sense of her life as a whole we should uphold the critical interests expressed in her maturity and not the merely experiential interests she now avows. Without the capacity to conceive of her life as a whole she can have no correct sense of what is good for her life as a whole: she cannot any longer espouse new critical interests. We therefore serve her best by upholding the critical interests she held to in the past.

This is Dworkin:

> by the time the dementia has become advanced, Alzheimer's victims have lost the capacity to think about how to make their lives more successful on the whole. They are ignorant of self—not as an amnesiac is, not simply because they cannot identify their pasts—but more fundamentally, because they have no sense of a whole life, a past joined to a future, that could be the object of any evaluation or concern as a whole. They cannot have projects or plans of the kind that leading a critical life requires. They therefore have no contemporary opinion about their own critical interests.
>
> (Dworkin, 230; quoted by Jaworska, 113)

And more tersely: 'Value cannot be poured into a life from the outside; it must be generated by the person whose life it is, and this is no longer possible for [the advanced dementia patient].'[24]

Jaworska disagrees. Critical interests are best understood as values, she argues. Drawing on her own observations of patients, on the evidence of doctors and carers, and on the evidence of neurophysiology, she urges that even people with advanced dementia of various kinds who have lost the ability to conceive of their lives as a whole and can no longer lay down new memories as part of a coherent narrative of self often retain values which go beyond mere present desires. They preserve values which they believe to be right, which relate to their sense of self, and the importance of which they understand as reaching beyond their own experience (altruism, for example, or a sense of humour). These are sufficient conditions for the possession of values. We should not insist upon the additional requirement, too strenuous in cases of advanced dementia though of clear importance in other contexts, that a person be able to originate critical interests through a correct view of their own complete life. Jaworska concludes: 'for a Dworkinian, the threshold capacity level necessary to lend prudential authority to a person's current wishes should not be set at the ability to grasp one's life as a whole, but rather at the ability to value' (124–5).

It follows that we should recognize and respect a capacity for autonomy as surviving, in many cases, well past the point where Dworkin recognizes it.[25] This means respecting convictions that a patient may hold without being able to carry them into action. It does not mean that we should give weight to all the desires or convictions a patient expresses in the here and now. Rather, we must learn to discriminate in specific cases when those desires and convictions amount to values: when they are coherent, consistent with what the patient holds to be right, and important to their sense of self-worth, and when they are not. A patient may, for example, have a strongly expressed desire to go on driving, because she believes this is crucial to her independence and to her ability to be of service to others, but she is no longer safe behind the wheel or capable of finding her way; in that case her carers are justified in overriding her contemporaneous interest in driving in order to serve her deeper values. 'The key insight', Jaworska summarizes, 'is that once a demented patient is recognized as a valuer, the problems are not, in principle, different from those encountered when working with ordinary competent people—these problems belong to an already familiar territory of practical reasoning' (135).

Jaworska's argument is attractively humane. It has significant implications for the application of prudential distributions. Plainly, it gives the prudential chooser a much more refined and generous set of criteria for recognizing autonomy in difficult cases such as Alzheimer's. In many, perhaps most, instances it would prevent any decision to withhold life-extending care until much later in the progress of the condition than Dworkin's case studies suggest. Would it obviate McKerlie's welfarist concern that the old and very infirm would be inadequately protected by prudentialism alone? Not entirely. The welfare needs of those as badly off in old age as the extreme cases McKerlie worries about will extend beyond any predictable prudential interest we can have, operating from behind the veil of ignorance. Precisely because they are the most unfortunate cases they require more than just the share of our resources that prudence alone would give.

The problem most often talked about in the media, politics, and public policy debates of recent years has been that such extreme cases are, however, becoming less exceptional: life-extending measures are keeping a larger proportion of us alive to experience dementia than would have survived to such an age, and in such a state, in the past. In Bernard Williams's phrase: more of us will in the future forfeit the 'moral luck' of dying naturally before that point.[26] But as that change happens—as the numbers suffering from dementia rise—their predicament comes the more fully within the view of what prudence, and not just kindness, will have to plan for.

As a monitory instance of how far from ideal the old age may be for which idealized philosophical choices are made, Dennis McKerlie asks us to contemplate Philip Larkin's poem about senility, 'The Old Fools'.

> What do they think has happened, the old fools,
> To make them like this? Do they somehow suppose
> It's more grown-up when your mouth hangs open and drools,
> And you keep on pissing yourself, and can't remember
> Who called this morning? Or that, if they only chose,
> They could alter things back to when they danced all night,
> Or went to their wedding, or sloped arms some September?
> Or do they fancy there's really been no change,
> And they've always behaved as if they were crippled or tight,
> Or sat through days of thin continuous dreaming
> Watching light move? If they don't (and they can't), it's strange:
>   Why aren't they screaming?
>
> At death, you break up: the bits that were you
> Start speeding away from each other for ever
> With no one to see. It's only oblivion, true:
> We had it before, but then it was going to end,
> And was all the time merging with a unique endeavour
> To bring to bloom the million-petalled flower
> Of being here. Next time you can't pretend
> There'll be anything else. And these are the first signs:
> Not knowing how, not hearing who, the power
> Of choosing gone. Their looks show that they're for it:
> Ash hair, toad hands, prune face dried into lines—
>   How can they ignore it?
>
> Perhaps being old is having lighted rooms
> Inside your head, and people in them, acting.
> People you know, yet can't quite name; each looms
> Like a deep loss restored, from known doors turning,
> Setting down a lamp, smiling from a stair, extracting
> A known book from the shelves; or sometimes only
> The rooms themselves, chairs and a fire burning,
> The blown bush at the window, or the sun's
> Faint friendliness on the wall some lonely

Rain-ceased midsummer evening. That is where they live:
Not here and now, but where all happened once.
                                        This is why they give

An air of baffled absence, trying to be there
Yet being here. For the rooms grow farther, leaving
Incompetent cold, the constant wear and tear
Of taken breath, and them crouching below
Extinction's alp, the old fools, never perceiving
How near it is. This must be what keeps them quiet:
The peak that stays in view wherever we go
For them is rising ground. Can they never tell
What is dragging them back, and how it will end? Not at night?
Not when the strangers come? Never, throughout
The whole hideous inverted childhood? Well,
                                        We shall find out.[27]

'These people will not be easy to help', McKerlie observes, 'But I hope
we will feel it is important to do them what little good we can.'[28] It is a
quaintly practical, cautiously optimistic philosophical response to a poem
very far from practicality and optimism, and explicitly unenchanted by at
least some of the standard consolations of philosophy.[29] McKerlie treats
'The Old Fools' as an unusually eloquent but, by implication, credibly
objective description of the problem of loss of choice in old age. So, in
keeping with his wish to defend a prioritarian welfarist approach to serious
incapacity in old age, he writes, compassionately, of 'the old fools' as
'them', where for Larkin, the 'they' mocked in the opening line will one
day be 'us'. Nevertheless, McKerlie recognizes that Larkin's negativity of
response to the sight of dementia, a response he assumes is shared by many
others, is based in subjective identification. 'Visitors to a nursing home
(like Philip Larkin)', McKerlie writes, 'are shaken by what they see. We
mind what we experience as much as we do, partly because we feel we are
witnessing our own future. It would be less disturbing if we believed that
it would not be us, but some other person or self marginally related to us
who would end his life in such an institution.'[30]

McKerlie is not a literary critic, nor pretending to be one, but his reading
of Larkin's poem is significantly off the mark in a way that demonstrates
the difficulty of moving between the philosopher's objective notion of
choice and choice as we may experience it subjectively in relation to our
own futures. 'The Old Fools' is by no stretch of the imagination a welfarist

poem. It is deeply sceptical of what 'choice' for old age can mean, given that old age (a very bad old age, that is, in which we will be gaga, but not so completely gaga as to have lost our apprehension of death) will define us as doubly without choice: not free before we are senile to choose a different future, and not able to choose at all once we are senile. (The final line in effect denies us the right to commit suicide at the point of old age.) More specifically, the poem opens up a gap—rhetorical, emotional, also logical—between two kinds of choosing: the choosing we can do (transitively) 'now' in midlife (as the poem imagines it) for old age; and choosing per se (intransitively) which is what age will take from us. The deprivation of choice *in* the future, and the absence of choice now *about* the future, Larkin suggests—caustically, fearfully—renders any operation of choice now in relation to that future at best ironic, at worst chillingly null. Given the rebarbativeness of many of the emotions and tones in 'The Old Fools', it is necessary to say, before going further, that this is a poem I like, but find problematic, and that though I refer frequently to 'Larkin' in what follows, it should be clear that what is meant is 'Larkin's imagined speaker'. That said, the diction and the postures adopted are consistent with those found in many of his poems, and familiar also from his correspondence: they are distinctively 'Larkinian', but no less an artifice in being so recognizable.

Structurally, 'The Old Fools' opens up a characteristic Larkinian gap between grace of form and charmlessness of content. Its twelve-line stanza (the last a half-line), with an elaborately constrained rhyme scheme (abacbdcedfef) but considerable freedom of metre, in this case both holds fear and revulsion in check and allows them unhindered expression. But although the poem's elegance of construction ironically offsets its abusive/disabusive ambiguities of tone, it does not offer to modulate or compensate for that tone as is often the case with Larkin, especially in the earlier poems (see e.g. 'An Arundel Tomb' (1956), or 'Talking in Bed' (1960), both written seventeen years or more before 'The Old Fools', but see also late poems, including 'Cut Grass' (1971), 'The Building' (1972), 'Love Again' (1979)). Nor does 'The Old Fools' suggest anything in the way of Yeatsian transcendence achievable through the power of one's rhetoric or one's own magus-like status as poet. Although Larkin's view of old age echoes that of Yeats in some ways—the congruence of biological age with 'an ingrained conservatism', the bitter consciousness that the ongoing practice of one's art is at the mercy of one's ageing body, the old man's relished licence for 'sexual frankness and irascibility'—there's no equivalently compensatory sense of a creative 'synergy between ageing and hatred'.[31] He lacks entirely Yeats's aristocratic assumption of authority in anger (his magisterial revival of the rhetorical tradition of the *senex iratus*). He lacks, especially, Yeats's confidence that mind and soul are in important respects independent of body. What Larkin captures are smaller, unlovely, but perhaps more commonplace emotions associated with the contemplation of age: pessimism, confusion, a wish for the future to be otherwise, just held in check by the desire to be understood to harbour no illusions (which is also, of course, a wish to be known to have the saving capacity for such illusions).

The opening of Larkin's poem is interrogative—'What do they think has happened, the old fools?'—but who is its addressee? Only the old fools themselves could answer this question, but they are evidently not its recipients. Like the subsequent questions this first stanza poses, it is rhetorical and has about it something of the posturing aggression of adolescence, though the speaker is plainly not adolescent. The poem mocks, but its mockery has no comprehending target, and the terms of abuse are oddly lame: 'the old fools', 'more grown-up', 'pissing yourself'. Sometimes, with Larkin, the poem's speaker seems to be trying to emulate a demotic speech he (and perhaps Larkin himself) is not quite competent at: 'she's taking pills', instead of 'she's on the pill' in the title poem of *High Windows*. Here something else is happening. The vocabulary—thin, bland as it initially seems—hardens into literalism; abuse becomes neutral objectivity (or ostensibly that). 'The old fools' are the senile. 'Do they somehow suppose | It's more grown-up when your mouth hangs open and drools?': 'more grown-up' is exactly it. At 'pissing yourself' the literal meaning pre-empts the metaphorical one altogether: only in a substantially different context could it mean 'laughing yourself stupid'.

These brutal actualizations of what at first seemed an underpowered lexis of abuse implicate the speaking voice from the start in what it pretends to reject. The exclusive 'they' of the first line soon gives way to the more inclusive 'you' (anyone) and then to the fully inclusive 'we'. The blame implied in the first hypothetical answer (they think it's more grown-up) undermines the blamelessness of the initial question (what do they think is happening to them?). The disgust, the paraded want of compassion, in what follows are calculated to provoke outrage, but whether from the reader or in the speaker—working himself into a state—is a moot point. Posturing outrage might be a bulwark, here, establishing a saving difference between 'us' and this drooling incapacity. But in tension with the will to provoke, the poem gradually exhibits a downward gravitational pull towards less strong reactions: contemplativeness, an attempt at sympathy, and (in direct contrast with the rhetoric of invective) the felt imaginative appeal of an agentless, objectless aesthetic of senility. These counterpoised tendencies—aggression and quieter reflection—already sit side by side in the final lines of the first stanza. The muted 'If they don't (and they can't) it's strange' precedes and provokes the half-protest, half-demand 'Why aren't they screaming?'

The repeated movement between fierce repudiation and a calmer curiosity almost bleached of emotion runs through all the responses the first stanza offers to its own opening question. The harsh response shifts gear rapidly to a quasi-sentimental one, and then back again, as if correcting errors of, respectively, emotional insufficiency and excess. Not knowing what memories these people (who never speak) could possess, the poem supplies a makeshift life-history: dancing all night, courting, getting married. Pouring value into a life from the outside, as Dworkin put it, is all this speaker can do—but he does it at best half-heartedly. As tokens of the lives that have been lost to memory the memories imagined for them are no more than generic: nostalgic, but without the emotional commitment of nostalgia. 'When they danced all night' translates action into a non-specific reference to the time at which it occurred; 'went to their wedding' is strangely skew in its phrasing (one doesn't usually 'go to' one's own wedding, one 'gets married'), 'sloped arms some September' is more evocative, possibly intended to suggest September 1914 or September 1939, but taken up by its own alliterative and imagistic effect, dissipating any sense of a specific event into vagueness (not 'that' September, but 'some' September).[32] By way of reaction, the question that follows counters sentiment with cynicism—but a cynicism still further divorced from any plausible account of what the 'old fools' could actually be thinking. 'Do they fancy...they've always behaved as if they were crippled or tight, | Or sat through days of thin continuous dreaming'? What kind of fancy would this be? Delusional, reparative perhaps (to an outsider's way of thinking), but not the kind of delusion a person would plausibly entertain about themselves.

The refinement of 'watching light move' anticipates the imaginative expansion of stanza three by offering temporary consolation in an aesthetic all but purified of any object. Compare the last lines of 'High Windows', gazing on 'deep blue air, that shows | Nothing, and is nowhere, and is endless'. But here the effect is not a last-stanza rising above the world but a reduction of metaphysics to the limited physical and mental capabilities of the senile. Watching light move is all they can do. 'The Old Fools' sees, as 'High Windows' did not, that, if old age is unkind to us, aesthetic transcendence may be beyond our powers. 'If they don't (and they can't)'. 'And', not 'or'. No choice here.

Having no access to the interior life of the senile, the poem shifts ground in the second stanza to contemplate their proximity to death. This, Larkin conceded to an early correspondent troubled by 'The Old Fools' aggression, was the nub of the poem. It is also the point at which the poem starts to show some strain between two not necessarily commensurate sources of concern: the degradations of dementia, and the extinction that is death. 'It is indeed an angry poem,' Larkin wrote, 'but the anger is ambivalent: there is anger at the humiliation of age (which I am sure you would share), but there is also an anger at the old for reminding us of death, an anger I think is especially common today when most of us believe that death ends everything.'[33] The assumption of a mutual anger *on behalf of* the old ('which I am sure you would share') distracts, courteously and a little too piously, from the less creditable assumption of shared anger *at* the old 'for reminding us' of what we prefer not to think about. The latent ambiguity of the phrase 'humiliation of age' has the same effect. Larkin, 50 at the time of writing 'The Old Fools', had already established a reputation as prematurely old. 'Apparently he is sixty', Alan Bennett remarked ten years later, 'but when was he anything else?... he has made a profession of it... he has been sixty for the last twenty-five years'.[34] Certainly he developed a well-honed poetic persona along those lines, and rage and dismay at the effects of time were among his most persistent themes.

There is then all the more reason to suspect that anger at, as well as on behalf of, old age has been overtaken or crowded out by fear of dying. Stanza two makes the connection explicit. Old age is the harbinger of death. Unlike the fathomless placidity of senility, death, as Larkin imagines it, is unstoppable, dismantling energy. 'At death, you break up', but as you break up 'you' cease to be the subject of the action: 'the bits that were you' are its agents, 'speeding away from each other for ever | With no-one to see'. 'For ever' may mean 'for good', but it sounds like the hyperbole of fear (you go on rapidly breaking up 'for ever'). What terrifies the speaker about death is our absence from it: we are not just dispersed, but unable to witness a dispersion which does not belong to us, because it is *of* us. Larkin presumably had Epicurean/Lucretian atomism consciously in mind at this point (the breaking up of the body into bits is precisely what Lucretius claimed will be our fate when we die), but the consolations of Lucretianism get a markedly prejudiced hearing:

> It's only oblivion, true:
> We had it before, but then it was going to end,
> And was all the time merging with a unique endeavour
> To bring to bloom the million-petalled flower
> Of being here.

McKerlie quotes these lines to illustrate the distinction we should be making between diminished quality of life in old age and the much greater harm done to us (*pace* Lucretius) by death. Death damages us more than Alzheimer's or other forms of senile dementia, he argues, because it eradicates us altogether where dementia only erodes us. To delay extinction and prolong old age would therefore be to secure a gain outweighing any impoverishment of our well-being that age brings. In the letter to his critic, Larkin does seem to have some sympathy with that view, disarmingly diagnosing his own 'selfish cruel anger' as 'typical of the first generation to refuse to look after its aged'.[35] But little if anything in 'The Old Fools' supports this private brandishing of a welfarist bad conscience about ageing. The grounds on which the poem argues its case against Lucretius are personal and subjective—not remotely motivated to try to do anything about the condition of the old in Britain generally. What Larkin fears about death, and what angers him about the old as a living *memento mori*, is not the loss of the goods of life but non-existence. There is a bleak joke in the double-think that puts us inside oblivion in order to confirm our own absence from it (Bellow's joke, again, but in a radically different tone (see p. 110 above)). This speaker knows the self-deceivingness of believing in a 'unique endeavour' to bring us into existence. Where death is we are not, Lucretius said: that we find this unthinkable is a sign of our folly (whatever our age) faced with oblivion. Hence the ambiguity in 'Next time you can't pretend': you've no justification for pretending; you won't be there to pretend. Hence also that bleaker repetition of 'being here' in the final stanza where it means, no longer, 'fully, beautifully, inside your own life' but 'ineluctably here and senile'.

Old age, even a very bad old age, is in McKerlie's view distinct from death and has a value that can be threatened by death, and Jaworska's defence of the margins of agency in cases of Alzheimer's gives that view strong and directly relevant support; but for Larkin the two are inseparable. Senility is death's portent. 'These are the first signs: | Not knowing how, not hearing who'. Life for the old fools is objectless, contentless (how *what*? *who* what or where?). 'The power | Of choosing gone' expresses a larger and more fundamental deprivation, the absolute loss of agency—for Larkin the defining characteristic of being human, Andrew Motion comments.[36] But unlike the other losses associated with age, 'the power of choosing' has a possible grammatical object: it may be read as 'choosing [rather to be] gone'. That buried implication comes out more openly in the doublespeak of the stanza's last sentence, especially its strained pun, 'Their looks show that they're for it': they are doomed to oblivion/(mockingly) they are in favour of oblivion. And, less crudely, 'How can they ignore it?': how can they not know?/how can they not respond? To be in such a state is to make a fool of one's own life through the signs of one's coming death, cremation, interment, desiccation: 'Ash hair, toad hands, prune face dried into lines'.

From this dehumanizingly external and fearful view of dementia in old age the poem turns back to ponder once again the interiority of the old. This time there is more of an effort at imagination, more resourcefulness of speculation. But being old, as Larkin imagines it, is not really a psychological state; it is a condition of alienation from one's own psyche, metaphorically rendered as geographical or spatial displacement from within one's own memories so that they are re-enacted piecemeal before one as a kind of theatre with actors one 'can't quite name'. The third stanza identifies a crucial gap between memory and recognition, knowing and naming, which takes the force out of the twice repeated word 'know'. 'People you know, yet can't quite name' are in effect unknown: the 'deep loss restored' that is their reappearance in memory remains a loss. 'Known doors' and a 'known book' sound more ontologically secure, but it's a trick of grammar: the adjectival form blurs the distinction between past and current knowing. Or perhaps Larkin's point here is that the known book and door are still genuinely recognized, by contrast with the people whose names have been forgotten: what matters more has been lost, what matters less retained. There is a possible aesthetic consolation, similar to that of the first verse, in the collocations of rooms, things, times, but the grammar of the phrases insists upon a troubling disappearance of agency. Implied verbal statements are compressed into adjectival ones. Past events survive only as images: 'A fire burning', 'the blown bush' (the 'million-petalled flower' now over-blown?), a 'rain-ceased midsummer evening'. Human emotions, no longer securely owned, have drifted into metonymic arrangements with things: 'smiling from a stair, … the sun's | Faint friendliness on the wall'. Unlike in 'High Windows', the poetic imagination is not eased by the beauty of this emptiness, but haunted by the loss of human habitation. 'Some lonely | Rain-ceased midsummer evening' raises and then annuls the expectation of a human presence. And once again, the seduction of sentiment prompts a countering austerity from the speaker—that hardening of attitude implied in the preference for saying 'all happened once' over the second- or third-hand emotion of Vita Sackville-West's (originally Milton's) 'all passion spent'.

The fact that 'The Old Fools' does not, like so many other Larkin poems, end by finding a kind of depersonalized aesthetic consolation in what remains for these people (light, glimpsed memories, remote but authentic beauty) has something to do with Larkin's 'anger at the humiliation of age', but the harshness of the final stanza has rather more to do with that other, more deeply felt source of anger: 'anger at the old for reminding us of death'. Its return to the rhetoric of blame ('the old fools') marks the point where this poem founders—where its exploration of the one kind of anger (on behalf of the old) becomes sabotaged rather than complexified by the other kind of anger (at the old). By the end of the penultimate stanza the poem has a conviction to declaim, one that carries it with rhetorical determination over the formal containment of the stanza break. 'This is why they give || An air of baffled absence, trying to be there | Yet being here.' The 'there' of memory retreats, in spite of efforts at resistance. And effort *is*, all of a sudden, attributed to the old—they 'give', they 'try'—but the stanza break puts a visible space between 'giving' and the little thing they can give: 'an air'. As their past becomes further and further removed from memory, the experience of the old becomes more and more compromised by the reduction of their agency. Not they themselves but their 'absence', or rather their attempt to be elsewhere, is baffled; the 'incompetence' registered is not theirs but a secondary attribute of the condition of being cold; the 'wear and tear of taken breath' leaves breath unowned, barely active ('taken' is another adjective derived from a verb, action reduced to inaction). The cliché, however, claims a kind of eloquence in the very banality of its statement about suffering. 'Wear and tear' is newly painful, newly literal if it expresses the struggle of the lungs for air.

This final stanza is an answer, at last, not to the question of what the old and senile 'think has happened' (a question that has no answer, for Larkin) but to the question of why they aren't screaming at the indignities of age and senility. Living not in the 'here and now, but where all happened once', they do not perceive how close they are to death. The extended metaphor of mountain climbing involves no heroic approach to oblivion. The old do not climb 'extinction's alp': the passage of time alone determines that they are on the steep slopes and no longer regarding death from a distance. They do not conquer the idea of extinction; the fact of it conquers them. As in stanza two, the speaker's mind rebels at its own coming obliteration, but the attempt to smooth over the fact rhetorically is too plainly that. 'Rising ground' initially sounds benign, but the meaning it belatedly yields, at 'falling back', is more suggestive of earthquake. The term 'strangers' might be a wry nod towards metaphysics, but refers instead to medical staff bringing death-speeding morphiates. The cadences could at a stretch be called consolatory, but there is no supporting consolation from the imagery—indeed barely any imagery at all by the end. The vituperative release of 'the whole hideous inverted childhood' prefaces a blankly certain conclusion: 'Well, | We shall find out'. That 'Well,' temporizes, establishing a limited pause, a last momentary respite, before the end, but there is no reassurance to be had, only a grimly bare statement of the obvious: we shall find out from first-hand experience.

The increasingly reduced mental capacities attributed to these people in the last lines ('the rooms grow farther') ultimately turn this poem away from 'the humiliations of age' altogether, towards the psychologically starker and for the speaker more self-interesting topic of death.[37] Larkin is not even confident that these people retain the capacity to understand death's nearness: 'Can they never tell | What is dragging them back, and how it will end? | Never, throughout the whole hideous inverted childhood'. On a generous reading, 'tell' might mean more than 'know'. Picking up and extending the earlier *doubles entendres* of 'they're for it' and 'ignore it', it could prompt the thought that the relevant gap is not between knowing and naming, but between knowing and saying. And if that were the case, there might be a worse explanation than want of comprehension, or being worn down by the sheer hard work of going on breathing, for why the old and senile keep quiet: what they know may be unspeakably bad. It seems more in keeping with the tone of 'The Old Fools'' ending to accept the bleaker reading: they just don't get it any more, not at any point.

The consequence of this privileging of the question of death over the question of what quality of life and mind might remain in a very bad old age, beset by dementia, is that anger *at* the old finally ousts anger *on behalf of* the old altogether, and with it any pretension the poem might have to expressing a welfarist concern for old age. 'The Old Fools' doesn't, in its ending, do anything like imaginative justice to the psychological state of the people Larkin is observing. Instead, it sacrifices the (very difficult) question of what they think, how much they remember, what they value, what their emotional state and rational capacities are, to the more salient thing (for Larkin, not yet definitively old) about their condition: their proximity to extinction. (One plausible answer to the question 'Why aren't they screaming?' is that Larkin is not observing closely enough.) Larkin, himself, seems to have felt that the poem didn't quite work: 'I don't think it entirely succeeded', he wrote to one friend; and to another, 'It's not very good.'[38] But if Larkin's own fear of death hijacked a poem ostensibly about fear of old age, 'The Old Fools' remains a potent evocation of the kind of bad old age we might, not irrationally, fear; not least because, both in the anticipation and in the living, it would leave us with so radically reduced a sense of our own life. It also makes it, as McKerlie recognizes, a potent, if worrying, imagining of the kind of old age that a just society needs to include in its planning. The question of how we would choose to live in old age is, after all, closely bound up with the generosity or otherwise with which we recognize 'margins of agency'. In Larkin's case, that generosity is painfully wanting. More oddly, what is also wanting (such is the fear of oblivion in 'The Old Fools') is any recognition that there may come a point at which the question of how we would choose to live in old age becomes a question about when we might rather, legitimately, choose to die.

By way of comparison, I turn to a poet whom Larkin admired, and to a poem directly focused on the question of choice in relation to length of life: specifically, when it is permissible to choose death rather than more of life. Stevie Smith's 'Exeat' (1965), written apparently when Smith was in her early to mid fifties,[39] accords with Larkin's view of old age as a looming threat to our 'power of choosing'. It is possible that Larkin had it in mind when writing 'The Old Fools' (1973), though there is no evidence that this is so.[40] Unlike Larkin, Smith detects an element of unkindness (that's about as strongly as one can put it) on the part of those poets and philosophers who place a high valuation on our ability to choose how long we go on living. The 'power of choosing' in 'Exeat' refers, more frankly than in Larkin's poem, to our ability to opt out—but for Smith that choice will be valid only 'after a long life', when we are on the verge of losing the capacity to exercise it. This seems, on the surface, almost the same emptying out of 'choice' that appals Larkin, but the tone and temper of Smith's poem are markedly unappalled, her ironic self-regard surprisingly, even perversely, reconciled to the narrow scope we have for exercising our power of choosing.

Exeat

I remember the Roman Emperor, one of the cruellest of them,
Who used to visit for pleasure his poor prisoners cramped in dungeons,
So then they would beg him for death, and then he would say:
Oh no, oh no, we are not yet friends enough.
He meant that they were not yet friends enough for him to give them death.
So I fancy my Muse says, when I wish to die:
Oh no, Oh no, we are not yet friends enough,

And Virtue also says:
We are not friends enough.

How can a poet commit suicide
When he is still not listening properly to his Muse,
Or a lover of Virtue when
He is always putting her off until tomorrow?

Yet a time may come when a poet or any person
Having a long life behind him, pleasure and sorrow,
But feeble now and expensive to his country
And on the point of no longer being able to make a decision
May fancy Life comes to him with love and says
We are friends enough now for me to give you death;
Then he may commit suicide, then
He may go.[41]

The poem has that characteristic ability of Stevie Smith's writing to make the naive and the fey bear weight. Like Christina Rossetti's voice, which seems to ghost the last lines ('Life comes to him with love and says ... '), it makes a virtue, but also a barrier, of simplicity. Less tightly constrained formally than Larkin's poem, the free verse adapts itself to the rhythms of a deceptively companionable speaking voice ('querulous and keening', is how Seamus Heaney described Smith's own reading style, 'inviting the audience to yield her their affection' yet 'keeping them at bay with quick irony'[42]). Rhyme lays traps for the ear: the dogmatically connective 'o's threading through 'So … Oh no, oh no … So … Oh no, Oh no … also … poet … tomorrow … poet … sorrow … go', and the more angular, insinuating half-rhyme in 'person/decision'. Simple repetition is even more extensively exploited, but so distributed and masked by the long phrases that the full extent of it is easily missed: 'So then … and then … ', but 'Oh no, oh no, we are not yet friends enough … Oh no, Oh no, we are not yet friends enough … We are not friends enough … not … still not', until we are at last given 'Yet … enough … then … then'. By these rhymes and repetitions, and the expansiveness of its rhythms in those early lines especially, 'Exeat' performs a tyrannous dilation of its own rhetorical time.

Smith's Roman Emperor is a figure 'remembered' as from a child's history book. Facetiously kind, insinuatingly polite, he is meticulous in the exercise of tyranny: 'Oh no, Oh no, we are not yet friends enough'. He personifies the power both to impose and to end suffering—a power the poem proceeds to attribute metaphorically first to the practice of poetry then to Virtue (how we make art, how we conduct life), before finally ceding it to Life itself. Even in the first verse, his cruel pleasure in making his poor prisoners suffer longer is implicitly shared with the speaker, who serves as the Emperor's interpreter and familiar ('He meant … '). She (or he) makes of him a figure for her own command over the desire for death. The relaxed, slightly eager expositoriness—'one of the cruellest … So then … and then … Oh no, oh no'—repeats his toying with his 'poor prisoners' as her teasing of the reader, his 'spurious' solicitousness ('spurious' a favourite word of Smith's) is also hers.

'Exeat' pivots on the difference between when we think we should choose, or fancy, to be done with life and what Life chooses, or fancies, for us. 'Fancy' does more overtly double work here than in 'The Old Fools'. Avowedly 'fanciful', and *inside* its fancies as Larkin's speaker is not (he conceives of fancy only as the diminished intellectual grasp of the old), Smith's poem speaks both of what is imagined, merely whimsically, and of what is wanted, ardently. It imagines, but crucially does not exercise, a choice. The only arbiter between what we might fancy and what Life fancies on our behalf would be 'the power of choosing'—or, in Smith's words, 'being able to make a decision'—but it is a power we can only have, and about which we can only really be serious, she claims, 'at the end of a long life' when Life is about to take from us the capacity to exercise it. The similarity to Larkin's thought is there, but Smith is less fearful. When it comes to choosing how long we should live, she agrees, we are not in control—but there are seductions for the poet and the philosopher, she slyly implies, in casting Life as a sadistically temporizing tyrant. If Life temporizes with us, drawing out our time longer than we would wish, we in our turn temporize with Life.

The parallel that 'Exeat' sets up between Poetry and Virtue is only playfully logical but, for all its flippancy, it is moral. 'How can any poet... | Or a lover of Virtue' commit suicide? The question here genuinely wants an answer as Larkin's questions do not ('What do they think has happened?', 'Why aren't they screaming?'). Both the poet and lover of virtue are in bad faith, the poem chides, when they express a wish to put an end to their own suffering: the former's desire for an *exeat* (permission to leave before his term is up) is not to be believed as long as he has not made the best of his talent; the philosopher's love of Virtue (Roman stoic Virtue, the context suggests) is similarly hypocritical as long as he holds back from the philosophic life. In so far as we do not make the best of our gifts or capacities, or are not fully serious (about poetry, about philosophy) it evidently suits us to be without this choice we claim to want over how long we have.

Only time and old age bring an end to such temporizing with death. 'Having a long life behind him', the 'poet or any person' may fancy—with less of the sense of wanting it to be so—that Life is at last ready to let him go. Smith's personifications and abstractions are robuster than Larkin's, but while they and the subordinate clauses lend an air of causal explanation to the final stanza the causalities are less than fully explicit. 'Pleasure and sorrow' appear to be integral to Life's offer, at long last, of an *exeat*, but on closer inspection they are incidental. Though they necessarily precede death, having experienced them is not in itself a licence to die. The word 'pleasure' especially disconcerts, associated as it was earlier with the Roman Emperor's tyranny. Has pleasure belonged, after all, to the poet or any person who has felt the potential of their own faculties while alive, or has he only been detained, sorrowfully, at the pleasure of a sadistic power? Being 'feeble now and expensive to his country' is similarly under-explained. Is the feebleness of the old the same thing as their expensiveness? Have we moved into the modern refusal to look after age that Larkin, not quite credibly, claimed to be deprecating? or is this a franker acknowledgement that the poet or any person accedes to their own detention for as long as they remain alive and so is, in effect, in a covertly friendly alliance with the Emperor all along?

The drive of these lines lies not in their imperfect rationality but rather in their mood, and in that vocal shift from 'long life' to 'no longer'. Like the word 'exeat' itself, the final lines blur and at last evade altogether the question of choice with which the poem has been preoccupied. 'Exeat' compounds what may be chosen with what will happen regardless of choice. It is both Latin verb and English noun: he/she may exit (present subjunctive) and his/her entitlement to exit; one's own agency and another's power of decision. The Victorian lyricism of 'Life comes to him with love', quaintly archaic in the context, suggests, as Larkin's poem did not, that there is room here for a religious interpretation of the injunction against taking one's own life (Smith held that to be the case). But it runs up hard against the bluntness of 'he may commit suicide'—so that the ending expresses at one and the same time the openness of possibility and the closure of imperial dictat: 'then | He may go'.

But this isn't to say that Smith views the question of choice for when to die as nugatory. We are, she suggests—and the irony is less bitter than it sounds in paraphrase—ethically entitled to choose that our lives should end only when we have persisted in living them through almost to the point where we are incapable of making that choice or any other. Almost, but not quite incapable. To be '[o]n the point of no longer being able to make a decision' is not the same thing as having lost the power of choosing. For Smith, in other words, we will have earned that permission only when we are very close indeed both to the end of the possibility of choice and to death from natural causes. Suicide, under those complex conditions—having lived a long life, having become enfeebled and expensive to one's country, wanting to die—becomes at last acceptable. It matters, however, that Smith appeals at that point not to morality or reason but to what we are at liberty to fancy that Life permits us. An important effect of that choice of lexis is that arguments which, mooted more directively in terms of rational life-planning, would be deeply troubling in their implications for social welfare[43] retain their integrity as potential but by no means requisite choices for an individual.

'Exeat's very narrow discrimination of the conditions for choice in a state of near choicelessness puts the poem in quite different tonal and philosophical territory from Larkin's pained disabusement. For Larkin, death was a fearful certainty, and the old and senile a source of anger in so far as they remind us of it: 'Well, | We shall find out'. For Smith, the choice for death at the end of a long life remains a possibility, a viable alternative to choiceless extinction ('a time may come'); and for her our relation with choice, and through it with death, is not simply linear but something that changes over time. What was an inadmissible choice for death, for most of our lives, becomes conceivably admissible under a specific mix of subjective and objective conditions in old age. Angular and deceptively slight as 'Exeat' is, its presentation of living out a long life as the only condition under which the wish to leave will be sanctioned by 'Life' is in one sense more devastated than 'The Old Fools' by the imagined loss, in old age, of our 'power of choosing'. It goes where Larkin, terrified of extinction, cannot go: towards the possibility of making our own choice of when to end. But in its imaginative opening out of the terms of that possibility, and the lightness (against all odds) of its tone, it is also finally much less devastated, and far more willing to take the question of choice seriously.

Dennis McKerlie reads Larkin's poem too restrictively—but in a sense also too generously—when he sees in it a welfarist warning of the limitations of prudential choice in relation to old age. He misses entirely the much larger challenge 'The Old Fools' presents for any 'chooser's' approach to ageing by its refusal to take its eyes off the fundamental threat a bad old age (senility, serious incapacity) poses in our subjective apprehension of our own futures. 'Exeat' is a timely reminder, not far from Larkin's moment or his poetic idiom, that our having drastically limited powers of choice for and in old age need not be cause for anger and despair: little choice is not no choice, and there are other kinds of accommodation—intellectual, moral, emotional, perhaps religious—that we can make with the idea of extinction, including irony, humour, and acceptance. It is far more attuned to what remains, even at a very late point, of our autonomy. Neither of these poems offers a positive view of old age, to be sure, but by putting the focus on how life may alter us, rather than how we would choose, in theory, to live, they open the door to a different philosophical approach to lives. What if the change old age brings to our capacities and/or our interests is not a gradual modification, but change so substantial, so disruptive of our psychological continuity and connectedness, that we may have reason not to think of our lives as unified? ('Change' here need not mean devastation, as it pre-emptively does in Larkin's poem.) What if that change is so profound or complex that it puts in question the continuity and coherence of our present and future selves? If this is so, we might need to rethink our reasoning about how we should conceive of self-interest, and our understanding of what it means to be a person. We might need a more radical theory altogether.

5

Where Self-Interest Ends

Some way into Balzac's *Le Père Goriot* (1834), Eugène de Rastignac, down on his financial luck and ambitious of moving up in the world with more speed and certainty than by grinding away as a student of the law, meets his good friend Bianchon in the Jardin du Luxembourg. Hearing that Eugène is plagued by temptations, Bianchon reminds him that there is one sure way of getting rid of them: 'By yielding to them'. 'Have you read Rousseau?', is Rastignac's reply. 'Do you remember the passage where he asks the reader what he would do if he could make a fortune by killing an old mandarin in China just by exerting his will, without stirring from Paris?... if it were proved to you that the thing was possible and you only needed to nod your head, would you do it?' Bianchon's response is of the 'It depends' kind: 'Is your mandarin really old?'—but even as he starts to follow Rastignac down that slippery moral slope, he recoils from (what he takes to be) the game. 'But, bless you, young or old, paralytic or healthy... Well, no.'[1]

The Chinese mandarin scenario is usually taken as a question about moral responsibility to others—a classic probing of 'the moral implications of distance', as Carlo Ginzburg puts it.[2] But in the context of Balzac's novel it is more immediately a question about the moral constraints on self-interest—and in that guise it bears a structural resemblance to another kind of dilemma, initially rational rather than moral in character. This is Derek Parfit, writing in *Reasons and Persons* (1984), on the way in which our reasoning about possible pain changes according to whether it is closer or further away in our future:

> [The following attitude to time] is extremely common: caring more about the nearer future. Call this the *bias towards the near*. Someone with this bias may knowingly choose to have a worse pain a few weeks later rather than a lesser pain this afternoon. This kind of choice is often made. [...] A similar

[case] would be th[is]. Many people care more about what happens to their neighbours, or to members of their own community.[3]

He continues: the bias towards the nearer future may be concealed by 'the *bias towards the future*' (a preference for postponing pleasures, and bringing forward pains)—but the deeper motivation is the same. 'We want to get the pains behind us and to keep the pleasures before us' (160). Neither bias is good for us. Were we to respond neutrally to time, Parfit argues, we would lose in some respects, but the gains would be much greater, especially 'in our attitude to ageing and to death' (175). We should cease to be troubled, as we entered old age, by the idea that our time is running out, for although there is little life left to enjoy we have the whole of the rest of our lives to look back upon. Our position within the temporal span of our lifetime would no longer be of particular importance to us.[4] We should, then, be 'much less depressed' by ageing and by the prospect of death (176).

Our future is to our present what the Chinaman is to Rastignac: we commonly give precedence to what is proximate over what is distant, temporally as well as spatially. The cost in the Balzac scene is a potential failure of moral responsibility; in the Parfit passage, a failure of rationality—but, in each case, the bias of self-interest is made conspicuous through the thought of old age. 'Is your mandarin really old?' Bianchon won't endorse any slackening of the moral prohibition on murder, but the joke tells us that he recognizes, even shares, Rastignac's intuition to view the death of an old person as less tragic than that of a younger (the same deeply problematic intuition behind Raskolnikov's murder of an old woman in *Crime and Punishment*[5]). In *Reasons and Persons*, the remoteness of our own old age while we are young opens the way for caring less about age, but if we were to consider our temporal location within our expected lifespan 'neutrally', Parfit suggests, we should put ourselves in the way of a much happier old age.

Theorists of self-interest seek to answer the question 'What would be best for someone, or would be most in this person's interests, or would make this person's life go, for him [or her], as well as possible?'[6] If Balzac and Parfit are right, our attitudes to time make it difficult for us to answer that question well with regard to our old age. Some caution is necessary here: the strength of the bias towards the near will of course differ according to the circumstances and perhaps the temperament of the individual. Any predilection I have for putting off writing my book will, for example, be modified if I have reason to believe someone else is writing one very like it. The strength of the bias may also be affected by our life history, by what we know of our genetic make-up, and by our social and historical context. Just how greatly it varies, within and between lives, may be left open to debate.[7] Assuming for now that it is plausible, and very widely if not universally exhibited, it has, as Parfit suggests, some important consequences for our thinking about old age.

For a start, it indicates a different rationale for ageism than those conventionally offered. Ageism is usually thought of as a matter of our conduct towards others—even by those who recognize our demonstrably ageist attitudes towards ourselves (trivially, our tolerance of certain kinds of birthday card; less trivially our willingness to curtail our expectations for our lives as we grow older, in advance of any necessity for doing so). Larkin's 'The Old Fools' (as we have seen) is a case in point. Readers who dislike it are often, I suspect, put off by its pessimism more than its unkindness, even if they recognize that its extreme negativity towards the old expresses the speaker's pre-emptive fears about his own future. Ageism towards ourselves, or ageism that expressly applies to ourselves, is harder to get a grip on morally, and may seem the more objectionable, because it pretends to a kind of neutrality in including itself as an object of its own negativity.

All this said, I want to leave the word 'ageism' behind here. It suggests one larger ramification of this chapter's arguments, but it is also potentially misleading. By reading Parfit in conjunction with Balzac, I want to think about whether many of the ills too often suffered in old age might not be more fundamentally a product of our perceptions of ourselves across our lifetimes: a consequence of how we think temporally about our own welfare; also, relatedly, a consequence of how we think rationally about what it is to be a person and to have a life. Neither Parfit nor Balzac is concerned with ageism as a large, politicized categorization of negative social attitudes to ageing. Their focus is rather on the rational justifications individuals have for acting in certain ways rather than in others, and the moral consequences of their reasoning. To approach old age initially in terms of rationality rather than morality is not to set aside the question of how prejudicially we may view the end of a longer, as opposed to a shorter, life. It is rather to ask, as I take Balzac and Parfit to be asking, whether our too often inadequate regard for old age, and perhaps our fear of it, do not have roots as firmly in our reasoning about, and attitudes towards, ourselves, as in our reasoning about, and attitudes towards, others.

Reasons and Persons is a deeply original, powerfully argued work by a philosopher in the analytic tradition. It has implications well beyond most of the philosophical works studied in *The Long Life* for how we may think about the consequences of old age for our understanding of what it means to be a person, to have a life, and to act justly towards the old. Four areas of its argument are especially relevant. First, Parfit's claims about time: that self-interest should be temporally neutral about the future, and that one's reasons for acting must be grounded in the present. Second, the removal of the metaphysical basis for personal identity. On Parfit's Reductionist View, what matters is not personal identity conceived of as a 'further fact' but only psychological connectedness and continuity. Psychological connectedness may, he argues, become weakened by events, especially over long stretches of time. When that happens, what we think of as a single self-identical person who persists through time may be better thought of as (by analogy) a series of selves differentiated over time. This second set of arguments has worrying implications for those concerned with justice between the young and the old. (Recognizing this, Norman Daniels explicitly criticizes Parfit in an appendix to *Am I My Parents' Keeper?*.[8])

The third aspect of *Reasons and Persons* with particular relevance for old age is the question of how, within the terms of the Reductionist View, I should choose rationally when my present decision will importantly affect my life at some later time when my values may be very different from the values I hold now. Parfit's argument, that it is reasonable for me to make the choice on the strength of my present values, is disputable—as is the fourth important aspect of his thinking: the argument that we should extend the field of morality to protect our future selves from grave imprudence. Specifically, he argues, we should broaden it to include a paternalistic concern for our future selves.

In all these ways Parfit's book has direct significance for the philosophical consideration of old age. Even so, reading *Reasons and Persons* for its account of ageing is (still more strongly than with Plato and Aristotle) a matter of bringing to the fore an element of the philosophical picture that, while evidently important, remains a minor concern, and, once examined in more detail, causes some trouble for certain of the arguments being advanced. Parfit makes, in passing, several explicit claims about the benefits and (with respect to imprudence) the dangers that his rational view could bring for old age, but they are very much 'in passing', and in the pursuit of broader arguments about our attitudes to time, about personal identity, and about reasons for acting.

Balzac, by contrast, makes old age his central, sustained subject in *Le Père Goriot*: the place where, were he a painter, he would have 'all the light of his picture fall' (42). In bringing these two works together, I am not arguing that Balzac anticipates Derek Parfit's exactingly rationalist approach to persons in any other than a very partial way, nor am I suggesting that Parfitian rationalism is really Balzacian cynicism under another name. I am looking to the combination to provide a fuller account than either alone gives of how deeply anchored our attitudes to old age may be in our reasoning, for most of our lives, about where our best interests lie. Both Parfit and Balzac see much of what is bad in those attitudes as intimately connected to our common but irrational bias towards the near, and implicitly at least both suggest that thinking more seriously about old age might operate as a check on that bias. Both also open the way to a psychologically discontinuous view of persons, in which actions are directed by present aims and desires. They are alike in recognizing that the full pursuit of such a discontinuous view would require the introduction of additional moral safeguards for the protection of old age. But this is also where they part company most strikingly. In Balzac's novel no moral safeguards are to be found. In *Le Père Goriot*, as in *King Lear*, old age is a state of 'misfortune', 'contempt', 'persecution'—with the difference that any dignity that it once gained along with pathos in Shakespeare is no longer secure. In Balzac's characteristically ambivalent gaze, age is at once a sublime tragedy and a grotesque comedy. Whatever one might hope for or from it, it is—cynically, and with the full semantic thickness of the phrase—where self-interest ends. For Parfit, there remains the hope that more impersonal reasoning could rescue us; but it is a hope, by his own account, still in need of a comprehensive theory.

Reasons and Persons is a sustained rebuttal of the classic theory of self-interest. That theory rests on the following claims:

> (S1) For each person, there is one supremely rational ultimate aim: that his life go, for him, as well as possible.
>
> (S2) What each of us has most reason to do is whatever would be best for himself, and
>
> (S3) It is irrational for anyone to do what he himself believes will be worse for himself.

(S4) What it would be rational for anyone to do is what will bring him the greatest *expected* benefit.   (Parfit, 4, 8)

Parts I and II of *Reasons and Persons* present extended, and complex, arguments for rejecting the classic Self-Interest Theory. First on the grounds that it is self-defeating. One important argument here is that the classic theory cannot survive a combined assault from morality (which is neutral about time and persons, taking interests and desires into account regardless of whose life it is and when in the life they occur) and from Present-Aim Theory (biased both towards the individual and temporally, in favour of present aims and desires). Secondly, the classic theory assumes, wrongly, that all desires are rational. Parfit argues that we should accept instead the 'Critical Present-Aim Theory', which (abbreviated) claims that some desires are intrinsically irrational and 'what I have most reason to do is what would best fulfil those of my present desires that are not irrational' (119). This appeal to a person's present desires may appear to be a breach of temporal neutrality, a 'bias towards the present', but Parfit adds the requirement that present aims be exercised with a temporally neutral concern for all parts of one's life (135). There are potential problems with that condition, and I shall come to them below.

The arguments in *Reasons and Persons* with most direct implications for old age arise in Parts III and IV, where Parfit defends a Reductionist View of Persons. According to the Reductionist View, we should reject the idea that personal identity is a 'deep-further fact' beyond psychological connectedness and continuity. Belief in a Cartesian ego, for example, or a 'spiritual substance' rests on common-sense, uncritical Non-Reductionism (210). We should admit, Parfit argues, that personal identity consists only in psychological connectedness and continuity, which will vary in strength depending on events. We are used to thinking about the identities of nations in such reductive terms: we readily accept that a nation does not exist as an entity distinct from its citizens and its territories. Analogously, we should accept that a person does not exist independent of 'a brain and body, and the occurrence of a series of interrelated physical and mental events' (211).[9]

At various points in Parts I and II, Parfit makes certain claims for the attractiveness of his revised reasoning about self-interest by comparison with what classic Self-Interest Theory can deliver. These include the claim, already quoted, that were we to respond neutrally to time we would lose in some respects, but the gains would be much greater, especially 'in our attitude to ageing and to death' (175).[10] But when he comes to consider the possible consequences of weakened psychological connectedness between one's present self and oneself in the further future it becomes clear that the implications of a Reductionist View of persons are not so good for old age.

According to classic Self-Interest Theory, a rational person should be equally concerned about all the parts of his or her future (Parfit calls this 'The Requirement of Equal Concern'). Not to be so would be imprudent. The Reductionist View makes it rationally defensible, though not compulsory, to accept 'The Extreme Claim': if personal identity does not involve a 'deep further fact', then we have no special reason to be concerned about our own futures (307 ff.). It also permits the more moderate, but (with a view to the happiness and welfare of the old) still worrying, claim that

> My concern for my future may correspond to the degree of connectedness between me now and myself in the future. Connectedness is one of the two relations that give me reasons to be specially concerned about my own future. It can be rational to care less, when one of the grounds for caring will hold to a lesser degree. Since connectedness is nearly always weaker over longer periods, I can rationally care less about my further future.   (313)

Parfit proposes, accordingly, 'a discount rate, not with respect to time itself, but with respect to the weakening of [psychological connectedness]' (314). The distinction here is important: temporal proximity alone does not determine strength of psychological connectedness. On the other hand there is likely to be a correlation between weakening of connectedness and length of time passed. Under normal conditions there will be no significant difference in connectedness between myself now and myself in a month's or even a year's time; the connections between myself now and myself in forty years, however, will be very much less close (314).[11]

So, where temporal neutrality earlier promised a happier relation to ageing, the 'discount rate' with respect to psychological connectedness seems likely to produce something less positive: a weakened regard for, or even recklessness of, the consequences one's present actions may have for oneself later in life. 'Since [psychological] connectedness is one of my two reasons for caring about my future, it cannot be irrational for me to care less, when there will be less connectedness' (318). The risk arises of grave imprudence: 'for the sake of lesser benefits now', I may rationally choose to impose greater burdens on myself in old age when I am likely to be less able to bear them well (319). 'I might, for instance, start smoking when I am a boy. I know that I am likely to impose upon myself a premature and painful death. I know that I am doing what is likely to be much worse for me. Since we must reject the Classical Theory [of Self-Interest], we cannot claim that all such acts are irrational' (317).[12]

The absence of a rational objection to great imprudence from within the Critical Present-Aim Theory produces a quite surprising turn in *Reasons and Persons*. The lack of protection from within rationality requires, Parfit argues, an expansion of morality into the terrain that the revised Self-Interest Theory has abandoned. (Great imprudence has conventionally been seen as irrational but not morally wrong, and though traditional 'Common-Sense Morality' recognizes some duties towards oneself, they are 'special duties, such as a duty to develop one's talents, or to preserve one's purity' (319).) There are two ways in which this expansion of morality might work. It could take the form of consequentialism: we could claim that by imposing greater burdens on myself in old age for the sake of lesser benefits now, I am increasing the sum of suffering in the world. This is a straightforward utilitarian claim, albeit superficially peculiar in that it relies on a non-self-regarding argument in order to save me from myself. The alternative would be to extend our sense of special obligations: we could claim that a person 'stands to himself in the future', as one stands towards certain other people for whom one is responsible, such as parents, children, pupils, clients, etc. (319).

The most tantalizing move in Parfit's arguments relating to ageing comes when he offers 'an easier' way of thinking about this newly moral sense of our relation to ourselves in the future. We might, he argues, think of a person's future self as, under certain conditions, subdivided into a series of successive selves. 'As I have claimed, this has long seemed natural, whenever there is some marked weakening of psychological connectedness. After such a weakening, my earlier self may seem alien to me now. If I fail to *identify* with that earlier self, I am in some ways thinking of that self as like a different person' (319).[13]

> We could make similar claims about our future selves. If we now care little about ourselves in the further future, our future selves are like future generations. We can affect them for the worse, and, because they do not now exist, they cannot defend themselves. [...]
>
> Reconsider the boy who starts to smoke, knowing and hardly caring that this may cause him to suffer greatly fifty years later. This boy does not identify

with his future self. His attitude towards this future self is in some ways like his attitude to other people. This analogy makes it easier to believe that his act is morally wrong. He runs the risk of imposing on himself a premature and painful death. We should claim that it is wrong to impose on *anyone*, including such a future self, the risk of such a death.... We ought not to do to our future selves what it would be wrong to do to other people.   (319–20)

Secondary accounts of *Reasons and Persons* often latch on too eagerly to the language of future selves, and (connecting it with the book's more imaginative thought experiments on brain replication and division) reduce the reductionism further to a kind of sci-fi escape from the constraints of a unitary model of a life.[14] It should be clear that the analogy is not to be taken literally, but is there, explicitly, to assist in changing our sense of what should be comprehended within the domain of moral beliefs: moral beliefs should include the belief that it is morally wrong to act in a way that is likely to cause harm to our future selves.

This analogy causes some difficulties with respect to Parfit's thinking about old age. The extension of the requirements for morality provides a highly desirable level of protection for old age, but not on terms that are entirely palatable. As Parfit himself acknowledges, we have a name for obliging people to act in their own interests: we call it paternalism, and we have some quite proper reservations about it. 'It is better if each of us learns from his own mistakes. And it is harder for others to know that these are mistakes' (321). Though Parfit does not spell it out, the same objections must then apply by analogy to the claim that our present self should act so as to prevent itself/us doing harm to a future self (that person, to whom we may not feel psychologically very strongly connected, who will be ourself in old age)—assuming we can get our head around the synchronic externality to the self *as well as* the diachronic disconnectedness from the self that such an application of paternalism requires.

Parfit does not say very much about paternalism, and he says nothing beyond this point in *Reasons and Persons* about ageing. He proceeds instead to a consideration of some other respects in which our moral views may need to change if we adopt the Reductionist View of personal identity: our views, for example, about abortion, about desert, commitments, and distributive justice. But some sharpening of the reasons not to be satisfied with paternalism as a safeguard for old age within the Reductionist View may be brought out by looking at the example (presumably an imaginative extrapolation from Tolstoy) that Parfit gives for how our understanding of moral commitments might change. Though it does not hinge upon old age, and is indeed articulated in relation to middle age, old age would seem to be an equally likely arena in which such a situation would be played out.

Consider

> *The Nineteenth-Century Russian.* In several years, a young Russian will inherit vast estates. Because he has socialist ideals, he intends, now, to give the land to the peasants. But he knows that in time his ideals may fade. To guard against this possibility, he does two things. He first signs a legal document, which will automatically give away the land, and which can be revoked only with his wife's consent. He then says to his wife, 'Promise me that, if I ever change my mind, and ask you to revoke this document, you will not consent.' He adds, 'I regard my ideals as essential to me. If I lose these ideals, I want you to think that I cease to exist. I want you to regard your husband then, not as me, the man who asks you for this promise, but only as his corrupted later self. Promise me that you would not do what he asks.' (327)[15]

The man's wife makes the promise, and in middle age he does indeed ask her to revoke her commitment. Assuming the husband to be of sound mind when he repudiates his youthful ideals, Parfit argues, the wife may reasonably consider that she is nevertheless *not* released from her promise: the young man she married has, in effect, ceased to exist.[16] She will be justified, in other words (and this is not a legalistic response but an emotional one) in treating the middle-aged man in front of her as though he were a different person from the man she married—one who has not the right to release her from a promise made to another.

One of the objections Bernard Williams made to the Russian nobleman scenario, when it first appeared in essay form in 1973, was that its (critical) present-aimism creates a serious problem with respect to the exercise of authority over one's future self. It is far from clear, he responded, why a person should regard his present aims and values as having higher authority than his future ones. '[W]hy should I hinder my future projects from the perspective of my present values rather than inhibit my present projects from the perspective of my future values? It is not enough in answer to that to say that evidently present action must flow from present values.'[17] If one believes that the future will bring greater enlightenment, one's present actions are likely to be shaped in order to assist that outcome. One is, to that extent, already dissatisfied with one's present values. For Williams, more needed to be said about why the Russian nobleman should therefore be so committed to his present aims. 'He may have, for instance, a theory of degeneration of the middle-aged; but then he should no doubt reflect that, when middle-aged, he will have a theory of the naiveté of the young.'[18]

Parfit's answer is not attached to the Russian nobleman passage itself, but can be found in an earlier chapter of *Reasons and Persons* entitled 'Different Attitudes to Time'.

> Suppose I believe that, with increasing knowledge and experience, I shall grow wiser. On this assumption, I should give to my *future* evaluative desires *more* weight than I give to my present evaluative desires, since my future desires will be better justified. [... But i]f I both assume that I am always growing wiser, and can now predict some future change of mind, I have in effect already changed my mind. If now I believe that some later belief will be better justified, I should have this belief now.
>
> [...] The contrary assumption is that, as time passes, I shall become less wise, and that the change in my ideals will be a corruption. The loss of ideals is commonplace; and judgement often goes. (In successive editions of their *Selected Poems*, many poets make worse and worse selections.) On this assumption, I should give greater weight to what I used to value or believe. But in the same way, if I accept this assumption, I would still believe what I used to believe, even if I care less. (155)

For Parfit, as we have seen, to have a theory of what will happen to oneself with the passage of time is to have, always, a present reason for acting accordingly. But belief and desire have here collapsed into one other. It is, surely, possible to believe, or for that matter (less strongly) to be able to *predict*, that one may come to change one's mind, without one's having 'in effect' already done so. The possibility of a change in one's values for better or for worse is both common knowledge and something we each of us learn for ourselves from routine observation of other people's lives (including reading about the lives and choices of poets).

Other philosophers have objected to the restriction of motives for action to one's present reasons. 'The hypothesis that all links to the future are made by present desires', Nagel writes in *The Possibility of Altruism* (1978),

> suggests that the agent at any specific time is insular, that he reaches outside himself to take an interest in his future as one may take an interest in the affairs of a distant country. The relation of a person to temporally distinct stages of his life must be closer than that. His concern about his own future does not require an antecedent desire or interest to explain it. There must already be a connection which renders the interest intelligible, and which depends not on his present condition but on the future's being a part of his *life*.[19]

But for Parfit, one can assume, the appeal to 'the *life*' may have insufficient grounds within the Reductionist View of persons. The relevant stress in Nagel's sentence, from Parfit's perspective, should be on 'his', not on 'life', because it is there that we must locate the degree of connectedness to our future self or selves, over whose life we may (or may not) claim possession from the vantage point of the present. In Parfit's own words, if 'what it is rational for me to do now depends on what I now want, or value, or believe' (445), I should now think of myself not in terms of my whole life but only of my present aims and actions. '[T]he fundamental unit is not the agent throughout his whole life, but the agent at the time of acting' (445).

The absence of old age from Parfit's discussion of morality after considering the possibility of grave imprudence should not perhaps surprise us. The passage of time alone is not assumed to bring discontinuity or a weakening of psychological connectedness. The two things are explicitly kept distinct. We may speculate that exposure to certain cultural prejudices and social realities as we grow older will carry some risk of psychological disconnectedness, but anyone, regardless of their age, may be exposed to events which will require a significant change in their beliefs and values or otherwise weaken psychological connectedness. There are also indications that, despite the need to safeguard old age against the imprudence of youth, Parfit sees the Reductionist View as 'liberating, and consoling' in ways that have further positive implications for our attitudes to ageing and death: when I believed that my existence was a deep 'further fact', 'I seemed imprisoned in myself.' Now, '[o]ther people are closer. I am less concerned about the rest of my own life and more concerned about the lives of others' (281, and see 347). Like other claims Parfit makes for the advantages of the Reductionist View of persons,[20] this can only be a psychological report on his own responses (282). Others may regard the reduction in what we mean by 'personal' identity as a loss.

It would enrich the (already very rich) argument of *Reasons and Persons* if Parfit were to consider more specific questions with respect to age: does ageing (rather than 'time') tend to weaken psychological connectedness, or is there no discernible correlation here? (Can it, equally, strengthen connectedness, and with it the sense of the 'unity of a life'?) Do negative cultural attitudes to ageing increase the likelihood of weakened connectedness? Should we treat any diminishment in connectedness differently when it is a consequence of mental pathology rather than of a change in 'values and attitudes'? (presumably so). More self-reflexively: does *Reasons and Persons* not problematically assume a young reader, both in its claims about our present-aimism and in its concern with the consequences of our present actions for our 'further future'? What difference would it make if Parfit were to assume a reader in his or her seventies or eighties, or older?

Above all, more needs to be said by Parfit about paternalism towards oneself as a necessary extension of our morality. He does, however, give some hint of what a fuller account of the problems with paternalism might be in the final section of the book. As we have seen, the language of future selves provides an *explicit* analogy for the relations between my present self and a future self with whom my psychological connections may be very weak. The treatment of future generations, in the final part of the book, may be read as an *implicit* analogy for the concept of paternalism towards oneself—an unintended analogy, presumably, but one that genuinely helps to clarify the nature of the problem, though it doesn't provide a solution.

Part IV, entitled 'Future Generations', addresses a problem that Parfit disarmingly admits he has been unable as yet to solve, though others, he believes, may do so: how are we to justify actions that will have consequences for future generations without referring to the identities of future persons? This final section of *Reasons and Persons* opens with the strongest version of Parfit's rational case for dispensing with persons as the objects of ethics. It is a scientific fact, he states, that if any given person had not been conceived within a month of the time when she or he was conceived that person would never have existed. We can therefore easily affect the identities of future people—that is, we can affect *who* will later live (351–5). We need, then, a reason to make certain choices rather than others as individuals, or adopt certain principles rather than others as societies, without relying on an appeal to the identities of persons. We cannot, he argues (it is one of his most contentious claims), rely on the language of the rights of people in the future when we can no longer refer to the existence of specific persons (364–6). What we need, according to Parfit, is a new theory of Beneficence which does not appeal to the identifies of particular people to be benefited or protected from harm. We need a way of securing both quality and quantity of life for future generations without speaking and thinking in terms of what is 'good or bad for those people whom our acts affect' (378).[21]

If there is an acknowledged gap in the theory of the relation between present and future generations, there is an analogous, but unacknowledged, gap with regard to old age, or 'later selves'. Just as we cannot know the identities of future persons, we cannot, on the Reductionist View, know the identities of our possible future selves. We cannot predict events that may weaken psychological connectedness, nor can we predict what the values or interests of a new self or selves, not strongly connected to our present self, will be. Parfit knows that he needs a new general social theory of beneficence that will secure the best quantity and value of life for future generations without appealing to the existence of given persons; but by the same reasoning (not followed through in *Reasons and Persons*) he needs a more specific theory of paternalism, or an alternative to paternalism, which will make it possible for our present self to do good on behalf of those future generations of ourself who are not necessarily to be thought of as, in any strong sense, 'ourself' at all.[22]

'Beneficence' is a stronger requirement than paternalism. It involves not only the prevention of harm (grave imprudence, when we are speaking of future selves) but the doing of good in situations where we have to make choices that will produce different outcomes. But the problem the theory of beneficence faces from the removal of identity is analogically equivalent to the problem paternalism faces from the removal of psychological connectedness and continuity. And the gap that remains in the theory of beneficence needs also to be acknowledged as a gap in the theory of paternalism. As it stands, the cautious endorsement of paternalism towards our future selves has something of the flavour of a moral stop-gap in *Reasons and Persons*.[23] Parfit seems to want to bind our future selves to our present selves much as the Russian nobleman seeks to pre-empt a possible later self from sabotaging his present socialist intentions.[24] In short, Parfit wants to supplement his own temporal neutrality and his critical present-aimism with a corrective (morally motivated) special concern for the further future, but in the absence, as yet, of a sufficiently explicit theory of what our grounds are for protecting persons whose identities are as yet unknowable.

Parfit's 'paternalism towards the self' opens up a number of further questions about the place of old age in a rational account of well-being. What is the status of the choices the old make for themselves? More nearly for those who are not yet old: exactly what part should the prospect of old age have in decisions taken earlier in life about what is and is not good for a person, or most likely to advance their happiness? Does 'paternalism' indicate, in effect, a reduction on what either Daniels's prudentialism or

McKerlie's welfarism, for example, would allow, or would the provision made for old age be comparable? I claimed in relation to Michael Slote's *Goods and Virtues* (p. 104 above) that a more persuasive argument for valuing the aims and interests of late life differently from those of our prime would require a narrower, more competence-based definition of 'age' than Slote's usage implies, and a more precise description of how our aims and interests relate to time's passage. Parfit provides the more detailed description of our attitudes to time, but if we follow him into a more impersonal account of our interests, we still need a fuller account of the effects of ageing on psychological connectedness.

Parfit's rational view of persons goes some considerable way towards correcting the bias against old age that is inherent in many of our dominant assumptions about self-interest. Certainly Parfit would like to think that his theory could produce a better old age in which the relatively little time left to the old would not diminish their claim to possess aims and intentions of equal significance to those they held in their prime. (I take that to be implicit in his reference to the better attitudes to old age which would result from temporal neutrality.) But, in its context, the invocation of paternalism looks like Parfit overcorrecting for his own presentism—and at the point when he considers most substantially what our relation to our 'further future' should be, he finds himself unable to complete the theory. 'Paternalism towards the self' is not a sufficiently persuasive or attractive recommendation. It seems to be there in *Reasons and Persons* only because, without it, and in the absence of the complete theory, it could be justifiably claimed that we have no good reason to care for our own old age much, or even at all. In Parfit's vocabulary, there would be inadequate reason not to inflict harm upon 'future generations' or our future selves. Our bias towards the near, unrestrained by any special concern for the further future, would open wide the doors to a bad old age for whichever self or selves may, in the future, go under our names.

We should find ourselves, morally speaking, in Balzac's Paris.

There is a moment, very near the end of *Reasons and Persons*, where Derek Parfit declares a motive for wanting to pursue impersonal reasons for acting. 'Life in big cities is disturbingly impersonal', he writes. 'We cannot solve this problem unless we attack it in its own terms. Just as we need thieves to catch thieves, we need impersonal principles to avoid the bad effects of impersonality' (444). Rarely does he sound more like Balzac: the

Balzac who imagined for Paris a thief to catch its thieves, and made him a disturbingly eloquent spokesman for a philosophy opposed to seeing life as 'a straight line', or a single unit.[25] As an analysis of age, Le Père Goriot reads at many points like certain parts of Parfit's view writ either much larger or with a great deal more scepticism about the capacity of our reason to protect us from harm. It is a distorted version of Parfit's view, certainly, and by no means as systematic, but it is hard to think of anything in literature that comes closer to expressing Parfit's sense that what is wrong with our common attitudes to old age begins in what is wrong with our reasoning about ourselves.

I am told that, in the lectures that evolved into key parts of Reasons and Persons, Parfit made extensive illustrative use of Proust. Little remains of the Proust discussion in the published version (see pp. 513–14 n. 42, 537) and I've chosen not to pursue those brief allusions further, although I am aware that Proust is especially beloved of many philosophers. Balzac seems to me a closer parallel to Parfit's interests in terms of the avowed concern with reasons for acting. He also shows a more direct, even polemical, concern with our common temporal bias towards the near future than Proust does. Balzac anticipates parts of Parfit's Reductionist View, too, when he describes the possibility that psychological connectedness from one's youth to one's further future may be so weakened as to make it easier to think of one's present and future self as different selves. And, like Parfit, he foregrounds the problem of what authority one has to make choices now that will affect oneself at a future date when one may have quite different aims and values. Finally, and crucially, the interest in paternalism as a moral protection against imprudence is there too (though it gets a deeply pessimistic and distorted hearing). In short, reading Balzac after reading Parfit is like watching many of Parfit's concerns mirrored back with the leer of satire.

I begin with the bias towards the near future.

The 'moral temperature'[26] of self-interest in Balzac's Paris can be most readily gauged by observing the direct connection between a pervasive bias towards the near future and the greatly reduced regard for old age. When the convict-in-hiding Jacques Collin, alias Vautrin, assumes the role of mentor to Eugène de Rastignac, he makes that bias explicit, and presents the young man with a stark rational choice: 'Voilà le carrefour de la vie, jeune homme, choisissez.' (There are the cross-roads of life, young man; choose!)

In fact you have already chosen; you went to your cousin de Beauséant's house and sniffed the sweet smell of luxury there; you went to Madame de Restaud, old Goriot's daughter, and there became conscious of the Parisian woman. That day you came back with one word written on your forehead [...] *Success!* [*Parvenir!*] success at all costs. [... But y]our fifteen hundred francs, squeezed out God knows how! [...] will slip away like marauding soldiers. And then what will you do? Will you work? Work, or what you understand by work at the moment, leads in old age to a room in Mamma Vauquer's boarding-house, for guys of Poiret's stature. (128–9/G139)

Rastignac has money enough (begged from his mother, aunt, and two sisters) to support his ambitions for perhaps a few months. Thereafter he has no social prospects beyond what he can make for himself. At which point, Vautrin offers a stark decision between rationality and morality: the 'quick road to success' (129) and the 'long' uncertain road laid out by duty (127). The choice he advocates would require killing the old Chinese mandarin: to drop the metaphor, acceding to the death of a young man whose inheritance will then pass to his sister and become available to Rastignac through marriage. Alternatively, Rastignac can hold to his principles and accept a life of drudgery with (Vautrin predicts) a wretched marriage for an ordinary dowry.

In Vautrin's preferred shorthand, it is a choice between a vigorous, well-rewarded prime and the squalid old age on display at the Maison-Vauquer. Being a 'guy of Poiret's stature' is not an attractive option. A 'kind of automaton', Poiret is to be seen

moving like a grey shadow along one of the pathways at the Jardin des Plantes, his head covered by a limp old cap, barely holding his stick with the yellow ivory knob in his hand, the rumpled tails of his frockcoat floating wide and ill-concealing his almost empty breeches, and his legs in blue stockings wavering like a drunk man's; his dirty white waistcoat showing, and his shirt-frill of coarse, crumpled muslin meeting up only imperfectly with the tie knotted round his turkey neck.[...]What toil could have shrivelled him so?

One can see here why Proust was drawn to Balzac, for all the 'massive vulgarity of mind'.[27] There is much of the 'cruelty' that Malcolm Bowie has identified in Proust's attitude to old age: the determination to 'do justice ... to [the writer's] knowledge that human mortality is an irremediable fact'.[28] Such an artist is no longer merely a reporter on death: he has become the 'agent' of mortality. But where Proust would probe beneath the skin in search of the 'impersonal' forces of nature ravishing the flesh (and in so doing return a perverse kind of individuality to the old),[29] Balzac sees the human body withered away to leave nothing but clothes and appendages: the social carapace. All that remains of Poiret, when the body is so reduced (a mere scrag end of flesh remaining, like a turkey neck), is the evidence of a former effort at respectability—shirt frill, frockcoat, cane—undercut by the age and poverty of the materials in which it was attempted: coarse muslin, rumpled cloth, yellowed ivory.[30] This is age as an unstoppable drift into the social abyss, the decline of the body refigured as, and reduced to, the wearing out of its social effects.

What exactly Poiret formerly did for his living the usually omniscient narrative voice affects not to know, but the insinuations of free indirect style in this early passage on old age at the Maison-Vauquer sound, in retrospect, very like the voice we will come to know as Vautrin's. The voice, that is, of a man with no illusions about society. Having pretended ignorance, it goes on to toy with a number of possibilities—all of them having to do with the social, functionary processing of death. Poiret was perhaps a minor official 'in the office to which public executioners send in their expense accounts … [p]erhaps … a receiver at the door of a slaughter house, or a sub-inspector in a Sanitary Department' (37). He has the look of 'one of the drudges of our great social treadmill[…]one of those[…]of whom we say, "The work can't be done without them, after all" ' (37). Which is why he can stand as so forceful a threat from Vautrin to Rastignac: look to your own interests, and start making some leeway in your principles! Society cares nothing for those who labour 'honestly' in its service.

But if a miserable old age at the Maison-Vauquer is the result of a life of public toil, it also appears to be the result of a life given over too much to pleasure. Poiret's companion, and later (not coincidentally) his confederate against Vautrin, is Mlle Michonneau.

> What acid had consumed the feminine curves of this creature? She must once have been pretty and well-formed. Was it vice, grief, greed? Had she loved too well? Had she been a dealer in second-hand clothing or simply a courtesan? Was she expiating the triumphs of an insolent youth when the world had run after her to offer pleasure [au devant de laquelle s'étaient rués les plaisirs], by an old age shunned by passers by?   (36/G57–8)

Here again, to look at old age is to be drawn to speculate. What life can once have inhabited so ruined a form? What passion or improvidence can have used up this flesh? 'The Venus of Père-Lachaise', Vautrin will dub her, brutally (199), for one can 'suppose that her body still retain[s] some vestiges of beauty' (37). She is a more embodied counterpoint to Poiret's shrivelledness (gender clearly plays a part here)—but she and Poiret come together in the logic that appears to underpin this version of the grotesque. Old age is presented as the outcome of a crude moral determinism in both their cases—yet the narrative is rather playing with than endorsing moralism. Is Mlle Michonneau expiating former triumphs? It is as good a theory as any other, and there are plenty of alternatives to hand if we do not like this one. The perceived condition of being old is here held up to us as the product of a grotesque because blunted social and moral logic that requires ageing to be spoken of in terms of ironic 'reward', 'expiation', 'end', but which knows and cares nothing of what went before.

What Vautrin offers to Rastignac, then, is not simply 'success' but release from so constrained and brutal a view of persons. Rastignac already, but too vaguely, wants a life in which his future will possess little or no connection to his present. Like Lucien Chardon (later de Rubempré) and so many other Balzacian heroes, he wants 'to reap without sowing',[31] to possess money without having to earn it, and to shed as quickly as possible his marginal status in Parisian society as the scion of a down-at-heel aristocratic family from the provinces. He has no 'ultimate goal' (241), only a strong desire for success in the near future. Vautrin offers a philosophy of the self that would make that possible. It is (emphatically) not Parfit's Reductionist View—rather, a cynically profiteering case against commitment to moral principles—but it too opens the door to seeing a person as, rather, a series of different persons, and it looks set to deliver some of the same outcomes for a person's further future as Parfit's 'Extreme Claim':

> 'don't stick any more firmly to your opinions than to your work. When you are asked for them, sell them. A man who boasts of never changing his opinions is a man who forces himself to move always in a straight line, a simpleton who believes he is infallible. There are no such things as principles, there are only events; there are no laws, there are only circumstances: the man who is wiser than his fellows accepts events and circumstances in order to turn them to his own ends [l'homme supérieure épouse les événements et les circonstances pour les conduire].' (134/G144)

In the French, the last phrase escapes the unwanted pun in the English. The word 'ends' has, after all, greatly diminished temporal range in such a philosophy. Vautrin would have Rastignac abandon the long view, substituting for the 'straight line' of duty the short-term improvisations of desire, and for the rule of law the flexibility of the marketplace. This is present-aimism in the form of a blatant bias towards the present, without the temporally neutral concern for the rest of one's life, and without the remotest concern for commitments, deserts, or justice. 'When you are asked for [your opinions], sell them.' At the end of *Splendeurs et misères des courtisanes* (1847), Vautrin/Collin/Carlos Herrera/Trompe-la-Mort/William Barker/M de Saint-Estève (and the many other aliases he has assumed) will do exactly that, poacher turning gamekeeper to become the head of the secret police.

Vautrin, not surprisingly, has no plan for his own old age. Not foreseeing his future career as 'the Figaro of justice',[32] he intends, as soon as he has secured his cut of the profit from Rastignac's marriage, to quit France for the American South where he will 'live the patriarchal life on a great estate' with 'two hundred negroes' to carry out his bidding. 'I shall be fifty years of age, not yet rotten [pas encore pourri]; I shall enjoy myself' (131/G142). One is ripe, and then one rots (Sainte-Beuve's riposte to Cicero[33]). This is a philosophy which says, in effect: old age will be wretched no matter what, so far better to seize the day and direct your ambitions towards your near future. It is also a philosophy underpinned by Balzac's historically contingent belief that each human being possesses a finite store of 'vital fluid'. If one wishes to live into old age one must guard that store as cautiously as possible. As the old shopkeeper explains to Raphaël in *La Peau de chagrin* (1831), one must invest one's energy not in the senses but in the mind, not in desire but in knowledge.[34] (This is why the old in Balzac's fiction tend to be, as if by definition, either impoverished or misers—eking out or hoarding their resources. Think of Grandet, Chardon senior, Pons, Schmucke...) Such restraint is, by definition, impossible for a man of passion such as Vautrin, or like Balzac himself.[35]

Sublimation not being an option in *Le Père Goriot*, a bad outcome for (or in) old age is ensured by both the available interpretations of self-interest. Work hard, live hard, and you may just be 'lucky' enough to reach old age—but it will be a miserable old age, the mere remnants of a life close to used up; live your life on the basis of present aims, as Vautrin recommends, and old age simply disappears from the equation (it is no longer a matter for consideration/you do not expect to have an old age/to age would be simply to rot). Hence the exactness of Rastignac's perception that old age is a particularly potent form of moral distance in Paris. And hence the peculiar force of the image with which the novel confirms his susceptibility to Vautrin's persuasions: 'Cynical as Vautrin's words were they effected a lodgement in the student's heart, as the sordid profile of an old crone hawking rags dwells in the memory of the girl for whom she had predicted "oceans of love and money" ' (140). It is a downgraded version of the early description of Mlle Michonneau: the old woman who may have been a dealer in second-hand clothes becomes an old crone hawking rags. The repressed returns, this time uglier and more intimately symbolic of the bias towards the present that Vautrin seeks to instil.

There is no move in *Old Goriot* to expand the terrain of morality in order to safeguard old age against a temporally foreshortened sense of one's own future interests. On the contrary, Old Goriot is himself a study in grave imprudence—as well as the generosity of paternal love. The novel might indeed justifiably be read as a meditation on the need for an expansion of the terms of morality such that the extent of his imprudence could be registered here as a moral problem and not simply irrational. One way of appreciating Goriot's centrality to the novel's analysis of the narrowly presentist self-interest that governs its society is to begin by noting how closely he is allied with Vautrin's case against morality. Vautrin himself finds out the likeness between them. In a passage whose homoerotic implications have tended to distract critics from what is being said about Goriot, the convict tells Eugène why he has decided to make him the heir to his (as yet imaginary) American millions. 'A man', he contends,

> 'is less than nothing if he is a Poiret [...] But a man is a god when he is like you; he is no longer a piece of mechanism covered with skin, but a theatre where the finest sentiments find play, and I live only for sentiments—fine thoughts and noble feelings. What is sentiment but the whole world in a thought? Look at old Goriot: his two daughters are the whole universe to him, they are the clue by which he finds his way through creation.'   (182)

One might expect to find Vautrin treating Old Goriot with the same disdain he accords to Poiret. Instead, he recognizes, with whatever degree of sentimental posturing, a kindred spirit. For Vautrin the ideal is 'friendship between man and man' (183), for Goriot it is the love between parent and child. These are sentiments, not morals or principles, and on the basis of them these two men stand in much the same relation to Rastignac. Both men seek to mentor his entry into society. Both adopt a paternalistic posture towards the young man who will act as their surrogate in society.

Both wish to lead him away from the values he has (at least theoretically) espoused thus far, the better to succeed.

Goriot's life reads—until his last years—like a textbook example of the flexibility with principles that Vautrin advocates. The now retired vermicelli-maker has been adept, until very lately, at turning 'events and circumstances … to his own ends'. Early in the novel the spiteful Duchesse de Langeais fills in his history. President of his district of Paris during the revolution, Goriot (whose name she repeatedly garbles) made a fortune profiteering from famine in the city, selling flour at ten times the price it cost him, and giving a sufficient slice of the proceeds to the Committee for Public Welfare to ensure his family's protection. Left a widower early in life, he brought up his two daughters alone. His wealth and his favour with the Napoleonic party enabled him to marry the elder to a hard-up aristocrat and the younger to a wealthy banker of Royalist leanings, but, with the return of the Bourbons to power, his welcome at the homes of both sons-in-law has been severely compromised (101–2). At the point where Le Père Goriot begins he is received by his daughters only when they have no other visitors, and his funds have sunk to the level where he must deprive himself in order to meet their constant demands.

According to the Duchess he is a willing 'accomplic[e] in this crime' (102). At the Maison-Vauquer he demotes himself to the poorest room in the house, and discards the remaining signs of the social standing he had achieved in his prime: the fine clothes, the powdered hair, the snuff, the trinkets, personal ornaments, and collection of silverware saved as a memento of his married life. After six years at the *pension*, Goriot's slide down the social scale is mirrored in his physique: from being a robust, well turned-out tradesman who at 62 looked about 40, he now appears 'at least 70'. His body has wasted away, his once 'fleshly' calves have shrunk, his forehead is wrinkled, his jaw prominent, and

> his blue eyes, formerly so lively, seemed to have turned a sad leaden grey; they had faded and dried up and their red rims seemed to ooze blood. People either pitied him or were shocked by him. Young medical students noticing the drooping of his lower lip and the conformation of his facial angle […] declared him to be declining into cretinism.   (53)

There is a grotesquely blunt logic of closed exchange at work here, as with M. Poiret and Mlle Michonneau. Goriot's decline is the price paid for his daughters' rise in society: their splendid residences are made possible by his reduction to a cheap garret, their immaculately dressed hair and fashionable gowns bought at the cost of his 'disgusting' unpowdered hair and cheap calico shirts, their robust health maintained at the price of his rapid degeneration. But the sharpest cut in Goriot's standard of living, and the one that takes him to his death, is brought about by the need to pay for the rent and furnishing of the house in which the young and ambitious Rastignac will live with Goriot's younger daughter for his first society mistress. Rastignac, in effect, occupies the berth Goriot might have hoped to be granted out of filial devotion or gratitude. The young lover will be the pampered object of Delphine's affection; her old father will be permitted a tenant's lodgings in one of the attics—and not even those for long, she suggests.

Such structural substitution is where Old Goriot's paternalistic concern for his children starts to look on the one hand like pimping and on the other like a vicarious acting out of incestuous desire. On Rastignac's first night in his lavishly appointed love nest, Goriot is there too, gloating over his daughter's beauty, straining her to him, kissing her feet, rubbing his head against her dress: 'no young lover could have been more foolish or more tender' (236). Rastignac, jealous, does not demur when Delphine complains that her father's attentions will soon grow tiresome, 'though the remark contain[s] the seed of all ingratitude' (236). This discomfitingly eroticized triangle, with Rastignac and Goriot in grossly unequal competition for Delphine, draws the morally abusive relation between youth and old age to the surface. Neglect of old age subtends Rastignac's view of his own aims and interests. As it is played out in his dependency on, and barely conscious antagonism to Goriot, it makes for a subtler but no less strong denigration of later life than Vautrin's comic brutalities ('the Venus of Père-Lachaise') or his frank dismissiveness ('not yet rotten'), or his postures of sentimental regard ('Look at old Goriot').

Goriot's paternalism towards his daughters and towards Rastignac is not, of course, paternalism in the sense Parfit means: obliging people to act in their own interests (applied by analogy to one's safeguarding, in the present, of the interests of one's future self). Goriot's paternalism is certainly not in his own interests, and in a strong sense it is not in the interests of his daughters or of Rastignac either: it confirms them in a path of gross ingratitude, materialism, greed, dishonesty, to the point of failing in the natural duty of care for their parent/mentor, and even hastening his death. But his version of paternalism nevertheless serves to cast a spotlight on the problem articulated by Parfit, of what authority we have for judging what is in another's interests. One of the few things we hear in Delphine's favour is, on Goriot's own testimony, that she did not want him to spend his money on rich apartments for herself and Rastignac: 'Well, Dephinette, Ninette, Dedel!', he crows when he makes the gift, 'wasn't I right when I said to you, "There are some fine rooms in the Rue d'Artois, let's furnish them for him!" You didn't want to' (231). We can treat with suspicion his explanation that 'she was afraid that people would say stupid things about her' (231), and imagine her coyly encouraging her father, but fear may also have been the voice of prudence, all too quickly suppressed by him. None of this means that a more rational and judicious paternalism would not have averted tragedy in *Old Goriot*, both for Goriot himself and for his daughters. But such a version of paternalism is conspicuous by its absence in a novel centrally about paternalism, and even if Goriot were to make better choices the question of how he can claim to know what are really his children's (no longer children's) best interests would remain.

Balzac recognizes two possible means by which both paternal love and old age might be rescued: one moral, the other rational. The former would require love and common kindness on the part of the young towards the old; the latter a more self-regarding sense of his own interests on Goriot's part. But Goriot neglects himself in order to be unstintingly generous to his daughters. They (and Rastignac too) have distinctly presentist ideas about what use they will make of the resources passed on to them by the previous generation, but the element of vicarious self-fulfilment in Goriot's benevolence grows stronger in proportion as he has less of a future to look forward to. His adoration of his daughters, Rastignac observes, draws 'its strength from the whole past, as well as from his anticipation of the future' (237)—only his future is not theirs, and his generosity can only be a temporary stop-gap against the effects of their disregard for him and their want of care for their own further futures.

The difficulty of articulating any form of rational resistance to this erosion of one's own resources in old age is starkly apparent. Quite simply, by the time one is old it is too late. If one spends one's life putting one's principles up for barter, and recognizing no interests beyond those that apply in the present or near future, there can be very few reasons to care about old age, either before it arrives or once one knows oneself to be old. As represented by Balzac, paternalism is not the answer. It is a mere simulacrum of morality—a sentiment rather than a moral force. It may be noble in the scale of its generosity, but it is fundamentally irrational—and ludicrous in its inability to judge the merit of its objects. An expense of generosity in a waste of others' self-interest, it is also the point at which one's own self-interest becomes self-annulling. No wonder that the critic who reviewed the novel for the *Courrier Français* felt that 'M. de Balzac [...] has accorded no honor to human nature [...] no honor to paternity [...] all his conclusions [...] lead to despair.'[36]

That last is not entirely true. Balzac does glance at ethical alternatives. Altruism, for example, in the person of Bianchon. And, in a characteristically sweeping gesture, we are told that an exceptional individual may 'strip himself of selfish desires and seek not his own greatness but the greatness of a whole nation' (242). But Rastignac is not a national hero in the making, and Bianchon's role is confined, as through much of the *Comédie humaine*, to that of benign observer. He can do nothing to save the old man; all he can do is register moral dissent, offer palliative care, and (with resilient, even jaunty, objectivity) seek to learn from the case.

The one thing no one, not even Bianchon, says when they contemplate Old Goriot, is 'This might be me.' The impossibility of such an act of imaginative projection (or prolepsis) is not just a failing on the part of the story's actors. It is integral to the novel's imagined relation with its readers, and stands at the core of Balzac's famous claim to realism:

> When you have read of the secret sorrows of old Goriot you will dine with unimpaired appetite, blaming the author for your callousness, taxing him with exaggeration, accusing him of having given wings to his imagination. But you may be certain that this drama is neither fiction nor romance. *All is true*, so true that everyone can recognize the elements of the tragedy 'chez soi', in his own heart perhaps.   (28)

Balzac here offers a general moral anatomy of selfishness but also a specific moral anatomy of his society's want of care for age. You, a leisured young reader, holding the book 'in your white hand, lying back in a softly cushioned armchair', are informed in advance that your callousness prohibits you from recognizing not only other people's suffering but a suffering that may—that will?—come to be your own. The Penguin translation renders that 'chez soi' as 'in one's own household', but the Norton edition's 'in one's own life', or even a more directive 'in one's own person', is closer to the moral thrust of the French. Old Goriot's secret sorrows are the disavowed potential sorrows (and the fears) of us all.

The claim to believability works, significantly, from the outside in: 'because old Goriot's story is true you can recognize it in your own heart' not 'because you can recognize it in your own heart you know old Goriot's story to be true.' 'Perhaps'. The wording places little if any faith in the ability of self-interest to see its own implication in what is being said. But that quieter-than-usual cynicism is in line with the novel's scepticism about how far the moral responsibility for the treatment of the old in this society should finally be taken to its source. Everyone (Goriot included) is understood to be complicit in Goriot's demise, just as everyone concurs in the social 'downfall' of Mme de Beauséant (Mme de Beauséant included). The *illusions perdues* strain of the novel consists in educating Rastignac into that confederacy, and Balzac declines to make him any more accountable for the death of Goriot than he makes himself. Similarly, at the crucial point where Rastignac could, in theory, force Delphine to go to her dying father's bedside rather than attend Mme de Beauséant's ball, he takes a conscious decision not to force her to the moral point. '[H]e felt instinctively that she was capable of stepping over her father's dead body to go to the ball; and he had not the authority to play the mentor, nor the courage to cross her, nor the strength of mind to leave her. "She would never forgive me for putting her in the wrong over this," he said to himself' (271). One can say, as generations of Balzac critics have done, that Balzac has insufficient faith in human nature; but one can also credit him with being prepared to imagine what Parfit finally is not, though he lays the theoretical grounds: a future generation equipped not only with its distinctive (not yet knowable) needs and desires, but (relatedly) with its own resilience.

It is in line with that disabused but ultimately non-judgemental view of the dominant morality that Balzac's most direct explanation of the human motives behind his story seems to turn us away from the significance of age altogether, and offer a general theory of social injustice: 'By what chance had this half-spiteful contempt, this half-pitying persecution, this lack of respect for misfortune buffeted the oldest lodger? Perhaps it is a part of human nature to pile burdens on those who make no protest because of their true humility, their weakness, or their indifference. Do we not all like to prove our strength at the expense of another person or a thing?' (42). Yet the metaphor that follows takes us back, unerringly, to injustice's source in the aspirations of youth: 'The puniest specimen of humanity, the brat in the street, knocks at all the doors when the streets are slippery with frost'. If Balzac is right (a bleak possibility), the desire to assert one's youth, and one's very existence, at the expense of others, is so fundamental as to deserve the name of human nature.

Balzac offers about as near an illustration as one could hope for of many of the aspects of self-interest Parfit seeks, much more systematically, to correct, and he does so by placing old age not on the margins of the debate but at the centre. The bias towards the nearer future is directly connected to a socially pervasive failure of concern, or even respect, for old age. *Le Père Goriot* toys, as Balzac does so often, with the idea that a person may under certain conditions be better described as a series of not-very-strongly psychologically connected selves (Eugène *en famille*, Eugène *à Paris*); and it recognizes a serious risk, then, of want of due care for one's further future—but also a major problem with advocating paternalism as an adequate answer. How can the paternalist know what is in another's best interests? More simply, in the choice with which Vautrin presents Eugène, between putting himself in the way of success now, and ploughing on in the honourable course, a choice then rendered very impure by the interventions of others, it dramatizes the great problem of knowing what one is doing when one makes choices that will affect a later self who may have different concerns, needs values.

And yet, for all Vautrin's eloquence on behalf of loosening up one's sense of oneself, and for all that events do change Eugène's outward life, Balzac preserved a strong sense of the persistence of personhood through all the events and the changes in circumstance that time can bring. The underlying joke of the *Comédie humaine* is that, notwithstanding its fascination with the loss of illusions (also its incompleteness and its numerous revisions and recastings of plots and characters), it offers so strong a portrait of the durability of personalities over long stretches of time: Vautrin, always charismatic, and ultimately recognizable, under however many layers of disguise; Baron Hulot, still womanizing after all these years ... The creed of self-liberation from principles turns out to be sustained by an exceptionally strong sense of self-interest and self-connectedness over time.

No scenes weigh more heavily in Balzac's fiction than those in which a protagonist is put to the ethical test—generally by someone who offers the seduction of a rationalist philosophy that would admit of a more self-serving and present-centred life than the one conventional morality would approve. In important respects *Old Goriot*'s young protagonist withstands that test. Whatever wrong Rastignac is prepared to do to Goriot (and he is prepared to do a great deal), he also does him much of the little good on offer, tending him as he lies dying, pawning his own watch to pay for Goriot's shroud, and making the arrangements for the funeral and burial; he also refuses (for now) Vautrin's incitements to kill the 'Chinese mandarin' by marrying Victorine and profiting from her brother's murder. Scornful though Balzac is of his reader's capacity to change his or her view of old age, it is therefore necessary to remember that enticing us towards rationality may (at the same time) be a form of moral persuasion by countersuggestion—an encouragement to resist.

For a literary critic there is obvious reason for, as well as attraction to, reading Parfit in company with a work of literature as fascinated as *Le Père Goriot* is with the relation between present self-interest and our prospects for our further future. If, as I have argued, the trouble with Parfit's view of old age is that he lacks a sufficient safeguard against serious imprudence, in the Reductionist View, then *Le Père Goriot* suggests an alternative answer to Parfit's own suggestions of paternalism and beneficence. And it does not come from the direction of morality, but from imagination.

Imagination is not, per se, a moral quality: it may, in theory, be directed towards good ends, but that will only happen if we discover reasons to want to direct it that way. Indeed, the inequity between the poorly imagined inner life of Père Goriot and the richly imagined inner life of Rastignac implicates not just Balzac's reader but his own narrative in the general bias towards the young.[37] And yet, this very shortfall in imaginative sympathy is accompanied always by an acute awareness of the failing, and awareness that it is built into the very fabric of 'our' desires—is even, perversely, a form of pleasure. The impression of Old Goriot's suffering, Balzac tells us on the first page of the novel, will 'vanis[h] as quickly as a delicious fruit melts in the mouth' (28). Exercising imagination, then, is not in and of itself a virtue, but for Balzac it would appear to be the only faculty capable of carrying us at least fleetingly over the moral gaps left by a purely rational account of how aims (and values) differ between persons, between our present and future selves, between present and future generations, and across geographical and historical divides—including those between Balzac and us.

Parfit is not far from proffering that answer himself. Artistic choice turns out to be, after all, the twist in the tail of his Reductionist View of persons and of the better old age that it hopes to offer. On the Reductionist View, his conclusion reminds us, 'the unity of our lives is a matter of degree, and is something that we can affect. We may want our lives to have greater unity, in the way that an artist may want to create a unified work. And we can *give* our lives greater unity, in ways that express or fulfil our particular values and beliefs' (446). In such cases, the impersonal view can claim after all to be a more personal view of life than the philosophies it opposes. And any persistence of the bias towards the near that may result from an as yet too weak theory of paternalism, or of beneficence towards the future, turns out to be a consequence we can resist.

6

The Bounded Life

Theodor Adorno's late lectures on *Metaphysics* propose a 'shocking thesis': 'metaphysics began with Aristotle'.[1] A 'doubly shocking' thesis, Adorno tells his audience, because it gives credit where credit is not usually given, and declines to give it where most students of philosophy would understand that it belongs—with Plato (18). The Platonic theory of forms, as Adorno interprets it, missed the essential criterion for metaphysics—that is, it missed the essential criterion for how Adorno himself, somewhat unorthodoxly, wants to redefine 'metaphysics'. Plato never fully accepted (Adorno claims) that the tension between the sphere of transcendence and the sphere of 'direct experience' is no mere adjunct of metaphysical inquiry but its defining subject matter (18). Aristotle, by contrast, understood that the proper goal of metaphysics is to present a non-transcendental essentialism: true metaphysics is an effort at once to define the limits of physical experience and to 'rescue' essence from the physical world. In his words, it is 'the exertion of thought to save what at the same time it destroys' (20).

I am not concerned, per se, with Adorno's highly tendentious reading of Aristotle and Plato. He is right to point out that Aristotle's *Metaphysics* attempts to avoid the transcendental metaphysics of Plato's theory of forms, but surely wrong to suggest either that Aristotle was criticizing Plato in the way Adorno proposes, or that Aristotle was providing an entirely new definition of what constitutes metaphysics. Aristotle explains metaphysics in, roughly, two (closely associated) ways: as (1) 'First Philosophy': the first or ultimate explanation of things (their being), (2) the science of being, especially primary being (*ousia*). Aristotle claims no novelty for this representation of metaphysics, and he counts Plato prominently among his precursors (see *Metaphysics* 1. 3–10, 983b6–993a23; also 7. 1. 1028b19). In short, one has to read Adorno's discussion of Plato and Aristotle as a flamboyantly non-conventional way into his own attempt to set metaphysics on a new path.

What interests me more is that, in the midst of Adorno's setting out of the definitional ground for metaphysics, another subject repeatedly comes into view: a subject not obviously germane to the philosophical work at hand. Investigating the definitional limits of 'direct experience', Adorno keeps being drawn to consider the limit of human life—not just in the general sense of mortality, but in the more specific sense of old age as a temporal and biological limit to experience. An early hint of that association comes in Lecture 4. Though he is not particularly concerned with philosophy as intellectual history, when accounting for Plato's contribution to the subject he takes a moment to refer his students to a line of historical argument that would allow Plato a firmer claim than he has allowed him to metaphysics proper. '[I]n the Anglo-Saxon countries', he notes, 'one not infrequently comes across the hypothesis that Plato as an old man was influenced retrospectively [*rückläufig* in the German (31)] by his pupil Aristotle; or that, as a result of his political disappointments in his attempts to set up the world purely on the basis of the Idea, he was forced to give greater recognition to that which is, the scattered, the merely existent' (17). One can, then, Adorno argues (tendentiously again) see signs in Plato of a late-life Aristotelian turn that, for want of time, never resulted in a fully reconceived metaphysics.

The word 'retrospectively'—'retroactively' would be a closer translation[2]—is not obviously necessary to the statement. Redundant, even misleading though it may seem (what does it mean to be 'influenced retroactively', given that the lives of Plato and Aristotle overlapped by some thirty-seven years?), its inclusion makes an issue of the philosopher's age. There are more obvious ways of presenting the trajectory of influence between Plato and Aristotle, but Adorno goes out of his way here to imagine the pupil–teacher relation from Plato's perspective as an old man: contemplating the limits Aristotle would impose on Platonic transcendentalism, yet unable, at the end of his life, to do justice to the challenge. 'I am only mentioning this to show you how complex these relationships are', Adorno tells his students (17). In the context of the whole lecture series, however, the glance towards Plato's last years is less incidental than he makes it sound. For Adorno, metaphysics has a recurrent connection to old age, as if—and the potential for embarrassment colours the suggestion throughout these lectures—reflecting on the temporal boundedness of human lives were a special imperative to reflecting on the boundedness of 'the sensible, empirical world' (20).

This chapter explores Adorno's perception of a link between the two kinds of boundary: the boundary between life and death as brought to mind by the decline of the very old, and the philosophical boundary between the physical and the metaphysical. It brings together the as yet little known lectures on metaphysics, delivered just four years before his death in 1969 at the age of 66, with two shorter works more likely to be familiar to literary critics: an essay on Charles Dickens's *The Old Curiosity Shop*, dating from the very start of Adorno's career (1931),[3] and a later lecture on Samuel Beckett's *Endgame* (1958).[4] The young Adorno was drawn to *The Old Curiosity Shop* in large part because he saw Dickens as having grasped the critical power of anachronism. In the story of the young girl who tries to rescue her grandfather from the death-ridden 'bourgeois object-world' but herself dies a symbolic victim to it, he found a powerful allegory of the damage done to human life by bourgeois capitalism, in which feeble-minded old age and overburdened youth were imaginatively inextricable. The older Adorno was more alert to the difference between youth and age and its capacity to draw us towards more complexly dialectical thinking. His reading of *Endgame*, with its emphasis on the loss of individual experience under late capitalism, and the necessity that art abandon naturalism in order to give expression to that loss, is much closer to the thinking of the *Metaphysics*. Like those lectures it finds an appropriate figure for the simultaneous abstraction and concretion of experience after World War II in the condition of the very old. It stops short of the *Metaphysics*' claim that the contemplation of old age can lead us to more radical thinking about the limits of thinking but it marks a significant step along the way to that position—and in so far as it misreads Beckett (as I shall be arguing) it does so very much as the lectures 'misread' Aristotle—in order to draw Beckett/Aristotle closer to his own anti-metaphysical metaphysics.

My interest in reading the later Adorno's philosophical writings about old age and metaphysics 'back' into these two earlier *Kulturkritik* essays does not rest on extended debate about his defence of metaphysics within the context of Frankfurt School philosophy, any more than it rests on an argument about the perversity of his reading of classical Greek philosophy. That is, I have no interest in rebuking the lingering strains of existentialism in his thinking: that post-World War II fixation on meaning's relation to death which, for many readers of Adorno, constitutes an 'incorrect' aspect of the late thought. This topic has been extensively explored by other critics.[5] I also have no wish to revisit the deconstructive/Heideggerian debate over the 'destruction' of metaphysics—or what sometimes looks like a competition for the credit of having murdered it (Derrida v. Nietzsche). My focus is simply on old age, and the part it has played in one line of enquiry into the limits on experience, and on thought.

Simon Jarvis has observed a tension within Adorno's philosophy of history between resistance to the concept of historical progress and almost equal dissatisfaction with 'the presentation of history as sheer disconnection'.[6] Appeals to historical discontinuity 'turn out to be no less metaphysical than a teleological insistence on historically unified progress'. In Adorno's own, more aphoristic phrase, 'History is the unity of continuity and discontinuity.'[7] So Jarvis goes on to present Adorno's major collaborative work with Horkheimer, *The Dialectic of Enlightenment* (1944) as 'a simultaneous construction and denial of universal history' (39). Following Adorno, this chapter pursues a sceptical approach to the notion of the writer's temporal development: one conceived in terms of both the connectedness and the disconnectedness of different moments of writing. It thus continues the discussion of discontinuous selfhood from Ch. 4, moving it from the psychological rationalism of Parfit into the very different priorities and rhetoric of late-Marxist dialectical reasoning. The Adorno of the *Metaphysics* evidently shares something with the Adorno who, more than thirty years earlier, had recognized the power of formal anachronism in Dickens's novel to 'dissolve the very bourgeois world' it depicted (172); also with the Adorno of 'Trying to Understand *Endgame*', who found in Beckett's geriatric Nell and Nagg a more authentic representation of the irrationality, after Auschwitz, of our will to go on living in the world. But the older writer also goes 'beyond' his younger self or selves in ways which allow for a reading more attuned to the critical valencies of age in Dickens's story and in Beckett's play. This is not to say that the *Metaphysics* points the way to a complete or sufficient reading of *The Old Curiosity Shop* or *Endgame*—but it assists in identifying a distinctively metaphysical turn to Dickens's thinking about old age, and a distinctively *anti*-metaphysical turn to Beckett's thinking about it. Beckett's anti-metaphysics, I argue, helped Adorno towards revising his own understanding of 'negative metaphysics', in which old age emerged as the symbolic prompt to thinking about the limits of thinking.

Part of what is in question here must be the concept of the philosopher's own old age—and more generally the integrity or otherwise of a writer's work when viewed from the perspective of his or her 'late writing'.[8] Here I confine that question to Adorno's career only because to extend it to Dickens and Beckett, and include, say, *Our Mutual Friend* and *Mal vu mal dit* alongside *The Old Curiosity Shop* and *Endgame*, would be unmanageable in the space of a single chapter. But it should be evident that I am not suggesting a necessary link between old age and either philosophical or literary alertness to old age. While it is true that Adorno became more aware of the critical potential of old age 'as' he grew older, the 'as' is not simply a 'because'. His ability to see more complex structural and political relations figured in old age and youth by the time of the essay on *Endgame* and then the lectures on *Metaphysics* was tied to the more general development of his thought away from the Hegelian Marxism of his youth towards the *Negative Dialectics*. But he was alert from very early on to old age as a potentially important subject for philosophy, writing his influential essay on 'Beethoven's Late Style' very soon after the essay on Dickens, probably when he was still in his late twenties.[9]

Dickens himself was 28 and 29 when he wrote *The Old Curiosity Shop*. Beckett was in his late forties and early fifties when he wrote *Endgame*, but 24 when he first gave sign of registering old age's potential as a subject for the theatre, playing the part of the hero's father, old Don Diègue, in *Le Kid*, a student spoof of Corneille's *Le Cid*.[10] This early interest shown in the subject by all these writers (though quite different in tone and accent) indicates that there is no 'natural' intellectual or attitudinal trajectory from obliviousness of old age to greater consciousness of it over time, nor from satire or irony to sympathy—or, indeed, the other way around. When a writer does, as in Adorno's case, come to think more intently about old age as he or she approaches it, that fact cannot be separated from the experience of ageing, but neither can it be purely or adequately traced to it. As ever, representations of old age are rarely 'just' about old age. They are about much else besides, including perceptions of the authentic practice of literature and of philosophy.

The concept of 'late writing' also has to be approached with caution. Lateness is obviously a relative thing: 'late Keats' a more limited notion than 'late Wordsworth'; 'late Dickens' more confined than 'late Beckett'. And 'late Adorno' has similarly less analytic potency than, say, 'late Kant'. This point may be banal, but it is not without weight—and for reasons

Adorno was especially attuned to. There is an ironically self-reflexive move early on in Lecture 17 of the *Metaphysics* when he reminds his audience of his 1955 introduction to Benjamin's *Schriften*, where he argued that 'a concept such as "the life's work" has become problematic today because our existence has long ceased to follow a quasi-organic law immanent to it, but is determined by all kinds of powers which deny it such an immanent unfolding' (133–4). So, when I propose reading the late Adorno back into the earlier Adornos, I do so on the assumption that they are and are not the same writers, and that there is no 'whole' or 'final' Adornian reading of *The Old Curiosity Shop* or *Endgame* to be achieved.

In taking seriously Adorno's strictures against the organic wholeness of a writer's life, much of what I have to say here about 'late style' is at odds with other recent writing on the subject, particularly the work of Edward Said. Said derived the term 'late style' from Adorno's essay 'Spätstil Beethovens', in which he speculated about the often antagonistic, and agonistic, nature of art produced under the experience of ageing, the decay of the body, the onset of ill health.[11] As Said summarized Adorno: the late music of Beethoven was deformed by mourning and anger. Phrases were 'left incomplete[…]suddenly, abruptly jettisoned[…]in marked contrast to the relentless quality of second-period works[…]where the composer cannot seem to tear himself away from the piece'.[12] Late style of this kind (Said sees it practised also by artists as diverse as Benjamin Britten, Giuseppi Tomasi, and Henrik Ibsen) combines the objective and the subjective, not leading to a 'harmonious whole' but (in Adorno's words) 'tear[ing the works] apart in time, perhaps in order to preserve them for the eternal. In the history of art, late works are the catastrophes'.[13]

Said both does and does not seem to want to acknowledge that 'lateness' here designates an aesthetic style or manner more than a stage of life:[14] it is the name Adorno (in his late twenties and early thirties) gave to the 'authentic' response of artistic form to late capitalism, and though the proximity of the artist to the end of his or her life was seen to be its prompt, it is not obvious that for Adorno the connection to time of life need be more than metaphorical or analogical. Said, however, insists upon a literal connection, acknowledging his own autobiographical reasons for doing so (his own proximity to death). In a striking metaphor he presents the fracturedness of Beethoven's late style as a kind of lapidary art, 'the mere phrase a monument to what has been, marking a subjectivity turned to stone'. In Adorno's original text that sentence applies only to artistic form—to what happens when expression is detached from its originating subjectivity. But when Said interprets these lines, they become more insistently about the artist's encroaching death; and as that happens, the structure of the artist's own life starts to reconfer wholeness. To be consciously at the end of one's time induces 'tragic self-awareness', Said writes. The artist's life is, accordingly, seen as integrated aesthetically but also temperamentally, by the force of its anger, its alienation, its anticipatory mourning. On that basis, Said takes Adorno's own essay to be an exercise in late style, apparently forgetting for the moment just how young he was when it was written:

> With old age and death before him, and a promising start years behind, Adorno uses the model of late Beethoven to come to terms with an ending. … Lateness is being at the end, fully conscious, full of memory, and also (even preternaturally) aware of the present. Thus, like Beethoven, Adorno becomes a figure of lateness itself, an untimely and scandalous, even a catastrophic commentator on the present.[15]

Said's insistence on old age, and proximity to death, as the literal basis of late style brings an unmistakeably moral as well as aesthetic accent to his essays on the subject, especially the posthumously published 'Thoughts on Late Style' (2004). 'Late style', in Said's deeply humanist reading of Adorno, is the outcome of an embodied predicament: being sick, dying—not necessarily old, but its characteristic temperament is familiarly that of old age. Its identifying traits are strongly reminiscent of Aristotle's composite rhetorical type of the old speaker, but it offers to revalue, even rescue, that characterization. Late style has 'a lamenting personality'. It is 'angry', 'disturbed', 'alienated', possessed of 'an increasing sense of apartness and exile and anachronism'. It thus feeds into Said's much wider efforts to define the writer and, especially, the intellectual as an heroically 'exilic' figure—a favourite word in his work, but nowhere more insisted upon than in 'Thoughts on Late Style'.

Such an artist is unseduced by the normative judgements or values of his or her time and place; unseduced also by any hope of transcendence. The practitioner of late style has 'surviv[ed] beyond what is acceptable and normal', Said comments of Adorno; 'he envisages nothing beyond lateness: it is impossible to surmount it; it can only be deepened'. And yet the notion of a 'beyond' keeps making itself heard in Adorno's essay. Said (emphatically secular and anti-metaphysical) does not pick it up, but it is there in the claim that late style refuses a harmonious aesthetic synthesis between the subjective and the objective so as perhaps 'to preserve them for the eternal'; and it comes up again in the description of Beethoven in his last years as a 'lonely prince of a realm of spirits'. The young Adorno nevertheless analysed this impulse towards the beyond in purely aesthetic/political terms. The later Adorno was willing to give it another name as well: metaphysics.[16]

Introducing the lecture series on *Metaphysics: Concepts and Problems* (delivered in Frankfurt in the winter term of 1965/6, first published in 1998, and first translated in 2000[17]), Adorno recollected his early, and thwarted, attempt to engage with metaphysics:

> I recall my own early experience as a schoolboy when I first came across Nietzsche, who, as any of you who are familiar with his work will know, is not sparing in his complaints about metaphysics; and I remember how difficult I found it to get my bearings with regard to metaphysics. When I sought the advice of someone considerably older than myself, I was told that it was too early for me to understand metaphysics but that I would be able to do so one day. (2)

The 'considerably older' adviser appears to have fobbed off the young Adorno with a platitude ('wisdom is the preserve of age'; perhaps more sourly, 'you will see the point of metaphysics when you come closer to dying'). But the older Adorno sees within or behind the deflective reply the germ of a more serious response.

Thirty-four years on, lecturing on metaphysics to an audience considerably younger than himself ('You are so young', he remarks at one point (127)), Adorno does indeed understand the modern problem of metaphysics in relation to age. In Lecture 17 he attributes the persistent appeal of metaphysical thinking, even within 'advanced' consciousness (135), to the inadequacy of modern culture in the face of death. Pitting himself, as so often, against Heidegger (his 'posture of tight-lipped readiness' (131); the 'impotence' of a metaphysics that has degenerated into 'a kind of propaganda for death' (131)), Adorno finds proof of the irreconcilability of life and death in the contemplation of extreme old age. The epic ideal of a wholeness to human life—Abraham dying 'old and sated with life'—is no longer tenable, he argues. We cannot today see age as a state of wisdom and plenitude, death as 'reconciliation', 'life [...] rounded and closed in on itself' (106–7). And this failure of our culture to 'integrate death' impels us towards metaphysics: 'thoughts which seek to penetrate beyond the boundaries of experience' (130–1).

Seen from this angle, metaphysical thinking is a confrontation with despair, imaged in the 'immeasurable sad[ness]' that attaches to age.

> [W]ith the decline of very old people, the hope of *non confundar*, of something which will be preserved from death, is [...] eroded, because, especially if one loves them, one becomes so aware of the decrepitude of that part of them which one would like to regard as the immortal that one can hardly imagine what is to be left over from such a poor, infirm creature which is no longer identical with itself. Thus, very old people, who are really reduced to what Hegel would call their mere abstract existence, those who have defied death longest, are precisely the ones who most strongly awaken the idea of absolute annulment. Nevertheless, [...] because the mind has wrested itself so strongly from what we merely are, has made itself so autonomous, this in itself gives rise to a hope that mere existence might not be everything.
>
> [...T]he very curious persistence of the idea of immortality may be connected to this.   (135)

This 'very curious' rising, or 'resurrect[ion]' (133), of hope flies in the face of strenuous post-Kantian efforts to eliminate a certain kind of metaphysical talk from philosophy, and to prohibit thinking 'beyond the boundaries of experience'. But by doing so it becomes, for Adorno, a means of bringing into focus his own wish not to rule out metaphysical speculation altogether, and to acknowledge instead its ongoing entanglement with materialism. Metaphysics does not require belief in an afterlife, he reminds his students at several points in the lecture series—but there are reasons why metaphysics and theology have so often found themselves on the same ground, and there is something to be rescued from the structure, though not the content, of that hope for something beyond 'mere existence' (a hope that Adorno himself seems to feel as a temptation[18]). Transcendental metaphysics shares with theology a disposition to think beyond the constraints of materialism and positivism: a 'manner of seeking to elevate itself above immanence, above the empirical world' (6).

In the closest thing to a definition of traditional metaphysics in these lectures, Adorno speaks of 'an attempt to determine the absolute, or the constitutive structures of being, on the basis of thought alone' (7). (The Platonic origins of that definition are not acknowledged.) Metaphysical systems are 'doctrines according to which concepts form a kind of objective, constitutive support on which what is naively called "the objective world" [...] is founded and finally depends' (8). '[W]hether concepts are real or are merely signs' is a metaphysical question whatever the answer—realist or nominalist (8). To the fundamental question of metaphysics as he defines it, 'whether thought and its constitutive forms are *in fact* the absolute' (99), Adorno's answer is an unhesitating 'no'—but a 'no' qualified by insistence that the business of metaphysics today is not to assert the autonomy of concepts, but to consider the possibility of their autonomy. 'To put it trenchantly: negative metaphysics is metaphysics no less than positive metaphysics'.[19] Or to put it simply: descriptive metaphysics is metaphysics no less than speculative metaphysics.

The sadness derived from the spectacle of advanced old age thus becomes, for Adorno, a means of acknowledging and then seeking to rescue something for philosophy out of the modern reduction of metaphysics to mere survivalist need, 'the material want of human beings'.[20] The wish to think the possibility of transcendence, of immortality, of something beyond the physical, becomes at that point no longer merely a panicked reflex of modernity, but the means to imagining the potential freedom of thought. This does not mean that he is, after all, defending a speculative metaphysics under cover of a descriptive metaphysics—though he comes very close indeed to doing so. On his own terms, this is not an endorsement of thinking beyond experience (especially not in the form of a hoped-for life after death), but it is an endorsement of the possibility of thinking that possibility, thereby enabling thought to think its own 'conditionedness'.[21] Metaphysics today 'can no longer be anything other than a *thinking* about metaphysics', Adorno says (99); it is now 'the thinking of thinking' (97), which means that it must also be, imperatively, thinking about the boundaries of thinking.

It is a substantively different view of the possibilities for transcendence of 'direct experience' from that to be found in Adorno's 1931 essay on *The Old Curiosity Shop*. Even as a much younger man he had recognized in old age a provocation to critical thought, but at that more Kierkegaardian stage in the development of his thinking he saw old age not in metaphysical terms but as a key to a Marxist-allegorical reading of Dickens's novel. As the young Adorno reads it, *The Old Curiosity Shop* belies the traditional view of Dickens as a founding figure of the realist social novel. Oddly baroque in many of its elements, it presents individuals not as psychologically internalized figures but as semi-stylized representations of 'objective factors'—representations of the damage done to human subjects by the greed-driven bourgeois object world. Projecting a pre-bourgeois view of the world into the bourgeois industrialized 'life space' of the nineteenth century, *The Old Curiosity Shop* makes visible the death-riddenness of the modern, commodified 'object-world'—rendered most obviously in the figure of Little Nell's feeble-minded, gambling-addicted, and guiltily exploitative grandfather. For Adorno, Little Nell is a 'victim of the mythic powers of bourgeois fate and at the same time the slender ray of light that fleetingly illuminates the bourgeois world' (172). Unable to 'take hold of the object-world' or to resist the injustices it has bred, she becomes a symbolic sacrifice to its power. But, the essay concludes gesturally, Dickens also recognized the possibility of 'transition and dialectical rescue' from within that world, figured in the 'powerful allegory of money with which the depiction of the industrial city ends: ' "two old, battered, smoke-encrusted penny pieces. Who knows but they shone as brightly in the eyes of angels as golden gifts that have been chronicled on tombs?" ' (177).

Despite the moral and spiritual difference between Nell and her grandfather, this reading sees no opposition between age and youth. They are, Adorno urges, constituent parts of one mythic pairing, 'the group portrayed in the old woodcut on the title page: Nell and her grandfather. Formed of the same material, the two remain inseparable; neither could exist as an autonomous human being' (172–3).[22] Adorno thereby subsumes the grandfather into the morally dominant figure of the child, burdened with his guilt and made its 'propitiatory sacrifice' (173). 'The novel is nothing but the story of her sacrifice', he says (173). So, he draws attention to the following lines, spoken by Old Trent on the eve of their flight from London:

> 'we will travel afoot through fields and woods, and by the side of rivers, and trust ourselves to God in the places where He dwells. It is far better to lie down at night beneath an open sky like that yonder—see how bright it is—than to rest in close rooms which are always full of care and weary dreams. Thou and I together, Nell, may be cheerful and happy yet, and learn to forget this time, as if it had never been.'[23]

Isolating that speech allows Adorno to establish a 'deep dialectical ambiguity' (174) in the novel: the 'somewhat romantic' and polemical vision, here, of an escape from the cares of the city, that is also an escape from old age back into childhood; and, opposed to it, the 'concrete presentation' of the city, which Adorno finds 'incomparably more powerful' (175). The grandfather's words are, in effect, Nell's too, expressing a mutual desire to escape the demonic world of industrial capitalism.

This reading would have been unlikely to satisfy the older Adorno of the essay on *Endgame*. Its fusion of the child and the old man into one figure ignores a marked concern in the novel itself to refute any impression of their romantic unity—not least by the echoes throughout the same chapter of Shakespeare's 'foolish fond' Lear, begging Cordelia to 'forget and forgive' (4. 6. 53, 76–7).[24] 'We'll […] be as free and happy as the birds,' the grandfather tells Nell at the end of his fleeting access of hope; 'We two alone will sing like birds i'th'cage' was Lear's more thinly strung line (5. 3. 9) (like Nell's bird, perhaps, left behind in London and returned to her only after her death). The young Adorno all but dismisses these lines. The older Adorno would have recognized the double movement of thought on the grandfather's part, or rather articulated through him, which can understand its own imprisonment only by expressing the impossible hope of escaping its bounds.

It is possible, in fact, to put together a reading of *The Old Curiosity Shop* in line with the thinking of Adorno's *Metaphysics*, which would do better justice to many of Dickens's own expressed concerns about old age and its relation to youth—and more especially to childhood. Time and again in *The Old Curiosity Shop* Dickens is verbally closest to Shakespeare when he seeks to express the old man's awareness that there can be no escape from material existence. Something akin to the 'immeasurable sadness' with which the Adorno of the *Metaphysics* contemplates old age speaks, at these moments, through the old man's querulous romanticism. 'Ah! poor houseless, wandering, motherless child!' he cries out, in one of Dickens's most verbally direct Shakespearean borrowings: 'clasping his hands, and gazing as if for the first time upon [Nell's] anxious face, her travel-stained dress, and bruised and swollen feet; "has all my agony of care brought her to this at last! Was I a happy man once, and have I lost happiness and all I had, for this!"' (340).[25] Dickens pays homage to Shakespeare (and possibly to Nahum Tate (see p. 87 above)) in such a way as to invoke the Lear of Act 5, brokenly leaning upon a daughter who, he knows too late, honoured and loved him. He consciously excludes the Lear of Act 3 who rages against his condition. So, immediately after the lines just quoted, Dickens cut several lines from the proof text of the story in order to fit Part 30 to the required space for serialization.

He could, he told John Forster, 'easily' lose them, though they might have been thought crucial to a psychological understanding of the old man.[26]

> His hat fell off as he raised his hands, pressed convulsively together, above his head, and, his white hair streaming in the wind, uttered this complaint with a passion and energy that shook him like an ague. Terrified to see him thus, the child clung to him and besought him to be calm. 'Brought me to this! To what?' she said cheerfully, 'one night without a bed to lie on! What matters that! We shall laugh at this one day; and when we are sitting before a good fire, we shall feel glad to think how cold and wet we were to-night. Come, let us find some corner where we can lie down to rest. There are many, many poor creatures in this town, dear, who will not sleep half so soundly as you and I to-night!' For a moment she turned away her face. There was something in the action with which she pressed her hand upon her drooping heart, sorely at variance with her speech; but next moment she looked with a smiling hope into the old man's face, and that was all he saw.   (585)[27]

If *The Old Curiosity Shop* is 'a Lear story […] virtually without a Lear',[28] it was this late-stage textual decision that secured it as such. When Dickens removed this passage, he cut out the most Lear-like scene he had imagined for Old Trent ('not ague-proof'), and the excision turned Nell's grandfather from a man capable in spirit, if not in rhetoric, of Lear's confrontation with the 'unaccommodated' human condition, to a senile figure who never gets beyond fitful and fearful expostulation. The cut lowers his register from tragedy to what Adorno saw as 'feeble-mindedness'.[29] It also excludes a speech in which Nell would have taken on more eloquently and deliberately than anywhere in the published text the redemptive function of Cordelia, seeking to give a future to the old man. Nowhere else does Nell come so close to Cordelia's tender (untruthful) reassurance 'No cause, no cause' (4. 6. 69).[30] The effect is to remove an exchange that could have been seen as strongly upholding the young Adorno's claim of her symbolic unity with the old man.

As the final text stands, the frailty and querulousness of the old man's hopes, and her almost silent assumption of his cares, debar identification of him with Nell's youth, opening up instead a dialectical fissure not just between the 'somewhat romantic' view and 'concrete presentation', but more ambiguously between the old man's nearness to death and the child's taking up of that burden—as it were, on his behalf. Immediately before the 'somewhat romantic' passage depreciated by Adorno, Dickens denounces as travesty the superficial likeness between Little Nell's childhood and her grandfather's age:

> he seemed unable to contemplate their real position more distinctly, and was still the listless, passionless creature, that suffering of mind and body had left him.
>   We call this a state of childishness, but it is the same poor hollow mockery of it, that death is of sleep. Where, in the dull eyes of doating men, are the laughing light and life of childhood [...]? Send forth the child and childish man together, and blush for the pride that libels our own old happy state, and gives its title to an ugly and distorted image.   (101–2)

This irreconcilable separation of youth and age offers as crucial and ambiguous a dialectic as the opposition the young Adorno more readily recognized between romance and concrete presentation of material life. Indeed, it is in significant measure a translation or extension of that other dialectic. One part of it prefigures the older Adorno's observation that, in the modern world, the old, 'too weak to preserve their own lives, are turned into objects' ('objects of science—the science of gerontology' (*Metaphysics* 106)). Nell's grandfather, first seen among the 'old and curious things' that clutter his shop, is one more 'thing' among them: 'There was nothing in the whole collection but was in keeping with himself; nothing that looked older or more worn than he' (9–10). This is the reduction of human life to the merely material: as the later Adorno put it, 'what we merely are' ushering in 'the idea of absolute annulment'. On the other side of the dialectic, childhood—or its allegorization in Little Nell—is made to seem the guarantor of something beyond this bounded existence. 'Beyond', both in the historically confined sense of 'an afterlife' and in the deeper sense of a something 'above immanence, above the empirical world'. Hence the inordinate burden of sentiment Nell has to bear on her grandfather's behalf. Heaven is where nothing dies or ever grows old, Dickens tells us (57). It is, in other words, for the young. Old age, by contrast, is face to face with the boundary of death and the inescapability of care (a word that shares the same Latin root as 'curiosity'[31]).

In practice the old are feeble parties to this moral and philosophical exploitation of children in *The Old Curiosity Shop*. Witness the many old men and women who mourn inconsolably the death of young loved ones, but whose hope for something beyond their histories of death amounts to no more than a very faltering stoicism. The old man in ch. 15 who lost his son; the old woman in ch. 17 whose husband died in their youth; the schoolmaster who has lost his favourite pupil; the Birmingham labourer who has seen all three of his children die: each of these people recalls a dead child or young lover or pupil with a pathos that has very little to do with the hope of an afterlife. The one who comes closest to looking for a 'beyond', the old woman in ch. 17, can still imagine a life after death only for the girl she was when her young husband died, not for the old woman she has become:

> now that five-and-fifty years were gone, she spoke of the dead man as if he had been her son or grandson, with a kind of pity for his youth, growing out of her own old age, and an exalting of his strength and manly beauty as compared with her own weakness and decay; and yet she spoke about him as her husband too, and thinking of herself in connexion with him, as she used to be and not as she was now, talked of their meeting in another world as if he were dead but yesterday, and she, separated from her former self, were thinking of the happiness of that comely girl who seemed to have died with him. (138)

Much the more determined sentimentalization of children comes from the narrative voice. Something might be made in this context of the dropping of Old Master Humphrey as the novel's narrator, and the taking up of that role by an anonymous voice, conventionally ascribed to Dickens himself. Leaving behind the 'infirm' and melancholic old man of the first pages of the story allows the novel to insist more strongly and more 'romantically' on Nell's positive connection to the metaphysical—what John Bowen has called her absorption in 'spirit' and her centrality to the novel's compulsion toward 'the Beyond'.[32] But the result is a discomfiting conflict of convictions. On the one hand, the narrative (Dickens, if you will) steers the child towards and then beyond her death to that triumph of early Victorian sentimentalism encapsulated in George Cattermole's woodcut of Nell, ascending to heaven in the arms of the angels. On the other, a gradually intensifying psychologization of Nell (*pace* the young Adorno) makes it plain that she fears death and feels its oppression.

Specifically, she fears what the adults around her fear: that death is categorically the end. There is nothing beyond the grave, and nothing that can rescue her from the death-ridden material world. When the old sexton tells her that the little shrubs and flowers she has seen in the churchyard 'grow but poorly' because those who have planted them quickly forgot the dead who lie below, she responds earnestly: 'I grieve to hear it [...] Perhaps the mourners learn to look to the blue sky by day, and to the stars by night; and to think that the dead are there, and not in graves.' 'Perhaps so,' replies the old man—but 'doubtfully' (418–19). And as the novel nears its conclusion, those doubts grow the more pressing in proportion as they are denied expression in the novel's 'official' passages of philosophy. 'A black and dreadful place!', Nell calls the deep, dark well in the crypt of the church—and Cattermole's illustration homed in intently on the ghoulish oppressiveness of the old man who forces her to look down into its grave-like depths, then wonders aloud 'on what gay heads other earth will have closed, when the light is shut out from here' (429–30).

In scenes such as these, the novel seems to be protesting against its own death-dealingness towards children: its wish to kill them off in order to set them up as guardians of the possibility that there may be something beyond our own existence, something beyond what old age (as represented here) tells us. Dickens himself was not unaware of his bad faith in the matter. After Nell's exchange with the sexton, he put words of eloquent consolation in the mouth of the schoolmaster:

'do you think [...] that an unvisited grave, a withered tree, a faded flower or two, are tokens of forgetfulness or cold neglect? Do you think there are no deeds far away from here, in which these dead may be best remembered? Nell, Nell, there may be people busy in the world at this instant, in whose good actions and good thoughts these very graves—neglected as they look to us—are the chief instruments.' (421)

Washington Irving wrote to Dickens to express his delight in this and other passages, 'which come upon us suddenly and gleam forth apparently undesignedly, but which are perfect gems of language'.[33] Privately, Dickens was prepared to confess that this was all they were. As he approached the writing of Little Nell's death, he admitted to John Forster that the situation threw him back into the distraught state he had been in after the death of her real-life counterpart, the 17-year-old Mary Hogarth: 'I am the wretchedest of the wretched. [...] Old wounds bleed afresh when I only think of the way of doing it [...] I can't preach to myself the schoolmaster's consolation, though I try.'[34]

That apostasy is the more pointed because the moral he sought to apply is essentially no more religious than the secular humanism preached by George Eliot. This is metaphysics of a markedly post-Kantian kind, in which what is sought is not theological truths, but rather a more expansive basis for the conceptualization of experience. And the pressure of the need for it—what the later Adorno would call the 'wresting' of the mind 'so strongly from what we merely are' (135)—can be felt not just in the text itself, but in those other writings that have become integral to *The Old Curiosity Shop*'s reception in English: the letters of the writer who confronted his own mortality, and the boundedness of his own life and thought, in the dialectical opposition between the old age towards which he felt himself to be slowly growing, and the youth of the dead girl he would like to have believed might have rescued him from his promised end.

Age thus operates as a deep fissure within the allegorical figure both the younger Adorno and Dickens himself wanted to identify in *The Old Curiosity Shop*'s imagined pairing of an old man and a young child.[35] The dialectical relation of age and youth certainly drives the novel's confrontation with early-industrial English society, but, from the vantage point of Adorno's later writing on metaphysics, it also suggests a revised Adornian reading of that confrontation. What would then emerge would be not only the child's sacrifice, but a larger philosophical and literary picture in which that sacrifice would be seen to be upheld but also denied: endorsed as the hope of a beyond, and exposed as the murderous proof that 'mere existence' is all we have.

And yet *The Old Curiosity Shop* also bears witness repeatedly to the resurrective powers of comedy (Dick Swiveller returned from the brink of death; the Marchioness as Little Nell's comic double).[36] What does this mean for the younger Adorno's and Dickens's thinking about old age and death? Is there any kind of dialectical relationship between the cruelty of Little Nell and her grandfather's story, and the novel's 'affirmative delight in linguistic and metaphysical play'?[37] There is a humanist protest to be made along these lines against emphasizing, as Adorno did, the 'immeasurable sadness' attached to old age, and the homicidal impulse implicit in its treatment of childhood. A redemptive reading could do much with the large cast of children, besides Little Nell and the young scholar, who are victimized by the 'material object-world' of adults, but whose response is of a very different mode and tenor.[38]

The Marchioness, for example, may, like Nell, be emotionally neglected and all but starved physically (her plight is even worse, locked into a dank basement and compelled to work as slavey to a grotesque amazon of a mother who has never named, let alone acknowledged, her child). But the Marchioness has a resilience, and 'cunning' (394, 445, 451), in addition to the capacity for love, which enable her to break free of her bondage. In connection with the dialectic of youth and old age, the closer analogies and richer counterparts to Nell's situation are the two boys roughly her own age whose lives are entwined with the demonic Quilp: Kit, who eludes the dwarf's plot to ruin him, and—more closely—Tom Scott, the child whom Quilp employs to run his errands and keep watch over his waste-ground 'summer house'. Critics rarely pick up on the statement of Quilp's age that accompanies his first appearance. 'The child [Nell] was closely followed by an elderly man of remarkably hard features and forbidding aspect, and so low in stature as to be quite a dwarf, though his head and face were large enough for the body of a giant' (26–7). No account of his appearance or behaviour thereafter reminds us of his age (though it adds a 'January and May' frisson to his sado-masochistic relationship with the young and pretty Mrs Quilp). Instead, everything about Quilp demonstrates extreme physical hardiness and savage energy. His relationship with Tom Scott brings to the surface of the plot the (half-) buried murderousness that characterizes the adult world's imaginative response to children. 'You dog,' Quilp snarls: 'I'll beat you with an iron rod, I'll scratch you with a rusty nail, I'll pinch your eyes [...] I'll cut one of your feet off' (47–8). He seems to take a perverse delight in having the boy mimic his own adult behaviour. Quilp's uncanny athleticism is mirrored in Tom Scott's passion for tumbling and for walking around on his hands, and on one occasion Quilp forces him to copy his habit of chain smoking: 'Luckily the boy was case-hardened, and would have smoked a small lime-kiln if anybody had treated him with it' (95).

In this parodic doubling of Nell's relationship with her grandfather, one might see writ large—and rebuked—the desire of the old to take the young as surrogates for, and symbolic defenders against, their own mortality. Like Mrs Quilp, Tom is in an evidently sado-masochistic relationship with the old man's desire to use and to wound him. He weeps, we are told, at Quilp's inquest. But at the end, when he disappears into the streets of London to earn his living as an 'Italian' tumbling boy, Tom Scott's resilience seems to have been offered to us, the readers, as compensation for the lack of a comparable hardiness in Nell. Not all children will fade away. There are those like Tom who exist under the protection of a comic view of the world as a place where death constantly threatens but is never realized, and in which a child can belong wholly and sufficiently to the 'material object world'.

There are several points in *The Old Curiosity Shop* where the question of comedy's alliance with death and metaphysics enters fully into the allegorical spirit of Nell and her grandfather's story. One of the most tonally agile of those scenes is the response of the grandfather to Short and Codlin's puppet theatre (a scene to which Adorno, in 1931, repeatedly alludes). Short and Codlin enter the novel as a strained but companionable pairing of the tragic and comic spirits. They are first seen labouring to repair the tools of their trade, one of them 'binding together a small gallows with thread' while the other repairs the 'radical neighbour' puppet (131). When they look up they encounter the 'curiou[s]' gaze of the old man and his young companion (132) (Dickens works the two meanings of 'curiosity' together throughout this chapter with more than usual deliberateness). Little Nell at this point recedes into the background, but the old man expresses 'extreme delight' at his first sight of Mr Punch off the stage, venturing to touch one of the puppets, and laughing 'a shrill laugh' (133). Phiz's illustration quietly underlined this unexpected moment of recognition and covert doubling, mirroring Mr Punch's hook nose, sagging jaw, and gangling limbs in the figure of the old man.

There is a strong humanist tradition of reading Dickens which would want to seize upon this scene, too, as a redemptive moment in tragedy. Such a reading would no doubt light upon Little Nell's volunteering to take over the mending of the puppets (so offering herself as a willing prop to the adult world), and it might well find support from Hablot Browne's sly signing of the illustration with his initials on a tombstone: 'H.B.' But if Old Trent and Mr Punch are on the same territory (allied, not least, in their unkindness to children), that doesn't mean that the novel's thinking about ageing, metaphysics, and death is overruled or negated by the energies of comedy. And if other children in *The Old Curiosity Shop* escape the deathly metaphysics that requires Little Nell to be sacrificed, that does not mean that they in any significant sense challenge it. Each of them who comes into contact with her casts off his or her comic role in response to her death. Nor does the presence of comedy obviate the later Adorno's case for old age's power to bring thought to a confrontation with its own limits.

Adorno himself was consistently clear about the limits of comedy's ability to rescue the world. In 'Is Art Lighthearted?', written in 1967, a year after the lectures on metaphysics, he quoted Hölderlin's 'Die Scherzhaften', or 'The Ones Who Make Jokes': 'Are you always playing and joking? You have to! Oh friends, this affects me deeply, for only the desperate have to do that'. Adorno was in agreement. Art as a whole is 'a critique of the brute seriousness that reality imposes upon human beings', he wrote, but the individual work of art cannot authentically be anything but serious. 'Where art tries of its own accord to be lighthearted […] it is reduced to the level of a human need and its truth content is betrayed. Its ordained cheerfulness fits into the way of the world. It encourages people to submit to what is decreed, to comply. This is the form of objective despair.'[39]

'What complicates Adorno's gravity is his levity', the literary critic Joseph Litvak writes: 'his Jewish […] way of developing the *comic* tendency of style's ontological lightness. I am aware that this may sound laughable'.[40] Not to a humanist reader of Adorno and Dickens, for whom it is necessary (as Adorno jibed) that there should be a connection—non-obvious but potent—between the critical work of old age and the work of comedy. In that tradition of criticism, there is a well-recognized kinship between age and comedy (Lear with flowers in his hair, pursued around the stage by the gentleman) and it would be entirely in accord with it to think that such yokings of tragedy and farce, by breaching the boundaries of decorum, might amount to a concept of freedom. But for Adorno, that reading can only be the knee-jerk reaction of those unwilling to face the 'brute seriousness of reality'. Comedy, in the single work of art, is only a way of shoring up our boundaries, not a way of putting them seriously to the test of thought.

In the introduction to the first English translation of Adorno's essay on *The Old Curiosity Shop*, Michael Hollington quotes a passage from Walter Benjamin's *The Origin of German Tragic Drama* (1963) which he sees as pointing back to Adorno on Dickens: 'Allegorical characters, these are what people mostly see. Children are hopes, young girls are wishes and requests.'[41] Adorno's later writing on metaphysics suggests a bleak end-point to that list: the very old are fears. But if—or indeed because—they are fears, they also generate in those who are neither children nor yet very old, hopes of a beyond. As Adorno put it, contemplating the 'near abstract' condition of the very old in Lecture 17 of the *Metaphysics*: 'the mind has wrested itself so strongly from what we merely are [that] this in itself gives rise to a hope that mere existence might not be everything'.

Reading Dickens through the Adorno of the lectures on metaphysics as well as the Adorno of the 1931 essay reveals one way in which those hopes have been expressed, and not just allegorically, in literature through reference to the temporality of human lives. For the young Adorno, old age and childhood seemed to have been bound by Dickens into one allegorical figure; for the older Adorno, that allegorical figure would have had to be seen as dialectically split. Reading *The Old Curiosity Shop* in the light of the late Adorno, one might then see a much darker playing-out of the impulse towards metaphysics. In Dickens's novel, contemplating the 'immeasurable sadness of old age' prompts the hope that there may be something beyond material existence, but it gives form to that hope only by enlisting the help of children. In other words, the need for something beyond material existence is met in this story only by taking mortality away from the very old and giving it instead to children, on whom its pressure seems so much less immediate and so much less necessary.

For Adorno (late Adorno), the spur old age gave to metaphysical thinking was illegitimate if it had the effect of encouraging us to believe, in spite of all that has been written and experienced, in some form of existence beyond death or beyond the material object world. It was legitimate if one took the structure of the impulse toward a 'beyond' and used it to push philosophy towards thinking about the limits of thinking. Reading Dickens, it would be easy to stop at the point where the version of metaphysics suggested by his novel is exposed as 'illegitimate' in those terms. And yet one of the aspects of *The Old Curiosity Shop* which drew it to the attention of the young Adorno, and which may have been part of its enduring appeal for him, is that it too reaches a point where it knows what it has imagined to be a kind of murder, and no rescue at all from the 'brute reality of existence' ('I am slowly murdering that poor child,' Dickens wrote to the actor William Macready[42]). It reaches a point, also, where it becomes caught in the double-bind that was, for Adorno, the definitive predicament of metaphysics: trying to save what at the same time it destroys.

Though his 1961 lecture on *Endgame* and his 1931 essay on *The Old Curiosity Shop* were widely separated in time, Adorno himself saw a connection between the two subjects. Pondering Beckett's Nagg and Nell in their dustbins, 'only torsos' without 'functioning bodies', and with 'mere stumps of names', he heard in Nell's name something 'somewhat familiar, if obsolete: [...] the touching figure of the child in *The Old Curiosity Shop*' (266). The reduction of Shakespeare's Hamlet to Beckett's Hamm ('hamming' it as a tragedian, blind, crippled, physically dependent on Clov) signals, Adorno argued, 'the now liquidated dramatic subject'; and Nell's transformation from the beautiful, spiritual child of Dickens's novel to an absurdist geriatric wreck renders her the equivalently liquidated sentimental and narrative subject.

The differences between Beckett's theatre of the absurd and Dickens's baroque fiction are enormous. *Endgame*, as Adorno sees it, overthrows traditional form entirely. Beckett's are 'the most advanced artistic techniques, those of Joyce and Kafka. His absurdism expresses the insight at the heart of existentialism, the 'irreducibility' of individual and material existence, but breaks any claim that existence might have to 'the universal and lasting'. In short, he denies any metaphysical basis either for existence or for thought, and in doing so assaults both traditional philosophical rationalism and traditional criteria for aesthetic judgement. What philosophy he presents has been reduced to 'cultural trash'; and artistic form—specifically, the form of the drama—can no longer be linked to 'any substantive, affirmative metaphysical meaning' as its 'law and its epiphany' (242).

Criticism and philosophy alike therefore face in Beckett the challenge of interpreting a drama whose strenuous confinement to the 'concrete' rejects in advance any claim of universal or abstract significance for that concreteness, and, in the same move, throws philosophy itself on the scrapheap. 'Beckett shrugs his shoulders at the very possibility of philosophy today, at the very possibility of theory', Adorno explains: 'The irrationality of bourgeois society in its late phase rebels at letting itself be understood; those were the good old days, when a critique of the political economy of this society could be written that judged it in terms of its own *ratio*' (244).

Philosophy and the old are thus equivalently situated in Adorno's reading of *Endgame*: both defunct, obsolete, thrown out by the play as garbage. Nagg and Nell crystallize for him Beckett's perception that the notion of the 'old and true' has 'deteriorate[d] to bourgeois sentiment' (244). 'HAMM: I love the old questions. (*With fervour*) Ah the old questions, the old answers, there's nothing like them!'[43] In effect, though not as explicitly as in the lectures on *Metaphysics*, Adorno takes Nagg and Nell as incitements to thinking about the limits of existence. Their proximity to death, the impossibility of imagining anything that can be 'left over' from their reduced lives, and yet their persistence in that state of reduction, offer a symbolic representation of the constitutive impossibility of symbolism itself—rescuing what at the same time it destroys. 'Everything waits to be carted off to the dump. This stratum is not a symbolic one but rather the stratum characteristic of a post-psychological condition such as one finds in old people and in those who have been tortured' (252).

'The old people' anchor Adorno's interpretation of the play as a challenge, and threat, to philosophy itself. For Nagg and Nell, *sans* legs, dependent for an ongoing existence on Hamm (their son), desire has been reduced to the most rudimentary of wants: 'more pap', sawdust not sand in their trashcans. Like children, they cry when their needs go unsatisfied, but their crying is merely functional, devoid of moral or emotional meaning: 'NAGG: Are you crying again? NELL: I was trying' (12). In many respects they resemble Hamm's toy dog, with its missing leg (just one) and no sex and no needs except those that Hamm attributes to it—an analogy underlined in the 1967 Berlin production, directed by Beckett, in which a 'Spratt's Bonio' replaced the 'Spratt's medium' given to Nagg in earlier versions of the text ('The change, Beckett felt, suggested both the bone shape of the biscuit offered to the toothless Nagg and its hardness.'[44])

The analogies are what matters, Beckett himself advised his actors— pointing them up in his production notebooks: ' "[A]nalogy N's knocks on lid, H's on wall"; "Analogy Clov-dog when trying to make it stand"; "Analogy voice and attitude [of Hamm during his narration] with N's tailor story" '. Analogies of movement (circles, arcs, crosses on the stage floor), of speech (echoes and repetitions),[45] and of situational dependency: Clov and Hamm, Nagg and Nell, Nagg and Nell and Hamm, Clov and dog, Nagg and Nell and dog—need in age, need in childhood, animal need. Analogy, in Beckett's hands, is a mode of theatrical and conceptual reductionism not expansionism, closing down historical allegory in favour of dramatic patterning. Also a way of stripping out emotion in favour of form. 'Pathos is the death of the play', Beckett warned his actors.[46] It survives in *Endgame* only as a series of theatrical postures and as the stuff of black comedy. This is comedy of a kind Adorno would have approved: 'Nothing is funnier than unhappiness', Nell concedes to Nagg at one point (11)—the most important line in the play, for Beckett. 'Please, no pathos',[47] he pleaded for the soliloquy in which Hamm imagines reaching the end (which, as ever in *Endgame*, he cannot actually imagine as an end): 'If I can hold my peace, and sit quiet, it will be all over with sound, and motion, all over and done with. (*Pause.*) I'll have called my father and I'll have called my ... (*he hesitates*) ... my son' (36). ' "Son" can have an ironic touch instead', Beckett indicated: 'What is meant here is that which has served me as a son.'[48]

Nagg and Nell present a special risk, in this regard, because the tempo of the play can so easily go slack around their geriatric condition and allow pathos in by default. The actor Alan Mandell, who played Nagg in the production at the Riverside Studios, Hammersmith, in 1980, made a note that 'Nagg should be nervous energy, frail, senile' (52).[49] The dialogue between him and Nell might look on the page like affectionate concern ('What is it, my pet?' (9)), but it must be 'without colour…Coloration is only for their memories.'[50] When they reminisce—'Ah yesterday!', 'Once!', 'Engaged!' (10, 11, 12)—they are audibly Hamm's begetters, hamming up the past as a practised method of passing the time. They have attitudes and postures, as they have physical situatedness, but they do not have naturalistic emotions.

As Adorno saw it, Beckett's achievement was to take literally the colloquialism, 'Today the old people are thrown on the rubbish heap.'

> *Endgame* is true gerontology. By the criterion of socially useful labor, which they are no longer capable of, the old people are superfluous and should be tossed aside; this notion is distilled from the scientific fussing of a welfare system that underlines the very thing it denies. *Endgame* prepares us for a state of affairs in which everyone who lifts the lid of the nearest trashcan can expect to find his own parents in it.   (266)

In reading *Endgame* this way, Adorno offers an analysis not so far removed from the allegorical Marxist interpretation he had earlier made of *The Old Curiosity Shop*. The old are, once again, symbolic representatives of the damage done to human subjects under capitalism, except that now they symbolize a more drastic loss of value. 'Gerontology' here condenses a much wider exposition of the culture's condition. Liberal welfarism, in offering to care for the old, exposes the refusal of 'modern culture' (the crudeness of historical description is still there) to care voluntarily for its weakest members—a refusal which became possible, Adorno asserts, only in the wake of World War II. 'The Nazis', he argues, 'have overthown the taboo on old age. Beckett's trashcans are thus emblems of the culture rebuilt after Auschwitz':

> This subplot […] extends all the way to the demise of the two old people. They are refused their baby food, their pap, which is replaced by a biscuit that the toothless old people can no longer chew, and they choke to death because the last human being is too squeamish to spare the lives of the next to last. This is linked to the main plot in that the deaths of the two old people move it forward to that exit from life whose possibility constitutes

the dramatic tension. This is a variation on *Hamlet*: to croak or not to croak, that is the question. (267)

Beckett, for one, thought that Adorno was wilfully and perversely overreading. He was in the audience when Adorno delivered his lecture at the Seventh Verlag evening in Frankfurt am Main on 27 February 1961, and appeared exasperated and embarrassed by it (though some of that exasperation was probably owing to his dislike of formal occasions in his honour). Over lunch together earlier the same day Beckett had listened to Adorno's claim that Hamm was a derivation from 'Hamlet', and told him bluntly that no such thought had been in his mind. When Adorno persisted, and went on to interpret 'Clov' as a mutilated form of 'clown', Beckett 'became a little angry', whispering a protest (in German) to his publisher: 'This is the progress of science, that professors can proceed with their errors!' After the lecture, a trembling and 'shaky' voiced Beckett thanked Adorno with 'as few words as he could decently employ'. He later gave away his presentation copy of the text to a friend.[51]

This non-meeting of minds between the writer and the philosopher could be brushed aside with the justification often resorted to by literary critics that writers are not necessarily the best readers of their own work—a justification that falls rather flatter than usual with Beckett. Adorno's overreading of *Endgame* so as to derive from it an allegorical representation of the condition of humanity, of authentic art, and of philosophy, in post-war Europe, while recognizing that it refuses such rational redescriptions, is nevertheless worth giving a little more time than Beckett gave it. Adorno persisted, in the *Aesthetic Theory*, in pursuing his own line of interpretation, rightly arguing that interpretation is not the same thing as explanation. And, though Beckett's objections have great weight, the essay is not uninstructive, both with regard to Beckett's play and with regard to the place of the old in the subsequent development of Adorno's thinking about metaphysics.[52] Put simply, the nature of Adorno's misdescriptions of Beckett marks an effort, though not, it would seem, a conscious one, to push Beckett closer to the position that, seven years later, Adorno would embrace, and would describe as 'negative metaphysics'.

The element of misdescription (or reinterpretation) in Adorno's reading of *Endgame* has much to do with inattentiveness to the specifics of Beckett's staging of 'the old people'—this despite Adorno's references to the strict 'concreteness' of the play. When Adorno comments that '[e]verything rests on the distinction between sawdust and sand' for Nagg and Nell's bins—'sawdust, wretched byproduct of the object-world, becomes a scarce commodity, and being deprived of it means an intensification of one's life-long death penalty' (266)—it is hard not to suspect that he has missed the scatological joke. Sawdust, one assumes, would be softer on the arse, mopping up excrement and piss and covering the smell more satisfactorily than sand. Similarly, when Adorno observes that '[b]y the criterion of socially useful labor, which they are no longer capable of, the old people are superfluous,' he gives Nagg and Nell a context and a history that are strictly absent from the play. They do not have histories of labour, or any reliable histories for that matter. Their 'past' exists as performance in the present—a series of seemingly well-worn gags about losing their legs in a tandem accident 'on the road to Sedan'; about rowing on Lake Como, the day after they got engaged, where Nagg first told the story of the tailor and Nell almost died laughing. Whether or not any of this is true is the wrong question to ask of *Endgame*.

Literalism, of the kind Beckett demanded, involves a particular kind of respect for linguistic and theatrical specificity: it can be an invitation—as with the sawdust, to go beyond what the play makes absolutely explicit, but only in obedience to the immediate implications of what is staged and said. The play may sometimes seem to hold out an invitation to allegory (as with the reference to Sedan—site of the defeat of the French in the Franco-Prussian war of 1870, and again in 1940 when the German army overwhelmed French forces and paved the way for the swift defeat of France[53]), but it blocks historical contextualization along with every other form of reference to a real 'outside'. The very few things that Beckett said by way of interpretation of the play for the assistance of his actors had to do with refusing or evading requests for more information or (not the same thing) less ambiguity. Adorno is strict about the second, but oddly cavalier about the first—for reasons which have to do, it would seem, with his wish to see Beckettian 'concreteness' as diagnosing a failure of metaphysics, with repercussions for the viability of philosophy generally.

One of the reasons why Adorno's reading of *Endgame* so irritated Beckett (it is safe to assume) is that in order to make this reading Adorno repeatedly describes the old as more definitively at the end of their existence than the play states. When he writes that 'Hamm lets the torsos of his parents, who have turned into babies in the garbage cans, starve to death' (258), or that Nagg and Nell 'choke to death because the last human being is too squeamish to spare the lives of the next to last', or again that 'the deaths of the two old people move [the main plot] forward', he is going further than *Endgame* permits. Nagg does not die, and Nell's death is deliberately unconfirmed in the play. Beckett's Berlin *Notebook* indicates, by way of shorthand, that she is dead, but when the German actress Gudrun Genest, who played Nell in Berlin in 1967, asked Beckett directly whether this was the case, he smiled and said 'So it seems, but no one knows.'[54]

The possibility, but also the uncertainty, of Nell's death are crucial to the theatrical playing of the endgame. In the earlier two-act version of the play, the first act ended with Nagg's recognition of her apparent demise. In the final text, he knocks on the lid of her bin:

> Nell! (*Pause. He knocks louder. Pause. Louder.*) Nell! (*Pause.* NAGG *sinks back into his bin, closes the lid behind him. Pause.*)
> HAMM: Our revels now are ended. (*He gropes for the dog.*) The dog's gone.   (30)

The pause before Hamm's response should be the longest in the play, Beckett told the London cast in 1980: but a silence of uncertainty, not pathos. For Nell to die would be clarifying. If she can die, an end becomes a dramatic, and (in the strictly limited terms the play makes available) a conceptual possibility. Hamm, hamming up Prospero, then implying 'Nagg, or perhaps Nell (the bitch?) is dead' registers as much, but registers also that until and unless Nagg and Nell die old age blocks the end. This in the sense that, having failed as yet to reach their own end, the old signal a longer endgame than Hamm likes the idea of; they indicate to him that there is more to be endured—misery not loftier but lowlier than his. 'Can there be misery—loftier than mine?' is his first rhetorical question of the play: 'No doubt. Formerly. But now? (*Pause.*) My father? (*Pause.*) My mother? (*Pause.*) My ... dog?' (4). Bathos notwithstanding, Hamm depends on Nagg and Nell for his sense of existing and being miserable in time, as he requires Clov for his sense of existing and suffering in a theatrical space. His cruelty towards all three arises because he sees them as analogously to blame for prolonging this 'thing' that—as long as it is unfinished—he cannot call his 'life'; but where Clov has a possible existence beyond and after Hamm's, Nagg and Nell symbolize the apparent unendingness of Hamm's own condition. Which is again why he needs them. He is 'the kind of man who likes things coming to an end but doesn't want them to end just yet', Beckett explained to Patrick Magee, who played the role in the Royal Court Theatre production in 1976.[55]

Adorno's reading of the play, rather than the play itself, moves Nagg and Nell 'forward to that exit from life whose possibility constitutes the dramatic tension' because he wants to see the philosophical 'endgame' as much more definitively at its end than it is. He wants to be able to take from *Endgame* a question much closer to a definition of negative metaphysics than anything Beckett asks: 'to croak or not to croak', as Adorno puts it in emulation of Beckett's anti-sentimentalism. Recognizing Beckett's refusal to permit us to go beyond the conditions of his characters' existence on stage and claim for them a universal significance, or to see in them concepts for which there could be a metaphysical foundation, he nevertheless tries to push that concreteness towards a clearer expression of the limits of existence and the limits of thought that would make of Beckett's hostility to metaphysics a metaphysics 'no less'. In the light of Adorno's later view in the *Metaphysics*, of the old as an incitement to thinking the 'beyond' of thought, this pulling of the play towards negative metaphysics is clearly predictive, but it could only find itself at odds with Beckett's more absolute resistance, in his depiction of old age, to thinking about a beyond to the limits of existence—a resistance that goes right back to his performance in the student spoof of Corneille at Trinity College, Dublin. Playing the part of *Don Diègue* in *Le Kid*, aged 24, he brought an alarm clock on stage with him and set it to go off midway through Diègue's celebrated lament at the powerlessness of old men, '*Ô rage! ô désespoir! ô Vieillesse!*', 'forcing him to go faster and faster until he built up a wild, crazy momentum'.[56]

The theatrical situatedness of old age in *Endgame* is similarly debunking of high rhetorical or philosophical loftiness. The play scrupulously closes down any suggestion that would give confirmation or even a conceptual content to a beyond. Hamm, recognizing in Clov a wish for such an elsewhere, orders him repeatedly and fearfully to take the stepladder over to the windows and report on what he sees 'outside':

> Look at the earth.
> CLOV: Again!
> HAMM: Since it's calling to you. (36–7)

Many of the revisions Beckett made to the play in 1967 and 1980 were aimed at reducing the evidence of even a very bare 'beyond'. So, Nagg's reference to Clov fetching sand from the shore for the bustbins went; also the picture with its face turned to the wall, Clov's song, and the much-quoted passage where Clov turns his telescope on the auditorium and announces 'I see ... a multitude … in transports … of joy.'[57] Beckett's directorial answers to actors' questions were in the same vein, declining to fill in any history or context that could constitute an 'elsewhere' or 'otherwise' for this play. Is Nell dead?: 'So it seems, but no one knows.' Is the little boy in Hamm's story the young Clov?: 'Don't know […] Simply don't know.'[58]

As Adorno saw it, Beckett's play is set in a conceptual halfway-house between existence and non-existence: a 'realm between life and death, where it is no longer possible even to suffer'. But this, too, is reinterpretation rather than a straight description of the play. One important corollary of Beckett's insistence on keeping the play this side of the philosophical borderline between the physical and the metaphysical, where the definition of metaphysics becomes *the* question, is that Nagg and Nell are more theatrically active than Adorno allows. They are certainly not just representations of the 'objective life'. Nagg, especially (who has a larger part in the play than Nell) is not merely a philosophical prop to Hamm's drama but 'in on the act', as it were: an old vaudeville performer, ready to fall into the familiar postures and banter on request—but not just on request (it takes persuasion, inducements, bribery). When Hamm plays the raconteur, he is doing something directly reminiscent of his father who has already told an old (or *faux* old) Jewish joke about a tailor and a pair of trousers. A squib on metaphysics:

> NAGG (*Customer's voice:*) 'In six days, do you hear me, six days, God made the world […] And you are not bloody well capable of making me a pair of trousers in three months!' (*Tailor's voice, scandalized:*) 'But my dear Sir, my dear Sir, look—(*disdainful gesture, disgustedly*) —at the world—(*pause*)—and look—(*loving gesture, proudly*)—at my TROUSERS!' (13)

A man without legs telling a joke about a perfectionist tailor who once made (or didn't make) him a pair of trousers. Beckett's old people do not, *pace* the Adorno of the *Metaphysics*, live a 'mere abstract existence' (though they do live an absurd one), nor have their minds 'wrested themselves from what they merely are'. They are, on the contrary, relentlessly embodied and repeatedly drawn to recollect their fuller embodiment in the imagined past.

Woken again later, and reluctantly, to stand in for Clov as the recipient of Hamm's story of the beggar father and his starving child, Nagg is also a dependable comic sidekick, laughing heartily, stifling a laugh, gabbling the Lord's prayer, delivering the punch line—all on cue: after prayer—'Wait!

(*Pause. Abandoning his attitude*) Nothing doing!' (29). Clov could perform all this in his stead, and the play would be that much more minimalist as a result, but without Nagg and Nell the time yet to be lived out would be another merely imaginary 'beyond'. With them, it has physical representation and generates much of the malice of the play's black comedy, its bathetic reductions of the idealistic to the material ('HAMM: We lose our hair, our teeth! Our bloom! Our ideals!' (8)), and its niggling puns ('NAGG: Are you cold? NELL: Yes, perished' (10); 'HAMM: What was she [Nell] drivelling about?' (14); 'That old doctor, he's dead, naturally?' (14); 'We're getting on' (35).)

'I didn't listen to you', Nagg tells Hamm just before he knocks on Nell's bin, gets no response, and disappears for the last time into his bin. 'I hope I'll live […] to hear you calling me like when you were a tiny boy, and were frightened in the dark, and I was your only hope' (29–30).[59] It's a threat, not a warning—but also not, *pace* Adorno, a death. For the parent not to come (not to be able to come) when the grown child calls, summons up a future in which death has not carried off the old people 'naturally', and where their ongoing and drastically reduced existence no longer protects one, if it ever did, from the dark—from the thought that there is no beyond to existence or to thought itself. According to Nagg, they never did.

The old, then, might seem to be, once again, fears. But this would be to read, as Adorno did, too allegorically. The threat they represent in *Endgame* is stripped of emotion. In his final soliloquy (the last speech of the play), Hamm turns Nagg's malicious projection of the future in on himself, taking up the position in relation to Clov that Nagg has held in relation to himself. Ostensibly he is recalling the story he told earlier of the father who came to him one Christmas, begging that his child be saved from starvation. There may be a suggestion of the death of Christianity here, but the more immediate structural parallel is closer at hand in Hamm's anticipation of his future relation to Clov, where he will play the part of the old person, Clov the part of the son: 'You want him to bloom while you are withering? Be there to solace your last million last moments? (*Pause.*)' Hamm then whistles—not for Clov but for Nagg. Once, then again 'louder': '(*Pause.*) [No?] Good. (*Pause.*) Father! (*Pause. Louder*) Father! (*Pause.*) [No?] Good. (*Pause.*) We're coming' (42). If Nagg is gone, the endgame can approach at last its finish (such tautologies pervade *Endgame*) instead of resting in stalemate. But the last words of the play are comically resurrective of

Nagg, after all. 'Old stancher! (*Pause*.) You … remain'. They refer to his handkerchief, his last remaining prop, but coming after Nagg's final speech reminiscing, unkindly, about the child Hamm crying and wanting his father to mop his tears, they also keep the old man in the frame even at the last—holding on, in spite of everything, to that hope of a beyond that has already been rejected.

Seven years later, Adorno would be clearer in his own mind about the double-move of thought to be found via that word 'old'. The end of his reading of *Endgame* is not quite there, seeing in Beckett's play only an unexpected (and—as a reading of the play—implausible) regress to stoicism: 'Hope skulks out of the world … and back to where it came from, death. From it the play draws its only consolation, a stoic one: [that] "there are not so many [terrible things] now"' (275). In the *Metaphysics* Adorno would recognize that the contemplation of the old does, after all, give rise to a form of hope: the hope of something beyond 'mere existence' even as we face up to 'the idea of absolute annulment'. He would recognize, too, what could be rescued for philosophy from the structure, though not the content, of that hope.

It is important to reiterate that there is a distinct tinge of embarrassment about this suggestion when it becomes explicit in Lecture 17. Adorno was acutely aware that the move from contemplating the old to contemplating metaphysics was, logically speaking, barely legitimate. This is why, when he raises it, the language he uses is not the language of logic (not, that is, the language of explicit analogy), but the language of imagination and speculation: 'one can *hardly imagine* what is to be left over from such a poor, infirm creature', 'the very old[…]most strongly *awaken the idea* of absolute annulment', 'the very curious persistence of the idea of immortality *may be connected*' to the hope the old prompt that our physical existence is not everything. This placing of the question of metaphysics within the domain of the imagination in turn explains why, until the very end of his career, its exploration should have found an intellectual home not in Adorno's philosophical writings but in his cultural criticism—and why, uniquely in this book, the connection to literature is already expansively there in the philosophy itself.

7

Now or Never

If contemplating old age was, for Adorno, a prompt to thinking afresh about metaphysics, for Bernard Williams it was rather an encouragement to thinking more deeply about our mortal condition. Williams's 'The Makropulos Case: Reflections on the Tedium of Immortality' is primarily about our attitude to death rather than ageing: even so, it is one of the very few works of moral philosophy in recent decades with new and substantive things to say about old age. Asked to contribute to a series of lectures at the University of California, Berkeley in 1972 'on the immortality of the soul or kindred spiritual subject',[1] Williams chose to set aside the metaphysical question of whether or not we are immortal and to put a case instead that we ought not to deplore the unavoidability of our death.

His arguments are not the Lucretian arguments. Lucretius, as we have seen (Ch. 3), sought to persuade us that we have no coherent reason for viewing death as a misfortune, because we do not know of our own death. Where death is we are not. He claimed also that a long life is no better than a short one: given that we shall be dead for eternity, the earliness or lateness of our dying should not matter to us.[2] Williams disposes of those arguments efficiently: if it is true that satisfaction of desires and possession of the *praemia* of life is a good thing, then, even if we retain the Lucretian requirement that the possessor of these things be conscious of the possession, it cannot be the case that a long life is no better than a short one: if the *praemia* are valuable, then getting to the point of possessing them, and possessing them for longer, must be better than not possessing them or possessing less of them (84). Williams then turns to the obvious counterproposition: that it will always be better to have more of life. But this, he observes, would be so only with 'other things being equal', and the fact that we grow old and our capabilities diminish is one reason we have to view 'other things' as *not* equal. 'No-one need deny that since, for instance, we grow old and our powers decline, much may happen to increase the reasons for thinking death a good thing' (89).

Suppose, then, that we did not age. Age and decline are, after all, usually taken to be contingencies. 'We might not age; perhaps, one day, it will be possible for some of us not to age. If that were so, would it not follow then that, more life being *per se* better than less life, we should have reason [...] to live for ever?' On the contrary, Williams argues 'that the supposed contingencies are not really contingencies; that an endless life would be a meaningless one; and that we could have no reason for living eternally a human life. There is no desirable or significant property which life would have more of, or have more unqualifiedly, if we lasted for ever' (89). If we think rightly about what it is to be a self and to have a life, Williams says, we shall recognize old age and decline as necessities, not contingencies. Given a long enough life, the categorical desire to carry on would cease: bluntly, we would bore ourselves to death—or, as he puts it more elegantly, 'I would eventually have had altogether too much of myself' (100). Either that or we should have to be willing to accept so much change in ourselves through the accumulation of experience and the passage of our lives through time that we should eventually cease to be recognizable *to* and *as* ourselves.

By way of lending imaginative depth to the possibility of going on forever unchecked by ageing or death, Williams recounts the story of Karel Čapek's play (later a Janáček opera), *The Makropulos Case*. Its heroine, Elina Makropulos, having taken an elixir of life, ages chronologically but not physically or, in important respects, psychologically. She possesses at 342 all the accrued knowledge and memories of her many years while retaining the physical and mental capacities of a 42-year-old. She retains also a certain character, seeming 'always to have been much the same sort of person'. The choice to be 42, 'if it was a choice', Williams declared himself 'personally, and at present, well disposed to salute' (he was 42 when he gave the lecture): 'if one had to spend eternity at any age, that seems an admirable age to spend it at' (90). 'EM' nevertheless destroys the elixir at the end of the play and takes her own life. Her problem, Williams remarks, was not 'that she was too old at the age she continued to be at. Her problem lay in having been at it for too long. Her trouble was it seems, boredom' (90).

Although Williams's essay has, as I began by noting, important things to say about old age, it is not primarily about that subject but about why we ought not to want to live forever. It is nevertheless well worth thinking harder about the implications of what he says, largely in passing, about old age. The passage in which he describes age and decline as necessities rather than contingencies is the most direct discussion of the subject in the essay. It is brief, and not entirely explicit about what Williams takes 'ageing and decline' to mean. The comments on EM's 'admirable age' are still briefer, and their implications almost entirely inexplicit. It is therefore clarifying to spell out the two quite distinct meanings 'age' possesses in 'The Makropulos Case'. In the first place, when Williams rebuts the view of old age as a contingency, it is coupled with decline and refers to the deteriorations in physical and mental capability that come with biological senescence. There is some ambiguity here about whether old age and decline is an objective or a subjective condition. Williams appears to be talking about objective decline, but would, I assume, agree that neither age nor decline are only objective states. In the second place, old age is a purely mathematical measure, a neutral count of the time one has spent alive. This kind of age is a literary and philosophical fiction. Thanks to EM's elixir, it has no implications for the heroine's physical ability to live well. The problem is psychological. After a while, albeit a long while, tedium sets in.

How long would it really take? Are EM's 342 years enough? Thomas Nagel is not the only respondent to Williams to feel that he underestimated the strength of the desire to go on being alive. 'Perhaps I shall eventually tire of life,' Nagel writes, 'but at the moment I can't imagine it, nor can I understand those many distinguished and otherwise reasonable persons who sincerely assert that they don't regard their own mortality as a misfortune.'[3] (This is of course a 'psychological report', rather than anything else.) 'Is it so clear', Stephen R. L. Clark asks in similar vein, 'that boredom is inevitable?'[4] Perhaps Williams had a low boredom threshold. But, like Williams, both Nagel and Clark suspend the problem of ageing in order to make these objections.[5] Only if 'old age' is definitionally separated from 'decline', as in *The Makropulos Case*, can the categorical desire to go on living be put to a purely psychological test, rather than the physical-cum-psychological test of incapacity, ill health, and pain—a test which, Williams and Nagel are agreed, commonly comes too soon.

Williams's description of the effects of ageing in the biological and not the fantasy sense is limited to two statements. One has already been quoted—'No-one need deny that since, for instance, we grow old and our powers decline, much may happen to increase the reasons for thinking death a good thing'; the other is similarly concerned with the limits of the categorical desire to be alive—'many of the things I want, I want only on the assumption that I am going to be alive; and some people, for instance some of the old, desperately want certain things when nevertheless they would much rather that they and their wants were dead' (85). One can imagine other reasons for reaching that position—living with chronic pain, perhaps most obviously. But given that old age is the only example Williams offers of why the categorical desire for life might leave us, it is worth taking the 'for instance' out of these sentences and considering the fact that 'we grow old and our powers decline' as the main foreseeable set of conditions under which many, perhaps most, of us may eventually come to think of death as 'a good thing'.[6] To do that, it is necessary to say more than Williams does about how his reading of Lucretius might or might not extend to the consideration of old age.

The Lucretian argument against regarding our own death as an evil does not apply to how we regard old age. The issue is one of consciousness: in death we are not, but in old age we remain. Unless seriously afflicted in our cognitive powers as we age we do know that we are losing capability, and once that loss begins significantly to impair our ability to live well and enjoy the good things of life we may justly regard our old age as deplorable. In the second case (the argument against preferring a long to a short life), it is not irrational, as Williams observes, to view a life that contains the enjoyment of good things 'to a ripe age' as better than a life which is 'very short and cut off before the *praemia* have been acquired' (84); it is also not irrational (here again I expand on Williams) to feel, even with many years behind one, that one has not yet reached 'a ripe age'. One may be acutely conscious that one has more to learn, greater emotional or intellectual 'maturity' to attain. But if Williams is right about categorical desire, the degree of impairment to our powers is likely at some point to become decisive. Once we decline severely the categorical desire to go on living will probably, though not certainly, desert us.

Given that we cannot, like 'EM', go on indefinitely with all our physical and mental powers intact until we are sated with life, are the reductions in capability which come with age then not rationally to be tolerated, if not quite welcomed? Do they not offer to take us out of life on terms that make the loss of it bearable? A significant element of Williams's argument is, to be sure, concerned with reconciling us to the inevitable (being in step with necessity is to an extent germane to his sense of right reasoning). He allows that individual responses will vary: the desire to go on living will be stronger in some people than in others. His comments on those who find comfort in the idea of life after death and those who find equal comfort in the conviction that death ends the only life there is (p. 83) also indicate scope for significant temperamental differences. But the final paragraph of 'The Makropulos Case' insists that some of the most important factors in whether our dying is for us a good or a bad thing are responsive neither to reason nor to the exercise of virtue, and have nothing to do with temperament. As in his influential essay on 'Moral Luck', Williams holds that, when all the philosophical arguments are in, the answer has much to do with chance.

'The Makropulos Case' ends with a brief meditation on whether advances in technology are not in danger of depriving many people of the good luck of happening to die at, or somewhere near, the moment when, through age and decline, the categorical desire to live abandons them.

> There are good reasons, surely, for dying before [one has had too much of oneself]. But equally, at times earlier than that moment, there is reason for not dying. Necessarily, it tends to be either too early or too late. EM reminds us that it can be too late, and many, as against Lucretius, need no reminding that it can be too early. If that is any sort of dilemma, it can, as things still are and if one is exceptionally lucky, be resolved, not by doing anything, but just by dying shortly before the horrors of not doing so become evident. Technical progress may, in more than one direction, make that piece of luck rarer. (100)

More than thirty years on, that conclusion looks prescient. Advances in medicine have, as Williams foresaw, made life-prolonging measures more successful and in some societies routine—to the point where many commentators on medical ethics are asking whether the old are not too often deprived of a good death.[7] Given medical interventions that can enable the very old to go on living what are in some cases barely functional lives, the dilemma of where to draw the line between palliative and life-extending care is if anything more difficult now to resolve, intellectually and ethically. The risk, Williams warned, is that we shall lose sight, as individuals and as a society, of the necessity of our own mortality. We shall also be in danger of forfeiting the moral luck that might once have been ours in the time of our deaths.

I take Williams, then, to be implying three things of special significance for the consideration of old age: first, that old age, understood as a process of biological decline, may have a decisive impact on the categorical desire to go on living, and that, *given that we are mortal, this deterioration of our capacities over time is not to be regretted*, though it is also not something most of us will welcome. Ideally, most of us would prefer a much longer life; but, as it is, our deterioration through old age may make our dying more acceptable to us than it would otherwise be. Second, the fact that I grow old and decline should not be thought of as a contingency, because the alternative—a life in which I went on forever—would be a 'meaningless' life, and incompatible with my retaining a sense of myself as a self. In this regard, too, old age and decline may be viewed, if not positively then without deep regret. MacIntyre's claim that 'unity of a life' and 'unity of self' require 'both childhood and old age' finds (limited) support, then, from Williams's view that old age and decline acclimatize us to the necessity of mortality, and thus help to give both formal integrity and value to a life. Third, I take Williams to be saying that, in the context of modern science's ability to prolong life, the chance of our recognition of our own terminal decline by reason of age coinciding nearly with our actual death is becoming less than it once was. As that happens, we stand to be less lucky in the time of our dying than we might formerly have been.

There are numerous directions in which one might pursue these thoughts. In my final chapter I take them in a direction Williams himself suggested (not only in 'The Makropulos Case'), considering how developments in science may affect our understanding of ageing. Specifically, I examine how recent advances in scientific theories of biological senescence could alter our perception of old age and decline, and how, if at all, they might affect our valuation of a long life. Here, I pursue Williams's view of ageing and decline as, rightly considered, necessities, which assist our ability to think of death as tolerable, and, in doing so, enable our lives to retain meaning for us, and ourselves to remain recognizable *as ourselves*. The question of the narrative unity (or otherwise) of lives (see Ch. 3) can be thought of as closely connected. The texts I have chosen are both narrative fictions. They both assume that lives may be made sense of as narratives; they both also show that the narrative model is under certain circumstances only sustainable over a long life with difficulty, with conscious and unconscious occlusions, sometimes only with misrepresentations. In this context, however, I am more interested in whether, and why, they encourage us to think of ageing and decline as either contingency or necessity.

The writers' concerns are not of course identical with those of Williams. They approach the subject of old age and decline not in the philosophical abstract, but by imagining specific modern contexts in which individuals, for different reasons, come to accept and even welcome the idea of their own mortality through what they themselves describe as growing old and declining. In the case of Coetzee's novel, that perception is likely to be viewed by most readers as inauthentic—as happening much too soon (in midlife rather than 'genuine' old age). This is part of *Disgrace*'s interest for me: it helpfully problematizes from the start the objective reality of old age, and fleshes out the important question, left ambiguous in Williams, of how far ageing and decline may be psychological rather than primarily physical. (It's not, of course, a pure distinction.) In the second case, the old age of the main protagonist and narrator is not in dispute, but the requirement that his life be adjusted in the light of it emphatically is. Where Williams identifies old age and decline as assisting the recognition that our mortality is not to be regretted ('since, for example, we grow old and our powers decline, much may happen to increase the reasons for thinking death a good thing'), these writers put more pressure on the idea of old age's causal relation to the acceptance of mortality (what does that 'since' mean?). They also do something to fill out the question of what other circumstances might contribute to that acceptance: the experience of ageing and decline is, in part, biological and objective, but it is also conditional on many other things, including personal, political, and historical circumstance. It is not only the pressure of biology that makes either a character in a novel, or a person in reality, feel themselves to be old and in decline and view the idea of their own death as tolerable, even welcome.[8] Williams would, I assume, agree with this, and it leads to an important deepening of his claims about how and why the categorical desire to go on living may come to wane 'with age'.

J. M. Coetzee's *Disgrace* (1999) and Philip Roth's *The Dying Animal* (1999) were published almost exactly contemporaneously. Each takes as its protagonist an ageing university lecturer in literature and/or creative writing, who makes much of his disenchantment with the profession and with the broader literary and intellectual culture around him. In each, sexual involvement between the male protagonist or protagonists and a much

younger lover or lovers becomes the means of representing—and disputing—his individual claim on the future. In each, the protagonist comes to
accept the necessity of his own mortality, and to express that acceptance as
an acceptance of ageing and decline; but they do so for different reasons,
and with very different degrees of willingness. Not least, the sense of the
necessity of their own dying is bound up with a newly pressing consciousness of the mortality of others in relation to which their length of life has
the stamp of privilege.

   Although it is not my principal concern, the professional context of
academia and the maleness of the protagonists matters (this is also true of
Bellow's *Ravelstein*, discussed in Ch. 3). Disenchantment with the profession takes the form in all these novels of dismay at the university's late
twentieth-century transformation into what *Disgrace*'s David Lurie calls 'an
emasculated institution of learning',[9] where the broadly humanist educa-
tional curricula of the past have been replaced by a free-market model
of learning and where the assumption of moral relativism is scarcely chal-
lenged. (Roth's narrator is less worked-up on that score, but only because
he has found in semi-retirement an ideally marginal relation to the university.) Within these fictions the university stands, albeit loosely, for the
society as a whole, being the institution through which the private 'agita-
tions' of these men translate into actions in the public sphere. ('Agitation' is
a favourite word of Roth, as also of Bellow.) But there is a more particular
argument being had here with the academy for its perceived failure to protect the tradition of serious, liberal thought it once fostered, and for having
caved in (allegedly) to a political correctness seen by these protagonists as
anti-individualist, illiberal, and anti-intellectual. The argument is evidently
culturally conservative, but not in all cases politically so, and in no case simply so. These novels are, as a result, not just (as I primarily take them to be)
reflections on the wider political and cultural discontents that may play a part
in an individual's recognition of the necessity of his or her own mortality and
the secondary expression of that truth as an awareness of old age and decline.
They are also specific addresses to the humanities faculties of our universities,
as if it is there that our thinking about mortality started to go askew.

A novel of 'mid-life crisis' is how one reviewer described J. M. Coetzee's
Disgrace:[10] David Lurie, formerly Professor of Modern Languages at Cape
Town University, now reluctant Professor of Communications Skills at
the renamed Cape Technical University, loses his job when he declines

to explain himself to the university's disciplinary committee for having sexual relations with a young female student and falsifying her academic record. 'David Lurie (1945—?), commentator upon, and disgraced disciple of, William Wordsworth' (46) is the epitaph he writes on his own career even before the hearing (which he treats with unconcealed contempt). Quitting Cape Town, he takes refuge at a smallholding in the Eastern Cape where his daughter Lucy farms alone, like a throwback, it seems to him, to the solid *boervrous* of the past. Any hope he has of building happier relations with her is destroyed when three black youths attack them, killing all but one of their dogs, badly injuring Lurie, and raping Lucy. Alienated by Lucy's refusal to press charges against her attackers or to terminate the pregnancy that follows, Lurie increasingly devotes himself—with a compassion surprising to him and the reader[11]—to the care of stray, sick, and ultimately condemned dogs.

Lurie's preferred idiom is not, however, that of mid-life crisis but of old age, retirement, more provocatively (in the political context) serving out the end of one's time. This is repeatedly how he explains any failure of historical and contemporary political imagination on his own part. Unwilling though he may be to justify himself to others officially, he is quick to produce the excuse—also, of course, a rejection of the need for excuses—that he is too old to change. He and his colleagues from 'the old days' are 'clerks in a post-religious age', 'burdened with upbringings inappropriate to the tasks they are set to perform' (4). The phrase 'after a certain age' is one of his hallmarks, mimicking the tact of the French (*d'un certain âge*) but making of it an aversion: 'One can't plead guilty to charges of turpitude and expect a flood of sympathy in return', he tells his daughter, 'Not after a certain age. After a certain age one is simply no longer appealing, and that's that. One just has to buckle down and live out the rest of one's life. Serve one's time' (67). The pun on 'appealing' sits heavily in the line: a manifestation of the 'terrible irony' from which Lucy will later beg relief (200).

Age is also Lurie's goadingly inadequate plea before the sexual harassment inquiry: 'I am a grown man [...] beyond the reach of counselling' (49). Near the end of the novel he reflects bitterly that what he did would of course be deemed punishably 'unnatural': 'On trial for his way of life:[... for] broadcasting old seed, tired seed, seed that does not quicken, *contra naturam*. If the old men hog the young women, what will be the future of the species?' (190). The distortive hyperboles and the jarring of elegant archaism against brutishness ('seed that does not quicken', 'the old men hog the young women') put ironic self-flagellation before self-pity. As throughout *Disgrace*, free indirect style holds Lurie at an ostensibly objectifying, intellectualizing distance on himself and the world—though one may suspect him (not Coetzee) of smuggling in a bid for pathos by the back door.

Contemplating with pain his daughter's willingness to humble herself before her attackers, Lurie, or 'Lourie', as the local paper prints his name in its Boer form, and as he later spells it himself, inwardly rebels all the same against being pushed to the side of his own life by the next generation. 'Du musst dein Leben ändern!' he reflects, quoting Rilke with characteristic mock-Romantic flourish: 'you must change your life. Well, he is too old to heed, too old to change. Lucy may be able to bend to the tempest; he cannot, not with honour' (209). That last phrase sounds again the note of end-of-the-line Romanticism to which he is given. The allegorical reading of *Disgrace* that it seems to gesture towards would extend beyond a personal failing on Lurie's part to the whole history of imperialism in South Africa—though a reading of *Disgrace* along these lines has to be chary of reductiveness. This is in part because Coetzee's scrupulous intelligence makes allegory seem too crude a word, in part because of his known antipathy to critical readings that make the novel subservient to history.[12] The allegorical mode is unquestionably there, in *Disgrace*, but it is perhaps better described, as James Wood suggests, as the 'allegorical ironical'.[13]

The valetudinarian rhetoric is objectively spurious. At 52 (though the student newspaper puts him at '53'), Lurie's declared inability to adapt to the changes shaping his family life, his profession, and his country can only register with others as a wishful and in some measure conscious refusal of where history is taking him, for in opting out of the present of South Africa, he also opts out of its future. An unpalatable note of Malthusian self-sacrifice hovers over Lurie's last meditations about his own place in the life of Lucy and the future for South Africa that she represents: 'The problem is with the people she lives among. When I am added in, we become too many' (209). Coetzee makes it altogether less easy than Thomas Hardy, whom he is alluding to here, to protest against the necessitarian conclusion. Self-consciously old before his time, Lurie may, like Hardy's Little Father Time, be vulnerable to the charge of melodrama,[14] but he is unlike him in having made, at some level, an adult's choice. To the classic philosopher's question 'How best can I live?', *Disgrace* thus appears to offer an uncomfortable answer, at once self-affirming and self-annulling: perhaps by ceasing to be; by dying when, or even before, one might have expected to go.

Viewing the ills of contemporary South Africa through the disappointed consciousness of a 'disciple of William Wordsworth' (46), unable to communicate the Romantics' appeal to his modern-day students, Coetzee (as befits the author of *Foe*) implies a literary/cultural as much as political/historical diagnosis of the late twentieth-century troubles of his country. The old South Africa stands exposed through Lurie's story as the ultimate sickness of a Romantic sensibility grown overripe and rank. 'I lack the lyrical', Lurie tells his students, even before his dismissal. Late Byron is his preference now, rather than the imperial sublime of, say, *The Prelude*, or (another poem he teaches) Shelley's 'Mont Blanc': Byron 'late' at 32, dead at 36, who knew that sympathy has its limits. It is 'not possible to love' Byron's Lucifer, Lurie explains to his seminar—'[h]e will be condemned to solitude' (34). And yet Byron went on to have a last, passionate, adulterous affair with the Italian Contessa Teresa Guiccioli.

Perhaps the 'lyric impulse', Lurie will reflect later, is not after all dead in himself either, but 'pinched, stunted, deformed' by 'decades of starvation' (214). He has hopes, in the last pages of the story, of composing 'an eccentric little chamber opera' (214), based on Byron's last love affair before dying a hero to a different nationalist cause, but he can find 'no action, no development' for the love situation, just a 'long, halting' banjo cantilena for the Contessa, punctuated by Byron's offstage 'groans and sighs'. This is Romanticism out of energy, no longer able to express (though still subject to) the 'swell [of] feeling', the 'hammer of blood in [the] throat' (215), and no longer likely to issue in political action.

For the David Luries of South Africa to retire prematurely from the country's future may be, some will feel, no tragedy. Lurie's assumption, before his time, of the postures of old age is, from a less sympathetic angle than Coetzee's, a mark of the most fundamental privilege he bears as a white South African: his expectation of living much beyond 50 at all. The official life expectancy rate for Black African men in 1945–7 (roughly corresponding to Lurie's generation) was thirty-six years: some twenty years lower than the figure, then, for white males. Demographic data for the following decades, until the mid-1980s, show white male life expectancy rising at roughly First World rates and Black African male life expectancy

rising rapidly, until the massively distorting impact of HIV-AIDS.[15] The
requirement until recently that South Africans identify themselves in the
census as 'white', 'coloured', 'black' is, of course, a prominent example
of an anthropological or proto-anthropological discourse that Coetzee has
criticized as a 'Discourse of the Cape'.[16] Nevertheless, it summarizes a
readily observable racial inequity, with respect to longevity, that never
seems to register with Lurie. If it did, he would probably respond with
more of the same self-flagellating ironies. What is one to do with one's
inheritance of an unjust share of life, he would presumably ask, except
serve out the time as though it were a punishment and not a good?

There is no evident compromise in *Disgrace* that would allow Lurie, and
by extension the South Africa he grew up with, to move into the future in a
form recognizable to him- or itself. Lucy's stoicism, more accurately a self-
abasing pragmatism, is not a choice Lurie can stomach, even if he thinks, at
the very end of the novel, that he might begin to recognize its beauty. She
will accept Petrus, the former farmhand, as her husband: an 'alliance', as she
sees it, 'protection' (Petrus is already married). She will become a tenant
on his land, assenting to her humiliation willingly, 'like a dog'. It is Lurie's
phrase, but she calmly allows it. In fact, she too has a limit beyond which
she will not go: she will give up her land, bear her rapist's child, but she will
not give up her house. The major difference between her and her father,
and indeed between her and everyone else in the novel (including Petrus,
who takes in Lucy's rapist, his wife's brother), is that she is capable of
ridding herself of the loyalty to family history that underpinned Lurie's old
South Africa and admitting the complicatedly miscegenated version of the
family that may be the country's future. Lurie cannot accept that outlook,
the only alternative he can see, until the very last pages of the narrative,
being to bide his time and wait for death. The end he faces is in his eyes
a necessary one—at the level of (ironic) allegory, he possesses a depressed
recognition of the choice Bernard Williams identified: either to accept the
necessity of his own mortality (literally, to die; figuratively, to give up on
his life in South Africa, perhaps to leave the country) or to be prepared to
submit to change without visible limits—change so comprehensive that he
would no longer be recognizable to himself.

Announcing the award of the 1999 Booker Prize to *Disgrace*, the Chair
of the judging panel, British Labour MP Gerald Kaufman, had no qualms
about using the term 'allegory'. 'This is a "millennial book"', he explained,
'an allegory about what is happening to the human race in the post-colonial

era.'[17] It's a reading that noticeably avoids commenting on the specificity of Lurie's position as a white South African, unable or unwilling to adapt himself to the new South Africa, and (understandably in the circumstances) avoids considering the implications of this novel for Coetzee's own positioning within South African politics. *Disgrace*'s reception in South Africa was deeply complicated by racialized readings—most prominently, an oral submission to the South African Human Rights Commission (SAHRC) by Jeff Radebe, Minister of Public Enterprises, describing the novel as, if not quite a racist text, a 'repor[t] on' continuing racism among white South Africans.[18] In South Africa especially, though by no means exclusively, the novel drew criticism for a perceived blurring of the line between the protagonist's voice and the authorial voice[19] (that blurring made easier, perhaps, by the fact that Coetzee, like Lurie, was Professor of Literature at Cape Town University and in his fifties, though his late fifties, when the novel was written). By refusing, or failing, to discriminate sufficiently between himself and David Lurie, perhaps even by establishing a provocative proximity between their situations, Coetzee could be seen to have laid himself open to suspicion on the question of how far he too was out of sympathy with the new South Africa.

It's an inadequate reading (too crude morally and much too crude artistically) of Coetzee's book to say that the only acceptable response in Lurie's situation should be to adapt 'constructively' to the new circumstances. Much of the power of *Disgrace* lies in elements that have evident historical and political importance in the South African context, but that also reach beyond that context: primarily, the rendition of an exemplary tension between a 'progressive' perspective of the necessity that one change in the light of circumstances, and a more Nietzschean ethic, a kind of individualism which won't consciously ask for pity but isn't willing to surrender its own dignity. This is one reason why reviewers and critics who identify Coetzee with Lurie do the book an injustice. It is also why *Disgrace* makes for difficult, gripping reading: it gives an exceptionally powerful representation of the resistance that certain kinds of call for apology and self-transformation necessarily set up in us if we are in any important sense to go on being us.

In that sense it chimes with Bernard Williams's argument that if we change too much we shall eventually cease to be recognizable as and to ourselves. It also requires an addendum to Williams: if our circumstances and environment change too much, the effect may be the same. And it draws out a more complex set of meanings to Williams's claim that age and decline may increase our reasons for 'thinking death a good thing'. Lurie's premature sense of his own old age suggests that the acceptance of one's own mortality may have other causes besides and *before* biological ageing and decline, but that *either* the sense we are growing old and our powers are declining is how we commonly experience that acceptance (how we internalize it as a necessity),[20] *or* old age and decline provide a language in which we express that sense to others and to ourselves. Or, perhaps, both. One can say, critically or even cynically, that Lurie dresses up his refusal to change as a case of 'being too old'; one can certainly accuse him of spurious self-righteousness; but one can also say (more revealingly, I think) that a deep need not to surrender the things that make him recognizable to himself as *himself* causes him to internalize his resistance to change as a sense of old age and decline. He may be partly aware of his own psychological motivation here—there is more awareness at the end of the novel—but only partly aware.

Lurie's will to hold on to his sense of his own life, even at the price of accepting that he will be viewed unsympathetically by most (rhetorically, that his life has not long to go), also requires a modification of Jacqueline Rose's argument that the core of this novel's reflection on the politics of post-apartheid South Africa is its depiction of apathy. Rose argues that the novel identifies in Lurie—and by extension in the old South Africa, its universities, and also in us, the novel's readers and witnesses to apartheid's history—a drastic failure to connect with the horrors going on around us. She reads *Disgrace* in tandem with the Report of the Truth and Reconciliation Committee, finding in both a recognition that apathy involves a consciousness of the arduousness of identification which may prove the seed of its own undoing.[21] There is much in this analysis that I find persuasive, but it gives too little recognition to the work of irony in the novel: that quality which defines in the intellectual's temperament something more actively resistant than apathy to the demand of others that one change; something other than fear, or the failure to make an effort of the moral imagination.

The self-protective character of irony comes to the fore when *Disgrace* first opens out the serious possibility that David Lurie might be capable of a more positive relation to the future. Growing old is the price of self-determination, he reflects as he contemplates the sheep that Petrus plans on slaughtering to celebrate the transfer of Lucy's land to him. 'When did a sheep last die of old age? Sheep do not own themselves, do not own their lives. They exist to be used, every last ounce of them […] Nothing escapes, except perhaps the gall bladder, which no one will eat. Descartes should have thought of that. The soul, suspended in the dark, bitter gall, hiding' (123−4). Again, the fierce resistance to having one's life taken away from one. But there is in addition here an explicit sub-Swiftian hope that gall, at least, and the 'terrible irony' that belongs to it, may remain intact when nothing else of the self is secure from assault.

Irony isn't solely in Lurie's control: for much of the novel it is his weapon against internalizing disgrace, but it is also a constant element in the reader's awareness of the gaps between his self-analysis and the reality. The hope, on his part, that it will work for him, not against him, and that it will be enough seems at last to weaken at the point when he breaks from his characteristic refusal to make himself answerable to others and (inexplicably to himself) seeks out the father of the girl with whom he had sexual relations. Invited to a meal with the family, he is acutely aware of the difference between the simple rural life he describes himself as living, and the complicated reality of his situation: 'He has a vision of himself stretched out on an operating table. A scalpel flashes; from throat to groin he is laid open; he sees it all yet feels no pain. A surgeon, bearded, bends over him, frowning. *What is all this stuff?* growls the surgeon. He pokes at the gall bladder. *What is this?* He tosses it aside' (171). The image represents the nadir of Lurie's felt removal from ownership of his own life—perhaps also a clinically remote reflection on his own capacity for bile. The vision is prefaced, significantly, by a reflection on his daughter's complexity, her lack of simplicity. 'He loves his daughter, but there are times when he wishes she were a simpler being: simpler, neater. The man who raped her, the leader of the gang was like that. Like a blade cutting the wind' (170−1). However appealing the *idea* of simplicity and neatness, of letting his irony go, tidying up 'all this stuff' would be an act of violence against the person. The surgeon cutting into the body; rape as 'cutting the wind' (the two images are clearly connected, but not a complete analogy). Melanie's father seems to read Lurie's mind, his next question quietly asking him to draw a connection, then, between the vulnerability of Lucy and the vulnerability of Melanie: ' "Your daughter—does she run her farm all alone?" ' (171).

When Lurie finds himself, against all his own expectations, expressing regret, Isaacs is once again acute. A practising Jew, he replies with (for

Lurie, the atheist) a taxingly theological question: ' "what does God want from you, besides being very sorry? Have you any ideas, Mr Lurie?" ' (172) The reply, compromised though it is by the circumstances in which it is spoken, is nevertheless the first sign that Lurie may be willing to make himself accountable for the past in a way that could open up the possibility of a less self-determined future: ' "Normally I would say [...] that after a certain age one is too old to learn lessons. One can only be punished and punished. But perhaps that is not true, not always. I wait to see" ' (172). Perhaps, that is, there will come a point when neither premature retirement nor its linguistic/tonal counterpart, the retreat into irony, will seem to him a sufficient response to disgrace.

If a vision of change is locatable at the very end of this novel, it is least ambiguous in Lurie's last meditations on old age. He reflects that he will probably be a less than satisfactory grandfather to Lucy's child, as he has been a less than satisfactory father to Lucy herself. '[H]e lacks the virtues of the old: equanimity, kindliness, patience. But perhaps those virtues will come as other virtues go: the virtue of passion, for instance. He must have a look again at Victor Hugo, the poet of grandfatherhood. There may be things to learn' (218). The idiom is still dryly ironic (the irony of meditation on virtues he does not have; perhaps also an irony in the identification of passion as a virtue). Nevertheless, this is part of a larger moment of self-criticism, in which—remarkably—Lurie acknowledges that, for all his expertise in Romanticism, he has never had an eye for simple, rural beauty of the kind his daughter (she of the Wordsworthian name) represents. 'Is it too late to educate the eye?', he asks: 'even city boys can recognize beauty when they see it, can have their breath taken away' (218). Taken (too) literally, to have one's breath taken away is to die, not by one's own agency: either to be killed by others, or to 'go to the Inevitable' (in Philip Larkin's deathbed phrase), but for once Lurie seems to be embracing cliché, and imagining for himself the ability to respond feelingly to the beauty of nature.

What does the inevitability of death mean to Lurie at the very end of *Disgrace*? Is he still narrowly possessed by a sense of his own redundancy, registered symbolically as a premature claim to be old, or is there any reinforcement for this tentative sense of the possibility of opening out to others in later life? In the last paragraphs of the novel, Lurie declines to spare the life of a young male dog with a withered hind leg, though the animal sanctuary rules would permit the dog a further week of life in which someone might adopt, and save, it—this despite the fact that he believes the animal has a special attachment to him ('the dog would die for him, he knows' (215)). The strictly premature giving over of the dog's life is represented as, inextricably, an act of (self-)betrayal and an act of (self-)love. Some readers will see in it nothing beyond the defensive self-regard that has characterized Lurie throughout. The dog's youth (repeatedly noted) would then be read as just a means of underlining Lurie's ongoing sense of his own old age. 'Yes, I am giving him up,' is the last line of the novel, and the unsympathetic reader will suspect that in taking the dog to its death now rather than allowing it its full span, Lurie is asking for grace, even so late on, on higher terms, in recognition of an exhaustive intellectual and emotional effort.

But the tone is markedly unlike what has gone before. Indeed, much of the power of *Disgrace*'s ending lies in a gentleness registered beneath an almost complete tonal self-effacement. Irony is not quite abandoned. It is there in Lurie's meditations on how uncomprehending the dog must be that it is entering the room where it will die: 'the dog will not be able to work [it] out (*not in a month of Sundays!* he thinks)' (219; emphasis Coetzee's). But the *corrosive* irony is gone, and it is not just weariness that takes its place. There is tenderness, and there is an intense imaginative identification with the animal that recapitulates the language of the earlier attack on Lurie himself: he will be 'burnt, burnt up' (220). The phrase eschews sentimentality, conveying, however, a new humility in Lurie's willingness to take mortality upon himself as part of his inevitable 'animal' condition, and an understanding, also new, that even a dog (metaphorically, even the lowest regarded human being) has a claim to be treated with dignity.[22] For a reader familiar with Coetzee's fiction, the scene recalls the recurrent use of animals, especially but not exclusively dogs, to take the measure of our human attitude to death. 'An animal likeness', is the term Dostoevsky, the protagonist of *The Master of Petersburg* (1994), gives this identification—at once deeply felt and deeply resisted by human beings.[23] '"Animals don't find it hard to die"', Dostoevsky consoles a dying woman (though he has himself seen evidence to the contrary): '"Perhaps we should take our lesson from them. Perhaps that is why they are with us here on earth—to show us that living and dying are not as hard as we think." '[24]

For Lurie to decide not to extend the life of this particular dog further might be taken as a symbolic choice for his own death sooner rather than later, but it equally suggests that Lurie may be giving up, symbolically, on the 'withered' life he has lived and loved. 'Giving [the dog] up' involves, in his own eyes, accepting that the time 'must come, it cannot be evaded' when this animal's life must come to an end. He has been eloquent on that theme all along, of course, but not in the mode of sympathy—not with the tender concern for another creature's living and dying evidenced in how he thinks through the death to come: 'he will have to bring him to [the] operating room (perhaps he will carry him in his arms, perhaps he will do that for him) and caress him and brush back the fur so that the needle can find the vein, and whisper to him and support him in the moment when, bewilderingly, his legs buckle [...]' (219). There is an intense act of identification in the word 'bewilderingly' here. It seems to me finally undecidable, how much self-regard is in it, also—and not at all to Lurie's discredit if there is a large component. The odd straining of Christian symbolism (a dog going, 'like a lamb', to the slaughter) should be a quiet warning against pressing his new sense of a shared animal condition towards a full-blown, self-effacing Christian martyrdom. Quieter still, and as important to the power of these last pages, is the departure of the language of old age, other than as Lurie's age continues to register by comparison with the dog's youth. In place of the rhetoric of old age is a language of endurance, which asks us to think not about ageing as a movement towards death, but about the human ability to go on living and suffering, in the knowledge that the end is inevitable: '*It gets harder all the time* [...] Harder, yet easier too. One gets used to things getting harder; one ceases to be surprised that what used to be as hard as hard can be grows harder yet. [...] But a time must come' (219). This is not, finally, Bernard Williams's sense that old age and decline may make our dying more acceptable to us than it would otherwise be. That sense has certainly been there in Lurie's pre-emptive sense of his age and decline until this point, but the major proof of how far he has changed is that, at the novel's conclusion, that rhetoric is let go.

Another novel about professor–student relations; another professor who prides himself on being an arbiter of cultural taste and defender of literary values, and who sees no good reason to restrain his desire to bed the more attractive of his female undergraduates—although, unlike David Lurie, David Kepesh pays careful attention to the letter of the university regulations. Not until the last paper is in and graded does he allow the teaching relation to become a sexual one. Philip Roth's *The Dying Animal* is a novel about ageing and, more explicitly than *Disgrace*, a millennial novel, its crisis taking place on 31 December 1999 as the television set in Kepesh's living room relays images of the celebrations taking place around the world. With him is one of his former student lovers, Consuela, a woman 38 years his junior. He was 62 when he first seduced her, she 24—though seduction is, emphatically, not his preferred term: 'The French art of being flirtatious is of no interest to me. The savage urge is. No, this is not seduction. This is comedy. [...] it's the radical inappropriateness that makes lust *lust*.'[25]

At the time of narration Kepesh is 70 and more than ever conscious that age will soon put such adventures out of his reach; Consuela is 32, and has just reappeared after an absence of eight years in which he suffered (almost unprecedentedly) from jealousy: an 'agitation that could have destroyed me' (113). Above all, she had 'the most beautiful breasts I've ever seen' (29). Much of *The Dying Animal* is a paean to the sexual liberation inaugurated by the 1960s, and which Kepesh intends to pursue into old age—but unlike most of Roth's recent work this is a slim novel, structured around one wrenching reversal of expectations. On the eve of the millennium Consuela has come to tell Kepesh that she has breast cancer and at best a 60 per cent chance of survival. With her arrival on his doorstep, already ravaged by chemotherapy and about to undergo a partial mastectomy, he is spun off his platform as tutelary seducer, obliged to concede that she, not he, may have the prior claim on the title of the novel: 'She, in fact, has overtaken me. Because I can still tell myself, "I'm not going to die in five years, maybe not in ten years, I'm fit, I'm well, I could even live another twenty," while she ...' (148).

Some reviewers of *The Dying Animal* have predictably found much to dislike here, accusing Roth of a failure to allow women fully to own their desire, and an unwillingness to think through the evidence that the sexual revolution has not distributed its rewards equally (it's an all too familiar knee-jerk reaction against Roth, and one he seems to have found galvanizing, as well as an irritant[26]). Kepesh in 1999 still has the seigneurially didactic way with his much younger lovers, his unnamed listener, and us that characterized him in the earlier novels, *The Breast* (1973), *The Professor of Desire* (1977), and *The Prague Orgy* (1985). Here: 'I am becoming a bit technical, but this is important' (103); 'The pubic hair is important because it returns' (28); 'And the aesthetic response to beauty alive is what, class? Desire. Yes' (46). Kepesh is incorrigible. Roth is incorrigible. But that, of course, is the point of the comedy and, on Kepesh's part, the self-parody.

The more astute of Roth's critics have been all too aware that objections on the grounds of sexism are naive. As one put it, Roth may not always be 'easy to pin down in these matters; but in this instance it is safe to say that he is wise to the piggishness of his man. […] The writer is never to be confused with his creations, of course. Roth has entrained in his readers a dread of being caught in that solecism'.[27]

Kepesh is plainly not Roth. His son Kenny, whose role in the novel is, apparently, to expose those aspects of Kepesh that his sexual vanity conceals, informs us that he is 'the very picture of a pathetic old fool. The long white pageboy of important hair, the turkey wattle half hidden behind the fancy foulard—when will you begin to rouge your cheeks, Herr von Aschenbach?' (89). On the other hand, Kenny is a biased witness, and, if Kepesh is at all to be believed, a prig and a hypocrite, ferociously quick to criticize his father for leaving the family home even as he is doing the same thing himself. Kepesh has no false illusions about his domestic virtues:

> Me and the sixties? […] I was determined, once I saw the disorder for what it was, to seize from the moment a rationale for myself, to undo my former allegiances and my current allegiances and not to do it on the side, not to be, as many my age were, either inferior to it or superior to it or simply titillated by it, but to follow the logic of this revolution to its conclusion, and without having become its casualty.   (62–3)

'I knew I could take only myself over the wall' (76).

What is one to say in response to so pre-emptive a narrator? In the course of his *Experience: A Memoir* (2000), Martin Amis offers a disarming (and disarmed) anecdote from his father's old age, in which Kingsley, paralytic with drink, collapsed in the middle of a traffic island on the Edgware Road in London, so helplessly incapacitated, and so physically vast, that his son was unable to move him. 'Dad, you're too old for this shit, I might have said to him. But why bother? Do you think he didn't know?'[28] Roth and Kepesh between them induce the same sense of wrongfootedness in the reader who feels the urge to take them to task. 'They should know better?' They do. 'You are too old for this shit'? Isn't that Kenny-speak for 'I don't want to have to deal with this shit? I don't want to have to think that there might be some of it in me.'

David Kepesh, unlike David Lurie, does not use old age as an excuse for 'premature' disengagement from a world he finds inhospitable to his values and interests. On the contrary, he is incurably dedicated to the world, the flesh, and what Kingsley Amis would cheerfully have called the devil. For Lurie, old age promised the gradual waning of sexual desire. For Kepesh, age and desire are farcically but inextricably twinned. So, where Lurie invoked Yeats's 'Sailing to Byzantium' to express a sense of his own superfluousness—'No country, this, for old men' (190)—Kepesh taps into the fiercer emotions that same poem expresses, and finds no Yeatsian transcendence in art: '"Consume my heart away; sick with desire | And fastened to a dying animal | It knows not what it is." Yeats. Yes, "Caught in that sensual music," and so on.' | | I played Beethoven and I masturbated' (102).

On the political front too, Kepesh puts himself forward as the most committed of all his contemporaries: the one still conscious revolutionary among all the sexual opportunists he knew in the 1960s, set apart even then by his age. 'People fifteen, twenty years younger than I, the privileged beneficiaries of the revolution, could afford to go through it unconsciously. [...] I had to think' (64). This devotion to the 'raucous repudiation, th[e] wholesale wrecking of the inhibitive past' (64) continues in old age, with an added claim to virtue. Age, according to Kepesh, brings with it unprecedented clarity of insight about oneself. So, where David Lurie presented ageing as an impediment to change, Kepesh sees in it a coming to remorseless acuity about change.

> It is, interestingly, the first time of life that you stand entirely outside of while you're in it. Observing one's decay all the while (if one is as fortunate, as I am), one has, by virtue of one's continuing vitality, considerable distance from one's decay—even feels oneself jauntily independent of it. [...] you stand outside. And the ferocity of the objectivity is brutal. (35)

Just a few paragraphs before this passage he has described sex in almost the same terms: sex is 'brutish', 'the forthright, incisive, elemental response'. (The echo of Hobbes on the state of nature is surely deliberate.) But in sex it is the ferocity of the other's response that matters—the desired ferocity of Consuela's response, to be precise, when Kepesh first claims, by fucking her hard in the mouth, to have broken through her well-bred self-control and 'freed her from her own surveillance' (31); in old age, by contrast, the ferocity lies in one's own attitude to oneself. Age offers a brutal self-directed objectivity, sex a more intimately brutish dismantling of the other's objectivity—and if Kepesh does that to Consuela, she does it still more emphatically to him from the moment he realizes that she

may be with him not because she desires him but because she desires to
be desired. Sex, one might then assume, one might hope even, frees the
old from a charmless self-scrutiny. Sex is 'the revenge on death', Kepesh
would have us believe (69); but it cannot undo ageing or prevent mortality.
What Kepesh gains (until Consuela's return) is not freedom but a fierce
objectivity about his own failure of objectivity, his own failure to give in
gracefully to old age. It is a kind of double-take on himself expressed less
as David Lurie's terrible irony and more as painful farce.

The collapse of this compromised objectivity, and with it the novel's
comic mode, matters not just for the novel's portrayal of eroticism and
ageing but for its thinking about mortality against the backdrop of the end
of the twentieth century. When Kepesh sits cradling Consuela in front
of the television on the eve of the millennium, they see a celebratory
wiping out of the last century of history and the collective embracing of
a new era from which, for different reasons, each of them may soon be
excluded.

> We watched the New Year coming in around the world, the mass hysteria of
> no significance that was the millennial New Year's Eve celebration. Brilliance
> flaring across the time zones, and none ignited by bin Laden. Light whirling
> over nighttime London more spectacular than anything since the splendors
> of colored smoke billowed up from the Blitz. And the Eiffel Tower shooting
> fire, a facsimile flame-throwing weapon such as Wernher von Braun might
> have designed for Hitler's annihilating arsenal [...] All evening long, on
> networks everywhere, the mockery of the Armageddon that we'd been
> awaiting in our backyard shelters since August 6, 1945. How could it not
> happen? Even on that very night, especially on that night, people anticipating
> the worst as though the evening were one long air-raid drill. The wait for
> the chain of horrendous Hiroshimas to link in synchronized destruction the
> abiding civilizations of the world. It's now or never. And it never came.
>
> Maybe that's what everyone was celebrating—that it hadn't come, never
> came, that the disaster of the end will now never arrive.   (144–5)

In Kepesh's—and at this point, one suspects, Roth's—disenchanted view
the millennium festivities turn history into parody. The violent confronta-
tions that shaped twentieth-century history are remembered, but robbed of
their reality. Here the fires of the Blitz are re-enacted as harmless 'splendors
of coloured smoke', Hitler's imagined arsenal becomes a show for the Paris
crowds. If the millennial doom-mongers had been right, this would have
been the moment at which the violence of Hiroshima came back to haunt
humanity on a global scale, but when the 'now or never' of 31 December

1999 passes without event, it appears that the West has been let off the consequences of its past, allowed to go scot free.

Not so Consuela, of course. Her 'revealed mortality' becomes Roth's rebuke both to this post-modern denial of history and to Kepesh's claim up till this point to 'jaunty independence' of his own 'decay'. The scenes from London and Paris are followed by the greatest affront of all to Consuela's sudden, unwanted knowledge that mortality is a necessity, and the future limited: the television coverage of the millennium shifts unexpectedly to a Havana night-club where a thousand tourists are corralled for 'an embalmed police-state embodiment of the Caribbean hot stuff that used to draw the big spenders in the days of the Mob. [...] The showgirls look like leggy Latino West Village transvestites walking around in a huff. [...] "My God," Consuela said, and she began to cry: "This," she said, and so angrily, "*this* is what he gives the world. This is what he shows them on New Year's Eve"' (146–7). While the rest of the 'civilized' world celebrates images of the old order of things successfully defended, as if the threat had never been real, Castro the revolutionary offers a camped-up mockery of their supposed security in the face of history. Or so Kepesh meditates: 'There are any number of things for Castro to choose from, any number of old-fashioned socialist-realism tableaux: a celebration at a sugar-plantation, in a maternity ward, at a cigar factory. Happy Cuban workers smoking, happy Cuban newborns nursing', but he has opted instead for the role of the parodist.

For Kepesh to be, symbolically if not politically, on the side of Castro, the great instigator of change, would make a great deal of sense, given Kepesh's dedication to 'the wholesale wrecking of the past' and his identification of himself till now as one of the few serious revolutionaries still around; but any such reading becomes unsustainable with Consuela's emergence as the emotional centre of the novel. Kepesh records without rebuke the deep and hopeless longing she has inherited from her parents and grandparents to return to the old Cuba. Hers is the history left behind by Castro's revolution, but Kepesh is not feminist enough to draw the conclusion, offered by analogy, that she has been left behind by *his* revolution—and surely not socialist enough to be suggesting an equivalent to Lurie's view of the absence of a political future for himself, in which Consuela must change or die because the Cuba of the twenty-first century has no place for her. Her background as 'the daughter of wealthy Cuban émigrés, rich people who'd fled the revolution' (11) may be one of disgrace seen through

Cuban revolutionary eyes, but not through Kepesh's American eyes. Not least, she had until now the presumption of a future.

In fact, Kepesh is tellingly unsure how far to credit Castro with knowing what he is doing. Is this display brilliant or stupid? a pointed satire on capitalism or unconscious self-satire by a revolutionary, a few years older than Kepesh, who has finally lost it? '[I]s Castro so out of touch?' (147). Is Kepesh? The kind of pressure that may be placed on the individual's understanding of the necessity or otherwise of their own end by historical and political circumstance is, consequently, elusive in *The Dying Animal*. At one level, Roth is clearly inviting a comparison between the end of twentieth-century history and his protagonist's old age and decline. But Roth is no more of a crude allegorist than Coetzee, and the point of that comparison is never simple—primarily because Kepesh's identification of himself as a revolutionary is so evidently and limitingly self-serving. What is wanted, Kepesh remarks glibly at one point, is 'lucidity about the misery made ordinary by our era' (145)—but what is to be done with such lucidity? And where does it stop? Does the misery include those ordinary unhappinesses generated not 'just' by the wars and revolutions of the twentieth century but (surely non-equivalently) by the sexual revolution, that sweeping aside of the 'inhibitive past' which *The Dying Animal* has hitherto celebrated as determinedly and as superficially as the rest of the world celebrates the passing of the twentieth century?

The identification of the end of a particular political or historical dispensation (the 1960s social and sexual 'revolutions') with the revealed mortality of individuals frays wherever one presses at it in *The Dying Animal*—which is not the criticism of Roth that it may sound. One of the consequences of Kepesh's devotion to the dying animal (both himself and Consuela) is that the undue pressure built into any analogy between an individual life, and the historical circumstances under which that life is lived, comes more obviously to the surface than in *Disgrace*, where it remains predominantly contained by the ironically self-Romanticizing idiom of David Lurie. The close of Roth's novel is as ambiguous as that of *Disgrace*, but tonally less controlled—frantic, indeed. The novel ends with David Kepesh, ten weeks into the new millennium, breaking off his narrative to take a phone call from Consuela. It is night, she is in hospital and has just been told that she must have a radical not a partial mastectomy the next day. Panic-stricken, she has asked him to come to the hospital and sleep beside her. At this point, Kepesh turns to address his unnamed listener and us, with what reads as a direct challenge:

> You? Stay if you wish. If you want to stay, if you want to leave … Look, there's no time, I must run!
>   'Don't.'
>   What?
>   'Don't go.'
>   But I must. Someone has to be with her.
>   'She'll find someone.'
>   She's in terror. I'm going.
>   'Think about it. Think. Because if you go, you're finished.'   (156)

The exchange loads the end of the novel with a sense of philosophical import, but, as at the close of *Disgrace*, there is some doubt about how we should read it. Is the unnamed listener finally urging a good hard look at death: 'Think about your own mortality. If you die, you're finished'—a brutal facing up to the inevitable which matches David Kepesh's earlier sense of the fierce objectivity of old age? Or does that final line express, as situationally it might, the listener's and our own ventriloquized resistance to Kepesh's sudden loss of objectivity, his internalization of the necessity of mortality: 'Think about it. Don't commit yourself to anything or anyone from your past, because if you do your future freedom of action is at an end'? The former is the more immediate reading, but the second is more plausible in the wider context.

In either case, the residual uncertainty fits with *The Dying Animal*'s conviction that old age and decline are not after all contingencies but necessities we cannot go on remaining unconscious of, even though we spend most of our lives doing everything we can to avoid confronting them directly. 'Obtuseness is de rigueur', Kepesh says at one point—until one grows old (35). This is close to but not the same as Coetzee's geographically specific claim that 'old age and decline' offer a psychological, and perhaps moral, vocabulary for relinquishing and at the same time defending the integrity of our lives. For Roth what is at stake is not the loss of the past, but the failure of a preferential version of the future in which one's own freedom was the overriding object. When the 'revolutionary' logic dictating 'eradication of the past' in the name of the future becomes unsustainable, the only course open will be to commit oneself to a version of selfhood in which one will have had too much of oneself before very long. Only when that knowledge comes home to us as feeling, Roth suggests, with his own version of Romanticism, do we truly apprehend the necessity of our own deaths. Only when the theoretical possibility of change becomes the felt necessity of change, and the contingency of mortality the felt necessity of mortality, does history cease to be mere rhetoric or image and become real lives, real deaths.

The fact that bin Laden subsequently made his mark on the new millennium after all would presumably not lead Roth to want to alter his conclusion. 11 September 2001 was, by many accounts, an inevitable end to obuseness. Of course, one then wants to protest—and loudly—that the mortalities generated by history are not necessities, not in the same way that our individual deaths will eventually be. And if obtuseness helps us to get through our personal lives, it is of less certain help to us, and no virtue, in our political lives. But this, too, Roth and even David Kepesh, at the very end, know. In *The Dying Animal* the reality of another loved person's impending death does not force one to accept the necessity of one's own death, but it does make one's own going on living seem suddenly too much—more than is necessary, more even than is wanted. 'The traumatic moment was upon us', says Kepesh, looking at what chemotherapy has done to Consuela's hair, 'when the change occurs, when you discover that the other person's expectations can no longer resemble yours and that no matter how appropriately you may be acting and you may continue to act, he or she will leave before you do—if you're lucky, well before' (154–5). That bitterly ironic inversion of the word 'luck'—unwilling assent to Williams's view, as it were—is where the comedy of *The Dying Animal* finally gives way to tragic necessity.

Disgrace and the *Dying Animal* enable us to extend Williams's reflections on ageing and decline in certain important ways. They show it to be not just an objective condition, but also, and sometimes primarily, a subjective one. There is a biological component to the experience of old age and decline in both novels—a clearer one on the part of Kepesh than on that of Lurie, whose early claim to ageing may appear spurious to others. In neither is biological age itself decisive for the protagonist's acceptance that his life is approaching a necessary end. His identification with the values of a particular culture is important; so are relations with family, friends, lovers; so, to an only slightly lesser degree, is the pursuit of a profession. For each of them there comes a point when a change in those circumstances gives rise to a choice: between submitting to change so significant that his life and himself will no longer be recognizable to him as his life and himself, and accepting that life and self must have an end, sooner rather than later.

Thinking of oneself as old and in decline may, they show, be a way of representing to oneself and (secondarily) to others the loss of the felt value and sustainability of the life one has had and the person one understands oneself to be. There is no suggestion that the perception has direct instrumental force, or even that it is conscious: neither of these novels is melodramatic enough to present the acceptance of mortality as producing death. The adjustment to mortality is psychological and to a degree rational. It has to do with, as Williams put it, a perceived increase in the reasons 'for thinking death a good thing': an increase expressed through, and assisted but not determined by, the experience of 'old age and decline'.

Coetzee and Roth thus also extend Williams's reflections on immortality by showing that 'boredom' is not the only reason we could have not to want to live forever. Other reasons would be the loss of a familiar environment (social, political, geographical); loss of the individual human relations important to one; loss of an audience for one's ideas. None of these entails boredom as such. As far as these reasons to want to go on living are concerned, boredom would kick in only in a fantasy scenario where they were retained indefinitely—and even Čapek and Janáček did not imagine that degree of stasis for Elina Makropulos.

Roth and Coetzee suggest one final and important addition to Williams on the part old age and decline may play in making our dying tolerable to us. Both these novels are centrally about the difficulty of a sufficient imaginative identification with others, less fortunate in the expected duration and the happiness of their lives, that would constitute a right response to human mortality throughout our lives. (This is not a correction to Williams, it is simply outside the purview of his essay.) In Roth's novel especially, accepting (which does not mean welcoming) the necessity of one's own death is a response to feeling deeply the *non*-necessity of the death of another—a premature death by comparison with one's own length of life. In Coetzee's novel, the gap between Lurie's privileged sense of having lived past his prime and the comparatively low life expectancy of those around him remains an irony never clearly accessed by Lurie himself.

A strength of both novels is that they do not close that perception down into a sentimental assertion that the appropriate response to the less good fortune of others is to accept one's own mortality gracefully. In each of them the categorical desire to go on living is not readily relinquished, even under the most pressing external circumstances. If it were not so, it would not be a categorical desire. Coming into step with the necessity of dying, they both suggest, is something that most of us do, if we do it at all, as late as possible. And from that perspective, yes, old age and decline may be the only conditions under which many of us shall find it tolerable. If we are lucky.

8

Evolved Senescence

All the philosophical writings discussed thus far in this book are, at the simplest level, trying to answer one question: What are the philosophical implications (in turn moral, rational, metaphysical) of the fact that the human animal grows old—that with time, after maturity, a human being's physical and mental capacities deteriorate? The causes of the deterioration lie in biology; the means of alleviating or postponing some of the effects, but not yet—and probably not ever—of preventing senescence altogether, increasingly seem to lie in science. But what contribution can science itself make to a philosophical understanding of ageing? As many writers have observed, Aristotle thought that he could rely on known scientific descriptions of 'human nature' as the basis for his ethics. The ethical demands and aspirations placed on human beings had to be consistent with what human beings are 'by nature'. But our understanding of nature is radically different from Aristotle's, and what kind of assistance (if any) contemporary biology can give to ethics is a major problem in philosophy today. As with other questions we might ask about the 'nature of human life', science's distinctive philosophical contribution to the understanding of ageing is epistemological: it offers to explain—most fundamentally through evolutionary theory—why and how human beings age (or, to use the more precise scientific term, how they senesce). In asking what scientific naturalism can contribute today to a philosophy of ageing, I start from the assumption—many will want to disagree with it—that, as with evolutionary theory generally, there is very limited, if any, justification for moving from statements of biology to claims about morality.

Some glossing of the room for disagreement is necessary. Evolutionary ethics asks whether we can base an account of morality on a post-Darwinian scientific description of how, as human animals, we behave, or think or feel we ought to behave. For an evolutionary naturalist the answer will be yes, but for probably the majority of moral philosophers evolutionary science is the major reason we have to depart from, or seriously revise, naturalism (the view that there is, innate in all natural beings, an appropriate, and appropriately moral, way for those beings to act[1]). The post-Darwinian philosopher knows, as Aristotle did not, that we evolve, both as a species, by means of natural selection, and as individuals, not preformed but developing from undifferentiated cells to complex organisms.[2] That we human beings are the dominant species on this planet is a consequence of our evolutionary success, but not one that comes with any guarantees. Evolution itself has no care for human needs or desires, and offers no promise that our special flourishing will continue. (Even statements such as that might mislead if they suggest an agency or principle capable of caring or not caring.) The evolutionary philosopher must, then, relinquish at least three assumptions central to Aristotle's view of nature: teleology, anthropocentrism, and the unchangingness of human biology over (evolutionary) time.

The case against naturalism has been much more fully and ably made by, among others, Janet Radcliffe Richards[3] and Peter G. Woolcock.[4] My own position is one of sceptical realism, as Bernard Williams denoted it, rather than the ethical non-realism associated with the work of Michael Ruse and others. Sceptical realism recognizes that biology produces certain tendencies in and constraints on our actions, but is as sparing as possible in its appeal to morality for explanations of human behaviour; it rejects the Naturalistic Fallacy of deriving 'ought' statements from 'is' statements, but finds that issue of less moment, and less interest, than the logical relation between *ought* and *can*.[5] This by contrast with the fuller-blown scepticism of the non-realist who remains focused on *ought* and *is*, and takes moral claims about what human behaviour ought to be as fictions—albeit sometimes useful and important ones.[6] I am not finally convinced by Ruse's argument that, though our moral claims are demonstrably non-objective, we have an evolved need to believe them objective. Like Woolcock, I assume that morality must finally rely on 'the hard grind of normative justification'.[7] These differences in emphasis and in wider explanatory framework aside, what I have to say about evolutionary theory of senescence and its implications for how we may think morally and rationally about a long life is unlikely to provoke disagreement from evolutionary non-realists.

Evolutionary ethics has a fairly well-established repertoire of topics: sexual behaviour, violence, competitiveness, altruism are all subjects about which it has had much to say. Senescence is not commonly part of that remit, and it is necessary at the outset to be clear about the kind and degree of relevance it can have. It is possible to imagine updating Aristotle's approach to the human lifespan to provide an account of how evolved senescence constrains the behaviour we can expect of the old (for example, their *capacity* for virtuous thought or action; or their *capacity* for sound reasoning). Alternatively we might think to produce a description of evolved constraints on the behaviour of the not yet old towards the old (affecting our notions of honour, respect, and duty). But even if naturalism had not been ruled out, there would be little or no value in such an endeavour. The evolutionary theory of senescence described and discussed here does not substantively alter the information about predictable behaviour that Aristotle worked with: it gives us a better explanation of how and why fitness declines in late life, but (unless used as part of a technology that postpones senescence) it does not change the behaviour we can expect to see from and towards the old.

Aristotle's observation that the ageing process is 'an act neither voluntary nor involuntary' remains true and is still an accurate mark of the dividing line between biology, attending to physiological 'acts' or processes, and ethics, which deals with the moral implications or consequences of behaviour as it occurs within, and is influenced by, culture. Evolutionary science can tell us much about the processes, but it says little if anything that is new about behaviour and does not, in and of itself, offer grounds for a moral response to old age: it does not tell us that ageing is a good or a bad thing; it does not automatically confirm or refute moral arguments about human flourishing; it does not tell us how we should live our own old age and/or treat others who are old.[8] Nor is there much ground for arguing that our broader moral intuitions about old age are themselves evolved characteristics. In so far as we have moral intuitions about it, they would seem to be covered by our more general intuitions, many of which appear to be culturally specific—the intuition, for example, that we have obligations to earlier generations and especially to our parents; or that abusing the weak is wrong; or that we should require less of those whose mental or physical capacities have been damaged; or that it is better to be reconciled than not to the inevitable drawing towards an end of a life.

As we shall see, the challenges evolutionary theory of senescence presents for ethics lie elsewhere, and were not envisaged by Aristotle or by any of the other schools of thought discussed hitherto. They are, first, conceptual, having to do with the ways in which we can think about old age in relation to the earlier stages of a life. Evolutionary theory tells us that some aspects of physical and mental decline in fitness over time may be the longer-term outcome of the same processes that have protected our ability to flourish in our youth and reproductive maturity: *not* flourishing in old age may be a consequence of—some theorists think *underwrites*—our flourishing earlier on. But evolutionary theory also tells us that the signs and symptoms of old age are mostly non-adaptive and, in that sense, singularly non-purposive. Moreover, all the evidence from cell biology, physiology, and ethology to date indicates that the ageing process is peculiarly 'plastic':[9] dependent upon numerous factors and by no means simply programmed into our genes (nothing is 'simply' programmed into our genes). Though there is a significant evolved genetic component to senescence, environment, diet, and stress are all known to have a major impact on rates and phenotypic profiles of senescence.

Evolutionary theory does, however, give us cause to think again about the scope of some of the philosophical accounts of old age discussed in earlier chapters, and the rational defensibility of others. It raises the possibility, though as yet a very slim one, that serious investment of financial and intellectual resources in biological research may, in time, enable us to reduce and even eradicate many of the ills of old age. It thus suggests a wider remit in the future for the ethical questions about distribution of social resources and planning of lives that were the subject of Ch. 4, though I shall not be revisiting that debate here. But recent evolutionary theory also predicts something not conceived of by any of the philosophers or literary writers in this book: namely, that in many animals, including humans, senescence is not an ongoing deteriorative process but a transition to a biologically 'immortal' phase (that is, a phase of 'late life' in which mortality rates are stable). This theory is at such an early stage that any philosophical conclusions from it would be grossly premature—but it does give us cause to modify some of the assumptions hitherto made about old age and check others. And it gives us, as we shall see, some additional, as yet tentative reasons to think again about the structure of lives, and about what it means to think of late life as a chronological end.

It needs to be said, at the outset, that the evolutionary theory of senescence is a rapidly evolving field. There have been several important developments during the period in which this chapter was written and revised (autumn 2004 to summer 2005), and there will no doubt have been more by the time it reaches publication. At the time of going to press there is broad agreement on many of the main lines of explanation, but lively debate and sometimes heated controversy about others. My conclusions are only as good as my understanding of the theory, and finally only as good as the theory itself, but where justified divisions of opinion exist I have tried to allow for subsequent verification of either side.

If this chapter were concerned with evolutionary science as it has been understood historically there would be no difficulty in drawing literature into debate with biological theory. Literary depictions of old age from the 1860s onwards often involved creative responses to Darwinian evolutionary theory and later subsidiary theories of 'organic memory' (unconscious, hereditary memory stored in the organism and exhibited as instinctual or otherwise atavistic behaviour).[10] Suzanne Raitt has shown that *The Picture of Dorian Gray* (1890) (Oscar Wilde's fantasy of arrested ageing by means of artistic replication of the body) and Freud's account of the death-drive in *Beyond the Pleasure Principle* (1920) both have connections with turn-of-the-twentieth-century research by August Weismann, Émile Maupas, and others into the possible 'immortality' of certain kinds of cell culture.[11] I have found no late twentieth- or early twenty-first-century literary writing that is comparably informed about contemporary evolutionary theory of senescence. One might expect science fiction to be ahead of the game, and there are indeed a few (a very few) novels in that genre trying to marry science fiction's long-established interest in immortality or extreme longevity stories with recent findings in biology. But even some of the best informed have a surprisingly persistent tendency towards ethical naturalism.

Take, for example, Greg Bear's *Vitals* (2002) which stands out among recent science fiction for its accurate knowledge of the biology of senescence up to *c*.2000. At a point of high narrative tension, Bear's protagonist, a cellular biologist specializing in senescence, comes face to face with the first trial candidate for an immortality procedure developed in Russia in the 1930s. Mrs Golokhova, also known as 'the Caretaker' (an allusion, I assume, to the 'caretaker genes' or proteins which protect the genome from damage or mutation), now runs her husband's secret laboratory in the heart of Manhattan:

> Out of the corner of my eye, I saw a little gray wisp emerge from the dark between the tanks. It walked with a quick, shuffling step along the platform. I craned my neck. At first I thought it was an old man, head small and wrinkled, eyes large, frame shrunken, walking along the upper ramp, skirting the aquariums. But something about the way the wisp moved, a sway of the shoulders with each step, made me think again about its sex. [...]
>
> She smelled like wine left in a glass after a party.
>
> [Some pages later:] A body lay in the white-enamel tub, curled in a frail, angular tangle of arms and legs. The wizened face appeared to float, like a lolling puppet's, above one end of an ill-fitting, calf-length black dress. Wide milky eyes stared up at the tiled ceiling with a squirrel-monkey expression of disappointment and surprise. [...] She was supposed to live forever. Perhaps her husband had promised her that much as a reward for being a guinea pig, for years of madness.
>
> [...] 'I'd like tissue samples from her,' I [said].   (Greg Bear, *Vitals* (2002))[12]

Behind Mrs Golokhova stands a long line of failed literary immortals, including H. Rider Haggard's Ayesha or 'She Who Must be Obeyed' (*She*, 1887), Aldous Huxley's Fifth Earl of Gonister (*After Many a Summer*, 1939), and numerous film and television derivatives. At the moment of truth in these narratives, as the immortality dream goes into reverse or is revealed to have gone badly wrong, the evolutionary paradigm starts to serve a blunt moral purpose. Men or women who have sought to evolve beyond senescence and death are returned, in the case of Haggard's novel at grotesquely accelerated speed, to the animal condition they hoped to escape: a baboon in *She*, a neontic ape in *After Many a Summer*, and for Bear a 'squirrel-monkey'—a distinctively simian 'guinea-pig'. It is debatable how much explanatory force the evolutionary paradigm can wield when Nature is given a punitive moral agency so entirely at odds with evolutionary theory. Bear's novel ends with humanity facing all-out war from the ancient bacterial colonies (stromatolites) which have enabled the scientist Golokhov to reprogramme gut bacteria, turning back the biological clock in chosen individuals, and making the whole of humanity receptive to new mind-altering genes. The stromatolites 'are not happy', Golokhov warns in the last pages: 'They are not happy with us at all. *We are a bitter disappointment to them*' (384).

This is a licensed joke in science fiction—a freedom flamboyantly taken with science. Bear's novel is much more inventive with the cellular biology of senescence than most novels; it is also reasonably frank about the super-imposition of an ethical on a scientific plot. But this aesthetic/moral/comic play with naturalism limits the interest of these anti-immortality stories for a literary-philosophical discussion of evolutionary theory.[13]

Behind every modern evolutionary anti-longevity plot there of course stands one commanding pre-evolutionary influence: Swift's *Gulliver's Travels* (1726), and the differences between it and more recent developments of the genre are instructive with regard to contemporary fiction and the evolutionary science of senescence. This is Swift on the Struldbruggs:

> At Ninety they lose their Teeth and Hair; they have at that Age no Distinction of Taste, but eat and drink whatever they can get, without Relish or Appetite. The Diseases they were subject to, still continue without encreasing or diminishing. In talking they forget the common Appellation of Things, and the Names of Persons, even of those who are their nearest Friends and Relations. For the same Reason they never can amuse themselves with reading, because their Memory will not serve to carry them from the Beginning of a Sentence to the End; and by this Defect they are deprived of the only Entertainment whereof they might otherwise be capable.
>
> The Language of this Country being always upon the Flux, the Struld-bruggs of one Age do not understand those of another; neither are they able after two Hundred Years to hold any Conversation (farther than by a few general Words) with their Neighbours the Mortals; and thus they lye under the Disadvantage of living like Foreigners in their own Country.   (272–3)

Swift had scientific targets of his own in view (the Struldbruggs are a satire on optimist reports of human longevity submitted to the Royal Society of London[14]) but he did not envisage science *producing* immortality. His Immortals are discovered, not made, and (like Tithonus and the Cumean Sybil of classical mythology) they age according to the normal tempo of human senescence. At 200 years or so they appear to reach a plateau of decrepitude. Science plays little part here. A ship's surgeon and amateur philosopher, Gulliver observes the Struldbruggs but does not intervene. There is no thought of taking tissue samples from them, no attempt at a mathematical analysis of their 'luck'—which is emphatically all it is. (Either thought would of course be anachronistic.)

Swift set the ethical perspective for subsequent fictional experiments with extended longevity: his strongly naturalistic and Christian reflex against living longer than our current span carries on into later works, and is often yoked to a naive Gulliver-like narrator who is at first delighted by the notion of avoiding death, then repelled by the reality. No subsequent work puts its finger as squarely on the moral and psychological questions raised by wanting to live forever: would individual identity be sustainable over the long historical *durée*? If not, how far could we go, as Bernard Williams put it, without ceasing to be, recognizably, ourselves? (See Ch. 5.)

Swift's answers were all restrictive: neither the body nor the psyche, as he saw it, can sustain itself meaningfully over much more than our given lifespan. For at least one recent philosopher, *Gulliver's Travels* thereby set a pattern in which modern science fiction has characteristically failed to imagine immortality as fully or seriously as it might. In *How to Live Forever: Science Fiction and Philosophy* (1995), Stephen R. L. Clark asks why it is that science fiction—which of all literary genres has thought hardest about the philosophical implications of eluding ageing and death—should have been so unwilling to give the idea scope.[15] Noting that Swift identified a 'serious problem' for the solitary immortal, in that he or she 'will always be losing friends, homes, civilizations', even language, he argues that this last failing is one 'we can perhaps think away': we could expect, if not infinite capacity, certainly more from our intelligence and curiosity than Swift did. And why assume a boringly finite world?[16] Clark is resourceful in suggesting conceptual routes beyond the standard limits, but can fiction really do more than gesture towards an infinite world or worlds? The novel as we know it is a finite form, limited by (amongst other things) the technology of print and (now) computer software, and the mind of its author or authors. If enough time passes, continuation of efforts to do immortality literary justice will require not only linguistic translation, as Swift foresaw, but more and more abbreviated or attenuated connection with past works in the series (in the generous world of e-composition, more and more hyper-links).

Modern science fiction's tendency to treat senescence as a technical challenge (something to be got around inventively) marks out a fundamental difference from Swift's fantasy. The portrait of the Struldbruggs is, first and foremost, moral: by retaining senescence alongside longevity it focuses on the link between a long life and a good life—the ability, or inability, to abide by—or after a certain point even to possess—virtues, values, and reason. By contrast, recent fiction's imagining of a science that could deliver ageless longevity and even immortality has not been accompanied by an equivalent interest in the possible ethical implications. In anti-mortality and anti-ageing narratives, the naturalistic message that we should not look to interfere too fundamentally with the ageing process is undoubtedly moral but crudely so, relegating to a much lower priority those other ethical questions which for Swift were primary: Why might we want to live forever? What difference in the quality of a life might be made possible by the extension of that life? How far is old age shaped by culture? How much of the behaviour of the old (and not just the old) is attributable to biology, how much to language, culture, and thought?

For Bernard Williams, this last question—*the representation problem*, as he called it—posed an enormous problem for human evolutionary ethics. 'Virtually no behavioural tendency which constitutes genuine action can just show up in a cultural context "as itself"', he remarked.[17] Taking that caution seriously, I do not pursue further here the more speculative perspectives on current biology of senescence offered by science fiction, but stay with what is known or credibly theorized. I begin with the science itself, discussing it first as science, then as rhetoric and then, relatedly, in its potential implications for ethics. I end with one recent literary work in which the question of how we should respond to science's improved understanding of the genetic mechanisms of senescence is put under close scrutiny. Michael Ignatieff's *Scar Tissue* (1992), at once memoir and novel, is an account of a mother's decline into and death from Alzheimer's-related dementia. It draws the ideas examined here into more personalized terrain, to reflect on how we can or should live with biology's ever-advancing ability to predict our individual old ages for us—without, as yet, saving us from most of the worst of them. It is also, explicitly, a meditation on both literature and philosophy in relation to science, and thus an apt place to finish.

First the science.[18]

Our power to alleviate many of the diseases and deteriorations in function that beset us in old age is an evolved characteristic of our species. It is a good example of why Darwinism should not be equated with determinism: if our biological conditioning does not always fit our needs and purposes as ideally as we wish it to, we are free to try to change it—and have already done so considerably. We have not, however, evolved to the point where we can ameliorate or stop biological senescence altogether. Indeed, by extending life expectancy, modern medicine has given greater room to the expression of diseases and deteriorations of function which would not have manifested themselves had those lives stopped sooner. Alzheimer's, Parkinson's, arthritis, heart disease are all more common in part because fewer individuals die of illness or accident before these pathologies have emerged.[19] This ironic correlation, if we wish to see it that way, between more longevity and more revealed 'unfitness' has been until recently at the core of the evolutionary biology of senescence.

In 1946, the future Nobel laureate Peter Medawar published an essay on 'Old Age and Natural Death'[20] in which he laid the foundations of thinking about the evolutionary theory of senescence for several decades thereafter. Drawing together and expanding on earlier observations by Alfred Russel Wallace, August Weismann, J. B. S. Haldane, and others, he argued that senescence—defined as an inevitable and irreversible deterioration in biological fitness due to age—is the consequence of the declining power of natural selection after reproductive maturity. From that stage onwards, deleterious genetic characteristics will have ever-decreasing impact upon an individual's ability to contribute to the evolutionary process. Increasingly irrelevant to successful continuation of the germ line, they are correspondingly less likely to be selected out.[21] Giving fuller expression to this theory (now known as the mutation accumulation theory) a few years later in a now classic text, *An Unsolved Problem in Biology* (1952), Medawar described old age pithily as a genetic 'dustbin'.[22] Because natural selection's effect on the organism becomes weaker with time—indeed, 'vanishingly small'[23]—old age, he argued, is in effect a biological dumping ground for unfavourable genetic effects.

Direct selection all but ceases, but indirect selection, as Medawar noted, continues, albeit increasingly weakly. George C. Williams argued in 1957 that if adverse genetic effects appear earlier or more strongly in one organ or body system than in others, they will be marginally selected against in favour of those expressed later or less strongly. (Mortality is always selected against, but ever less effectively at ages ever less likely to be reached.) Senescence should therefore 'always be a generalized deterioration, and never due largely to changes in a single system'.[24] Williams also added a refinement to the 'dustbin' theory. In old age, 'antagonistic pleiotropy' can start to show itself: genes that have been advantageous early in life may prove disadvantageous with the passing of time. He gave the hypothetical example of an allele (or gene) which improves calcium take-up being beneficial initially, assisting the development of bone structure, but in later years leading to arteriosclerosis.[25] Subsequent laboratory experiments have discovered an allele in one strain of fruit fly that increases early reproductivity but pleiotropically reduces longevity:[26] another study has indicated a similar genetic basis to Huntington's chorea in humans (though the apparently enhanced early fertility of Huntington's carriers is unproven).[27]

An obvious gap (though not necessarily an error) in Medawar's theory was its silence on the difference between male and female senescence in humans.[28] For women, 'reproductive senescence' occurs long before the deterioration of other body functions. (The only other species for which this is clearly true are some kinds of whale.[29]) However, a midlife reduction in female fecundity is common among mammalian species for which we have enough data.[30] Two theories have been offered to explain this gendered divergence. One holds that female menopause is a product of our evolutionary success in extending the average human lifespan. In primitive societies, where few if any individuals are assumed to have lived beyond reproductive maturity, the notion of menopause simply did not apply. Steven Austad captures the commonsense tenor of this theory ('the dominant one', he suspects, in the medical community): 'women's bodies have been designed by evolution to produce about as many eggs over as long a period as they would ever need to, and menopause is just an incidental by-product of the extra longevity of modern life'.[31] Among anthropologists, however, there is some scepticism about the supposed near-certainty of early death in primitive societies—and scepticism, too, about the accuracy of age attributions to fossilized skeletons. Several cases have been found of indigenous, pretechnological peoples living 'considerably longer than the evidence of the bones suggests they should'.[32] This is a hotly disputed subject.

Female menopause is universal. Why should it have proved more advantageous under natural selection than continued reproduction across the lifespan? A different attempt to answer this problem was put forward by Williams in the same essay. The 'Grandmother Theory' hypothesizes an adaptive advantage to female menopause in that it releases a woman, after a sufficient period of being reproductively active, to care for the next generation of children, thus shifting her energy from child-bearing to raising her own younger children and helping to raise her children's children.[33] The 'Good Mother' variant on this theory (sometimes mistakenly elided with it) disputes the reproductive or survival value of caring for other offspring than one's own (one's genetic interest in one's grandchildren is substantially less than one's genetic interest in one's own offspring), and sees the advantage as lying more nearly at hand in the ability of menopausal and post-menopausal mothers to devote maximum care to their children until fully adult. Both these theories have also been criticized by anthropologists and comparative zoologists.[34] The jury remains out.[35] (Indeed, Williams himself now finds the evidence for adaptive menopause inconclusive.[36])

Medawar and Williams's accounts of senescence provided an evolutionary mechanism for senescence and, as mathematically established by W. D. Hamilton, Brian Charlesworth, and others, a credible explanation for why natural selection should always favour youth over old age, and senescence over potential immortality. To date, however, the supporting evidence from genetics for the mutation accumulation theory has been slight, for antagonistic pleiotropy stronger but 'as yet lacking in details'.[37] The disposable soma theory of ageing, first put forward by Tom Kirkwood in 1979, sought to provide a further rationale that made more direct reference to biological complexity. Senescence, he suggested, is advantageous to complex multicellular organisms, because it allows them to devote less energy to preserving the individual body (or soma), and more to transmitting the germ line as accurately as possible. As Medawar and Williams recognized, even a theoretically immortal individual will die sooner or later from injury: 'might it not be better to save energy and make somatic cells in a more economical way, even if this results in them ageing?' (65). Immortality, then, is sacrificed not just to reproduction per se, but to greater accuracy of reproduction in a species for which accuracy is especially important.[38] Kirkwood at first saw the Disposable Soma Theory as supporting the 'error catastrophe' mechanism of senescence—that is, senescence as the outcome of cumulative errors in cell replication—but later revised it to include antagonistic pleiotropic effects.[39] More accurately, his theory is a special case of antagonistic pleiotropy, which in turn is a special case of the still more general theory now in play.

The cellular biological study of ageing is at present so much in flux (and likely to remain so) that any summary would rapidly be out of date. To take one example, the 'Hayflick Limit', discovered in 1961 (which describes the regulation of cell-replication by means of DNA-protein structures called telomeres that stabilize the ends of linear chromosomes and protect them from damage or fusion[40]) looked for some time as if it might provide a connection between organismal senescence and 'cellular senescence'.[41] That interpretation has now been exploded, and the Hayflick Limit is understood simply as one of the vertebrate body's mechanisms for controlling malignant proliferation—a piece of our chemistry that allows us to live longer. There is ongoing investigation into possible links between cancer control mechanisms and mechanisms controlling senescence. Some of that work makes large claims about its potential to explain human ageing to us,[42] but for anyone interested in what science can reliably say at present to assist philosophical or literary thinking about old age, it is a field best avoided.

There is, however, a recent development in the evolutionary theory of ageing that has provoked excitement and intense argument among those at the cutting edge of scientific debates about senescence. It concerns a growing body of evidence for the stopping of senescence, and for a phase of 'late life', distinct from 'ageing', in which mortality rates become stable rather than (as one might expect) increasing incrementally. There is also strong evidence for the stabilization in late life of reproductive ageing. In other words, with respect to two major components of ageing (mortality rates and fecundity) there occurs something like the plateau-effect that Swift depicted in the Struldbruggs.[43]

'Late life' was first 'definitively observed' in two dipteran species (two-winged insects) in 1992. Data from various laboratories has subsequently suggested that it is generally present among organisms which senesce. There are two main theories that might explain this plateauing: evolutionary theory, based on the force of natural selection; and what is called 'lifelong heterogeneity theory', based on the supposition that differences in individual robustness within a population are sufficient to cause it. To date, theoretical results and experimental findings seem to favour the evolutionary explanation. That explanation rests on W. B. Hamilton's mathematical formula for quantifying the weakening force of natural selection with age. Once reproduction stops, natural selection cannot distinguish fitness differences in survival at different ages. 'Mortality rates do not necessarily have to reach zero, because beneficial genetic effects that are not age-dependent will continue to benefit individuals who remain alive' even though the direct effect of natural selection has become vanishingly small (4–5). Evolutionary theory also predicts correctly that fecundity will be high in early ages, decline rapidly, then plateau at late ages.

In humans, what studies have been done so far indicate that the decline in mortality rates starts above 75 years. Analysis of the American Cancer Society's findings, from a comprehensive epidemiological investigation begun in 1959 of more than one million (mainly middle-class) men and women, showed that the Gompertz model of mortality, often used in actuarial calculations, was not valid above that age. The Gompertz model predicts exponential rises in mortality across the human life course.[44] The ACS study showed that, on the contrary, human mortality declines more slowly at late ages.[45] There are, to the best of my knowledge, no equivalent studies of male human fecundity in late life.

Unlike the theories addressed earlier, 'late life' evolutionary theory does not appeal to the concept of specific physiological trade-offs; nor (unlike the heterogeneity theory) does it rest on the idea of differences in robustness within populations. It is compatible with the mutation accumulation and antagonistic pleiotropic effects discussed earlier, but the mathematical explanation of the phenomenon also puts some emphasis on age-independent effects and *positive* pleiotropy.[46] The fact that mortality plateaux do not occur only at 100 per cent mortality depends on such benefits continuing to operate at late ages.

A great deal more mathematical analysis and experimental testing, and a great deal more biological research, remains to be done, but it seems safe to say that the existence of a 'third phase' of life presents a major avenue for further advances in the evolutionary theory not only of why ageing happens, but of why ageing also stops. Any broader philosophical conclusions would be greatly premature. Late life evolutionary theory is a *general* theory in the strict sense of the term. It makes no claim to predict individual or even large group patterns of ageing. It does, however, suggest one important change to how we standardly think about old age in human lives: it gives us reasons to defend the idea that late life should be described as a stage or phase of life, not an ever more precipitous slope of decline. Collectively, and on average, we are not racing ever faster towards death, though psychologically that is most people's experience;[47] biologically, at least, we are for the first time in our lives fairly stable.

The science is, as science, absorbing enough—but what difference, if any, does it make to already existing ways of thinking about what it means to age physically, or to be a member of a species that experiences senescence? For a start, many of the theoretical premises currently in play for evolutionary biologists substantially complicate the challenges biology posed for Aristotelian naturalism. We now have an understanding of biological senescence that strongly underlines the absence of teleology.[48] For Aristotle, old age presented a threat to character, and hence a threat to the capacity to flourish; for the evolutionist, the very existence of old age is evidence that the end of the lifespan matters least in terms of genetic adaptability. So, to the threat of old age eroding character must we now add the idea of senescence as, in Medawar's phrase, a genetic 'dustbin'—the time of our lives when, metaphorically speaking, we are most likely to be dumped on by biology?

Medawar's ear-catching metaphor is an apt illustration of how —unfortunately—statements that seem to encourage an inherently evaluative or even ethically driven aspect to nature can enter through the rhetoric of science. In theory, the rhetoric of evolutionary biology should be free of any implication of agency in nature; in practice, agency tends to creep in—and it takes constant vigilance with one's prose to exclude it. Figurative language can be a creative stimulus in science but it can also at times look more like a necessary evil. Without it there can be very little in the way of explanation; but metaphor and analogy readily become, as Darwin put it, 'presumptuous'.[49] The solution within many areas of science is the mathematical expression of theories—though the move to express biological theories in mathematical language is a fairly recent 'paradigm shift', and not all biological theories can be so expressed. For those who can now operate in that language, Medawar's essays were 'really distraction'.[50] The genetic dustbin metaphor particularly has raised eyebrows over the years (two recent commentators call it 'a moment of figurative zeal').[51] A muted echo can be heard in Kirkwood's naming of the 'Disposable Soma Theory'. But this is not the most significant example of language going beyond explanatory neutrality in the evolutionary literature on senescence, and if it sounds like an invitation to pessimism, it might equally be taken as provocation for science to work harder at reducing the amount and offensiveness of the biological 'rubbish' our species has accumulated on its way to longevity. Thinking about old age as a biological rubbish heap is in practice less deeply entrenched in scientific language, less clearly proven, and less fundamentally ethically directive, than certain other terms.[52]

Potentially more misleading for non-scientists, and for scientists at the point of explaining the theory to those not trained in biology or mathematics, are two terms more deeply embedded in evolutionary theoretical language: 'antagonism' (as in antagonistic pleiotropy) and 'trade-off'. When George Williams introduced the idea that senescence could be partly attributed to 'the natural selection of pleiotropic genes' he did not use the phrase 'antagonistic pleiotropy'. Nor did he use the term 'trade-off'. 'Antagonistic' pleiotropy entered the vocabulary only subsequently through the work of Michael Rose and Brian Charlesworth.[53] 'Trade-off' (with its near synonym 'pay-off'), now a standard term in evolutionary biology, is also of fairly recent origin—an import from the language of economics.[54] Williams's essay employs in its stead the terms 'expense' (as in 'at the expense of') (410) and 'price' ('favoring vigor in youth at the price of vigor later on' (402)), and, importantly, puts cautionary quotation marks around the latter (402).[55] 'Price' arguably conveys less of the sense of an inescapable exchange involved in 'trade-off', though one might equally claim that it underlines the suggestion of moral consequentialism, of 'having to pay'. Subsequent writers have been less wary—or have felt no need to be wary. These are clearly defined concepts within genetics. In most of the current biological literature on senescence, 'trade-off' and 'antagonism' are, like Hayflick's 'senescent' and 'ageing' cells, unquestioned components of the vocabulary.

But the terminology matters, in the context of a discussion of evolutionary ethics, because it can easily appear to enshrine a perceived logic of ageing that was not present in any of the earlier philosophical models.[56] It can also seem to convey implicit attitudes to that logic; occasionally, in the public explanation of science especially, it becomes hooked up to explicit attitudes. What would it mean to think that we 'trade off' our old age for our youth or 'pay' for our youth with our old age? Or (not proven) that we 'trade off' our ability to take up calcium in earlier life for arteriosclerosis in later life? There is a fundamental difference here from looking at old age as an end, or a last 'stage', or a mere contingency, or even one half of a dialectical pairing with youth and/or a metaphysical 'beyond'. These are all structural ways of thinking about a life (and not all mutually exclusive), but only the last of them expresses a causal view of old age. The notion of 'trade-off' or payment for early benefits in life by later disadvantages is, in contrast, strongly causal. It tells us, that *because* our species enjoys certain protections up to reproductive maturity, we may *by the same mechanisms*, suffer for them later, other things being equal (it also tells us that other things almost never are equal). It may be that science will succeed in altering the lived experience, and even the biology, of old age, so that the human species evolves away from its current experience of senescence, but at present that is a very distant possibility.

In a recent review of developments in the science of ageing, Tom Kirkwood goes further, suggesting that 'part of the attraction of antagonistic pleiotropy to many, both within and beyond the aging field, may be the way in which it suggests that aging happens for a *purpose*. The purpose is not aging, per se, but the early benefit for which the pleiotropic gene is selected. In this sense, it is possible even to see aging as being program driven, like development, even though the program evolved for some other reason.'[57] Kirkwood's main worries about this interpretation are that antagonistic pleiotropy cannot explain the 'extraordinary variability of the aging phenotype', and that the idea of 'antagonism' does not fit well with the disposable soma theory's emphasis on beneficial repairs. He finds it 'easier to talk simply in terms of trade-offs' (445).

Kirkwood is right that the evolutionary theory of senescence is starting to interest people beyond the field of science itself, and if and when the terms 'antagonistic pleiotropy' and 'trade-off' start to enter popular consciousness it will matter, not least to the scientists themselves, whether they are taken to express a simple logical relation, or causal process, or (non-neutrally) a purposive programme. Certainly the notion of 'antagonism'—not there in Williams's original 1957 paper—is where the language of evolutionary biology can seem to push furthest beyond neutral explanation into implied ethics, apparently suggesting that our evolved genetic mechanisms of replication and repair amount to a hostile trade, or an unwelcome but contractually necessary 'paying off' of our metaphorical account with life. No serious scientist would endorse such a reading. 'Antagonistic pleiotropy' is an explicitly genetic concept: one allele substitution having multiple effects on the phenotype. 'The use of the term "pleiotropy" alone is preferable', Michael Rose notes, 'when one is attempting to avoid misleading metaphors.'

Scientists know, or think they know, what their own language means, and to draw attention to its metaphors will seem exiguously literary to most of them. But it may be partly because the language of evolutionary theory of senescence seems to carry an element of negativity that Kirkwood and others have been keen to help us see 'trade-offs' other than neutrally. An 'optimal balance' is how one recent paper in evolutionary theory of senescence describes the 'trade-off' it posits between sensence and earlier protection against cancer. ('It is not clear there is much room for improvement.')[58] A 'double edged sword' is the more dramatic metaphor prefered by a prominent cell biologist.[59] These statements are partly driven by a desire on the part of the writers to distance themselves from the buoyant optimism of much popularizing writing about the developing science of senescence, where it is standard practice to tell us that there is no quick fix for old age now but that the future looks bright and it is not absurd to imagine a world in which our biological resources will no longer be as limited. Talk of 'trade-offs' that becomes coloured in this way is not philosophically explicit, but it could easily be seen as opening the door to a neo-Stoic conclusion, in which we recognize the rationality of taking Nature as our guide, accepting that old age is the biological outcome of great benefits earlier in life, and in a strong sense our biological protection against worse outcomes later in life. But we understand nature very differently now from how Cicero understood it, and our revised understanding means that we cannot look either to nature or to science to do the work of moral justification for us. There is a room for a (separate) argument that our felt obligation to care for the old has arisen as an evolved characteristic of our species. But the basic premise of evolutionary theory of senescence remains that the evolutionary process itself is not purposive, not morally motivated, and that the so-called 'optimal balance' natural selection has produced thus far is descriptive only of current outcomes not intentions, let alone ideals.

To date, there is no literary work that I am aware of that reflects directly on evolutionary theories of senescence—nor would one necessarily expect there to be. The significance of cancer in scientific research on senescence is also not matched by any especially noticeable literary interest in cancer in old age. In fiction, poetry, drama, and biography the representative disease of old age has, instead, become Alzheimer's Disease. Elie Wiesel's *L'Oublié* (1989), Tony Harrison's poem and film for television *Black Daisies for the Bride* (1993), John Bayley's *Iris: A Memoir of Iris Murdoch* (1998), Jonathan Franzen's *The Corrections* (2001), Bryony Lavery's play *A Wedding Story* (2000), Julian Barnes's short story 'Appetite' (2000),[60] Kate Jennings's *Moral Hazard* (2002), are just a few of the recent works to have reflected social concerns, and personal fears, about the rise in incidence of Alzheimer's-type dementia in old age that has accompanied the rise in longevity.

At present in the UK, one in twenty people over the age of 65 and one in five over the age of 80 is affected by dementia, 55 per cent of those cases being of the Alzheimer's type.[61] The risk is higher for people with specific combinations of gene defects, but no one has a certainty of contracting it. Even for those with a family history of the form most strongly linked to specific gene defects (early onset Alzheimer's), the risk is 50 per cent—high, but not as high as is commonly presumed. The general trajectory of Alzheimer's is well known: it is a progressive disease, in which 'plaques' and 'tangles' develop in the brain tissue and neurotransmitters gradually deteriorate. A person with Alzheimer's has an increasingly impaired capacity to remember, understand, communicate, and reason. The cause is not yet fully known, but it is likely to involve a combination of factors, including genetic makeup, lifestyle, and age.[62]

The correlation with old age is strong—the chances of developing the condition increase significantly after 65—but it is by no means absolute. One of the major questions for Alzheimer's researchers at the moment is whether the disease is in fact at all related to normal neuronal degeneration in old age (an accelerated or extreme form of it), or whether it is a specific condition, distinct from the ageing process. In the absence, as yet, of a clear answer to that question, Alzheimer's represents what many people most fear from old age: a too early, too rapid, unavoidable, and drastic loss of mental capacity that will take away much of what makes them recognizable to themselves, and to others. This is the worst version of what, black-comically, and in the way of commonplace conversation, we often predict for ourselves: 'losing our marbles', 'going gaga', 'going batty', 'going senile'.

There have been several authoritative studies in recent years demonstrating the mismatch between many people's expectations for old age and the statistical realities.[63] In the context of thinking about current scientific theories of senescence, however, the more interesting problem extends beyond Alzheimer's (or cancer, or any other specific pathology to which we become more prone with age) to how we think about the part biology, and especially genetics, plays in shaping our capacities. The perception that old age is where we become most unhappily vulnerable to the genetic draw is rationally not fully justified, but it is a strong presupposition nonetheless. Michael Ignatieff addresses it unusually directly in his novel about Alzheimer's, *Scar Tissue* (1992), one of the best informed and most intelligent of recent literary responses to the science of ageing.

In the opening pages of the novel, Ignatieff's first-person narrator (sometimes hard to distinguish from Ignatieff himself) describes the potency for him of the notion of fate. He discovered fate, we are told, when his grandmother Nettie died of the disease that would later wreck his mother's mind, and which he comes to fear will also wreck his own. Childhood ended, for this man, with the coming into awareness of an unwanted but ineluctable inheritance, passed from mother to daughter, and from mother cell to daughter cell:

> It was as if I discovered, in my innocence, that there was such a thing as fate and that it could take a life and dismember it.
>
> My brother [a neuropathologist] hates it when I use the word fate. But then he is a doctor. He believes that they are bringing fate around, getting it under control. [...]
>
> When I try to imagine fate, I think of it as a bullet leaving a smoking chamber, perforating the flesh of our ancestors, exiting in spray and resuming its flight towards the expectant canopy of our skin. Thanks to genetics, we can see the bullet coming, estimate its likely impact and the path it will cut through our viscera. We can even calculate the pattern of the exit spray. The one thing we cannot do is duck.
>
> When I tell my brother this, he says I am talking bad science. We do not know enough. Look at you and me, he says. Ninety-nine per cent the same genetic material. Yet a stranger couldn't tell we were brothers.[64]

'When ... when ... when.' The word sounds like a bass note through *Scar Tissue*. Memory hinges on it—identifying retrospectively the moment at which the mother's mind began to falter, her personality to crumble, and, later, when the corrosion passed on to himself. But 'when' is also implicitly interrogative. When will be his moment? 'When', not 'if'. How soon?

Anyone with a knowledge of genetics would, indeed, want to resist this fatalism. Genes, as we have seen, are not deterministic in the way or to the degree feared by Ignatieff's philosopher protagonist. There are probabilities, likelihoods, but no bullet with our name on it guaranteed to strike us. A genotype requires the 'right' phenotypic and chemical environments to achieve expression, and we do not yet know how those environments are shaped—how sensitive they are to our diet, our environment, our mode of living, our emotions and general psychic state. As *Scar Tissue* progresses, it in fact becomes harder to tell whether the speaker's mounting fatalism is in good faith or whether it is exaggerated for the purpose of establishing a dialogue between fear and science, and (relatedly but not synonymously) between fiction and reality.

The fear is getting the upper hand by the time he is given an introduction by his brother to the histological and DNA profiles of an Alzheimer's patient (he realizes only belatedly that it is his mother):

> The cells on the glass slide—magnified six hundred times—are from the temporal lobe of a patient in her late sixties. The cells have been stained in order to highlight her neurons, axons and dendrites, the structural architecture of her brain. [...] At the centre of the image is a compacted black mass surrounded by a halo of inflammation. This is a deposit of amyloid protein, a form of scar tissue deep within this patient's brain. Under the microscope, it resembles a galactic storm, a starburst from an extinguished universe.   (130)

A DNA scan, 'an X-ray like transparency', records the genetic sequencing of the same patient:

> Notice the difference? my brother says, pointing to row six, her scan. I notice nothing. There, he says, pointing out the defect on the middle arm of chromosome 21. The cascade begins there, he says.
>
>   To my brother the word cascade means only the sequence of pathological effects, but for me the word has menace. I see a body tumbling down a black, liquid-filled shute. I catch him watching me. He raises his voice to bring me back to myself.   (131)

If there is a claim being made here for the priority of the literary and aesthetic perspective over the scientific one it is by no means straightforward. We should, surely, be cautious of the simile produced in response to the histology slide—'starburst from an extinguished universe'—and distrust its easy pathos. When the philosopher speaker observes that the histology slide 'looks beautiful' the doctor brother's agreement is also quietly levelling: 'everything becomes more beautiful the more closely you observe it' (130). Don't turn scientific fact into pathetic fallacy, is the implied rebuke. He is similarly quick to restrain the philosopher's Gothic turn of response to the vocabulary of DNA sequencing. 'Cascade' has no metaphorical burden for the neurologist. Allowing it to do so would itself be a sign of a mind in need of 'bringing back' to itself.

   There is genuine sympathy here, on the novel's part, with the scientist's materialism, and with the combination of pragmatism, stoicism, and optimism that in this case goes with it. And the novel also allows him a sensitivity to the aesthetic—plus the ability to ignore it when taking account of it would amount to sentimentalism. There is a good measure of irony attached to the narrator's aesthetic febrility, by contrast. But the novel does want us to take philosophy seriously (not surprisingly, given Ignatieff's background). If the philosopher brother's aestheticizing tendency regularly detracts from his observations, colouring them with egoism and no small measure of sentimentalism, that tendency nevertheless remains essential to *Scar Tissue*'s attempts to fashion an adequate ethical response to the modern science of ageing.

For Ignatieff, as for many before him, the philosophical tradition that comes most readily to mind in the face of age's possible—for some individuals genetically quite strongly possible—erosion of our capacities is stoicism. *Scar Tissue*'s protagonist has two explicit attempts at it. The first, uncomfortably, is in the form of a lecture to his parents' local Rotary Club: an audience comprised of their neighbours, the parents themselves, and his wife, who is alert, as he is not, to his mother's un-derstanding that she is the real subject under discussion here. The lecture takes a dismissive view of the North American cultivation of health as a stand-in for philosophy, pointing out the 'contradiction at the heart' of a self-help regime that only pretends to make us masters of a fate that biology tells us we cannot possibly control. It is 'one thing to argue that distress or low mental states can *affect* immunological responsive-ness', he admonishes his audience, quite another to claim that 'emotions *cause* disease' or that 'a positive mental attitude can reverse biological processes' (66). No, what is needed is a rigorously non-metaphorical ap-proach to disease, a relation of trust and shared understanding between patient and doctor, and mutual recognition of what medicine can and cannot do.

> The 'last men' of modernity have junked the culture of endurance for the sake of a culture of complaint. They go into illness as rights bearers, as vigilant bundles of informed consent. The stoic tradition, on the other hand, did address itself to a question the culture of complaint cannot answer: when should I struggle and when should I give in? [...]
>
> The real problem, of course, is what we are to think of death. [...] We are addicted to a vision of life as narrative, which we compose as we go along. In fact, we didn't have anything to do with the beginning of the story; we are merely allowed to dabble with the middle; and the end is mostly not up to us at all, but to genetics, biological fate and chance. Accepting death would mean giving up on the metaphor of life as narrative. Accepting illness would mean living ironically, accepting that we go into battle against biological fate as underdogs. We can struggle, but we are likely to lose. (67–8)

If this is stoicism it is not of the Ciceronian or any other classical kind, where resistance meant that one did not, in any important sense, 'lose'. One had moral dignity, rather more valuably than irony, on one's side. It is also, despite the preliminary protestations, thoroughly metaphorical: 'we go into battle … as underdogs'. Romantic fatalism not realism. The philosopher is of course being a bit of a jerk on this occasion. Or, to be fair, the narrative is setting him up as a jerk in order to sort out his thinking later, and in doing so talk the reader through the strengths and limitations of various possible moral stances. (There is a strong stamp of the Oxbridge or Harvard philosophy tutorial about these sections of *Scar Tissue*.) The case against the 'rights-bearer' approach to health is sound, as far as it goes. We are presumably intended to see the shortcomings in his remodelling of stoicism, and certainly intended to see the unkindness of his preaching it before (not even 'to') his mother. And in due course the philosopher/narrator gets the correction he deserves, not only from experience, which shows him that he cannot achieve the moral distance on his mother's or his own suffering requisite for stoicism, but also in the form of a necessarily brief corrective tutorial from a man with advanced motor neurone disease.

Moe, a patient of the scientist brother, has read the Rotary Club lecture (with considerable difficulty) and gives his response to it in the only way he can now communicate, by blowing through a straw onto a computer keyboard:

> if i had become a stoic or a fighter, i would probably be gone by now. rather, i face each day with a prayer. i try to be completely open to whatever christ brings.
>
> [...] better to know and grow from the experience than to remain aloof and have no basis for wisdom. stoicism. not much of a motivator. perhaps the unsung reason for searching out one's spirituality. (139–40)

The philosopher, in return, translates Moe's Christianity, to a degree sympathetically, into his own literary attentiveness to 'the word'. '[W]hen you strip us right down', he thinks and tries awkwardly to say, 'we remain creatures of the word. Nothing can save us but the word, the messages we send from deep in the shaft of sickness' (140–1).

This valuation, above all else, of the power to communicate is underlined by the Acknowledgements page to *Scar Tissue*, where Ignatieff thanks 'the family of Maurice des Mazes, of Kamloops, British Columbia' for permission to quote from des Mazes's private correspondence with him. It should not detract from these quotations' status as testimony (that is, as more than fiction) to observe that they have a crucial narrative function in the novel. Physically reduced though he is, des Mazes is an authoritative witness to the experience of 'radical and irreversible' neurological deterioration. He can do what the writer's mother cannot: put into words what it is like to be on the inside of biological disaster. Where her awareness of the world was and still is most keenly visual (she has been a painter), his is, like the philosopher's, verbal. He has composed a poem: a modernist prose poem written out of illness, which implicitly rebukes the victim mentality of the earlier Gothic riff on 'cascade':

> what are these flashes crashing noiselessly from side
> to side in my mind? spells of brownout follow
> ozone cinders down the unknown path   (142)

'Neurological disease' is a capacious category. In Moe's case the central nervous system supplying the muscles has been devastated, but his brain function remains unimpaired. The doctor brother sees the difference between Moe's and their mother's situations much more clearly than the narrator, who wants to find greater similarity than there is. Moe is losing his body, not his mind. Their mother is losing her mind. His illness has struck him in his prime, hers has struck with the onset of old age, and 'old age', rather than Alzheimer's, is what she herself calls it, quoting, loosely, Bette Davis: 'Old age ain't for cowards, kid' (28).[65] Old age, the narrator agrees, is what his mother suffers from—but brutally accelerated, like 'slipping down a steel ramp' (28).

Her sons can (and do) dispute how far their mother is conscious of her own deterioration, but there is no dispute over her inability, in the midst of illness, to have and hold on to a philosophy of her own too rapid senescence. This conviction is not explicitly articulated, though almost every other aspect of the situation is. When having or not having a philosophy is in question, the focus tends to veer towards the philosopher: '*my* "stoicism" now seemed to me nothing more than surrender' (144; my emphasis). As far as he is concerned, his mother may or may not have a worked-out philosophy, but she has what may be just as valuable: moments of access to Truth. Even this late in the novel and in her illness she can tell him that she sees her son/his brother, the doctor 'walking through the gates of truth' (146). Usually she is less verbally gifted than Moe, but like the abstract painter Willem de Kooning she remains capable until very near the end of producing art: she can be given a pencil and produce an 'accurate, graceful' though incomplete representation of her scientist son's face. One of the things experimentalism with style thus allows in *Scar Tissue*, both in art and in the use of language, is the investing of residues of capability, and of fragments of expression, with the value of whole things—though in the mother's case, only the narrator requests this status for her last drawing.

The risk of course, as with de Kooning, is that we shall see more than is there, invest what is broken with the mystique of the deliberately fragmented. There is an object lesson in that danger, though perhaps not one Ignatieff consciously designed, in the scene where the philosopher attempts to impress upon his young students his personal (that is, familial) knowledge of how minds break up: a knowledge, or rather a burden of emotion, that they are not equipped to deal with in the classroom. He gives them Act 4 scene 6 from *King Lear*—the speech in which Cordelia is reunited with her father who only very falteringly begins to recognize her. 'Pray do not mock me', is the passage singled out for special attention, and all but enacted in front of the students: 'I would be up there [...] patting my old tweed jacket, running my hands across my own arms' (164). In the real world, the philosopher son is in the role of Cordelia, but in the classroom he takes on, or wishes to take on (the grammatical mood of 'would' is unclear) the role that he believes and fears is more properly his: that of Lear himself.

Loss of identity threatens on every side. His mother is now failing to recognize him; his students, too, are alarmed: 'Who is this? Why is he like this?' (164). The only slip in his recollection of the Shakespeare scene, unremarked and perhaps unnoticed by Ignatieff, comes when he interpolates a stage direction into the play: 'The king lifts his hand towards his daughter. Think, I tell my class, of the way infants grab a finger when it is extended to them. This is the primary identification process' (165). It is all his mother can, at the end, do. But the direction is not there in *Lear*. In *Lear* Cordelia asks for the king's benediction. It is not given. Even at the end of the speech under discussion Lear has only just been brought to understand that this is his child, and when he does grasp that knowledge he fears that she will poison or abuse him. Reawakened trust comes much later. But the philosopher son, and perhaps Ignatieff himself, needs it now—needs to believe that the fuller capacity is still there, and that it only requires a sufficient intensity of love or belief to elicit the occasional, saving sign.

After his mother dies, the narrator becomes obsessed with people who vanish. He starts a book on the subject, recalls a man in his college dormitory who won a scholarship to Oxford but failed ever to show up, and for all anyone knows is dead. His mother, he feels, did something similar when she compelled him, as a teenager, to destroy all her paintings—not just accepting but pre-empting the obliteration of mind and memory and communicative powers to come. *Scar Tissue*'s closing chapter takes a similar risk with its reader. Instead of having its narrator reach some kind of philosophical accommodation with what may be to come, it allows him to spiral into a fatalism that appears unjustified, egoistic, but which the final paragraphs suggest may be symptomatic of early-onset Alzheimer's. In muddying the line between the egoism of fear and the courage of prediction ('I want to predict it in every particular', he tells us—'What else is the examined life for?' (196)) Ignatieff makes it all but impossible for the reader to judge these closing pages. Not many of us will have equivalent familial cause for this specific fear, though most of us are perhaps assailed from time to time by fear of our biological inheritances in some form, so this may be as close as we can be brought to feeling rationalism assailed at its core by the passage of time. The alternative, perhaps, would be to hand over the ending of this novel/memoir/philosophical essay to the doctors, but that would be melodramatic—and, the narrative implies, will happen soon enough anyway.

If it is hard to know whether to believe in this ending—whether to take it as the onset of Alzheimer's or 'only' the fear of Alzheimer's—this is largely because the narrator never relinquishes the faith in the power of words that has pitted him against both brother and mother. Helen Vendler picked up on his problematic quasi-mystification of words in a review for *The New York Review of Books*, where, after admiring the book's depiction of the mother's illness, and taking issue with the schematism that sets the philosopher/literary man against the scientist (as if artists do not have equally much to hope for from the progress of science),[66] she complained of a Hemingwayesque portentousness that increasingly colours the prose. She quotes from the scene describing the death of the mother: 'in truth we make nothing. We live, and we cannot shape life. It is much too great for us, too great for any words. A writer must refuse to believe this' (172).[67]

In fact, the passage goes on and the 'fuzzy sonorousness' of which Vendler complains attaches also to the collapse of a writerly *non credo* at the moment of his mother's death: 'I knew that all my words could only be in vain, and that all that I had feared and all that I had anticipated could only be lived'. These sentences drive a double wedge between science and art. Having told us, all the way through, that science is committed to describing processes that deprive us of the power to make sense of our lives, the philosopher/narrator first insists that the writer must refuse to give in—then immediately gives in. (Some will see an allegory here of philosophy's relations with science much more broadly: most obviously, philosophy of mind's relations with cognitive science.) His rapid decline follows. But the more persuasive passages in Ignatieff's book encourage us to read matters differently, seeing literature and philosophy and science as engaged in a common endeavour to press beyond the question of whether words have (ideally) the power to 'shape' and give meaning to a life. All these fields want also to test the power of words to record unsentimentally, unportentously, the ways in which age may deprive our lives of the shapes we have sought to give them in our earlier years, and take on other shapes not entirely, or not at all, of our choosing.

The loss of that power of choosing from within a life (one's own life) can become, as Larkin knew, the subject of too oppressive fears. Ignatieff is good on fear: the acceleration towards us, in a compulsively entertained fantasy, of what we believe will destroy us. 'She is ageing at a terrifying rate', one passage of *Scar Tissue* reads: 'There is nothing graceful or gentle about it. Everything is accelerated, like those ghastly time-lapse films of flowers pushing through the soil, flowering and dying in a single moment' (49). Ignatieff's achievement is to have shown that the fear mimics the disease itself: it is of the nature of Alzheimer's to make us age before we should, and of the nature of fear to do the same. In that sense, Alzheimer's gives a name and a specific pathology to a more general fear of ageing. Most readers will probably find themselves resisting the end of *Scar Tissue*, with its narrator running to meet the unconfirmed future: 'No one will stop me now' (199). But the writer/philosopher's failure here is not the same thing as the novel's, and there is a case for saying that the narrator's failure is necessary if the reader is to feel the need for resistance.

But resistance sends us back to stoicism—and faced with the emotional and rational free fall of *Scar Tissue*'s ending, that seems much the better philosophy to inhabit. It cannot save us from the deteriorations that may come with age, but it can lead us to a rational assessment of the risks, an understanding of how we can best hope to improve them, and a just valuation also of the potential goods. As quietly practised by the scientist brother, yoked to the 'serenity' of a belief that science will at some point in the future tell us the whole story, it has been a position of some envy to the narrator: 'My brother isn't bothered by what he doesn't know. The answers will surrender themselves eventually. There is a serenity in his science which makes me envious and unhappy. "I wish I knew how to change my life," I say' (132). A flailing punch or two at the imperialism of science follows ('doctors are the ones who make the rules' (133)), but science comes out of this novel largely unscathed—not least because the stoicism his brother has achieved is not inherent in the science but in his attitude to it and the use he puts it to. It is also clear that the narrator's belief in the primacy of the word is absolutely shared by his brother: ' "Speech can matter more than life itself," I said. | "Exactly," my brother said ... "The word. Believe in the word" ' (143). Tritely, it's a recognition that science, as much as philosophy, or novel-writing for that matter, can only be done from within language. Less tritely, it is the best defence (a notably non-imperialist one) of the thought experiments in ageing, before one's time, in which the philosopher-novelist and the scientist have an equal interest: 'We're all moral tourists here. ... None of us has any idea. That's what thought experiments are for' (144).

Conclusion

No grand conclusions—not because I do not feel some pressure to make them. I have been acutely aware while writing this book of how intensely many people feel that there should be strong conclusions about old age, especially with respect to our individual ethical outlooks and our expectations of social justice. How we can cope best with loss (which is, in one form or another, what most fear from old age) and how we should respond to the increasing proportion of old to young in our society are hard questions. There seems to be widespread feeling that any book on old age should deliver answers. I have to put up some resistance, particularly on the question of how we should respond to loss in late life. I do not think that this question *can* be answered meaningfully without reference to our wider views about what life is, and what we want from it. To perceive ageing as a loss is already to have decided in favour of one set of options rather than another. Similarly, to regard the problem of social justice as one of distributions between competing parties is already to have made some fundamental choices, albeit unconsciously.

Like Simone de Beauvoir, I am, more simply, wary of grand pronouncements about old age. One of the problems with and for old age is that, while there has been too little serious thinking about it over the years, there have been quite enough pronouncements. A reason for making this book a dialogue of literature and philosophy was that when philosophy offers to take us towards schematism, literature (if it is worth reading) reminds us that not many aspects of human lives are satisfactorily described by schemata. This is, of course, why philosophers themselves have often seen literature as a way out of the reductiveness of theory.

Some synthesizing comments at the end of a book that spreads its attention so widely are, however, needed. The first aim of *The Long Life* has been to extend the range and deepen the content of current thinking about old age. Philosophy seems to have been (with rare exceptions) the missing figure at the table when supposedly 'cross-disciplinary' debates about old age have taken place. Literature, as I said in starting, is rich in accounts of long lives; philosophy relatively poor, as yet. Given how little modern philosophical writing, outside medical ethics and life-planning theories, focuses directly on old age, taking account of what philosophy has said about late life has required drawing out often very minor strands within much larger arguments about ethics, epistemology, rational self-interest theories, metaphysics, and so forth. Literary critics (also historians and social scientists) will perhaps be more comfortable with this method than philosophers, who may feel that the purpose of a philosophical argument, aimed at a normative description of people or lives, is distorted when the minor strand or passing gesture is given such prominence.

In concentrating on minor, or apparently marginal, references to old age in philosophical works not primarily about that subject, I have tried to show that we understand old age best when we view it, not as a problem apart, but as always connected into larger philosophical considerations. As I have argued throughout this book, the really interesting questions about old age arise out of how we think more generally about lives and persons. For example, Bernard Williams's remarks about the parts old age and decline play in our ability to think of our own mortality as a tolerable necessity are a passing gesture in an argument about why we should not want to live forever—but they are, nevertheless, saying something about old age and decline in their own right that has not, to my knowledge, been said with as much clarity anywhere else. Derek Parfit's 'impersonal theory' of self-interest similarly has important implications for our reasoning both about the temporal dimension of self-interest and about what we think it means to be a person: it says relatively little that is explicit about ageing and decline, but what it does say is forceful and rewards more expansive consideration.

My second aim has been to show that, in some (not all) cases, bringing old age to the forefront of the discussion causes difficulties for a general theory of how we should live, or how we should think about our values, interests, selfhood. A theory, such as Aristotle's account of virtue ethics, that is coherent when applied to one's prime may prove incoherent, or at least in need of rather more being said, when its principles are extended into old age. Or, a theory explicitly directed at old age, such as Plato's repeated references to late life as the best place from which to do philosophy, may need one to read widely in Plato to discover what the limits are on such a claim. Clearly, Plato did not want to deny that very old age (sometimes relatively early old age) brings a decline in one's intellectual powers, and yet he places an unusually high valuation on the long life.

'It is a reasonable demand that what one believes in one area of philosophy should make sense in terms of what one believes elsewhere', Bernard Williams remarked in a reply to a collection of essays in his honour. 'One's philosophical beliefs, or approaches, or arguments should hang together (like conspirators, perhaps), but this demand falls a long way short of the unity promised by a philosophical system.'[1] There is certainly no hidden 'unity' in the eclectic range of philosophical and literary texts I have written about here. Nevertheless, I have defended some ways of thinking about old age, and rejected others, and I believe that the claims I have defended hang together.

Chapter 1's reading of Plato and Mann shows that there are good philosophical reasons to value old age highly, but that the conventional association of old age with wisdom and authority is not a decontextualizable ideal. Wherever it arises, it inevitably has roots in specific understandings of what knowledge and wisdom are. Plato's and Mann's exploitation of old age in the service of describing and defending (respectively) philosophy and art is also a reminder that rhetoric must be a component in any critical vocabulary for thinking about old age. We need, as a bare starting point, to be able to dissociate claims about what human beings are really like in old age, or what they should aspire to be like, from attempts to persuade us of something else, not strongly related to how we may actually live. Plato's wish to define philosophy as a sublimation of desire into truth-seeking, is one example; Mann's self-consciously Neoplatonic desire to see art as an escape from the constraints of form and the burden of labour is another.

This distinction between what is rhetoric and what is held out as lived reality is also an important element in my reading of Aristotle. The *Rhetoric* is (deliberately) typologically reductive, but its view of ageing as a diminishment of character is less a betrayal than an addition to and intensification of the worries about old age that one finds in the *Ethics*. Aristotle's perception that the weakness of age tends to reduce our capacity for virtue, and makes us vulnerable to disaster in ways we were not in our prime, is undoubtedly bleak. For many it is uncongenial. It is not, I think, obviously wrong—so long as we are clear that physical and mental capacity will differ widely between individuals, and that we can sustain considerable diminishment in our capabilities before biological senescence becomes seriously destructive of our ability to live well. Where I find the Aristotelian view of old age not only bleak but wrong is in the absence of any explicit discount on the criteria for virtue in old age. A virtue ethics that relies heavily on practical wisdom and the active pursuit of virtue must make some allowance for likely diminishment in power and energy in late life, and Aristotle does not do this. Virtue ethics also needs, in my view, a more flexible sense of the effects of age. How unsteady and complex character may be, even or especially in an apparent state of deterioration, is richly expressed by Shakespeare's *Lear*. Its refusal to rewrite the vulnerability of old age as a source of moral good should also check any philosopher who, like Alasdair MacIntyre, wants to redeem Aristotle's account of old age through a positive revaluation of our dependency upon others in late life.

Relaxing the criteria for virtue in old age would not eliminate the possibility for tragedy on an Aristotelian or neo-Aristotelian view. But the tragic case is, we should remember, exceptional. Michael Slote's claim that, in general, we should apply less exacting criteria for a good life in old age seems to me sensible and appropriate—not only as a corrective to the pressure Aristotle places upon the end, but as a check on the very widespread belief today that lives are comparable to narratives, and that the best lives have the form of a progress narrative. Once again, we need to be able to discriminate finely between different degrees and kinds of impairment. But we also need to be alert to the reductiveness of the narrative view per se. To say that a life has the structure and the temporal logic of a narrative is to describe that life by means of an analogy that will always be at best simplifying. In the case of old age, the benefits of that analogy (its ability to help us aim for better goals, and to shape our lives so that we are more effective in pursuit of those goals) are less evidently appropriate than in our youth and our prime. One can recognize the efficiency and sometimes the instrumental value of describing lives narratologically in particular contexts (philosophical and literary) while also recognizing—with Saul Bellow—the limited purchase of that description on how we actually experience our lives, and, in old age, how we may *want* to experience them. Bellow's is an idiosyncratic meditation on old age and philosophy (including his revision of Epicurean hedonism), but he puts some serious challenges in the way of the narrative view through his sense that, in old age, there may be special reasons to resist both its future-directedness and its focus on the unity of the single life.

One of the fields in which the narrative view does retain instrumental value is the field of prudential life-planning. In my discussion of Daniels's lifespan allocation model for distributing social resources between age groups, and McKerlie's prioritarian welfarist objections, I see the really difficult cases for establishing fairness, on either basis, as being those where agency is gravely impaired in late life. These are the cases where both the prudential reasoner and the prioritarian reasoner could hold that we are justified in withholding life-extending care. Such cases, though distressing, will, I think, prove less distressing, and less numerous, if we accept Agnieszka Jaworska's argument that the threshold level necessary to lend prudential authority to a person's current wishes should be set at the ability to espouse coherent and consistent values, and not at the ability to grasp one's life as a whole. Here, as in my reading of Aristotle and of Slote, I am suggesting that our sense of the depletions of old age is sometimes so pre-emptively strong that it overrules a just recognition of how much remains. Philip Larkin's 'The Old Fools' is an extreme instance of a prejudicial fear of loss, where old age becomes a cipher for the coming obliteration that is death. Stevie Smith's 'Exeat' is a reminder that even if, like Larkin, we greatly fear age and death, choosing for or against more life is not something we ever do simply on the basis of thinking that we want to live or to die. Our choices are too embedded in other values besides the value we place on life alone—also, to put it more explicitly than she does, too embedded in the lives of other people (family, friends, communities), whose values help to shape our sense of what actions are available to us.

Derek Parfit's arguments about our attitudes towards time, our inter-pretations of self-interest, and the possible consequences of psychological discontinuity and disconnectedness for our moral thinking, all considered in Ch. 5, unsettle much of what has been assumed up to that point in *The Long Life*. They put some fundamental challenges in the way of the narrative view of lives, and the assumption of unity of lives and unity of personhood, with which Chs. 1 to 4 worked—and which, they increasingly suggested, was inadequate in some ways, misleading in others. I am persuaded by Parfit's argument that our attitudes to ageing and to death would change for the better were we to respond more neutrally to time. I'm less persuaded (and, it should be said, he is himself less than fully satisfied) that, if we adopt his Reductionist View of persons, thinking and acting in terms of paternalism towards our future selves would be a sufficient protection against grave imprudence. *Le Père Goriot* is not a correction or extension of the philosophy here—rather a bracing imaginative justification of some of its concerns about where our bias towards the near future leaves old age, and where a less continuous view of persons might also leave it. I hold back from the Reductionist View myself. I believe psychological continuity and connectedness are much stronger in the vast majority of cases than many of Parfit's admirers enjoy imagining that they might be. In other words, the idea that our further future self should, under certain conditions, be considered as like another person is rationally defensible, but has, I think, limited applicability in the world. Secondly, I argue here that, just as his theory of beneficence towards future generations remains (avowedly) incomplete, the Reductionist View will have worrying implications for old age unless it is supplemented by a fuller theory of how we are to protect our future selves from harm.

Adorno is the wild card in this book. Whether or not his account of metaphysics (including his account of its history) is plausible is not my concern in Ch. 6. I am not persuaded by it, but Adorno contributes a very clear example of old age playing a significant role in the shaping of a philosophical argument to which it is not obviously germane. Adorno's *Kulturkritik* readings of *The Old Curiosity Shop* and *Endgame* are important preparatory pieces for the rhetorical deployment of old age in his lectures on *Metaphysics*: that is, for the contemplation of old age as a prompt to thinking about the limits of thought. Such a rhetorical use of old age would barely raise an eyebrow within literary criticism. Few literary readers will have any difficulty with the idea that figures of old age in Dickens and Beckett are, inter alia, a means to thinking about the limits of human experience, and the limits (necessary and imposed) of literary and theatrical forms. In philosophy this, essentially metaphorical, use of old age is a less 'legitimate' move—and one Adorno himself presents with some apparent embarrassment, knowing full well that old age has no actual relation to metaphysics.

The philosopher who comes closest to expressing my own sense that we should not merely tolerate the necessity of ageing but recognize that we have cause to value it is Bernard Williams. My phrasing here is stronger than his: he adduces the fact that we grow old and decline as one possible inducement among others (unspecified) that we may have to make our accommodation with mortality. Age-related decline seems to me the *best* reason many of us will have to see our death as tolerable for us—if we are fortunate. Great and chronic pain could have the same effect on our categorical desire to go on living, but before old age we may justifiably feel aggrieved at facing a premature death. Not least, our too early death, in such cases, will mean that we have had less chance to enjoy the goods of life than most of the people we encounter in life have had, or will have. In the chapter on Williams's essay 'The Makropulos Case', I argue that his view of age and decline should be expanded to include, explicitly, a subjective as well as objective perception of growing old. Though a purely subjective sense that one is old, before one has observably begun to decline physiologically, will probably seem spurious to others, even the questionably authentic case may express a sense of having run out of time or licence to enjoy the things we value and consider constitutive of ourself. These include environment, family, friends, lovers, having an audience for our ideas. Although old age and death, in this view, preserve a basic kind of coherence to one's sense of having a life and being a self, they do not imply a narrative view of either in any but a very trivial sense of establishing an end.

My final chapter is speculative in its philosophical conclusions. Its account of current evolutionary theory of senescence considers whether very recent developments in that theory should lead us to revise our assumptions of what is 'natural' for us in old age. Evolutionary theory removes any basis in nature for claiming that old age has a purpose, or is part of a design for our lives. It tells us that the physical and mental deteriorations of old age are mostly non-adaptive. But recent work in science also tells us things that we might conceivably find helpful in making our own old age and decline tolerable to us. If there is truth in the idea supported by some evolutionary theorists that some aspects of our late-life loss of fitness are the result of the same processes that protected our ability to flourish in our youth, then I find that this leads me to accept the prospect of ageing a little more willingly. This is no more than a 'psychological report': others will think that possessing a scientific explanation along these lines does nothing to make our loss of biological fitness less regrettable. My view is less affected by very recent theorizing about a 'plateau' effect in late life, whereby our rate of decline in key respects levels out rather than accelerating. There may be minor cause there for gratification, if one reaches one's later eighties, but population statistics have no simple or direct bearing on our individual life expectancies. I'm happy for scientists to go on working on possibilities for ameliorating the ills of age, but that is in part because I greatly doubt that science will ever eliminate old age.

One important observable change that ageing brings is not biological but psychological—one might call it (sacrificing elegance) proto-philosophical. Many people report that, as one approaches old age, it becomes less and less possible not to think about the limited and ever-diminishing time available to one, and to give more and more space in one's mental life to the main questions this book has been preoccupied with: what a good life is, how we measure happiness, what a person is, when we are at our best, what thinking can and cannot achieve. But the reverse is also true: many of us strongly prefer to avoid thinking about it 'too much', and are, so far as one can tell, successful in doing so. I keep coming back to the perversity, as it still seems to me, of Simone de Beauvoir's conclusion for *La Vieillesse*: 'far better not to think about it too much'. It's an irony, of course, as much as a perversity. She had by then spent 541 pages thinking about it, and would expend many more in her autobiographical writings. She was right, though, that the double-think exists: many of us spend more and more time, as we grow older, thinking about the fact that we are growing older and what it implies, but we also spend a great deal of time trying, more or less strenuously, *not* to think about that fact and what it implies.

This ambivalence about dwelling too much on the subject of ageing is another reason for trying to expand the terms for our thinking about later life. Old age, I have been arguing, is not only of interest because it comes to us all in the end, if we are fortunate enough not to die first, or because we must expect that it will bring more of the ills of life as well as more of the goods. These are large elements in why it matters or will come to matter to us individually, but old age is, as I hope I have shown, a subject with much wider dimensions. It has repercussions for what we deem to be a good life, how we measure happiness, what we think a person is, when we think we are at our best, what we consider thinking can and cannot achieve. It touches on, and makes a difference to, how we understand epistemology, virtue, justice, self-interest, metaphysics, and, not least, what is natural for us. These are not narrow problems, as the question of how we can sustain loss would be, if that were all we thought was meant by growing old. They are good reasons for pressing past any natural reluctance to start thinking about old age seriously now.

Bibliography

ADORNO, THEODOR W., *Aesthetic Theory*, ed. Gretel Adorno and Rolf Tiedemann, newly translated, edited, and with a translator's introduction by Robert Hullot-Kentor (London: Athlone, 1997).

—— *Beethoven: The Philosophy of Music*, ed. Rolf Tiedemann, tr. Edmund Jephcott (Cambridge: Polity, 1998).

—— *Metaphysik: Begriff und Probleme*, ed. Rolf Tiedemann (Frankfurt am Main: Suhrkamp, 1998); *Metaphysics: Concepts and Problems*, 'Editor's Afterword' by Rolf Tiedemann, tr. Edmund Jephcott (Stanford, Calif.: Stanford University Press, 2000).

—— *Moments Musicaux: Neu gedruckte Aufsätze 1928–1962* (Frankfurt am Main: Suhrkamp, 1964).

—— *Negative Dialectics*, tr. E. B. Ashton (London: Routledge, 1973).

—— 'Rede über den Raritätenlanden von Charles Dickens', *Frankfurter Zeitung und Handelsblatt*, 18 Apr. 1931, 1–2; 'On Dickens' *The Old Curiosity Shop*: A Lecture', in Adorno, *Notes to Literature*, ed. Rolf Tiedemann, tr. Shierry Weber Nicholsen, 2 vols. (New York: Columbia University Press, 1991–92), ii. 171–7.

—— 'Trying to Understand Endgame', in Adorno, *Notes to Literature*, i. 241–75.

ALBIN, ROGER L., 'Antagonistic Pleiotropy, Mutation Accumulation, and Human Genetic Disease', *Genetica* 91 (1993), 279–86.

—— 'The Pleiotropic Gene Theory of Senescence: Supportive Evidence from Human Genetic Disease', *Ethology and Sociobiology* 9/6 (1988), 371–82.

ALTER, ROBERT, Response to Michael Ignatieff, *Berlin in Autumn: The Philosopher in Old Age*, Doreen B. Townsend Center for the Humanities, Occasional Papers, 16 (Berkeley: University of California, 1998).

AMIS, MARTIN, *Experience* (London: Jonathan Cape, 2000).

ANNAS, JULIA, *The Morality of Happiness* (Oxford: Oxford University Press, 1993).

A Profile of Older Americans: 2002 (Administration on Aging, US Department of Health and Social Services, 2003), <http://www.aoa.gov/prof/Statistics/profile/profiles2002.asp>, last accessed 15 Feb. 2007.

ARISTOTLE, *The 'Art' of Rhetoric*, with English tr. by John Henry Freese, Loeb Classical Library (Cambridge, Mass.: Harvard University Press, 1926).

—— *Aristotle's Eudemian Ethics, Books I, II and VIII*, tr. with a commentary by Michael Woods (Oxford: Clarendon, 1982).

ARISTOTLE, *The Complete Works of Aristotle*, Revised Oxford Translation, ed. Jonathan Barnes (Princeton: Princeton University Press, 1984).

——*Nicomachean Ethics*, with English tr. by H. Rackham, Loeb Classical Library (Cambridge, Mass.: Harvard University Press, 1934).

——*Nicomachean Ethics*, tr. with introduction and notes by Terence Irwin (Indianapolis: Hackett, 1985).

——*Nicomachean Ethics*, tr. (with historical introduction) by Christopher Rowe, philosophical introduction and commentary by Sarah Broadie (Oxford: Oxford University Press, 2002).

——*Rhetoric*, tr. W. Rhys Roberts, *Poetics*, tr. Ingram Bywater, with introduction by Edward P. J. Corbett (New York: Random House, 1954).

ATLAS, JAMES. *Bellow: A Biography* (London: Faber & Faber, 2000).

AUSTAD, STEVEN A., *Why We Age: What Science is Discovering about the Body's Journey through Life* (New York: John Wiley & Sons, 1997).

BAILEY, CYRIL, *Epicurus: The Extant Remains* (Oxford: Clarendon, 1926).

BALDWIN, T. W., *William Shakspere's Small Latine and Lesse Greeke*, 2 vols. (Urbana: University of Illinois Press, 1944).

BALZAC, HONORÉ DE, *A Harlot High and Low*, tr. Rayner Heppenstall (London: Penguin, 1970).

——*Cousin Pons*, Part II of *Poor Relations*, tr. Herbert J. Hunt (London: Penguin, 1968).

——*Lost Illusions*, tr. Herbert J. Hunt (London: Penguin, 1971).

——*Le Père Goriot*, in *La Comédie humaine*, iii. *Études de mœurs: Scènes de la vie privée; Scènes de la vie de province*, ed. Pierre-Georges Castex et al. (Paris: Gallimard, 1976); *Le Père Goriot*, tr. Marion Ayrton Crawford (London: Penguin, 1951); *Le Père Goriot*, tr. Peter W. Lock (London: Macmillan, 1968).

BANDURA, A., 'Self-Efficacy Mechanism in Human Agency', *American Psychologist* 37/2 (1982), 122–47.

BANNER, L. W., *In Full Flower: Aging Women, Power and Sexuality* (New York: Vintage, 1992).

BARNES, JONATHAN (ed.), *The Cambridge Companion to Aristotle* (Cambridge: Cambridge University Press, 1995).

BARNES, JULIAN, 'Appetite', *Areté* 2 (Spring/Summer 2000), 53–61; repr. in *The Lemon Table* (London: Jonathan Cape, 2004).

BARROLL, J. LEEDS, 'Gulliver and the Struldbruggs', *PMLA* 73 (1958), 43–50.

——*Shakespearean Tragedy: Genre, Tradition, Change in* Antony and Cleopatra (Washington, DC: Folger, 1984).

BAYLEY, JOHN, *Iris: A Memoir of Iris Murdoch* (London: Duckworth, 1998).

BEAR, GREG, *Vitals* (New York: Ballantine, 2002).

BEARON, LUCILLE B., 'Successful Aging: What Does the "Good Life" Look Like? Concepts in Gerontology', *The Form for Family and Consumer Issues* 1/3 (1996). <http://www.ces.ncsu.edu/depts/fcs/pub/aging.html>, last accessed 15 Feb. 2007.

BEAUVOIR, SIMONE DE, *The Prime of Life*, tr. P. Green (Cleveland, Ohio: World Publishing, 1962; London: André Deutsch and Weidenfeld & Nicolson, 1965).

——— *La Vieillesse* (Paris: Gallimard, 1970); *The Coming of Age*, tr. Patrick O'Brian (New York: G. P. Putnam's Sons, 1972); published in England as *Old Age* (London: André Deutsch and Weidenfeld & Nicolson, 1972).

BECKETT, SAMUEL, *The Theatrical Notebooks of Samuel Beckett*, ii. *Endgame, with a revised text*, ed. with introduction and notes by S. E. Gontarski (London: Faber & Faber, 1992).

BEGAM, RICHARD, 'Interview with J. M. Coetzee', *Contemporary Literature* 33/3 (1992), 419–31.

BELL, E., et al., 'Loss of Division Potential In Vitro: Aging or Differentiation?', *Science* 202 (1978), 1158–63.

BELLOW, SAUL, Preface to Bloom, *The Closing of the American Mind*, 11–18.

——— 'Problems in American Literature', in Todd Breyfogel (ed.), *Literary Imagination, Ancient and Modern: Essays in Honor of David Grene* (Chicago: University of Chicago Press, 1999), 375–88.

——— *Ravelstein* (2000; London: Penguin, 2001).

——— 'Saul Bellow—Nobel Lecture', 12 Dec. 1976, <http://nobelprize.org/nobel prizes/literature/laureates/1976/bellow-lecture.html>, last accessed 15 Feb. 2007.

BERGOFFEN, DEBRA B., *The Philosophy of Simone de Beauvoir: Gendered Phenomenologies, Erotic Generosities* (Albany: State University of New York Press, 1997).

BERTMAN, STEPHEN, *The Conflict of Generations in Ancient Greece and Rome* (Amsterdam: Grüner, 1976).

'Bette Davis: The Official Website'. <http://www.bettedavis.com>, last accessed 15 Feb. 2007.

BIDDER, G. P., 'Senescence', *British Medical Journal* 2 (1932), 583–5.

BIGELOW, JOHN, CAMPBELL, JOHN, and PARGETTER, ROBERT, 'Death and Well-Being', *Pacific Philosophical Quarterly* 71 (1990), 119–40.

BLACKBURN, SIMON, *Ethics: A Very Short Introduction* (Oxford: Oxford University Press, 2003).

BLOOM, ALLAN, *The Closing of the American Mind: How Higher Education Has Failed Democracy and Impoverished the Souls of Today's Students* (New York: Simon & Schuster, 1987).

BOUCE, PAUL GABRIEL, 'Death in Gulliver's Travels: The Struldbruggs Revisited', in Rudolf Freiburg, Arno Löffler, and Wolfgang Zach (eds.), *Swift: The Enigmatic Dean. Festschrift for Hermann Josef Real* (Tübingen: Stauffenburg, 1998), 1–13.

BOWEN, JOHN, *Other Dickens: Pickwick to Chuzzlewit* (Oxford: Oxford University Press, 2000).

BOWIE, MALCOLM, *Proust Among the Stars* (London: HarperCollins, 1998).

BRADEN, GORDON, *Renaissance Tragedy and the Senecan Tradition: Anger's Privilege* (New Haven: Yale University Press, 1985).

BRADLEY, A. C., *Shakespearean Tragedy: Lectures on* Hamlet, Othello, King Lear, Macbeth (1904), 2nd edn. (London: Macmillan, 1905).

BRISON, SUSAN J., 'Beauvoir and Feminism: Interview and Reflections', in Claudia Card (ed.), *The Cambridge Companion to Simone de Beauvoir* (Cambridge: Cambridge University Press, 2003), 189–207.

BROCK, DAN W., *Life and Death: Philosophical Essays in Biomedical Ethics* (Cambridge: Cambridge University Press, 1993).

BROOK, PETER (dir.), *King Lear* (Columbia Pictures, 1970).

BROOME, JOHN, *Weighing Lives* (Oxford: Oxford University Press, 2004).

BUFFIÈRE, FÉLIX, *Éros adolescent: la pédérastie dans la Grèce antique* (Paris: Belles Lettres, 1980).

BULLOUGH, GEOFFREY (ed.), *Narrative and Dramatic Sources of Shakespeare*, 8 vols. (London: Routledge & Kegan Paul, 1973).

BUTLER, R., and GLEASON, H. (ed.), *Productive Aging: Enhancing Vitality in Later Life* (New York: Springer, 1985).

CALLAHAN, DANIEL, *Setting Limits* (New York: Simon & Schuster, 1987).

CAMPBELL, LILY B., *Shakespeare's Tragic Heroes: Slaves of Passion* (London: Methuen, 1930).

CAMPISI, JUDITH, 'Aging, Tumor Suppression and Cancer: High Wire-Act!', *Mechanisms of Ageing and Development* 126/1 (Jan. 2005), 51–8.

_____ 'Cancer and Ageing: Rival Demons?', *Nature*, Review sect. 3 (2003), 339–49.

_____ 'Did You Ever Wonder…? …Why People Age?', Lawrence Berkeley National Laboratory website, <http://www.lbl.gov/wonder/campisi.html>, last accessed 15 Feb. 2007.

_____ 'Senescent Cells, Tumor Suppression, and Organismal Aging: Good Citizens, Bad Neighbors', *Cell* 120 (25 Feb. 2005), 513–22.

CASEY, JOHN, *Pagan Virtue: An Essay in Ethics* (Oxford: Clarendon, 1990).

CHARLESWORTH, BRIAN, 'Patterns of Age-Specific Means and Genetic Variances of Mortality Rates Predicted by the Mutation-Accumulation Theory of Ageing', *Journal of Theoretical Biology* 210 (2001), 47–65.

_____ and PARTRIDGE, LINDA, 'Ageing: Levelling of the Grim Reaper', *Current Biology* 7/7 (1997), R440–R442.

CICERO, *Cato Maior de Senectute*, ed. with an introduction and commentary by J. G. F. Powell (Cambridge: Cambridge University Press, 1988).

_____ *Selected Works*, tr. and with introduction by Michael Grant, rev. edn. (London: Penguin, 1971).

CLARK, STEPHEN R. L., *How to Live Forever: Science Fiction and Philosophy* (London: Routledge, 1995).

CLÉNARD, NICHOLAS, *Institutiones linguae grecae* (London: Thomas Marshe, 1572).

COETZEE, J. M., *Age of Iron* (London: Penguin, 1990).

_____ *Disgrace* (1999; New York: Penguin, 2000).

_____ *Elizabeth Costello: Eight Lessons* (London: Secker & Warburg, 2003).

_____ *The Master of Petersburg* (London: Secker & Warburg, 1994).

_____ 'The Novel Today', *Upstream* 6/1 (1988), 2–5.

_____ *White Writing: On the Culture of Letters in South Africa* (New Haven: Yale University Press, 1988).

_____ et al., *The Lives of Animals* (Princeton, NJ: Princeton University Press, 1999).

COHEN, LEE (ed.), *Justice Across Generations: What Does It Mean?* (Washington DC: American Association of Retired Persons, 1993).

COKAYNE, KAREN, *Experiencing Old Age in Ancient Rome* (New York: Routledge, 2003).

COLE, THOMAS R., *The Journey of Life: A Cultural History of Ageing in America* (Cambridge: Cambridge University Press, 1992).

COLE, THOMAS R., KASTENBAUM, ROBERT, and RAY, RUTH E. (eds.), *Handbook of the Humanities and Aging*, 2nd edn. (New York: Springer, 2000).

COOKE, RACHEL, 'The Amis Papers' (Interview with Martin Amis), *The Observer Review*, 1 Oct. 1986, <http://observer.guardian.co.uk/review/story/0,1884637, 00.html>, accessed 15 Feb. 2007.

COOPER, JOHN, *Reason and Human Good in Aristotle* (Cambridge, Mass.: Harvard University Press, 1975).

CROLL, ELIZABETH, 'Ageing in Asia: Culture, Generations and Policy', paper delivered at a conference on *Ageing in Asia*, School of Interdisciplinary Area Studies, Oxford Institute of Ageing and Asian Studies Centre, St Antony's College, Oxford, 18–19 Feb. 2005.

DANIELS, NORMAN, *Am I My Parents' Keeper? An Essay on Justice between the Young and the Old* (New York: Oxford University Press, 1988).

_____ *Just Health Care* (Cambridge: Cambridge University Press, 1985).

_____ 'The Prudential Lifespan Account: Objections and Replies', in *Justice and Justification* (Cambridge: Cambridge University Press, 1996), 257–83.

DARWIN, CHARLES, *The Descent of Man, and Selection in Relation to Sex*, A Facsimile of the 1871 First Issue, 2 vols. in 1, with an Introduction by John Tyler Bonner and Robert M. May (Princeton, NJ: Princeton University Press, 1981).

_____ *On the Origin of Species*, A Facsimile of the First Edition, with an Introduction by Ernst Mayr (Cambridge, Mass.: Harvard University Press, 1964).

DAWKINS, RICHARD, *The Selfish Gene*, 2nd edn. (Oxford: Oxford University Press, 1989).

DERRIDA, JACQUES, 'The Pharmakon' (Part 4 of 'Plato's Pharmacy'), in *Dissemination*, tr. Barbara Johnson (Chicago: University of Chicago Press, 1981), 61–171.

DEUTSCHER, PENELOPE, 'Beauvoir's Old Age', in Claudia Card (ed.), *The Cambridge Companion to Simone de Beauvoir* (Cambridge: Cambridge University Press, 2003), 286–304.

_____ 'Bodies, Lost and Found: Simone de Beauvoir from *The Second Sex* to Old Age', *Radical Philosophy* 96 (1999), 6–16.

_____ 'Three Touches to the Skin and One Look: Sartre and Beauvoir on Desire and Embodiment', in Sara Ahmed et al. (eds.), *Thinking Through the Skin* (London: Routledge, 2001), 143–59.

DICKENS, CHARLES, *Hard Times*, ed. with an introduction and notes by Paul Schlicke, Oxford World's Classics (Oxford: Oxford University Press, 1998).

DICKENS, CHARLES, *The Letters of Charles Dickens*, Pilgrim edn., ed. Madeline House, Graham Storey, et al., 12 vols. (Oxford: Clarendon, 1965–2002).

——— *Master Humphrey's Clock and Other Stories*, ed. Peter Mudford (London: J. M. Dent, 1997).

——— *The Old Curiosity Shop*, ed. Elizabeth M. Brennan (Oxford: Clarendon, 1997).

DIERKS, MANFRED, 'Der Wahn und die Traüme in "Der Tod in Venedig": Thomas Manns folgenreiche Freud-Lektüre im Jahr 1911', *Psyche* 44 (1990), 240–68.

DODD, WILLIAM, 'Impossible Worlds: What Happens in *King Lear*, Act 1 Scene 1?', *Shakespeare Quarterly* 50 (1999), 477–507.

DOREY, T. A. (ed.), *Cicero* (London: Routledge & Kegan Paul, 1964).

DOSTOEVSKY, FYODOR, *Crime and Punishment*, ed. with an Introduction and notes by David McDuff, rev. edn. (London: Penguin, 2003).

DOVER, K. J., *Greek Homosexuality* (London: Duckworth, 1978).

DRAAISMA, DOUWE, *Why Life Speeds Up as You Get Older: How Memory Shapes Our Past*, tr. Arnold and Erica Pomerans (Cambridge: Cambridge University Press, 2004).

DRABBLE, MARGARET, *The Witch of Exmoor* (San Diego, Calif.: Harcourt Brace, 1996).

DRESSER, REBECCA, 'Life, Death, and Incompetent Patients: Conceptual Infirmities and Hidden Values in the Law', *Arizona Law Review* 28/3 (1986), 373–405.

DWORKIN, RONALD, *Life's Dominion: An Argument about Abortion and Euthanasia* (London: HarperCollins, 1993).

——— *Sovereign Virtue: The Theory and Practice of Equality* (Cambridge, Mass.: Harvard University Press, 2002).

ELIOT, T. S., *The Complete Poems* and *Plays* (London: Faber and Faber, 1969).

ELLIOTT, MICHAEL (dir.), *King Lear* (BBC Television, 1984).

ELTON, W. R., 'Aristotle's *Nicomachean Ethics* and Shakespeare's *Troilus and Cressida*', *Journal of the History of Ideas* 58/1 (1997), 331–7.

ERIKSON, ERIC H., ERIKSON, JOAN M., and KIVNICK, HELEN Q., *Vital Involvement in Old Age* (New York: W. W. Norton, 1986).

EVERETT, BARBARA, 'The Treasurer's Son—Money, Worth, and the Inner Life in Philip Larkin', *Times Literary Supplement*, 19 Sept. 1997, 3.

FAULKNER, THOMAS M., *The Poetics of Old Age in Greek Epic, Lyric, and Tragedy* (Norman: University of Oklahoma Press, 1995).

FAULKNER, THOMAS M., and DE LUCE, JUDITH (eds.), *Old Age in Greek and Latin Literature* (Albany, NY: State University of New York Press, 1989).

FEATHERSTONE, MIKE, and WERNICK, ANDREW (eds.), *Images of Aging: Cultural Representations of Later Life* (London: Routledge, 1995).

FINCH, C. E., *Longevity, Senescence, and the Genome* (Chicago: University of Chicago Press, 1990).

FINCH, JOCELYN SCOTT, 'Menopause: Adaptation or Epiphenomenon', *Evolutionary Anthropology* 10 (2001), 43–57.

FOSSHEIM, HALLVARD, 'Mimesis in Aristotle's Ethics', in Øivind Andersen and Jon Haarberg (eds.), *Making Sense of Aristotle: Essays in Poetics* (London: Duckworth, 2001), 73–86.

FRANZEN, JONATHAN, *The Corrections* (New York: Farrar, Straus & Giroux, 2001).

FRIEDAN, BETTY, *The Fountain of Age* (London: Jonathan Cape, 1993).

GARLAND, ROBERT, *The Greek Way of Life: From Conception to Old Age* (London: Duckworth, 1990).

GINZBURG, CARLO, 'Killing a Chinese Mandarin: The Moral Implications of Distance', *Critical Inquiry* 21 (1991), 46–60.

GRAZIA, MARGRETA DE, 'The Ideology of Superfluous Things: *King Lear* as Period Piece', in Margreta de Grazia, Maureen Quilligan, and Peter Stallybrass (eds.), *Subject and Object in Renaissance Culture* (Cambridge: Cambridge University Press, 1996), 17–42.

GREENBLATT, STEPHEN, 'Shakespeare and the Exorcists', in Patricia Parker and Geoffrey Hartman (eds.), *Shakespeare and Question of Theory* (London: Routledge, 1985), 163–87.

GRIFFIN, JAMES, *Well-Being: Its Meaning, Measurement, and Moral Importance* (Oxford: Clarendon, 1986).

GRIFFIN, JASPER, *Homer on Life and Death* (Oxford: Clarendon, 1980).

GULLETTE, MARGARET MORGANROTH, *Aged by Culture* (Chicago: Chicago University Press, 2004).

—— *Declining to Decline: Cultural Combat and the Politics of the Midlife* (Charlottesville, Va.: University Press of Virginia, 1997).

—— 'The Exile of Adulthood: Pedophilia in the Midlife Novel', *Novel* 17/3 (1984), 215–32.

GUTMAN, D., *Reclaimed Powers: Toward a New Psychology of Men and Women in Later Life* (New York: Basic Books, 1987).

HALL, G. STANLEY, *Senescence: The Last Half of Life* (New York: Appleton, 1922).

HALPERIN, DAVID, *One Hundred Years of Homosexuality* (New York: Routledge, 1990).

HARRIS, JOHN (ed.), *Bioethics* (Oxford: Oxford University Press, 2001).

HARRISON, TONY, *Black Daisies for the Bride* (London: Faber, 1993).

HAWKES, K., O'CONNELL, J. F., BLURTON JONES, N. G., ALVAREZ, H., and CHARNOV, E. L., 'Grandmothering, Menopause, and the Evolution of Human Life Histories', *Proceedings of the National Academy of Sciences, USA* 95 (1998), 1336–9.

HAWLEY, KATHERINE, *How Things Persist* (Oxford: Clarendon, 2001).

HAYFLICK, LEONARD, *How and Why We Age* (New York: Ballantine, 1996).

'The Limited In Vitro Lifetime of Human Diploid Cell Strains', *Experimental Cellular Research* 37 (1965), 614–36.

—— 'Living Forever and Dying in the Attempt', *Experimental Gerontology* 38 (2003), 1231–41.

—— and MOORHEAD, P. S., 'The Social Cultivation of Human Diploid Cell Strains', *Experimental Cellular Research* 25 (1961), 585–621.

HEANEY, SEAMUS, 'A Memorable Voice', in *Preoccupations: Selected Prose 1968–1978* (London: Faber & Faber, 1980), 199–201.

HEIDEGGER, MARTIN, *Being and Time, A Translation of* Sein und Zeit, tr. Joan Stambaugh (Albany, NY: State University of New York Press, 1996).

HEILBRUN, CAROLYN, *The Last Gift of Time: Life Beyond Sixty* (New York: Ballantine Books, 1997).

HEILBUT, ANTHONY, *Thomas Mann: Eros and Literature* (New York: Alfred A. Knopf, 1996).

HELLER, ZOË, 'The Ghost Rutter', *The New Republic* 224/21 (21 May 2001).

HERODOTUS, *The Persian Wars*, tr. G. C. Macaulay (London: Macmillan, 1890).

——— *The Persian Wars: Books I–II*, with an English tr. by A. D. Godley (Cambridge, Mass.: Harvard University Press, 1926).

HILL, KIM, and HURTADO, A. MAGDALENA, 'The Evolution of Premature Reproductive Senescence and Menopause in Human Females: An Evaluation of the "Grandmother Hypothesis"', *Human Nature* 2 (1991), 313–50.

HITCHENS, CHRISTOPHER, 'The Egg-Head's Egger-On', *London Review of Books*, 22/9 (27 Apr. 2000), <http://www.lrb.co.uk/v22/n09/hitc2209.htm>, last accessed 15 Feb. 2007.

HOBSBAWM, ERIC, *Age of Extremes: A History of the Short Twentieth Century, 1914–1990* (1994; London: Abacus, 1995).

HOFMILLER, JOSEF, 'Thomas Manns neue Erzählung', *Süddeutsche Monatshefte* 10 (1931), 218–32.

HOLLINGTON, MICHAEL, 'Adorno, Benjamin and *The Old Curiosity Shop*', *Dickens Quarterly* 6/3 (1989), 89–95.

HOMER, *The Iliad*, tr. Samuel Butler (1898; New York: Barnes & Noble, 1995); *The Iliad*, tr. E. V. Rieu (Harmondsworth: Penguin, 1950).

HONIGMANN, E. A. J., *Myriad-Minded Shakespeare: Essays on the Tragedies, Problem Comedies and Shakespeare the Man*, 2nd edn. (London: Macmillan, 1998).

HUME, DAVID, *A Treatise of Human Nature: Being an Attempt to Introduce the Experimental Method of Reasoning into Moral Subjects*, ed. David Fate Norton and Mary J. Norton, Oxford Philosophical Texts (Oxford: Oxford University Press, 2000).

HURKA, THOMAS, *Perfectionism* (Oxford: Oxford University Press, 1993).

HURSTHOUSE, ROSALIND, *Beginning Lives* (Oxford: Basil Blackwell, 1987).

——— *Virtue Ethics* (Oxford: Oxford University Press, 1999).

HUSSERL, EDMUND, *On the Phenomenology of the Consciousness of Internal Time* (1928), tr. Richard Rojcewicz and André Schuwer (Dordrecht: Kluwer, 1989).

IGNATIEFF, MICHAEL, *Scar Tissue* (1992; London, Vintage, 1993).

JAMESON, FREDRIC, *Late Marxism: Adorno, or, The Persistence of the Dialectic* (London: Verso, 1990)

——— 'Longevity as Class Struggle', in George Slusser, Gary Westfahl, and Eric S. Rubkin (eds.), *Immortal Engines: Life Extension and Immortality in Science Fiction and Fantasy* (Athens, Ga.: University of Georgia Press, 1996), 24–42.

JARVIS, SIMON, *Adorno: A Critical Introduction* (Cambridge: Polity, 1998).

JAWORSKA, AGNIESZKA, 'Respecting the Margins of Agency: Alzheimer's Patients and the Capacity to Value', *Philosophy and Public Affairs* 28/2 (1999), 105–38.

JECKER, NANCY S. (ed.), *Aging and Ethics: Philosophical Problems in Gerontology* (Clifton, NJ: Humana, 1991).

JENNINGS, KATE, *Moral Hazard: A Novel* (London: Fourth Estate, 2002).

KANES, MARTIN, *Père Goriot: Anatomy of a Troubled World* (New York: Twayne, 1993).

KATZ, STEPHEN, *Disciplining Old Age: The Formation of Gerontological Knowledge* (Charlottesville, Va.: University Press of Virginia, 1996).

KAUFMAN, S. R., *The Ageless Self: Sources of Meaning in Late Life* (New York: New American Library, 1986).

KAY, N. M., *Martial Book XI: A Commentary* (London: Duckworth, 1985).

KENNEDY, GEORGE A., *Aristotle on Rhetoric: A Theory of Civic Discourse* (New York: Oxford University Press, 1991).

KENNY, ANTHONY, *Aristotle and the Perfect Life* (Oxford: Oxford University Press, 1992).

KERRIGAN, JOHN, 'Old, Old, Old, Old, Old', Review of R. F. Foster, *W. B. Yeats: A Life*, ii. *The Arch-Poet 1915–39* (2004), *London Review of Books*, 3 Mar. 2005, 7–10.

KINSELLA, KEVIN, and FERREIRA, MONICA, 'International Brief: Aging Trends: South Africa' (US Department of Commerce, Economics and Statistics Administration, Bureau of the Census, August 1997), <http://www.census.gov/ipc/prod/ib-9702.pdf>, last accessed 15 Feb. 2007.

KIRKWOOD, T. B. L., *The End of Age: Why Everything About Aging is Changing* (London: Profile, 2001).

—— 'Evolution of Aging', *Nature* 270 (1977), 301–4.

—— *Time of Our Lives: The Science of Human Aging* (New York: Oxford University Press, 1999).

—— 'Understanding the Odd Science of Aging', review article, *Cell* 120 (25 Feb. 2005), 437–47.

KNOWLSON, JAMES, *Damned to Fame: The Life of Samuel Beckett* (London: Bloomsbury, 1996).

KRAUT, RICHARD (ed.), *The Cambridge Companion to Plato* (Cambridge: Cambridge University Press, 1992).

KUKLICK, BRUCE, *A History of Philosophy in America, 1720–2000* (Oxford: Clarendon, 2001).

KURZKE, HERMANN, *Thomas Mann: Life as a Work of Art. A Biography*, tr. Leslie Willson (Princeton: Princeton University Press, 2002).

LARKIN, PHILIP, *Collected Poems*, ed. with an introduction by Anthony Thwaite (London: The Marvell Press and Faber & Faber, 1988).

—— 'Frivolous and Vulnerable', review of Stevie Smith, *Selected Poems* (1962), *New statesman*, 28 Sept. 1962, 416, 418.

LARKIN, PHILIP, *Further Requirements: Interviews, Broadcasts, Statements and Book Reviews*, ed. and with and introduction by Anthony Thwaite (London: Faber and Faber, 2002).

—— *High Windows* (London: Faber & Faber, 1974).

—— *Selected Letters of Philip Larkin, 1940–1985*, ed. Anthony Thwaite (London: Faber and Faber, 1992).

LAVERY, BRYONY, *A Wedding Story* (London: Faber & Faber, 2001).

LEW, E., and GARFINKEL, L., 'Mortality at Ages 75 and Older in the Cancer Prevention Study. (CPSI)', *Cancer Journal for Clinicians* 40/4 (1990), 210–24.

LITVAK, JOSEPH, 'Adorno Now', *Victorian Studies* 44/1 (2001), 33–9.

LONG, A. A., and SEDLEY, D. N., *The Hellenistic Philosophers*, 2 vols. (Cambridge: Cambridge University Press, 1987).

LUKÁCS, GEORG VON, *Die Seele und die Formen: Essays* (Berlin: Egon Fleischel, 1911); *Soul and Form*, tr. Anna Bostock (Cambridge, Mass.: MIT, 1974).

LUCRETIUS, *De Rerum Natura*, with an English translation by W. H. D. Rouse, rev. Martin Ferguson Smith, Loeb Classical Library (1975; rev. Cambridge, Mass.: Harvard University Press, 1992).

McCONICA, JAMES, 'Elizabethan Oxford: The Collegiate Society', in McConica (ed.) *The History of the University of Oxford*, iii. *The Collegiate University* (Oxford: Clarendon Press, 1986), 645–732.

McDONALD, PETER, 'Disgrace Effects', *Interventions* 4/3 (2002), 321–30.

MACINTYRE, ALASDAIR, *After Virtue: A Study in Moral Theory*, 2nd edn. (London: Gerald Duckworth, 1985).

—— *Dependent Rational Animals: Why Human Beings Need the Virtues* (London: Duckworth, 1999).

McKEE, PATRICK L., *Philosophical Foundations of Gerontology* (New York: Human Sciences, 1982).

McKERLIE, DENNIS, 'Equality and Time', *Ethics* 99 (1989), 475–91.

—— 'Justice Between Age Groups: A Comment on Norman Daniels', *Journal of Applied Philosophy* 6/2 (1989), 227–34.

—— 'Justice Between the Young and the Old', *Philosophy and Public Affairs* 30/2 (2002), 152–77.

MACKIE, JOHN L., 'The Law of the Jungle: Moral Alternatives and Principles of Evolution', *Philosophy* 53 (1978), 455–64.

McSHEA, DAVID W., 'Complexity and Evolution: What Everybody Knows', in David L. Hull and Michael Ruse (eds.), *The Philosophy of Biology* (Oxford: Oxford University Press, 1998), 625–49.

MANN, THOMAS, 'Die Erotik Michelangelos', in *Altes und Neues: Kleine Prosa aus fünf Jahrzehnten* (1953; Berlin: Aufbau, 1956).

—— *Essays of Three Decades*, tr. H. T. Lowe-Porter (New York: Alfred A. Knopf, 1947).

—— *Reflections of a Nonpolitical Man*, tr. with an introduction by Walter D. Morris (New York: Frederick Ungar, 1983).

—— *Sämtliche Erzahlungen* (Frankfurt am Main: S. Fischer, 1963).

_____ 'Der Tod in Venedig', in *Sämtliche Erzahlungen* (Frankfurt am Main: S. Fischer, 1963); *Death in Venice and Other Stories*, tr. and with an introduction by David Luke (New York: Bantam, 1988).

MARCUS, JUDITH, *Georg Lukács and Thomas Mann: A Study in the Sociology of Literature* (Amherst: University of Massachusetts Press, 1987).

MARKS, ELAINE, *Simone de Beauvoir: Encounters with Death* (New Brunswick, NJ: Rutgers University Press, 1973).

MARKUS, H., and NURIUS, P., 'Possible Selves', *American Psychologist* 41 (1986), 954–69.

MARS JONES, ADAM, 'Stands of Reason: Disgrace by J. M. Coetzee', *The Observer*, 18 July 1999, http://books.guardian.co.uk/reviews/generalfiction/0,6121,96805.00html, last accessed 15 Feb. 2007.

MAUS, KATHERINE EISAMANN, *Inwardness and Theatre in the English Renaissance* (Chicago: University of Chicago Press, 1995).

MEDAWAR, P. B., *An Unsolved Problem in Biology* (London: H. K. Lewis, 1952).

_____ 'Old Age and Natural Death', *Modern Quarterly* 1 (1946), 30–56.

MELTON, LISA, 'How Brainpower Can Help You Cheat Old Age'. *New Scientist*, 17 Dec. 2005, <http://www.newscientist.com/channel/health/mg18825301.300.html>, last accessed 15 Feb. 2007.

METCHNIKOFF, ÉLIE, *The Nature of Man: Studies in Optimistic Philosophy* (New York: G. Putnam's Sons, 1903).

_____ *The Prolongation of Life: Optimistic Studies*, ed. P. Chalmers Mitchell (New York: G. Putnam's Sons, 1908).

MILLER, JONATHAN (dir.), *King Lear* (BBC Television, 1982).

MILLER, SARAH CLARK, 'The Lived Experience of Doubling: Simone de Beauvoir's Phenomenology of Old Age', in Wendy O'Brien and Lester Embree (eds.), *The Existential Phenomenology of Simone de Beauvoir* (Dordrecht: Kluwer, 2001), 127–48.

MILO, DANIEL S., *Trahir le temps (histoire)* (Paris: Belles Lettres, 1991).

MINDON, MICHAEL (ed.), *Thomas Mann* (London: Longman, 1995).

MITSIS, PHILLIP, 'Epicurus on Death and the Duration of Life', in John J. Cleary and Daniel C. Shartin (eds.), *Proceedings of the Boston Area Colloquium in Ancient Philosophy* IV (New York: Lanham, 1988).

MODELL, JOHN, FURSTENBERG, FRANK, and HERSHBERG, THEODORE, 'Social Change and Transitions to Adulthood in Historical Perspective', *Journal of Family History* 1/1 (1976), 7–32.

MOI, TORIL, *Simone de Beauvoir: The Making of an Intellectual Woman* (Oxford: Basil Blackwell, 1994).

MONTAIGNE, MICHEL DE, 'De L'Âge', in *Œuvres complètes*, ed. Albert Thibaudet and Maurice Rat, introduction et notes par Maurice Rat (Paris: Gallimard, 1962).

MOTION, ANDREW, *Philip Larkin: A Writer's Life* (London: Faber & Faber, 1993).

MYERS, J. E., *Empowerment for Later Life* (Ann Arbor: University of Michigan, 1990).

NAGEL, THOMAS, *Mortal Questions* (Cambridge: Cambridge University Press, 1997).

_____ *The Possibility of Altruism* (Princeton, NJ: Princeton University Press, 1970).

NAGEL, THOMAS, *The View from Nowhere* (New York: Oxford University Press, 1986).

NEHAMAS, ALEXANDER, *Nietzsche: Life as Literature* (Cambridge, Mass.: Harvard University Press, 1985).

NEUBERGER, JULIA, *The Moral State We're In: A Manifesto for a Twenty-First Century Society* (London: HarperCollins, 2005).

NICOLSON, MARJORIE, and MOHLER, NORA M., 'The Scientific Background of Swift's "Voyage to Laputa"', *Annals of Science* 11 (1937), repr. in A. Norman Jeffares (ed.), *Fair Liberty Was All His Cry* (New York: St Martin's Press, 1967), 231–3.

NIETZSCHE, FRIEDRICH, *Basic Writings of Nietzsche*, tr. and ed. Walter Kaufmann (New York: The Modern Library, 2000).

———— 'On the Uses and Disadvantages of History for Life', in Nietzsche, *Untimely Meditations*, ed. Daniel Breazeale, tr. R. J. Hollingdale, Cambridge Texts in the History of Philosophy (Cambridge: Cambridge University Press, 1997), 114–23.

NULAND, SHERWIN B., *How We Die: Reflections on Life's Final Chapter* (1993; New York: Vintage, 1995).

NUSSBAUM, MARTHA C., *The Fragility of Goodness: Luck and Ethics in Greek Tragedy and Philosophy*, updated edn. (Cambridge: Cambridge University Press, 2001).

———— *Poetic Justice: The Literary Imagination and Public Life* (Boston: Beacon, 1995).

———— *Upheavals of Thought: The Intelligence of Emotions* (Cambridge: Cambridge University Press, 2001).

O'BRIEN, MICHAEL J., ' "Becoming Immortal" in Plato's Symposium', in Douglas E. Gerber (ed.), *Greek Poetry and Philosophy: Studies in Honour of Leonard Woodbury* (Chico, Calif.: Scholars Press, 1984), 185–205.

OLSHANSKY, S. JAY, and CARNES, BRUCE A., *The Quest for Immortality: Science at the Frontiers of Aging* (New York: W. W. Norton, 2001).

PACKER, C., TATAR, M., and COLLINS, A., 'A Reproductive Cessation in Female Animals', *Nature* 392 (1998), 807–11.

PARFIT, DEREK, 'Comments', *Ethics* 96/4 (1986), 832–72.

———— 'Equality and Priority', *Ratio* NS 10 (1997), 202–21.

———— 'Later Selves and Moral Principles', in Alan Montefiore (ed.), *Philosophy and Personal Relations* (London: Routledge & Kegan Paul, 1973), 137–69.

———— *Reasons and Persons* (1984; rev. edn. Oxford: Clarendon, 1987).

PARKIN, TIM G., *Old Age in the Roman World: A Cultural and Social History* (Baltimore: Johns Hopkins University Press, 2003).

PLATO, *The Collected Dialogues of Plato*, ed. Edith Hamilton and Huntington Cairns, Bollingen Series LXXI (Princeton: Princeton University Press, 1961).

———— *Lysis, Symposium, Gorgias*, tr. W. R. M. Lamb, Loeb Classical Library (Cambridge, Mass.: Harvard University Press, 1925).

———— *The Symposium of Plato*, ed., with introduction, critical notes and commentary, R. G. Bury, 2nd edn. (Cambridge: Heffer, 1932).

PLETCHER, SCOTT D., and CURTSINGER, JAMES W., 'Mortality Plateaus and the Evolution of Senescence: Why are Old-Age Mortality Rates So Low?', *Evolution* 52/2 (1998), 454–64.

PLUTARCH, *The Life of Cicero*, tr. Bernadotte Perrin, in *Plutarch's Lives*, 11 vols. (London: William Heinemann, 1919).

POOLE, ADRIAN, 'The Shadow of Lear's "Houseless" in Dickens', *Shakespeare Survey* 52 (2000), 103–13.

POSNER, RICHARD, *Aging and Old Age* (Chicago: University of Chicago Press, 1995).

PROUST, MARCEL, *By Way of Sainte-Beuve*, tr. Sylvia Townsend Warner, with a new Introduction by Terence Kilmartin (London: The Hogarth Press, 1984).

RAITT, SUZANNE, 'Freud's Theory of Metaphor: *Beyond the Pleasure Principle*, Nineteenth-Century Science and Figurative Language', in Helen Small and Trudi Tate (eds.), *Literature, Science, Psychoanalysis, 1830–1970* (Oxford: Oxford University Press, 2003), 118–30.

RAUSER, CASANDRA L., MUELLER, LAURENCE D., and ROSE, MICHAEL R., 'Aging, Fertility, and Immortality', *Experiential Gerontology* 38 (2003), 27–33.

—— 'The Evolution of Late Life', *Ageing Research Reviews*, 5/1 (2005), 14–32.

RAWLS, JOHN, *A Theory of Justice*, rev. edn. (Cambridge, Mass.: Belknap Press, 1999).

REED, T. J., *Thomas Mann: The Uses of Tradition*, 2nd edn. (Oxford: Clarendon, 1996).

RICHARDS, JANET RADCLIFFE, *Human Nature after Darwin: A Philosophical Introduction* (2000; London: Routledge, 2004).

RICHARDSON, BESSIE ELLEN, *Old Age Among the Ancient Greeks* (Baltimore: Johns Hopkins University Press, 1933).

RIDLEY, MATT, *The Origins of Virtue* (London: Penguin, 1996).

RILEY, PATRICK (ed.), *The Cambridge Companion to Rousseau* (Cambridge: Cambridge University Press, 2001).

ROBB, GRAHAM, *Balzac: A Biography* (London: Picador, 1994).

ROGERS, ALAN R., 'Why Menopause?', *Evolutionary Ecology* 7 (1993), 406–20.

RORTY, AMÉLIE OKSENBERG, 'Improvisatory Accident-Prone Dramas of (What Passes for) a Person's Life', in Cynthia Lightfoot, Chris Lalonde and Michael Chandler (eds.), *Changing Conceptions of Psychological Life*, Jean Piaget Symposium Series 30 (Mahwah, NJ: Laurence Erlbaum, 2004), 243–54.

ROSE, JACQUELINE, 'Apathy and Accountability: The Challenge of South Africa's Truth and Reconciliation Commission to the Intellectual in the Modern World', in Helen Small (ed.), *The Public Intellectual* (Oxford: Blackwell, 2002), 159–78.

ROSE, MICHAEL R., 'Antagonistic Pleiotropy, Dominance, and Genetic Variation', *Heredity* 48 (1982), 63–78.

—— *Evolutionary Biology of Aging* (New York: Oxford University Press, 1991).

—— and CHARLESWORTH, BRIAN, 'Genetics of Life-History in *Drosophila melanogaster*. I: Sib Analysis of Adult Females' and 'II. Exploratory Selection Experiments', *Genetics* 97 (1981), 173–85, 187–96.

Rose, Michael R., Passananti, Hardip B., and Matos, Margarida (eds.), *Methuselah Flies: A Case Study in the Evolution of Aging* (Singapore: World Scientific, 2004).

——Rauser, Casandra L., and Mueller, Laurence D., 'Late Life: A New Frontier for Physiology', *Physiological and Biochemical Zoology* 78 (2005), 869–78.

Rosen, Charles, 'Should We Adore Adorno?', *New York Review of Books*, 24 Oct. 2002, 59–66.

Rosenbaum, Stephen, 'Epicurus on Pleasure and the Complete Life', *The Monist* 73/1 (1990), 21–41.

Rosslyn, Felicity, 'Pope on the Subject of Old Age: The *Iliad* Translation, Books xxii–xxiv', in Howard Erskine-Hill and Anne Smith (eds.), *The Art of Alexander Pope* (London: Vision, 1979), 119–31.

Roth, Philip, *The Breast* (London: Jonathan Cape, 1973).

——*Deception: A Novel* (London: Cape, 1990).

——*The Dying Animal* (Boston: Houghton Mifflin, 2001).

——*The Human Stain* (Boston: Houghton Mifflin, 2000).

——*The Prague Orgy* (London: Jonathan Cape, 1985).

Rozanov, V. V., *Solitaria*, with an 'Abridged Account of the Author's Life', by E. Gollerbach, and other biographical material and matter from *The Apocalypse of our Time*, tr. S. S. Kateliansky (London: Wishart, 1927).

Ruse, Michael, *Evolutionary Naturalism* (London: Routledge, 1995).

——review of William D. Casebeer, *Natural Ethical Facts: Evolution, Connectivism, and Moral Cognition* (Cambridge, Mass.: MIT, 2003), *Evolutionary Psychology* 2 (2004), 89–91.

——*Taking Darwin Seriously: A Naturalistic Approach to Philosophy* (Oxford: Basil Blackwell, 1986).

——and Wilson, E. O., 'Moral Philosophy as Applied Science', in Elliott Sober (ed.), *Conceptual Issues in Evolutionary Biology* (Cambridge, Mass.: London: MIT, 1994), 421–38.

Safranski, Rüdiger, *Nietzsche: A Philosophical Biography*, tr. Shelley Frisch (London: Granta, 2002).

Said, Edward, 'Adorno as Lateness Itself', in *Adorno: A Critical Reader*, ed. Nigel Gibson and Andrew Rubin, Blackwell Critical Reader (Oxford: Blackwell, 2001), 193–208.

——*On Late Style* (London: Bloomsbury, 2006).

——'Thoughts on Late Style', *London Review of Books* 26/15 (5 Aug. 2004), <http://www.lrb.co.uk/v26/n15/said01_.html>, last accessed 15 Feb. 2007.

——'Untimely Meditations', *The Nation*, 14 Aug. 2003, <http://www.thenation.com/doc/20030901/said>, last accessed 15 Feb. 2007.

Salingar, Leo, *Dramatic Form in Shakespeare and the Jacobeans: Essays* (Cambridge: Cambridge University Press, 1986).

Sartre, Jean-Paul, *L'Être et le néant: essai d'ontologie phénoménologique* (1943), ed. and corr. with index, Arlette Elkaïm-Sartre (Paris: Gallimard, 1976).

SCHMITT, CHARLES, *Aristotle and the Renaissance* (Cambridge, Mass.: Harvard University Press, 1983).

SCHOENBAUM, S., *William Shakespeare: A Compact Documentary Life*, rev. edn. (New York: Oxford University Press, 1987).

SCHOFIELD, MALCOLM, 'Religion and Philosophy in the *Laws*: The C. J. de Vogel Lecture, 2001', in *Plato's Laws: From Theory into Practice, Proceedings of the VI Symposium Platonicum Selected Papers*, ed. Samuel Scolnicov and Luc Brisson (Sankt Augustin: Academia, 2003), 1–13.

SCHOLES, ROBERT, 'Language, Narrative, and Anti-narrative', *Critical Inquiry* 7/1 (1980), 204–12.

SCHWARTZ, HILLEL, *Century's End: A Cultural History of the Fin de Siècle from the 990s through the 1990s* (New York: Doubleday, 1990).

SEEDAT, ABIZA, *Crippling as Nation: Health in Apartheid South Africa* (London: International Defence & Aid Fund, 1984).

SEN, AMARTYA, *Commodities and Capabilities* (Amsterdam: North Holland, 1985).

—— *Development as Freedom* (Oxford: Oxford University Press, 1999).

—— 'Utilitarianism and Welfarism', *The Journal of Philosophy* 76/9 (1979), 463–89.

—— 'What Difference Can Ethics Make?', closing speech to the International Meeting on Ethics and Development of the Inter-American Development Bank in collaboration with the Norwegian Government, <www.iadb.org/etica/documentos/dc_sen_queimp-i.doc>, last accessed 15 Feb. 2007.

SHAKESPEARE, WILLIAM, *King Lear*, ed. Kenneth Muir, Arden (Cambridge, Mass.: Harvard University Press, 1952).

—— *King Lear: A Parallel Text Edition*, ed. René Weis (London: Longman, 1993).

—— *King Lear* (Folio text), in *The Complete Works*, Compact Edition, gen. eds. Stanley Wells and Gary Taylor (1988; rev. edn. Oxford: Clarendon, 1998).

—— *The Riverside Shakespeare*, 2nd edn., gen. and textual ed., G. Blakemore Evans, with the assistance of J. J. M. Tobin (Boston: Houghton Mifflin, 1997).

—— *Troilus and Cressida*, ed. Kenneth Palmer (London: Methuen, 1982).

SHEFFIELD, FRISBEE C. C., 'Psychic Pregnancy and Platonic Epistemology', *Oxford Studies in Ancient Philosophy* 20 (2001), 1–33.

SHIFFRIN, SEANA VALENTINE, 'Autonomy, Beneficence, and the Permanently Demented', in Justine Burley (ed.), *Dworkin and His Critics, with Replies by Dworkin* (Oxford: Blackwell, 2004), 195–218, and Dworkin's reply, 366–70.

SHOOKMAN, ELLIS, *Thomas Mann's 'Death in Venice': A Novella and its Critics* (New York: Boydell & Brewer, 2003).

SHOWALTER, ELAINE, 'Critical Cross-Dressing: Male Feminists and the Woman of the Year', *Raritan* 3/2 (1983), 130–49.

SILK, M. S., 'Nestor, Amphitryon, Philocleon, Cephalus: The Language of Old Men in Greek Literature from Homer to Menander', in Francesco de Martino and Alan H. Sommerstein (eds.), *Lo Spetta delle Voci* (Bari: Levante Editori, 1995), 165–214.

SIMPSON, G. G., *Tempo and Mode in Evolution* (New York: Columbia University Press, 1944).

SIPRIOT, PIERRE, *Balzac sans masque: Splendeurs et misères des passions 1799–1850* (Paris: Robert Laffont, 1992).

SLOTE, MICHAEL, *Goods and Virtues* (Oxford: Clarendon, 1983).

SMALL, HELEN, 'Tennyson and Late Style', *Tennyson Research Bulletin* 8/4 (2005), 226–50.

——— ' "The Unquiet Limit": Old Age and Memory in Victorian Narrative', in Sally Shuttleworth, Jackie Labbe, and Matt Campbell (eds.), *Memory, 1789–1914* (London: Routledge, 2000), 60–79, 214–16.

SMITH, STEVIE, *The Collected Poems of Stevie Smith* (London: Allen Lane, 1975).

SMITH, THOMAS W., *Revaluing Ethics: Aristotle's Dialectical Pedagogy* (New York: State University of New York Press, 2001).

SNEAD, JAMES A., 'The Vision of Desire in *Death in Venice*', in Kara Keeling, Colin MacCabe, and Cornel West (eds.), *Racist Traces and Other Writings: European Pedigrees/African Contagions* (London: Palgrave Macmillan, 2003), 59–80.

SOBEL, J. H., 'Ends and Means: Aristotle on Happiness and Virtue', <http://www.utsc.utoronto.ca/~sobel/Means_Ends/Arist_5.pdf>, last accessed 23 Mar. 2007.

SOPHOCLES, *Oedipus the King, Oedipus at Colonus, Antigone*, tr. F. Storr (Cambridge, Mass.: Harvard University Press, 1912).

SOUTH AFRICAN DEPARTMENT OF JUSTICE AND CONSTITUTIONAL DEVELOPMENT website (African Charter on Human and People's Rights), <http://www.doj.gov.za/2004dojsite/policy/african%20charter/africancharter.htm>, last accessed 20 Mar. 2007.

STOCKTON, DAVID, *Cicero: A Political Biography* (Oxford: Oxford University Press, 1971).

STRAWSON, GALEN, 'A Fallacy of Our Age: Not Every Life is a Narrative', *Times Literary Supplement*, 15 Oct. 2004, 13–15.

STRIKER, GISELA, 'Commentary on Mitsis', in John J. Cleary and Daniel C. Shartin (eds.), *Proceedings of the Boston Area Colloquium in Ancient Philosophy* IV (New York: Lanham, 1988), 323–38.

STURGIS, JON, 'Little Nell: The Monster with Two Heads', *Victorian Literature and Culture* 19 (1991), 293–314.

SUNSTEIN, CASS, 'Lives, Life-Years, and Willingness to Pay', *Columbia Law Review* 104/1 (2004), 205–54.

TATE, NAHUM, *The History of King Lear*, ed. James Black, Regents Restoration Drama (London: Edward Arnold, 1976).

TAYLOR, GARY, *Moment by Moment by Shakespeare* (London: Macmillan, 1985).

——— and WARREN, MICHAEL (eds.), *The Division of the Kingdoms: Shakespeare's Two Versions of 'King Lear'* (Oxford: Oxford University Press, 1983).

TEMPLETON, A. R., and RANKIN, M. A., 'Genetic Revolutions and Control of Insect Populations', in R. H. Richardson (ed.), *The Screwworm Problem* (Austin: University of Texas Press, 1978), 81–111.

____CREASE, TERESA J., and SHAH, FAITH, 'The Molecular through Ecological Genetics of Abnormal Abdomen in *Drosophila Mercatorum*. I. Basic Genetics', *Genetics* 111 (1985), 805–18.

THANE, PAT, *Old Age in English History: Past Experience, Present Issues* (Oxford: Oxford University Press, 2000).

THEOPHRASTUS, *The Characters of Theophrastus*, ed. with an introduction and commentary, R. G. Ussher (London: Bristol Classical Press, 1993).

THOMAS, DYLAN, *Collected Poems 1934–1952* (London: J. M. Dent, 1990).

THWAITE, ANTHONY (ed.), *Larkin at Sixty* (London: Faber and Faber, 1982).

TIDD, URSULA, 'For the Time Being: Simone de Beauvoir's Representation of Temporality', in Wendy O'Brien and Lester Embree (eds.), *The Existential Phenomenology of Simone de Beauvoir* (Dordrecht: Kluwer, 2001), 107–26.

VELLEMAN, J. DAVID, 'Well-Being and Time', *Pacific Philosophical Quarterly* 72 (1991), 48–77.

VENDLER, HELEN, 'Death of a Soul', *New York Review of Books*, 20 Oct. 1994, 9–13.

VINCENT, JOHN A., *Old Age*, Key Ideas (London: Routledge, 2003).

VISCONTI, LUCHINO (dir.), *Death in Venice* (Alfa Cinematografica, 1979).

WARREN, JAMES, *Facing Death: Epicurus and his Critics* (Oxford: Clarendon, 2004).

WEBBER, ANDREW J., 'Mann's Man's World: Gender and Sexuality', in Ritchie Robertson (ed.), *The Cambridge Companion to Thomas Mann* (Cambridge: Cambridge University Press, 2002), 64–83.

WEDBERG, ANDERS, *History of Philosophy*, 3 vols. (Oxford: Clarendon, 1982–4).

WEINERT, BRIAN T., and TIMIRAS, POALA S., 'Physiology of Aging: Invited Review: Theories of Aging', *Journal of Applied Physiology* 95 (2003), 1706–16.

WEINSTEIN, BRET S., and CISZEK, DEBORAH, 'The Reserve-Capacity Hypothesis: Evolutionary Origins and Modern Implications of the Trade-off between Tumor-Suppression and Tissue-Repair', *Experimental Gerontology* 37 (2002), 615–27.

WELSH, ALEXANDER, 'King Lear, Père Goriot, and Nell's Grandfather', in Joseph P. Strelka (ed.), *Literary Theory and Criticism: Festschrift Presented to René Wellek in Honor of His Eightieth Birthday*, 2 vols. (Frankfurt am Main: Peter Lang, 1984), ii. 1405–25.

WELLS, STANLEY, and TAYLOR, GARY, *William Shakespeare: A Textual Companion* (Oxford: Oxford University Press, 1987).

WHITE, R. S., *Natural Law in English Renaissance Literature* (Cambridge: Cambridge University Press, 1996).

WIESEL, ELIE, *L'Oublié* (Paris: Éditions du Seuil, 1989).

WILLIAMS, BERNARD, 'Evolution, Ethics, and the Representation Problem' (1983), in *Making Sense of Humanity, and Other Philosophical Papers* (Cambridge: Cambridge University Press, 1995), 100–10.

____ 'The Makropulos Case: Reflections on the Tedium of Immortality' (1972), in *Problems of the Self: Philosophical Papers 1956–1972* (Cambridge: Cambridge University Press, 1973), 82–100.

WILLIAMS, BERNARD, 'Nietzsche's Minimalist Moral Psychology' (1993), in *Making Sense of Humanity*, 65–76.

——— 'Persons, Character and Morality', in Amélie Oksenberg Rorty (ed.), *The Identities of Persons* (Berkeley: University of California Press, 1976), 197–216.

WILLIAMS, GEORGE C., *Plan and Purpose in Nature* (1996; New York: Phoenix/HarperCollins, 1997).

——— 'Pleiotropy, Natural Selection, and the Evolution of Senescence', *Evolution* 11 (1957), 398–411.

——— 'The Tithonus Error in Modern Gerontology', The 1999 Crafoord Prize Lectures, *The Quarterly Review of Biology* 74/4 (1999), 405–15.

WILSON, EMILY R., *Mocked with Death: Tragic Overliving from Sophocles to Milton* (Baltimore: Johns Hopkins University Press, 2004).

WOLF, SUSAN, 'Self-Interest and Interest in Others', *Ethics* 96/4 (1986), 704–20.

WOLOCH, ALEX, *The One vs. the Many: Minor Characters and the Space of the Protagonist in the Novel* (Princeton, NJ: Princeton University Press, 2003).

WOOD, JAMES, 'Coetzee's *Disgrace*: A Few Skeptical Thoughts', in *The Irresponsible Self: On Laughter and the Novel* (New York: Farrar, Straus & Giroux, 2004), 246–57.

WOOD, JAMES W., O'CONNOR, KATHLEEN A., HOLMAN, DARRYL J., BRINDLE, ELEANOR, BARSOM, SUSANNAH H., and GRIMES, MICHAEL A., 'The Evolution of Menopause by Antagonistic Pleiotropy', Working Paper 01–4, 2001, <http://www.csde.washington.edu/pubs/wps/01-04.pdf>, last accessed 13 Aug. 2004.

WOODWARD, KATHLEEN B., *Aging and its Discontents: Freud and Other Fictions* (Bloomington: Indiana University Press, 1991).

——— 'Late Theory, Late Style: Loss and Renewal in Freud and Barthes', in Anne Wyatt-Brown and Janice Rossen (eds.), *Aging and Gender in Literature: Studies in Creativity* (Charlottesville: University of Virginia Press, 1993), 82–101.

——— 'Youthfulness as a Masquerade', *Discourse* 11/1 (1988–9), 119–42.

WOOLCOCK, PETER G., 'The Case against Evolutionary Ethics Today', in Jane Maierschein and Michael Ruse (eds.), *Biology and the Foundation of Ethics* (Cambridge: Cambridge University Press, 1999), 276–306.

WOOLF, VIRGINIA, *The Common Reader* (London: The Hogarth Press, 1925).

XENOPHON, *Memorabilia; Oeconomicus*, with an English tr. by E. C. Marchant, *Symposium; Apology*, with an English tr. by O. J. Dodd (Cambridge, Mass.: Harvard University Press, 1979),

YEATS, W. B., *The Poems*, ed. Daniel Albright (London: J. M. Dent, 1990).

YOUNG, BRUCE W., 'Shakespearean Tragedy in a Renaissance Context: *King Lear* and Hooker's *Of the Laws of Ecclesiastical Polity*', in Robert H. Ray (ed.), *Approaches to Teaching Shakespeare's 'King Lear'* (New York: The Modern Language Association of America, 1986), 98–104.

Notes

INTRODUCTION

1. Dylan Thomas, 'Do Not Go Gentle into That Good Night', *Collected Poems 1934–1952* (London: J. M. Dent & Sons, 1990), 116; W. B. Yeats, 'Her Vision in the Wood', *The Poems*, ed. Daniel Albright (London: J. M. Dent & Sons, 1990), 325.

2. Robert Alter, Response to Michael Ignatieff, *Berlin in Autumn: The Philosopher in Old Age*, Doreen B. Townsend Center for the Humanities, Occasional Papers, 16 (Berkeley: University of California Press, 1998), 40.

3. Alter, Response, 39.

4. The title of Thomas Nagel's 1979 book (Cambridge: Cambridge University Press).

5. I have referred to '*La Vieillesse*' throughout in the main text because the English and American translations are differently titled: *The Coming of Age*, tr. Patrick O'Brian (New York: G. P. Putnam's Sons, 1972); published in England as *Old Age* (London: André Deutsch and Weidenfeld & Nicolson, 1972).

6. See Ronald J. Manheimer, 'Aging in the Mirror of Philosophy', in *Handbook of the Humanities and Aging*, 2nd edn., ed. Thomas R. Cole, Robert Kastenbaum, and Ruth E. Ray (New York: Springer, 2000), 77–92: 'apart from those engaged in bioethics [...] relatively few contemporary academic philosophers participate in critical discourse on aging and later life' (78).

7. I am not including in this statement the specialist philosophical literature on Beauvoir. See 11–15 below for discussion.

8. Michel de Montaigne, 'De L'Âge', in *Œuvres complètes*, ed. Albert Thibaudet and Maurice Rat, introduction and notes Maurice Rat (Paris: Gallimard, 1962), 311–14: 'C'est un sien rare privilège de nous faire durer jusque l'à [à l'âge]. C'est une exemption que [donne la nature] par faveur particulière' (312); 'la vivacité, la promptitude, la fermeté, et autres parties bien plus nôstres, plus importantes et essentielles, se fanissent et s'alanguissent' (313).

9. 'L'alacrité'. Quoted by Beauvoir, *The Coming of Age*, 401; *La Vieillesse*, 424.

10. See esp. Betty Friedan, *The Fountain of Age* (London: Jonathan Cape, 1993) and Margaret Morganroth Gullette, *Aged by Culture* (Chicago: Chicago University Press, 2004), both of which wage impassioned war against the 'declinism' associated with old age. Since the early 1980s there has been a huge proliferation in the literature promoting 'vital' old age. For a concise overview, see Lucille

B. Bearon, 'Successful Aging: What Does the "Good Life" Look Like? Concepts in Gerontology', *The Forum for Family and Consumer Issues* 1/3 (1996) <http://www.ces.ncsu.edu/depts/fcs/pub/aging.html>, last accessed 15 Feb. 2007.

11. See also the observation, credited to Kathleen Woodward, that 'the word "age" itself (because it serves also as another euphemism for "old age") [may] weig[h] in too late in the young/old dichotomy to ever shake that binary'. Gullette, *Aged by Culture*, 105.

12. 'Wear and tear' is a phrase used by cellular biologists to describe the organic processes of the body wearing out—as distinct from the genetic 'time clock' theory, which says that a genetic mechanism triggers ageing at a certain point or points in the life cycle.

13. *Aging and Its Discontents: Freud and Other Fictions* (Bloomington: Indiana University Press, 1991), 4.

14. See, *inter alia*, Thomas K. Hubbard, 'Old Men in the Youthful Plays of Aristophanes', in Thomas M. Faulkner and Judith De Luce (eds.), *Old Age in Greek and Latin Literature* (New York: State University of New York Press, 1989), 90–131.

15. 'East Coker' (II. 25), *Four Quartets*, in T. S. Eliot, *The Complete Poems and Plays* (London: Faber & Faber, 1969), 179.

16. Another example, also from the phenomenological tradition, is Edmund Husserl, *On the Phenomenology of the Consciousness of Internal Time* (1928), tr. Richard Rojcewicz and André Schuwer (Dordrecht: Kluwer, 1989).

17. The omission of ageing from the terms of reference is similarly true in arguments about how things persist: the question of how a person persists is usually taken to be an impure problem by comparison with how a material object persists. We can, of course, talk about our bodies and even ourselves as material objects, but metaphysicians, like phenomenologists, tend not to. In her book on *How Things Persist* (2001), for example, Katherine Hawley acknowledges the relevance of the questions she is asking to issues of personal persistence, identity, and survival, but chooses a non-animate example (a ripening banana) over the complexities of human existence in time. (Oxford: Clarendon, 2001), 3–4, 48.

18. See Stephen Katz, *Disciplining Old Age: The Formation of Gerontological Knowledge* (Charlottesville: University Press of Virginia, 1996), ch. 1 (esp. p. 28). There are rare exceptions. Two (not cited by Katz) are Patrick L. McKee's critical anthology *Philosophical Foundations of Gerontology* (New York: Human Sciences, 1982) and a collection of essays on *Aging and Ethics: Philosophical Problems in Gerontology*, ed. Nancy S. Jecker (Clifton, NJ: Humana, 1991). Neither is confined to academic philosophy and Jecker, especially, includes a significant component of medical ethics and sociology.

19. e.g. Pat Thane, *Old Age in English History: Past Experience, Present Issues* (Oxford: Oxford University Press, 2000), 35–7, 40–2, 56–60; Thomas

R. Cole, *The Journey of Life: A Cultural History of Ageing in America* (Cambridge: Cambridge University Press, 1992), pp. xxxii (on Aristotle and Cicero), 6 (on Aristotle), 30 (on Bacon); Cole makes no mention of Montaigne or Beauvoir, and none of more recent philosophy.

20. For a critical overview see Gullette, *Aged by Culture*, ch. 6. Gullette dates the emergence of 'age studies' to 1993.

21. For overviews, see Katz, *Disciplining Old Age*, 5–7; and Thomas R. Cole, Andrew Achenbaum, Patricia L. Jakobi, and Robert Kastenbaum (eds.), *Voices and Visions of Aging: Toward a Critical Gerontology* (New York: Springer, 1993).

22. 'Cato the Elder on Old Age (On Old Age)', in Cicero, *Selected Works*, tr. with an introduction by Michael Grant, rev. edn. (London: Penguin, 1971), 211–47 (215).

23. Simon Blackburn, *Ethics: A Very Short Introduction* (Oxford: Oxford University Press, 2003), 61.

24. See J. G. F. Powell, Introduction to Cicero, *Cato Maior de Senectute*, ed. with an introduction and commentary by J. G. F. Powell (Cambridge: Cambridge University Press, 1988), 3–4. See also H. H. Scullard, 'The Political Career of a "Novus Homo"', in T. A. Dorey (ed.), *Cicero* (London: Routledge & Kegan Paul, 1964), 1–25.

25. Plutarch, *The Life of Cicero*, tr. Bernadotte Perrin, in *Plutarch's Lives*, 11 vols. (London: William Heinemann, 1919), vii. 207.

26. David Stockton, *Cicero: A Political Biography* (Oxford: Oxford University Press, 1971), 305–6.

27. Martha C. Nussbaum, *Upheavals of Thought: The Intelligence of Emotions* (Cambridge: Cambridge University Press, 2001), 357.

28. There is a large literature on the philosophical foundations of *La Vieillesse*, much of it written as a critical extension of debates about Beauvoir's feminism. See esp. Penelope Deutscher, 'Bodies, Lost and Found: Simone de Beauvoir from *The Second Sex* to *Old Age*', *Radical Philosophy* 96 (1999), 6–16, 'Three Touches to the Skin and One Look: Sartre and Beauvoir on Desire and Embodiment', in Sara Ahmed et al. (eds.), *Thinking Through the Skin* (London: Routledge, 2001), 143–59, and 'Beauvoir's Old Age', in *The Cambridge Companion to Simone de Beauvoir*, ed. Claudia Card (Cambridge: Cambridge University Press, 2003), 286–304; Toril Moi, *Simone de Beauvoir: The Making of An Intellectual Woman* (Oxford: Basil Blackwell, 1994), 217–52; Ursula Tidd, 'For the Time Being: Simone de Beauvoir's Representation of Temporality', and Sarah Clark Miller, 'The Lived Experience of Doubling: Simone de Beauvoir's Phenomenology of Old Age', both in Wendy O'Brien and Lester Embree (eds.), *The Existential Phenomenology of Simone de Beauvoir* (Dordrecht: Kluwer Academic, 2001), 107–26, 127–48; Debra B. Bergoffen, *The Philosophy of Simone de Beauvoir: Gendered Phenomenologies, Erotic Generosities* (Albany: State University of New York Press, 1997), 186–90; and Elaine Marks, *Simone de Beauvoir: Encounters with Death* (New Brunswick, NJ: Rutgers University Press, 1973).

29. Beauvoir's ostensibly objective description of the actual condition of old people in different societies should be read with scepticism. She is especially critical of the United States, for example (see her comments in the Introduction and Appendix II), although many historians and sociologists would point out that the decade at the end of which her book was published (1960–70) saw the start of major pressure to improve the lives of old people. The term 'ageism' was coined by the psychiatrist Robert Butler in 1968. Thomas R. Cole rightly points out, however, that the opposition to age discrimination produced its own pressures in the form of increased expectations that the old should be healthy, socially engaged, self-reliant. Cole, *The Journey of Life*, 227–9.

30. *The Prime of Life*, tr. P. Green (Cleveland, Ohio: World, 1962; London: André Deutsch and Weidenfeld & Nicolson, 1965), 290.

31. Susan J. Brison, 'Beauvoir and Feminism: Interview and Reflections', in Card (ed.), *Cambridge Companion to Simone de Beauvoir*, 189–207 (195–6).

32. *Nicomachean Ethics*, 1100a1–1101a20 (1. 9. 10–1. 10. 16).

33. 'Trying to Understand Endgame', and 'On Dickens' *The Old Curiosity Shop*: A Lecture', in Adorno, *Notes to Literature*, ed. Rolf Tiedemann, tr. Shierry Weber Nicholsen, 2 vols. (New York: Columbia University Press, 1991–2), i. 241–75, and ii. 171–7. Discussed at 187–208 below.

34. Amartya Sen, 'Utilitarianism and Welfarism', *The Journal of Philosophy* 76/9 (1979), 463–89 (470–1).

35. Bernard Williams, 'The Makropulos Case: Reflections on the Tedium of Immortality' (1972), in *Problems of the Self: Philosophical Papers 1956–1972* (Cambridge: Cambridge University Press, 1973), 82–100.

36. *Well-Being: Its Meaning, Measurement, and Moral Importance* (Oxford: Clarendon, 1986), 318 n.

37. *Fragility of Goodness*, 13. The criticism does not fit her more recent work.

38. Ibid. p. xxix.

39. Ibid. 15.

40. Beauvoir, *The Coming of Age*, 543.

CHAPTER I

1. In *Death in Venice and Other Stories*, tr. and with an introduction by David Luke (London: Secker & Warburg, 1990), 195–267 (238). German references are to 'Der Tod in Venedig', in Thomas Mann, *Sämtliche Erzählungen* (Frankfurt am Main: S. Fischer, 1963) (hereafter *SE*).

2. The word usually, though not definitively, implies respect. Both *presbyteros* and *geron* (and cognates) are commonly translated as old or elderly. Neither necessarily implies greater age than the other. Michael Silk uses them interchangeably in his discussion of the rhetoric of the old in Greek literature. See M. S. Silk, 'Nestor, Amphitryon, Philocleon, Cephalus: The Language

of Old Men in Greek Literature from Homer to Menander', in Francesco de Martino and Alan H. Sommerstein (eds.), *Lo Spetta delle Voci* (Bari: Levante Editori, 1995), 165–214 (166), as does Thomas M. Faulkner, *The Poetics of Old Age in Greek Epic, Lyric, and Tragedy* (Norman: University of Oklahoma Press, 1995), 72, 56. For wider discussion of old age in ancient Greece, see Bessie Ellen Richardson, *Old Age Among the Ancient Greeks* (Baltimore: Johns Hopkins University Press, 1933); T. M. Faulkner and J. De Luce (eds.), *Old Age in Greek and Latin Literature* (Albany, NY: State University of New York Press, 1989); Robert Garland, *The Greek Way of Life: From Conception to Old Age* (London: Duckworth, 1990).

3. *Phaedrus*, tr. R. Hackforth (Cambridge, 1952), in *The Collected Dialogues of Plato*, ed. Edith Hamilton and Huntington Cairns, Bollingen Series LXXI (Princeton: Princeton University Press, 1961), 475–525.

4. David Halperin, 'One Hundred Years of Homosexuality', in *One Hundred Years of Homosexuality* (New York: Routledge, 1990), 15–40, 113 n. and 160 (n. 26), citing K. J. Dover, *Greek Homosexuality* (London: Duckworth, 1978), 85–7; Félix Buffière, *Éros adolescent: la pédérastie dans la Grèce antique* (Paris: Belles Lettres, 1980), 605–15; N. M. Kay, *Martial Book XI: A Commentary* (London: Duckworth, 1985), 120–1.

5. The *Phaedrus* forms, with the *Republic, Parmenides*, and *Theaetetus*, the later work of Plato's middle period. In the *Parmenides*, Socrates is very young. In all the others he is mature and, though he speaks of himself as 'old' in the *Phaedrus*, clearly much younger than, for example, Lysias' aged father Cephalus (discussed at pp. 27–8 here).

6. Tr. W. H. D. Rouse and ed. Philip G. Rouse, in *Collected Dialogues of Plato*, ed. Hamilton and Cairns, 385–420.

7. Tr. Hugh Tedennick (Penguin Classics, 1954), in *Collected Dialogues of Plato*, ed. Hamilton and Cairns, 3–26.

8. Diotima, in the *Symposium*, may be an exception (see pp. 31–2 and n. 25) below), but she is a wise woman (her name and origin associate her with prophecy and with religious mysteries) rather than a philosopher. See *Lysis, Symposium, Gorgias*, tr. W. R. M. Lamb, Loeb Classical Library (Cambridge, Mass.: Harvard University Press, 1925), 173 n. 1.

9. Tr. Paul Shorey, Loeb Classical Library (1930), in *Collected Dialogues of Plato*, ed. Hamilton and Cairns, 575–844. (See also *Republic* 7 (540a–b), *Laws* 2 (653a–b).) Socrates has just complained that present practice is exactly the reverse: 'those who do take [philosophy] up are youths, just out of boyhood, who in the interval before they engage in business and money-making approach the most difficult part of it, and then drop it—and these are regarded forsooth as the best exemplars of philosophy. By the most difficult part I mean discussion. In later life they think they have done much if, when invited, they deign to listen to the philosophical discussions of others. [...] And toward old age, with few exceptions, their light is quenched more

completely than the sun of Heraclitus, inasmuch as it is never rekindled' (498a–b).

10. Relatedly, book 5 of the *Republic* defines a man's maturity as 'from the time he passes his prime in swiftness of running to fifty-five' (460e).

11. See Richard Kraut, 'Introduction to the Study of Plato', in Richard Kraut (ed.), *The Cambridge Companion to Plato* (Cambridge: Cambridge University Press, 1992), 1–50 (35 n. 17).

12. Men are permitted to go on serving in some physically and politically demanding civic capacities (as the envoys, commissioners, or ambassadors of the state) until their sixtieth year (951d–e). It does not, of course, follow that they cannot start philosophy before then.

13. Schofield, 'Religion and Philosophy in the *Laws*: The C. J. de Vogel Lecture, 2001', in *Plato's Laws: From Theory into Practice, Proceedings of the VI Symposium Platonicum Selected Papers*, ed. Samuel Scolnicov and Luc Brisson (Sankt Augustin: Academia, 2003), 1–13 (3).

14. Schofield, 'Religion and Philosophy in the *Laws*', 5–6.

15. Ibid. 11–13.

16. *The Republic*, 575–844 (578).

17. Shorey's translation adds an intensifier not present in the original: 'very aged'.

18. For Plato's influence on Cicero, see *Cato Maior de Senectute*, ed. with an introduction and commentary by J. G. F. Powell (Cambridge: Cambridge University Press, 1988), 5–6, 9, 15, 17 n. 46, 21, 24, and (in the commentary) *passim*.

19. Patrick L. McKee observes that Cephalus' interests are ethical and religious but his command of knowledge is particular and personalized rather than general; and his mental powers are 'integrative rather than analytic'. *Philosophical Foundations of Gerontology* (New York: Human Sciences, 1982), 187–8.

20. Xenophon, *Memorabilia*, in *Memorabilia; Oeconomicus*, with an English tr. by E. C. Marchant, *Symposium; Apologia*, with an English tr. by O. J. Dodd (Cambridge, Mass.: Harvard University Press, 1979), 353 (bk. 4, ch. 8, sect. 1, ll. 5–13).

21. Thomas Hurka, *Perfectionism* (Oxford: Oxford University Press, 1993), 72 and n. And see the *Apology* (41d) and the *Republic* (486a).

22. I assume, in common with the majority of writers on Plato, that the *Symposium* was composed before the *Phaedrus*.

23. Plato, *Symposium*, ed. with an introduction, translation and commentary by C. J. Rowe (London: Aris & Phillips, 1998). All quotations are from this edition unless specified otherwise.

24. In Michael Joyce's still widely available 1935 translation for Everyman, Socrates first gives his audience a prod in the ribs to remind them of his own old age: 'I'm not going to make a fool of myself, at my age, trying to imitate the grand manner that sits so well on the rest of you' (199b) (*hina me gelota ophlo*). Joyce has imported 'at my age' from nowhere, perhaps recalling the Socrates of the

Phaedrus. Plato's Symposium, repr. in *Collected Dialogues of Plato*, ed. Hamilton and Cairns, 526–74 (551).

25. It is natural to assume that, as Socrates' teacher, Diotima speaks from a vantage point of age, but we are not told either how old she is or how young Socrates was. The result is that she can be taken to have, but isn't explicitly accorded, the authority of an age advantage over Socrates. If (as David Halperin has argued) Diotima has to be a woman, because only by making her female can Socratic philosophy 'seem to leave nothing out' and lay claim to being a 'universalising discourse', then the omission of any reference to her age may play a similar part in broadening out the terms of the male pederastic scene. It certainly supports Halperin's claim that by characterizing her as thinly as he does, Plato avoids contaminating Socrates' authority with the notion that he was himself once an object of teaching and of love. See 'Why is Diotima a Woman?', in Halperin, *One Hundred Years*, 113–51 (144).

26. On the narrow application of the concept of immortality here to the continuation after death achievable through 'generation' (*genesis*) and through posthumous reputation, see Michael J. O'Brien, ' "Becoming Immortal" in Plato's *Symposium*', in Douglas E. Gerber (ed.), *Greek Poetry and Philosophy: Studies in Honour of Leonard Woodbury* (Chico, Calif.: Scholars Press, 1984), 185–205 (182). I agree with his argument that, unlike the *Phaedrus*, the *Symposium* is concerned with 'the never-ending blessedness to be achieved through a life of philosophy' (201) rather than with establishing the imperishability of the soul—but the latter doctrine is not, as some commentators have thought, denied.

27. 'The Pharmakon' (Part 4 of 'Plato's Pharmacy'), in *Dissemination*, tr. Barbara Johnson (Chicago: University of Chicago Press, 1981), 61–171 (109).

28. It is the 'boundary (between inside and outside, living and nonliving)', Derrida writes, which 'separates speech from writing but also memory [...] from rememoration' (108–9). He says nothing about age as the enactment or making visible of the boundedness of mortality (age is not itself the boundary in Plato). The omission is the more tantalizing in view of his observation that ungrounded assumptions about Plato's own age played a role in the largely negative response to the *Phaedrus* for much of its history: Diogenes Laertius recorded a traditional view that 'the *Phaedrus* was Plato's first attempt [to construct a well-made object] and thus manifested a certain juvenile quality (*meirakiodes ti*). [...] In 1905, the tradition of Diogenes Laertius was reversed, not in order to bring about a recognition of the excellent composition of the *Phaedrus* but in order to attribute its faults this time to the senile impotence of the author: The *Phaedrus* is badly composed. [...] But the inability to accomplish what has been well conceived is precisely a proof of old age" (*Dissemination*, 66–7). (As a corrective to Derrida's emphasis on age, it should be noted that the key factors in dating the *Phaedrus*, from the late 1860s onwards, have been stylometrics, and the relative complexity of its treatment of the soul and rhetoric.)

29. See Frisbee C. C. Sheffield, 'Psychic Pregnancy and Platonic Epistemology', *Oxford Studies in Ancient Philosophy* 20 (2001), 1–33, for Plato's use of another complex biological analogy for epistemology, that of pregnancy, in the *Symposium, Meno*, and *Phaedo*.

30. Joyce's translation.

31. As many commentators have noted, the *Symposium* offers a vision which is much more in the manner and idiom of a religious mystery than the *Phaedrus*. See *The Symposium of Plato*, ed. with introduction, critical notes, and commentary by R. G. Bury, 2nd edn. (Cambridge: Heffer, 1932), pp. xlviii–xlix, and 124 (re 210a), O'Brien, ' "Becoming Immortal" ', and G. R. F. Ferrari, 'Platonic Love', in Kraut (ed.), *Cambridge Companion to Plato*, 248–76 (255–61).

32. Ferrari, 'Platonic Love', 262.

33. Joyce's translation.

34. Joyce's translation, but with the more literal 'till I grow old' in place of Joyce's 'till I'm positively senile'.

35. The miseries of 'old old age' are not denied by Plato. They can be discerned in the commonplace jibes about the diminished physical capacities of the old lover. In *The Laws*, Megillus and Cleinias recognize that their intellectual faculties are not as quick as they once were and that there will soon come a day when they must resign their places at the head of the state (see especially 892d, 770a). They also make provision for the possibility that the 'extremely aged' will lose their powers of reason, and hence their ability to abide by the rules of the republic (864e). But nothing in Plato's writing comes near Aristotle's long list of complaints about old age in the *Rhetoric* (discussed in Ch. 2).

36. Biographers and critics have identified Aschenbach's brief essay with the note on Wagner that Mann composed while in Venice, in which he acknowledged his 'affinities' with the composer: 'the *leitmotif*, the self-quotation, the symbolic phrase, the verbal and thematic reminiscence across long stretches of text'. Anthony Heilbut, *Thomas Mann: Eros and Literature* (New York: Alfred A. Knopf, 1996), 249, and T. J. Reed, *Thomas Mann: The Uses of Tradition*, 2nd edn. (Oxford: Clarendon, 1996), 74, 145–6, 154. I have substituted Reed's more Wagnerian term 'leitmotif' (74) for Heilbut's 'recurrent motif'.

37. See Reed, *Thomas Mann*, 156–8. Mann also took notes on Plutarch's late 'essentially Platonic' *Erotikos* and on Georg Lukács's *Die Seele und die Formen* (1911) (discussed below), and there is one quotation in *Death in Venice* from Xenophon's *Memorabilia of Socrates* (226). Reed suggests a process of retreat from Platonism during the composition of the novella as Mann's naturalistic and analytic turn of mind gradually predominated (156). Cf. Luke, Introduction, pp. xlii–xliii.

38. Especially Goethe's and Platen's commingling of *eros* and *thanatos*. Mann reread *Elective Affinities* 'at least five times' while writing *Death in Venice*. See Heilbut, *Thomas Mann*, 248.

39. Mann read Freud closely, but there is an ongoing debate over how much of the available work he had encountered by 1911. Most critics have assumed not much, but for the 'pro-Freudian' view see Andrew J. Webber, 'Mann's Man's World: Gender and Sexuality', in Ritchie Robertson (ed.), *The Cambridge Companion to Thomas Mann* (Cambridge: Cambridge University Press, 2002), 64–83, and Manfred Dierks, 'Der Wahn und die Traüme in "Der Tod in Venedig": Thomas Manns folgenreiche Freud-Lektüre im Jahr 1911', *Psyche* 44 (1990), 240–68 (cited in Webber, p. 73). *Beyond the Pleasure Principle* (which is indebted to Plato, and, like the *Symposium*, links its theory of desire to the biological processes of ageing) was not published until 1920.

40. Many critics have noted Aschenbach's misrepresentation of Plato, but not in this detail. For a succinct summary of references, see Ellis Shookman, *Thomas Mann's 'Death in Venice': A Novella and its Critics* (New York: Boydell & Brewer, 2003), 96–7, 152–4, 191.

41. James A. Snead, 'The Vision of Desire in *Death in Venice*', in Snead, *Racist Traces and Other Writings: European Pedigrees/African Contagions*, ed. Kara Keeling, Colin MacCabe, and Cornel West (London: Palgrave Macmillan, 2003), 59–80 (60). Luchino Visconti (dir.), *Death in Venice* (Alfa Cinematografica, 1979).

42. See Webber, 'Mann's Man's World', 65.

43. The pedagogic and collective context of Socrates' death is described in the *Phaedo*.

44. Aschenbach has noted with alarm that his observation of the boy has 'attracted attention and aroused suspicion' (248).

45. Homosexual acts were illegal from 1871 under Paragraph 143 (later 175) of the German Constitution. Italy had adopted liberal legislation from 1889, but Aschenbach carries his German background with him, especially in a hotel with many other German guests (until the presence of cholera becomes known). See Heilbut, *Thomas Mann*, 40, 251, and (on successful prosecutions of public figures in the years immediately before *Death in Venice*), 210–11.

46. 'Impossible that any young man could love me', Mann himself would write, in his late seventies—but old age lent plausibility, Heilbut argues, to a posture of exclusion habitual from much earlier on. *Thomas Mann*, 15 and *passim*. Heilbut memorably describes Mann as 'the poet of the half-open closet' (251). See also Hermann Kurzke, *Thomas Mann: Life as a Work of Art. A Biography*, tr. Leslie Willson (Princeton: Princeton University Press, 2002), 534–52 and *passim*. There are far fewer detailed critical discussions of old age in *Death in Venice* than there are discussions of homosexuality in the novella. Significant exceptions include Josef Hofmiller, 'Thomas Manns neue Erzählung', *Süddeutsche Monatshefte* 10 (1931), 218–32 (on Goethe's old age as an influence on the novella); Margaret Morganroth Gullette, 'The Exile of Adulthood: Pedophilia in the Midlife Novel', *Novel* 17/3 (1984), 215–32; Kathleen Woodward, 'Youthfulness as a Masquerade', *Discourse* 11/1 (1988–9), 119–42.

47. See Reed, *Thomas Mann*, 144–78 (144).

48. See Heilbut, *Thomas Mann*, 247.

49. Mann makes prominent use of the threshold metaphor, but applies it to desire and death rather than to old age. Tadzio turns back from the door of the dining room, when Aschenbach first sees him, and his 'strangely lit twilight-gray eyes' meet the older man's (218). At the end of the novella, the boy seems to stand on another threshold, pointing Aschenbach towards death and the infinite possibility of desire (236). The German equivalent, *Schwelle*, is the word used in the standard German translation of the *Republic*. I am assuming that Mann read Plato's *Republic* in Karl Preisendanz's translation, *Platons Staat* (Jena: E. Diederichs, 1906). He owned Rudolf Kassner's German translations of the *Symposium* and the *Phaedrus* in the same series: Platons, *Gastmahl*, ins Deutsche übertragen von Rudolf Kassner (Jena: E. Diederichs, 1906); Platons, *Phaidros*, ins Deutsche übertragen von Rudolf Kassner (Jena: E. Diederichs, 1910).

50. Usually translated as 'late in the morning', but equivalent to the English 'late in the day'.

51. See Reed, *Thomas Mann*, 174, and Webber, 'Mann's Man's World', 64.

52. Heilbut, *Thomas Mann*, 49. See also 42 and 248, and Reed, *Thomas Mann*, 165, on Mann's penchant for the word.

53. I have restored the final ellipsis, present in Mann's text (394) but not given in Luke's translation.

54. 'Metaphysik der Tragödie: Paul Ernst', in *Die Seele und die Formen* (Berlin: Egon Fleischel, 1911); *Soul and Form*, tr. Anna Bostock (Cambridge, Mass.: MIT, 1974), 152–74.

55. Quoted (and tr.) Judith Marcus, *Georg Lukács and Thomas Mann: A Study in the Sociology of Literature* (Amherst: University of Massachusetts Press, 1987), 33.

56. On the possible timing of Mann reading the book, see Reed, *Thomas Mann*, 166.

57. Mann subscribed to the journal and seems to have read it avidly. See Marcus, *Georg Lukács and Thomas Mann*, 30–1. The direct evidence in Mann's working notes of Lukács's influence on *Death in Venice* is summarized by Heilbut, *Thomas Mann*, 248, and Reed, *Thomas Mann*, 164–9.

58. G. E. Lessing is the only one not explicitly acknowledged, but the influence of *Laocoon: On the Limits of Painting and Poetry* (1766) on 'Longing and Form' especially is evident. (See *Soul and Form*, 102–3.)

59. Mann used almost exactly the same words of Goethe more than a decade later. See 'Goethe and Tolstoy', in *Essays of Three Decades*, tr. H. T. Lowe-Porter (New York: Alfred A. Knopf, 1947), 93–175 (107).

60. Lukács, 'Metaphysik der Tragödie', 153.

61. James Snead remarks on the repression of the artist's labour in *Death in Venice* and sees the return of the repressed in the unnamed workers, especially servants, who quietly help shape the plot (sending Aschenbach's luggage to

the wrong destination, for example, and so providing him with the excuse he wants to return to Venice). *Racist Traces*, 74. He makes no connection with Aschenbach's and the novel's construction of old age as the end of the artist's labour. Again, it is striking that so many of the servants in *Death in Venice* are old—as if age displaces his own labour or makes labour invisible for Aschenbach.

62. It is distinct from the attraction towards death: a state of suspension, of pleasure in 'lying hidden', rather than a drive towards extinction.

63. In Luke (tr.), *Death in Venice and Other Stories*, 135–94 (191).

64. Quoted in Heilbut, *Thomas Mann*, 21, and Kurzke, *Thomas Mann*, 19.

65. Quoted in Heilbut, *Thomas Mann*, 155.

66. Mann does not explain his statement to Heinrich, but this gloss fits with the letter, and with his habit, even in his twenties, of using his own ageing as a means to critical self-reflection. See Heilbut, *Thomas Mann*, 15, 45.

67. 'The Old Fontane' (1910), in Mann, *Essays of Three Decades*, 287–306 (287).

68. Quoted in Heilbut, *Thomas Mann*, 156.

69. Mann wrote extensively about Nietzsche, including in *Reflections of a Non-political Man* (1918) which co-won the Nietzsche award. See especially 'Soul-Searching', and (on his preference for young over old Nietzsche, 'Politics'. *Reflections of a Nonpolitical Mann*, tr. with an introduction by Walter D. Morris (New York: Frederick Ungar, 1983), 160–272 (224). See also Heilbut, *Thomas Mann*, 372.

70. *Beyond Good and Evil*, in *Basic Writings of Nietzsche*, tr. and ed. Walter Kaufmann (New York: The Modern Library, 2000), 90.

71. On Nietzsche's hostility to Socrates as 'the rage of Caliban seeing his own face in a glass', see Alexander Nehamas, *Nietzsche: Life as Literature* (Cambridge, Mass.: Harvard University Press, 1985), 24–38.

72. 'On the Uses and Disadvantages of History for Life', in *Untimely Meditations*, ed. Daniel Breazeale, tr. R. J. Hollingdale, Cambridge Texts in the History of Philosophy (Cambridge: Cambridge University Press, 1997), 114–23 (117, 116). On Nietzsche and the beginnings of youth culture, see also Rüdiger Safranski, *Nietzsche: A Philosophical Biography*, tr. Shelley Frisch (London: Granta Books, 2002), 320.

73. *Essays of Three Decades*, 93–175 (120, 119).

74. 'Die Erotik Michelangelos', in *Altes und Neues: Kleine Prosa aus fünf Jahrzehnten* (1953; Berlin: Aufbau, 1956); summarized and translated in extract in Heilbut, *Thomas Mann*, 264–5.

75. Mann's work notes for *Death in Venice*, as quoted and tr. by Marcus, *Georg Lukács and Thomas Mann*, 33.

76. Heilbut, *Thomas Mann*, 232.

77. There are also passing references to works Mann had written: *Buddenbrooks*, the drama *Fiorenza*. For a full list, see Kurzke, *Thomas Mann*, 178.

78. *On Myself*, a lecture delivered at Princeton in 1940. Quoted in Luke, Introduction, p. xlvi.

79. 'What I Believe', quoted in Kurzke, *Thomas Mann*, 524–5. It is also the case that Mann was drawn to different versions of Goethe as he himself aged. At 35 he was attracted to Goethe as a figure of morbidity and impossible longing: the Goethe of *Elective Affinities*, in love, at the age of 59, with an 18-year-old girl. The Goethe Mann admires in 1938 is the one who extolled and exemplified the power and pleasures of old age, its force of 'Mind' and its 'mighty emotions'. See 'Goethe's Career as a Man of Letters', and 'Goethe as a Representative of the Bourgeois Age', in *Essays of Three Decades*, 43–65, 66–92. See also Heilbut, *Thomas Mann*, 456–8 and 516.

80. See Kurzke, *Thomas Mann*, 533.

81. Diary entry for 6 July 1953, quoted ibid. 559. See also Friedrich A. Wagner, 'Thomas Mann at 80', in Michael Mindon (ed.), *Thomas Mann* (London: Longman, 1995), 49–50.

82. See Gullette, 'The Exile of Adulthood'.

CHAPTER 2

1. I have preferred the traditional translation of *eudaimonia* as 'happiness' in these first sentences, and occasionally hereafter, to the now widely preferred 'flourishing'. The notion of duration implied by the verbal noun is problematic, as this chapter seeks to demonstrate, in connection with Aristotle's insistence on seeing complete lives. Standard caveats nevertheless apply: 'happiness' introduces a notion of subjective pleasure or contentment absent from the original Greek. The alternative, 'human flourishing' was made current by John Cooper, *Reason and Human Good in Aristotle* (Cambridge, Mass.: Harvard University Press, 1975), 89 (he tentatively attributes its first use to G. E. M. Anscombe). Martha Nussbaum suggests that a fuller rendition would be 'something like "living a good life for a human being" '—with the additional requirement that, for the Greeks, *eudaimonia* was a state of activity, not of passive satisfaction or virtue. *The Fragility of Goodness: Luck and Ethics in Greek Tragedy and Philosophy*, updated edn. (Cambridge: Cambridge University Press, 2001), 6 n.

2. Aristotle, *The Nicomachean Ethics* [hereafter *EN*], with an English translation by H. Rackham, Loeb Classical Library, rev. edn. (Cambridge, Mass.: Harvard University Press, 1934), 47 (1. 9. 10–11). All Greek citations are from this edition.

3. Homer, *The Iliad*, bk. 22. 59–6; tr. Samuel Butler (1898; New York: Barnes & Noble, 1995), 338; I also borrow here from E. V. Rieu's translation (Harmondsworth: Penguin Books, 1950), 398. The lines are sometimes dismissed as being 'late'. See Jasper Griffin, *Homer on Life and Death* (Oxford: Clarendon, 1980), 117.

4. *EN* 1. 9. 10–1. 10. 16 (1100a1–1101a20). *Athlios* (wretched) is not an ethical term. It designates miserable circumstances, but not a failure of virtue. In this instance I have adopted Martha Nussbaum's expository translation (*Fragility of Goodness*, 328).

5. In the *Rhetoric*, Aristotle puts a man's bodily prime at from 30 to 35, his mental prime at about 49 (1390b).

6. Herodotus, *The Persian Wars: Books I–II*, with an English translation by A. D. Godley (Cambridge, Mass.: Harvard University Press, 1926), 30–41 (1. 30–4). I have also drawn on G. C. Macaulay's more poetic translation (London: Macmillan, 1890), but with my own translation of *olbion* and *eutukhea*. 'Call no man happy until he is dead' is also the last line (spoken by the Chorus) in Sophocles' *Oedipus Rex*.

7. Aristotle, *Nicomachean Ethics*, tr. (with historical introduction) by Christopher Rowe, philosophical introduction and commentary by Sarah Broadie (Oxford: Oxford University Press, 2002). Hereafter, unless indicated otherwise, references are to this edition.

8. *Aristotle and the Perfect Life* (Oxford: Oxford University Press, 1992), 35. Kenny is here contesting Martha Nussbaum's claim that the Priam passage is a good example of Aristotle's tendency to use *eudaimonia* and *makariotes* interchangeably—her point being that it matters that *eudaimonia*, and not just the more exacting criteria for supreme blessedness, is sensitive to contingency. Kenny argues that the same deduction can be made more securely if one recognizes the absolute requirement, for *makariotes*, of a good end. *Eudaimonia* admits of a less than ideal end, but not of a very bad one. A similar argument is made by J. H. Sobel, 'Ends and Means: Aristotle on Happiness and Virtue', <http://www.utsc.utoronoto.ca/~sobel/Means_Ends/Arist_5.pdf>, last, accessed 2002; rev. version available at <http://www.scar.utoronoto.ca/~sobel/Means_Ends/Arist_5.pdf>, last accessed 23 Mar. 2007. See also *Nicomachean Ethics*, tr. with introduction and notes by Terence Irwin (Indianapolis: Hackett, 1985).

9. In addition to Nussbaum and Irwin (n. 8), see Julia Annas, *The Morality of Happiness* (Oxford: Oxford University Press, 1993), 44. Annas describes *eudaimonia* and *makaria* as essentially interchangeable, though *makarios* is 'a loftier and more pretentious word'.

10. 'Virtue ethics' refers to 'an approach in normative ethics which emphasizes the virtues, or moral character, in contrast to an approach which emphasizes duties or rules (deontology) or one which emphasizes the consequences of actions (utilitarianism)'. Rosalind Hursthouse, *On Virtue Ethics* (Oxford: Oxford University Press, 1999), 1.

11. The case of Priam leads him, for example, to ponder whether a good life may be vulnerable to contingency even after a person's death. We cannot dismiss this question, he argues, because few of us would concede that disgrace on the part of our descendants does not diminish the value of our own life. Aristotle

prefers to think of that effect as 'feeble or small […] at any rate of such a size and such a sort as not […] to take blessedness away' (1101b1–4)—but the impression is of a question abandoned rather than cleanly refuted.

12. *The Morality of Happiness*, 34.

13. *Reason and Human Good in Aristotle*, 87–8. (The inset quotation is from Rawls.) And see Thomas W. Smith, *Revaluing Ethics: Aristotle's Dialectical Pedagogy* (New York: State University of New York Press, 2001), 170.

14. I set aside, here, Aristotle's pondering on the vulnerability of *eudaimonia* to the actions of our descendants.

15. Or last months, or perhaps even last days. Aristotle never specifies just how short a time may suffice to do substantial damage to a good life. A 'bad' but quick death unconnected to virtue (falling from a building, for example) would presumably not erase a person's claim to *eudaimonia* in Aristotle's eyes, though it would impair it. For the virtuous character to be damaged, some duration of suffering or ill-fortune is presumably necessary.

16. 'So then, man is wholly accident,' he concludes. Herodotus, *Persian Wars*, 38–9 (1. 32).

17. Eight are explicit references; one implicit (1165a22). Book 1's commentary on Priam and the 'complete life' is the only discussion of any length.

18. 'One should give honour to every older person, too, in accordance with their age, by getting up as they approach, giving up one's couch at table, and so on.'

19. 1165a22 asserts that our parents have first claim on us for maintenance, because they are 'the authors of our being'.

20. Aristotle's physiological understanding of the natural process of ageing can be found in 'On Length and Shortness of Life', and 'On Youth, Old Age, Life and Death, and Respiration', where he describes the gradual exhaustion of the vital heat supplied by the heart. Old age is the internal cause of death 'involved from the beginning in the constitution of the organ. […] The source of life is lost to its possessors when the heat with which it is bound up is no longer tempered by cooling [by the lungs], for, as I have often remarked, it is consumed by itself. Hence when, owing to lapse of time, the lungs […] get dried up, these organs become hard and earthy and incapable of movement and cannot be expanded or contracted. Finally things come to a climax, and the fire goes out from exhaustion. Hence a small disturbance will speedily cause death in old age. Little heat remains, for the most of it has been breathed away in the long period of life preceding, and hence any increase of strain on the organ quickly causes extinction.' Tr. G. R. T. Ross, in *The Complete Works of Aristotle*, The Revised Oxford Translation, ed. Jonathan Barnes (Princeton: Princeton University Press, 1984), i. 740 4, 745–63 (760).

21. *Fragility of Goodness*, 361. The example under discussion is intimate love (*philia*).

22. Aristotle is not much drawn to the Pindaric grace of the plant metaphor that gives Nussbaum her title. He virtually dismisses it in book 1 of the *Nicomachean Ethics*, noting that 'we share with plants the mere act of living'. He explores the biological likenesses closely in 'Youth, Old Age, Life and Death, and Respiration'.

23. *The 'Art' of Rhetoric*, tr. John Henry Freese, Loeb Classical Library (Cambridge, Mass.: Harvard University Press, 1926), 227.

24. 1169b10: 'It seems strange to assign all good things to the happy person and not give him friends, something that seems greatest of the external goods'. In book 4 Aristotle says that honour is the greatest of external goods for the magnanimous man (1123b20). The two are clearly related, the greatness of the good being dependent on how the person manifests their virtuous character. *Philia* is usually translated as friendship; Nussbaum finds the greater semantic breadth of 'love' more accurate. (354)

25. See also Nussbaum, 418, on the *Rhetoric*'s discussion of youth and age as an example of Aristotle's mining of the 'traditions of his culture, preserving what is deepest'.

26. *Apology* 41d.

27. The claim in book 4 that, as a cause of meanness, age is like other (unspecified) forms of weakness does not negate this point. See 1121b14.

28. See *Nicomachean Ethics* 1138a5−14, 1116a15.

29. At Athens, however, slaves rowed in the fleet.

30. Homer, *Iliad*, bk. 23. 74−6; tr. Butler, 365.

31. I am indebted here and in the following comment on Nestor to Felicity Rosslyn's elegant essay, 'Pope on the Subject of Old Age: The *Iliad* Translation, Books XXII−XXIV', in Howard Erskine-Hill and Anne Smith (eds.), *The Art of Alexander Pope* (London: Vision, 1979), 119−31 (esp. 120−2). The wording draws on her translation, and that of Rieu, 399.

32. Aristotle, *Rhetoric*, tr. W. Rhys Roberts, *Poetics*, tr. Ingram Bywater, Introduction by Edward P. J. Corbett (New York: Random House, 1954), 123−5 (2. 13. 1389b−1390a). See also the passage on prejudice against aged speakers in 'Rhetoric to Alexander', tr. E. S. Forster, in *Complete Works of Aristotle*, ii. 2210−315 (2298).

33. M. S. Silk, 'Nestor, Amphitryon, Philocleon, Cephalus: The Language of Old Men in Greek Literature from Homer to Menander', in Francesco de Martino and Alan H. Sommerstein (eds.), *Lo Spetta delle Voci* (Bari: Levante Editori, 1995), 165−214 (178).

34. Ibid. 178, 181.

35. Exploited, for example, in Theophrastus' characterization of the *opsimathes* (late learner, or elderly pedant). See *The Characters of Theophrastus*, ed. with an intro. and commentary by R. G. Ussher (London: Bristol Classical Press, 1993), 226−34.

36. Christopher Rowe, 'Historical Introduction' to *Nicomachean Ethics*, 3. See also Jonathan Barnes (ed.), *The Cambridge Companion to Aristotle* (Cambridge:

Cambridge University Press, 1995), 18–22, on the impossibility of a secure dating, or even a chronology.

37. For a summary of the arguments about dating, see Appendix II to George A. Kennedy, *Aristotle on Rhetoric: A Theory of Civic Discourse* (New York: Oxford University Press, 1991), 299–305.

38. Cf. Hursthouse, *On Virtue Ethics*, 73: 'the concept of the virtuous person does not figure, in virtue ethics, riding on the back of a prior concept of right, or wrong, action. A virtuous agent is one who has the character traits of, for example, charity, honesty, justice.' Hursthouse is describing the conditions for irresolvable and tragic dilemmas; it is this same weighting of character that determines Aristotle's view of old age as (too often) an irresolvable and tragic 'thing'.

39. See *EN*, esp. 1103a15–b25 and 1143b8–14; but also 1095a3–4, 1142a15–20, 1151a18–19, 1179b25. Book 2 is devoted to the promotion of excellence of character through experience, practice, habituation, and training. The closest thing I have found to the comments here on time's positive role in Aristotelian ethics, prior to old age, is Hallvard Fossheim's brief discussion of habituation, 'Mimesis in Aristotle's Ethics', in Øivind Andersen and Jon Haarberg (eds.), *Making Sense of Aristotle: Essays in Poetics* (London: Duckworth, 2001), 73–86.

40. Rosalind Hursthouse, *Beginning Lives* (Oxford: Basil Blackwell, 1987), 237. She goes on: 'Notoriously, Aristotle himself did not, in fact, believe that we could all flourish.'

41. See esp. Nussbaum, *Fragility of Goodness*, 391–4.

42. See Barnes (ed.), *Cambridge Companion to Aristotle*, 12–14, for the argument against the standard earlier theory that these were lecture notes.

43. Richard A. Posner takes a similar view, in *Aging and Old Age* (Chicago: Chicago University Press, 1995), observing that the element of truth in Aristotle's rhetorical stereotyping tends now to be suppressed. Given the paucity of equivalent modern studies of the effects of ageing on personality, character, and the emotions (most psychological studies have focused on reasoning and cognitive powers), he argues that Aristotle's age profiling of innate capacities still has value as an indicator of why standard economic theories of human capital need refining to take account of the effects of age. See esp. pp. 6, 101–15.

44. Silk, 'Nestor, Amphitryon, Philocleon, Cephalus', 209. Silk, too, emphasizes the continuities with modern profiles of the old, more than the disparities. Cf. Robert Garland, *The Greek Way of Life: From Conception to Old Age* (London: Duckworth, 1990), 271.

45. See Bessie Ellen Richardson, *Old Age Among the Ancient Greeks* (Baltimore: Johns Hopkins University Press, 1933), esp. 7–8, and chs 2 and 6; T. M. Faulkner and J. De Luce (eds.), *Old Age in Greek and Latin Literature* (Albany, NY: State University of New York Press, 1989); Garland, *The Greek Way of Life*. None of these standard works discusses Aristotle's *Ethics* in any detail.

46. T. W. Baldwin, *William Shakspere's Small Latine and Lesse Greeke*, 2 vols. (Urbana: University of Illinois Press, 1944) (still the first resort for scholars of this subject) is more briefly dismissive than most recent scholarship, claiming that 'If Shakspere ever heard of Aristotle, it was the Aristotle of his own age, not that of Greece, still less that of the latest expert' (ii. 667). His transcription (i. 500) of the patent for school books held by Thomas Marshe from 1572 nevertheless suggests that Shakespeare is likely, at the very least, to have learned brief passages of Aristotle as grammatical examples in Nicholas Clénard, *Institutiones linguae grecae* (London: Thomas Marshe, 1582). He would also have encountered the term *eudaimonia* there, but via Hesiod rather than Aristotle (pp. 145, 146).

47. As a schoolboy, he is more likely to have encountered Aristotelian ideas via the Latin curriculum than through the introductory course in the Greek language. A few scholars have attempted to demonstrate specific references to the *Nicomachean Ethics* in Shakespeare's plays—the most persuasive instance being Hector's speech on morality and justice in *Troilus and Cressida*, 2. 2. Kenneth Palmer argues that the speech demonstrates Shakespeare's familiarity with at least the first half of the *Nicomachean Ethics*. See *Troilus and Cressida*, ed. Kenneth Palmer (London: Methuen, 1982), Appendix 3. W. R. Elton, 'Aristotle's *Nicomachean Ethics* and Shakespeare's *Troilus and Cressida*', *Journal of the History of Ideas* 58/1 (1997), 331–7, argues, similarly, that Act 1, sc. 2 contains a knowing inversion of the discussion of voluntary and involuntary actions in the *Nicomachean Ethics*. J. Leeds Barroll thinks that Shakespeare knew Aristotle, including the principles of the *Ethics*, via Plutarch (*Shakespearean Tragedy: Genre, Tradition, Change in* Antony and Cleopatra (Washington: Folger Books, 1984), 36–51. Even in such a relatively strong case as *Troilus and Cressida*, identifying the *Nicomachean Ethics* as a source is notoriously difficult unless it is explicitly acknowledged, both because Aristotelian idiosyncrasies of style were flattened by the process of transmission, and because Aristotle deals with common and durable (though not inevitable) perceptions about lives: what 'most people are agreed about' (*EN* 1095a18). More simply, Aristotle's views on the good life were, by the early seventeenth century, so diffusively part of the general vocabulary of moral thought, so mixed with its other main lines of inheritance from Roman Stoicism and Judaeo-Christian religion, that argument by way of one-on-one influence is in danger of missing the point. On the wider Renaissance reception of Aristotelian ideas, see *Aristotle and the Renaissance* (Cambridge, Mass.: Harvard University Press, 1983). Also James McConica, 'Elizabethan Oxford: The Collegiate Society', in McConica (ed.), *The History of the University of Oxford*, iii. *The Collegiate University* (Oxford: Clarendon, 1986), 645–732 (699–716), on the revival of Aristotelianism in Britain in the final quarter of the sixteenth century.

48. References are to the modernized Folio text of 1623, in *King Lear: A Parallel Text Edition*, ed. René Weis (London: Longman, 1993), unless otherwise

indicated. For a concise account of the textual and editorial problems posed by *Lear* see Weis's Introduction; and for the key arguments (still disputed) in support of seeing the Folio as Shakespeare's revision in 1609–10, of an earlier text (thought to have been composed in 1605–6, and published in 1608), see Stanley Wells and Gary Taylor, *William Shakespeare: A Textual Companion* (Oxford: Oxford University Press, 1987); also Gary Taylor and Michael Warren (eds.), *The Division of the Kingdoms: Shakespeare's Two Versions of 'King Lear'* (Oxford: Oxford University Press, 1983).

49. Weis (ed.), *King Lear*, 303.

50. On the theme of over-living (not just through old age, but through the experience of intolerable suffering and loss) and the challenge it poses to Aristotelian notions of tragic structure, see Emily R. Wilson, *Mocked with Death: Tragic Overliving from Sophocles to Milton* (Baltimore: Johns Hopkins University Press, 2004). As Wilson points out, '[r]elatively few tragic characters who live too long are old in years. Tragic overliving is the result not of a gradual natural decline, but of a single sharply defined event or action after which it seems that life ought to be over—and yet it goes on' (3). See her ch. 5 (113–28) on *King Lear* as a case of tragic overliving in old age, and its relation to Sophoclean and Senecan treatments of the theme.

51. *OED* online, definitions 6, 9c, 8b, 2d.

52. 'Expropriate' not in the Lockean sense of owning a property in oneself, but in the earlier sense of having a monarchic inheritance, or tenure over one's lifetime, of a property and powers that will pass to others with one's death. Cf. Margreta de Grazia, 'The Ideology of Superfluous Things: *King Lear* as Period Piece', in Margreta de Grazia, Maureen Quilligan, and Peter Stally-brass (eds.), *Subject and Object in Renaissance Culture* (Cambridge: Cambridge University Press, 1996), 17–42.

53. William Shakespeare, *The Complete Works*, gen. eds. Stanley Wells and Gary Taylor (Oxford: Clarendon, 1986), 1124.

54. Michael Warren argues that the change is part of a shift towards greater emphasis on Edgar as the representative of youth in the Folio. 'The Diminution of Kent' in Taylor and Warren (eds.), *The Division of the Kingdoms*, 59–73 (70).

55. Albany comes closer to it if we take 'Fall and cease' (5. 3. 238) to be addressed to Lear.

56. Though whether Kent means there 'endured all his life' or 'endured in old age' is disputable.

57. Gary Taylor argues that the Folio here has Kent voice the audience's incredulity at Lear's 'abdication', forcing him to 'make the decision to abdicate again, before our eyes, resisting advice to the contrary'. In Q that decision is 'a necessary given, […] in the Aristotelian sense, "outside the plot"'. *Moment by Moment by Shakespeare* (London: Macmillan, 1985), 180–1.

58. In Geoffrey of Monmouth's *Historia regium Britanniae* (*c*.1135), a probable source, though less obviously close to Shakespeare's *Lear* than those listed

here, Lear is more active: he fights alongside the French forces to regain the kingdom, and rules for three years thereafter. For the relevant extract, see Geoffrey Bullough (ed.), *Narrative and Dramatic Sources of Shakespeare*, 8 vols. (London: Routledge & Kegan Paul, 1973), vii. 315.

59. Quoted in Bullough (ed.), *Narrative and Dramatic Sources*, 401 (ll. 2633–46).

60. Quoted ibid. 358 (ll. 860–1). And again, without self-pity, at 378 (l. 1672): 'I have lived too long.'

61. Quoted ibid. 355 (ll. 755–6).

62. A. C. Bradley, *Shakespearean Tragedy: Lectures on* Hamlet, Othello, King Lear, Macbeth (1904), 2nd edn. (London: Macmillan, 1905), 307.

63. *Shakespearean Tragedy*, 307.

64. *King Lear* (Columbia Pictures, 1970).

65. Many theatre and film productions cast Kent in disguise as a young man, little older than Edgar and Edmund. See e.g. Brook (dir.), *King Lear*, and Jonathan Miller (dir.), *King Lear* (BBC Television, 1982). Michael Elliott's 1984 film for the BBC, with Sir Laurence Olivier in the title role, takes the more textually defensible route of casting Kent as a man of indeterminately late middle years, apparently older than 48, and (in disguise) with the stubbled beginnings of a grey beard.

66. 'Ancient' puns perhaps on 'old' and 'experienced'; the phrasing suggests that it does not mean 'standard bearer', as in *Othello*.

67. 'The Diminution of Kent', *Division of the Kingdoms*, 59–73 (63). Kent's actual age is never stated. He is usually cast as younger than Gloucester, and older than Albany and Cornwall. Bradley assumes that he is 'much older than eight and forty': 'not so old as his master, who was "four-score and upward" and whom he "loved as a father," [1. 1. 139] but, one may suppose, three score and upward' (*Shakespearean Tragedy*, 308). This is considerably more specific than anything in the text substantiates. An additional problem arises with what is usually taken to be Kent's assumed name: 'Caius'. It is mentioned only once in the text, when Kent asks the dying Lear 'Where is your servant Caius?' The timing is strained, Kent seeming to want to test the King's capability, in these last moments, of recognizing his own loyal service throughout. The name itself is an oddity in a play set in ancient, pre-Roman Britain. There is no obvious source for it in classical literature, unless it is intended to remind the audience that, even in disguise, Kent is one of the nobility. It may stand more gesturally for Roman virtue, and thus as a pointer to Kent's Stoicism.

68. Kenneth Muir (ed.), *King Lear*, Arden (Cambridge, Mass.: Harvard University Press, 1952), p. xxxii. Muir notes that 'A *king leare* was performed at the Rose Theatre by the combined Queen's and Sussex's men during an unsuccessful season in April 1594', and that the play probably belonged to the Queen's Men. His speculation about Shakespeare's playing of Perillus is based partly on the fact that Perillus is on stage during all but one of the *Chronicle* passages closest to *King Lear*. On late seventeenth- and eighteenth-century reports

of Shakespeare playing Adam and the Ghost in *Hamlet* see S. Schoenbaum, *William Shakespeare: A Compact Documentary Life*, rev. edn. (New York: Oxford University Press, 1987), 201–2.

69. In the Quarto text, 'Lear's shadow' is spoken by Lear himself—less far gone, one could argue, though it is more likely a case of a missing speech prefix in Q.

70. One can argue—as Lily B. Campbell did in *Shakespeare's Tragic Heroes: Slaves of Passion* (London: Methuen, 1930)—that Lear's downfall stems from immoderate anger, but this leaves open the question of what the sources of anger are: specifically, how far they reside in age.

71. *Myriad-Minded Shakespeare: Essays on the Tragedies, Problem Comedies and Shakespeare the Man*, 2nd edn. (London: Macmillan, 1998), 75.

72. Ibid. 74 (quoting Bradley), 76.

73. *Shakespearean Tragedy*, 262. See also Wilson, *Mocked with Death*, 114–19.

74. Bradley, *Shakespearean Tragedy*, 262, 264.

75. See Katherine Eisamann Maus, *Inwardness and Theatre in the English Renaissance* (Chicago: University of Chicago Press, 1995), 35, 48.

76. See Stephen Greenblatt, 'Shakespeare and the Exorcists', in *Shakespeare and the Question of Theory*, ed. Patricia Parker and Geoffrey Hartman (London: Routledge, 1985), 163–87 (178) on the possible origins of this line in Samuel Harsnett's *Declaration of Popish Impostures* (1603). Also Leo Salingar, 'King Lear, Montaigne and Harsnett', in *Dramatic Form in Shakespeare and the Jacobeans: Essays* (Cambridge: Cambridge University Press, 1986).

77. My argument here fits with R. S. White's description of *King Lear* as the play in which Shakespeare examines most starkly 'the rival claims of Natural Law and positive law in effecting "poetic justice"'. *Natural Law in English Renaissance Literature* (Cambridge: Cambridge University Press, 1996), 185–215 (185).

78. See e.g. *Macbeth* 5. 3. 27 on the 'honour, love, obedience, troops of friends' that should accompany old age; *A Lover's Complaint*, on the 'reverence' and 'privilege' of age (ll. 57, 62).

79. The last of these has been seized on by those wanting evidence that Shakespeare knew Aristotle's *Ethics*.

80. Gary Taylor makes the same point, more generally, in *Moment by Moment*, 227, 235.

81. There is a vast literature on the concept of nature in *Lear*, but among more recent work see Bruce W. Young's comparison of *Lear* with Hooker's account of nature as 'ordered structure and life-giving force', but like 'human nature' corrupt, and imperfect. 'Shakespearean Tragedy in a Renaissance Context: *King Lear* and Hooker's *Of the Laws of Ecclesiastical Polity*', in *Approaches to Teaching Shakespeare's 'King Lear'*, ed. Robert H. Ray (New York: The Modern Language Association of America, 1986), 98–104 (99).

82. Weis mistakenly prints the Quarto reading 'not been little' in the Folio text here.

83. See Gordon Braden, *Renaissance Tragedy and the Senecan Tradition: Anger's Privilege* (New Haven: Yale University Press, 1985), esp. 2, 216.

84. *Dependent Rational Animals: Why Human Beings Need the Virtues* (London: Duckworth, 1999), p. x.

85. Ibid. 1.

86. The strangeness of the word 'animal' for the play's first audience is hard now to recapture. The *OED* notes that, as a noun, it is hardly in English before the end of the sixteenth century, and not in the 1611 Bible, and gives its etymology as from the Latin root *anima*, 'air, breath, life'; so, animal: 'anything living'.

87. 'On Youth, Old Age, Life and Death, and Respiration', 760.

88. See p. 7 above.

89. Cf. John Casey, who argues that 'our pity for Priam includes a sense of the common fate of man' whereas *Lear*'s 'greatness' is that it leads us rather to ethical confusion. He sees the play as caught in an unreconciled and perhaps irreconcilable conflict between pagan and Christian values. *Pagan Virtue: An Essay in Ethics* (Oxford: Clarendon, 1990), 224. See also Wilson, *Mocked with Death*, on Lear's desire to transfer his living to his daughter. As Wilson notes, the repeated punning in the play on 'living' (being alive | possessing the material wherewithal to support life) underscores this desire, and Lear's and Gloucester's growing concern with the unjust superfluity of their wealth (120–5, 116).

90. Again, the reference is to the Folio text. The Quarto Lear's last line is 'Break, heart, I prithee break' (given in the Folio to Kent).

91. Bradley, famously but (to me) unpersuasively, wrests an optimistic reading from this line, suggesting that Lear sees life returning to Cordelia. *Shakespearean Tragedy*, 291.

CHAPTER 3

1. *De Finibus* (*On Final Ends*), quoted and translated by Julia Annas, *The Morality of Happiness* (Oxford: Oxford University Press, 1993), 344. For a more detailed consideration of the context of these views see ibid. 334–50. See also Phillip Mitsis, 'Epicurus on Death and the Duration of Life', in John J. Cleary and Daniel C. Shartin (eds.), *Proceedings of the Boston Area Colloquium in Ancient Philosophy* IV (New York: Lanham, 1988), 303–22, and Gisela Striker, 'Commentary on Mitsis', ibid. 323–38.

2. Stephen E. Rosenbaum, 'Epicurus on Pleasure and the Complete Life', *The Monist* 73/1 (1990), 21–41 (37); quoted in Annas, *Morality of Happiness*, 347. See also Epicurus, 'Letter to Menoeceus', 126: 'Just as with food, [the wise man] does not seek simply the larger share and nothing else, but rather the most pleasant, so he seeks to enjoy not the longest period of time but the most pleasant.' Cyril Bailey, *Epicurus: The Extant Remains* (Oxford: Clarendon, 1926), 85.

3. Annas, *Morality of Happiness*, 348.

4. Ibid. 350.

5. 'Letter to Menoeceus', in A. A. Long and D. N. Sedley (eds.), *The Hellenistic Philosophers*, 2 vols. (Cambridge: Cambridge University Press, 1987), i. 154–5. This edition gives only a portion of the letter, but the translation is more elegant than Bailey's (used in n. 3).

6. *After Virtue: A Study in Moral Theory*, 2nd edn. (London: Gerald Duckworth, 1985), 204.

7. MacIntyre acknowledges that the quest is 'not for something already adequately characterized, as miners search for gold or geologists for oil' (219)—but his emphasis on 'incidents and goals' (219) repeatedly pulls the Aristotelian sense of *telos* towards a temporally end-directed reading.

8. 'A Fallacy of Our Age: Not Every Life is a Narrative', *Times Literary Supplement* 15 Oct. 2004, 13–15 (13)—a shorter edited version of 'Against Narrativity', *Ratio* 17 (2004), 428–52.

9. There is a huge literature on narratology, a subject that was at the height of its popularity in literary studies in the 1980s. A good introduction to the subject is Shlomith Rimmon-Kenan, *Narrative Fiction: Contemporary Poetics* (London: Methuen, 1983).

10. James Warren, *Facing Death: Epicurus and his Critics* (Oxford: Clarendon, 2004), 118.

11. Ibid. 119.

12. Ibid.

13. *Pacific Philosophical Quarterly* 72 (1991), 48–77.

14. 'Well-Being and Time', 72 n. 9.

15. Ibid. 49–50.

16. Ibid. 54–5.

17. Ibid. 50.

18. *A Treatise of Human Nature*, 2. 3. 7, 'Of Contiguity and Distance in Space and Time', ed. David Fate Norton and Mary J. Norton, Oxford Philosophical Texts (Oxford: Oxford University Press, 2000), 276.

19. C. D. Broad, *Examination of McTaggart's Philosophy*, 2 vols. (Cambridge: Cambridge University Press, 1933–8), ii. 532–3 (532).

20. Ibid. 532.

21. Velleman, 'Well-Being and Time', 50.

22. Ibid. 54 and *passim*.

23. Much more could be said, of course, about the role of old age in the Holy Grail legend. For some thoughts on that subject in relation to Tennyson's handling of it, see my essay 'Tennyson and Late Style', *Tennyson Research Bulletin* 8/4 (2005), 226–50.

24. Velleman's essay is partly an argument with Slote.

25. 'Goods and Lives', in Michael Slote, *Goods and Virtues* (Oxford: Clarendon, 1983), 9–37 (23). Aristotle does not, however, defend pure time preference

for what comes later in life. Slote (23 n. 22) gives as an example of that extreme position, J. N. Findlay, *Values and Intentions* (London: Allen & Unwin, 1961), 23 ff.

26. 'Improvisatory Accident-Prone Dramas of (What Passes for) a Person's Life', in Cynthia Lightfoot, Chris Lalonde, and Michael Chandler (eds.), *Changing Conceptions of Psychological Life*, Jean Piaget Symposium Series 30 (Mahwah, NJ: Laurence Erlbaum, 2004), 243–54 (252–3).

27. See Christopher Hitchens, 'The Egg-Head's Egger-On', *London Review of Books* 22/9 (27 Apr. 2000) <http://www.lrb.co.uk/v22/n09/hitc01_.html>, last accessed 15 Feb. 2007. Hitchens was prominent among those who thought the novel a falling-off in Bellow's old age.

28. Quoted in James Atlas, *Bellow: A Biography* (London: Faber & Faber, 2000), 598.

29. 'Modern Fiction', in *The Common Reader* (London: The Hogarth Press, 1925), 184–95 (189).

30. 'Saul Bellow—Nobel Lecture', 12 Dec. 1976, <http://nobelprize.org/nobel_ prizes/literature/laureates/1976/bellow-lecture.html>, last accessed 15 Feb. 2007.

31. Saul Bellow, *Ravelstein* (2000; London: Penguin, 2001), 16.

32. 'The function of anti-narrative', Robert Scholes writes, 'is to problematize the entire process of narration and interpretation for us'—but he is sceptical that narrativity can ever be renounced entirely. 'Language, Narrative, and Anti-Narrative', *Critical Inquiry* 7/1 (1980), 204–12 (211).

33. Rozanov is perhaps an unlikely source for Bellow, given his notorious propagandization against Jews and what is often seen as the cynicism of his later retraction. See S. S. Koteliansky, 'A Note on V. V. Rozanov' and E. Gollerbach, 'V. V. Rozanov: A Critico-Biographical Study', both in V. V. Rozanov, *Solitaria,* with an 'Abridged Account of the Author's Life', by E. Gollerbach, and other biographical material and matter from *The Apocalypse of Our Times*, tr. S. S. Koteliansky (London: Wishart, 1927), p. vii.

34. Saul Bellow, 'Problems in American Literature', in *Literary Imagination, Ancient and Modern: Essays in Honor of David Grene*, ed. Todd Breyfogel (Chicago: University of Chicago Press, 1999), 375–88 (387).

35. For a succinct summary, see Victor Gourevitch, 'The Religious Thought', in Patrick Riley (ed.), *The Cambridge Companion to Rousseau* (Cambridge: Cambridge University Press, 2001), 193–246 (212–15).

36. The name 'suggests innocence, even infantility' Atlas comments. *Bellow*, 594.

37. Allan Bloom, *The Closing of the American Mind: How Higher Education Has Failed Democracy and Impoverished the Souls of Today's Students* (New York: Simon & Schuster, 1987), 277.

38. *Experience: A Memoir* (New York: Hyperion, 2000), 202.

39. 'Saul Bellow—Nobel Lecture'.

40. Rachel Cooke, 'The Amis Papers' (Interview with Martin Amis), *The Observer Review*, 1 Oct. 2006, <http://observer.guardian.co.uk/review/story/0,, 1884637,00.html>, accessed 15 Feb. 2007.

CHAPTER 4

1. (San Diego, Calif.: Harcourt, Brace, 1996), 4.
2. Ibid., 6–7.
3. Important recent work relating the philosophical problem of intergenerational distributive justice into the area of practical economic decision-making includes John Broome, *Weighing Lives* (Oxford: Oxford University Press, 2004), and Cass Sunstein, 'Lives, Life-Years, and Willingness to Pay', *Columbia Law Review* 104/1 (2004), 205–54.
4. (Oxford: Oxford University Press, 1988), 45. See also (in response to criticisms of *Am I My Parents' Keeper?*): 'The Prudential Lifespan Account: Objections and Replies', in *Justice and Justification* (Cambridge: Cambridge University Press, 1996), 257–83. Wilfred Beckerman points out to me that Daniels's argument admits of a stronger interpretation which Beckerman himself derives from a reading of Sunstein, 'Lives, Life-Years, and Willingness to Pay': 'Sunstein discusses the question of whether, in deciding whether to, say, spend resources on saving lives of young people or old people one ought to value the options in terms of life years saved, rather than just lives. Sunstein points out that using this approach does not really discriminate against old people because they were young once, so taking their lives as a whole there can be no net discrimination against them. I interpret this to mean that if one makes the value judgement that the question ought to be examined in terms of people's whole life spans, rather than some particular segment of it (i.e. when they were young or old or in the middle) then the question of distributive justice simply does not arise. One cannot discriminate between people on age grounds.' Beckerman, personal communication, 2 Nov. 2006.
5. Rawls himself mentions age only once, and without further comment, among the stipulations for the veil of ignorance: 'The persons in the original position have no information as to which generation they belong.' *A Theory of Justice*, rev. edn. (Cambridge, Mass.: Belknap, 1999), 118.
6. Daniels is not explicit about this last point (see p. 75) but I take it to be a necessary condition of the theory. Without it the constructed anonymity of the position of choice will fail, and with it the secondary unanimity of decisions.
7. A version of Pascal's wager applies here: the consequences of getting it wrong by living into an old age one has provided for too parsimoniously would be worse than the consequences of providing resources one turns out not to need and might beneficially have used earlier.

8. See *Am I My Parents' Keeper?*, 83–102 (esp. 87–91). See also Dan W. Brock, *Life and Death: Philosophical Essays in Biomedical Ethics* (Cambridge: Cambridge University Press, 1993), which broadly agrees with Daniels's defence of age-rationing, and argues that it can be extended to apply not just to general health care, as in Daniels, *Just Health Care* (Cambridge: Cambridge University Press, 1985), but 'to morally differentiate the claims to life-extending health care up to, as opposed to beyond, the normal lifespan' (396–7). A more controversial extension of this line of thinking, supporting 'strong age rationing', under which the elderly would have *no* entitlement to life-extending care once they reached a normal lifespan (late seventies or early eighties) is pursued by Daniel Callahan, *Setting Limits* (New York: Simon & Schuster, 1987). For discussion, see Brock, ch. 13. Another, only slightly less controversial, line of reasoning is pursued by Ronald Dworkin in *Sovereign Virtue: The Theory and Practice of Equality* (Cambridge, Mass.: Harvard University Press, 2002), 314–15, and discussed in relation to Daniels by McKerlie, 'Justice Between the Young and the Old', *Philosophy and Public Affairs* 30/2 (2002), 152–77 (159).

9. *Well-Being: Its Meaning, Measurement, and Moral Importance* (Oxford: Clarendon, 1986), esp. 144–9.

10. See esp. *Am I My Parents' Keeper?*, 35–6.

11. 'Justice Between the Young and the Old', 161.

12. Ibid. 160. Where I have written 'we must experience thirty consecutive years of success [and] thirty years of failure' McKerlie writes 'we must experience thirty consecutive years of success *followed by* thirty years of failure' [my emphasis]. I take this to be a mistake, since the scenario depends upon the movability of these units of thirty years relative to each other.

13. 'The Prudential Lifespan Account', 265.

14. In *Justice and Justification*, Daniels replies to earlier critical objections (not quite the same, but similar) from McKerlie: 'Equality and Time', *Ethics* 99 (1989), 475–91, and 'Justice Between Age Groups: A Comment on Norman Daniels', *Journal of Applied Philosophy* 6/2 (1989), 227–34.

15. Daniels, *Am I My Parents' Keeper?*, 75.

16. See George C. Williams, 'The Tithonus Error in Modern Gerontology', The 1999 Crafoord Prize Lectures, *The Quarterly Review of Biology* 74/4 (1999), 405–15 (410).

17. 'Justice Between the Young and the Old', 165. See also McKerlie, 'Equality and Time', and 'Dimensions of Equality', *Utilitas* 13 (2001), 263–88.

18. *Ratio* NS 10 (December 1997), 202–21; repr. in John Harris (ed.), *Bioethics* (Oxford: Oxford University Press, 2001), 347–86.

19. Note, though, that there are occasional areas of apparent contradiction. See esp. 163: 'we must supplement the lifetime perspective. A consideration of justice is discovered by comparing life-stages, not lifetimes.' The logic of McKerlie's argument is that we compare both.

20. *Life's Dominion: An Argument about Abortion and Euthanasia* (London: Harper-Collins, 1993), 218–41, 256–9. See also Dworkin, 'Justice and the High Cost of Health', in *Sovereign Virtue*, 307–19.

21. *Aging and Old Age* (Chicago: University of Chicago Press, 1995), 256–7. Posner's comment, that such a conclusion is 'beyond the gravitational field of American morality' (McKerlie, 162), is applied to Dan Brock, whose argument Posner aligns with Dworkin's.

22. 'Respecting the Margins of Agency: Alzheimer's Patients and the Capacity to Value', *Philosophy and Public Affairs* 28/2 (1999), 105–38.

23. *Life's Dominion*, 218–37 (230–2).

24. Ibid. 230.

25. Jaworska's arguments find support from Seana Valentine Shiffrin, 'Autonomy, Beneficence, and the Permanently Demented', in Justine Burley (ed.), *Dworkin and His Critics, with Replies by Dworkin* (Oxford: Blackwell, 2004), 195–218, and Dworkin's reply, 366–70. Shiffrin argues (*inter alia*) that the reasons for respecting the autonomy of the fully competent do not extend to allowing their prospective control over what happens to them should they become permanently demented. She also argues that Dworkin misconceives of autonomy in a way that 'leads him to disregard the autonomy that demented people may be capable of exerting' (196).

26. See Ch. 7.

27. Philip Larkin, *Collected Poems*, ed. with an intro. by Anthony Thwaite (London: Marvell and Faber & Faber, 1988), 196–7. Dated 12 Jan. 1973; first published in *The Listener* that year and reprinted in *High Windows* (London: Faber & Faber, 1974).

28. 'Justice Between the Young and the Old', 161.

29. The Epicurean view of death is Larkin's main target here (see below). Elsewhere in *High Windows* (1974), the collection from which 'The Old Fools' comes, he is also a savage critic of prudential thinking for old age. See esp. 'Money', (the poem which follows 'The Old Fools' in *High Windows*: 'You can't put off being young until you retire, | And however you bank your screw, the money you save | Won't in the end buy you more than a shave.' And see Barbara Everett, 'The Treasurer's Son—Money, Worth, and the Inner Life in Philip Larkin', *Times Literary Supplement* 19 Sept. 1997, 3.

30. 'Justice Between the Young and the Old', 170.

31. See John Kerrigan, 'Old, Old, Old, Old, Old', Review of R. F. Foster, *W. B. Yeats: A Life*, ii. *The Arch-Poet 1915–39* (2005), *London Review of Books*, 3 Mar. 2005, 7–10 (8).

32. If there is an allusion to the mobilization of British troops in one or other of the world wars, the 'some' also strikes the self-conscious yob-smug note of Larkin's persona, a little guilty at having missed World War II.

33. To Robert Giroux, 14 Apr. 1983; quoted in Andrew Motion, *Philip Larkin: A Writer's Life* (London: Faber & Faber, 1993), 425–6.

34. 'Instead of a Present', *Writing Home* (London: Faber & Faber, 1994), 320–4 (320); originally written for *Larkin at Sixty*, ed. Anthony Thwaite (London: Faber & Faber, 1982). See also Motion, *Philip Larkin*, 421–2, 448.

35. Motion, *Philip Larkin*, 426.

36. Ibid. 426. Motion also links the poem to Larkin's complicated relationship with his mother.

37. It is worth noting, in this regard, that when Larkin turned the question back on himself, some years later, and before the onset of his final series of illnesses—'Why aren't I screaming?'—he was referring to death, not illness or old age. See Motion, *Philip Larkin*, 520. He described himself, at the same time, as 'spiralling towards extinction' (ibid.).

38. Motion, *Philip Larkin*, 425; *Selected Letters of Philip Larkin, 1940–1985*, ed. Anthony Thwaite (London: Faber & Faber, 1992), 472 (I am assuming that he is referring here to 'The Old Fools', whose completion he describes on the previous page).

39. The poem was first published in the *Times Literary Supplement*, 29 July, as part of a group of 'Poems of the Sixties' by various authors.

40. Larkin reviewed Smith's *Scorpion* in 1972. The review does not mention 'Exeat'. See 'Stevie, Goodbye', in *Further Requirements: Interviews, Broadcasts, Statements and Book Reviews*, ed. and with an introduction by Anthony Thwaite (London: Faber and Faber, 2002), 263–5. In an article, 'Frivolous and Vulnerable', written in 1962, he told how he found her collection of poems *Not Waving but Drowning* in a bookshop, and was 'sufficiently impressed' to buy copies for his friends for Christmas. He goes on to say that this caused surprise, his friends 'were, I think, bothered to know whether I seriously expected them to admire it. The more I insisted that I did, the more suspicious they became. An unfortunate episode' (*New Statesman*, 28 Sept. 1962, 416, 418) Larkin also wrote an entry on Smith for Jenny Stratford's 1974 catalogue of MSS acquired through the Arts Council 1963–72, and mounted a manuscript exhibition in Hull (Smith's birth town) in 1980. See *Letters*, 511 n., 555, 615.

41. Repr. in *The Collected Poems of Stevie Smith* (London: Allen Lane, 1975), 414.

42. 'A Memorable Voice', in Heaney, *Preoccupations: Selected Prose 1968–1978* (London: Faber & Faber, 1980), 199–201 (199).

43. If the imperatives of virtue and the dignity of a person's critical interests—in e.g. the pursuit of poetry—conceivably expire in old age once capacity diminishes past a certain point, one then needs other welfare arguments, other arguments about the retention of dignity.

CHAPTER 5

1. Honoré de Balzac, *Le Père Goriot*, in *La Comédie humaine*, iii. *Études de mœurs: Scènes de la vie privée; Scènes de la vie de province*, ed. Pierre-Georges Castex et al. (Paris: Gallimard, 1976). I have drawn on Marion Ayrton Crawford's

translation (London: Penguin, 1951) (here, 157), and on Peter W. Lock's 1968 translation for Macmillan, but have preferred a more literal rendition in several places. Page references hereafter are to the Penguin and (where directly cited) the Gallimard (G) editions.

2. 'Killing a Chinese Mandarin: The Moral Implications of Distance', *Critical Inquiry* 21 (1991), 46–60.

3. Derek Parfit, *Reasons and Persons* (1984; rev. edn. Oxford: Clarendon, 1987), 124–5. Parfit sets the bias towards the near alongside a more plainly irrational bias towards time or distance within a specified limit: e.g. a 'bias towards the next year', or—its correlative—'Within-a-Mile Altruism'. There are good reasons, according to Hume, why the bias towards the near should be stronger with time than with geography—or, why the mandarin's oldness might be doing more moral work in *Le Père Goriot* than his Chineseness. Spatially, several things can be simultaneously present to our senses or emotions, Hume argues; but temporally, no more than one thing can be present to us at any one time. *A Treatise of Human Nature*, 274–6. And see 98–9 above.

4. There may be other reasons to rue the consequences for old age of our temporal bias, but Parfit does not enumerate them: worse health, one might imagine (if we have put off painful medical intervention which could have done us more good if we had accepted it earlier); greater dependency perhaps; even a premature or less good death.

5. On Dostoyevsky's debt to Balzac, see Joseph Frank, *Dostoevsky*, 5 vols. (London: Robson Books, 1977–2002), esp. iv. 73.

6. See Appendix I to *Reasons and Persons*. Parfit identifies three types of self-interest theory: *Hedonistic Theories*, which hold that 'what would be best for someone is what would make him happiest'; *Desire-Fulfilment Theories*—'what would be best for someone is what, throughout his or her life would best fulfil his desires'; and *Objective List Theories*—'certain things are good or bad for us, whether or not we want to have the good things or avoid the bad things' (493).

7. One objection to any claim for the general truth of that bias is that our attitudes to the future are a form of gamble, in which the odds are different for different individuals. Balzac, for example, began writing *Le Père Goriot* when he was 35. (See Tim Farrant, *Balzac's Shorter Fictions: Genesis and Genre* (Oxford: Oxford University Press, 2002), 173 n. 78, re the difficulty of exact dating.) For him, the likelihood of not being around at 80 to reap the consequences of a presentist self-interest was higher than for most readers at the equivalent life stage now. Moreover, it is a matter of biographical curiosity that gambling on the likelihood of living to be old was not, in his experience, merely a metaphor: late in life his father invested seriously in an insurance scheme (the *tontine Lafarge*) whereby the last man left alive took all. Balzac père died in a coach accident shortly before his 83rd birthday—old, but not old enough to have realized his hope of great wealth in his final years. See Pierre Sipriot, *Balzac sans masque: Splendeurs et misères des passions 1799–1850* (Paris: Robert

Laffont, 1992), 143–4, on the tontine Lafarge, and Robb, *Balzac*, 160, on the death of Bernard-François Balzac.

8. See 'Appendix: Problems with Prudence', *Am I My Parents' Keeper?*, 157–76.

9. For objections to that analogy, see Susan Wolf, 'Self-Interest and Interest in Selves', *Ethics* 96/4 (1986), 704–20 (717–18).

10. I am struck, in this context, by the moving opening tribute to Gareth Evans, with whom Parfit travelled by car to Madrid sixteen years before the first publication of *Reasons and Persons*, who supported and tested the budding philosopher's ideas, and who died at 34.

11. I ignore Parfit's analogy with the growth of an acorn into an oak tree (322), which seems to me misleading, applied to persons, especially if we are allowing for cases of extreme psychological discontinuity.

12. Norman Daniels suggests that Parfit is 'equivocating over personal identity' when he proposes a discount rate. Are the future interests that are being discounted 'really my own interests'? or are they no longer 'mine' because of weakened psychological connectedness? See Daniels, 'Appendix', 162–3. I understand this to be a dilemma, rather than an equivocation, in Parfit—answered, though not entirely satisfactorily, by the appeal to paternalism.

13. Hence Galen Strawson's enlistment of Parfit in the group of writers opposed to a narrative view of lives. Parfit's recognition of possible psychological discontinuity and disconnectedness within lives does not rest on the idea that there are different kinds of psychology or temperament, some more invested in connectedness than others. 'A Fallacy of our Age: Not every life is a Narrative', *Times Literary Supplement*, 15 Oct. 2004, 13–15 (13).

14. One of those sci-fi experiments involves Nagel's concept of a series-person. Nagel imagines a community in which everyone over the age of 30 enters a Scanning Replicator which produces a Replica exactly similar to the original 'except that it has not aged or decayed'. The original is destroyed in the production of the Replica (290). Parfit disputes Nagel's claim, via this fiction, that each person is essentially his brain in order to refine his own concept of psychological relatedness. I do not discuss this passage in any detail because the avoidance of old age is essentially decorative to the fiction.

15. An earlier version of this passage can be found in his 'Later Selves and Moral Principles', in Alan Montefiore (ed.), *Philosophy and Personal Relations* (London: Routledge & Kegan Paul, 1973), 137–69.

16. One might argue, on the same grounds, that she should also consider herself released from her marriage. Parfit stops short of that conclusion, instead taking the wife as an example of how 'sincerity' may reinforce the argument for thinking in terms of earlier and later selves as distinct persons. If the woman chooses not to obey her middle-aged husband, this is because she considers herself married to the young man who preceded him, to whom she wishes to be loyal, just as we may 'love, and believe we are committed to' someone who is dead.

In the event of such a response on her part, the argument becomes one about her emotional commitment to the past (*her* 'psychological connectedness and continuity') rather than the rational justification for how she might act now.

17. Bernard Williams, 'Persons, Character and Morality', in *The Identities of Persons*, ed. Amélie Oksenberg Rorty (Berkeley: University of California Press, 1976), 197–216 (206). See also Shelly Kagan, 'The Present-Aim Theory of Rationality', *Ethics* 96/4 (1986), 746–59. Kagan argues that Parfit needs to explain why only currently held desires should be held to generate reasons for acting.

18. Ibid. Parfit is also exposed, here, to a different kind of objection: namely, that the shift from reflection on a cognitive state—enlightenment—to a moral claim—change of values—is unjustified.

19. (Princeton, NJ: Princeton University Press, 1970), 38–9.

20. For example, the claim that the Critical Present-Aim Theory of self-interest allows room for a person to question the 'presumptuousness' of their own certainties. Why should other people's values not have equal standing to mine, so long as they can be shown to be rational? 'Why should I assume that *I* am more likely to be right?' (156).

21. I am necessarily omitting the details of Parfit's arguments about the obstacles that must be overcome in order to reach such a theory: the Non-Identity Problem, the Repugnant and Absurd Conclusions, and the Mere Addition Paradox. See *Reasons and Persons*, 352–441. Because they refer mostly to many-person rather than single-person scenarios, they have no clear analogical import for paternalism towards oneself.

22. It is not as clear as Parfit wants us to think it is that the language of rights could not do some of this work. Rights, contrary to his claim, can be (and in international law are) held to pre-exist individual people. They attach, in law, to the idea of people, not to actual people.

23. Consequentialism, Parfit himself warns in response to one critical reading of *Reasons and Persons*, 'is not the whole truth about rationality'—but it can be a significant component, and the paternalism argument itself is surely a consequentialist one. 'Comments', *Ethics* 96/4 (1986), 832–72 (833).

24. To put this point another way: Parfit wants to make a protectionist attitude to one's own future interests a compulsory component of present-aim self-interest, in a way that threatens to deprive present-aimism of its meaning.

25. See esp. Carlos Herrera (Vautrin)'s lecture on ethics to Lucien Chardonin; ch. 33 of *Lost Illusions*.

26. Honoré de Balzac, *Cousin Pons*, Part 2 of *Poor Relations*, tr. Herbert J. Hunt (London: Penguin, 1968), 30.

27. *By Way of Sainte-Beuve*, tr. Sylvia Townsend Warner, with a new Introduction by Terence Kilmartin (London: The Hogarth Press, 1984), 118: 'a vulgarity of mind so massive that a lifetime could not leaven it'.

28. *Proust Among the Stars* (London: HarperCollins, 1998), 285.

29. *Ibid.*, 285.

30. The Penguin translation misleadingly puts the body back in. 'Une culotte presque vide', for example, becomes 'breeches much too big for his shrunken thighs'.

31. *Lost Illusions*, tr. Herbert J. Hunt (London: Penguin, 1971), 102.

32. *A Harlot High and Low*, tr. Rayner Heppenstall (London: Penguin, 1970), 529.

33. See Introduction, 12.

34. Quoted, with commentary, in Graham Robb, *Balzac: A Biography* (London: Picador, 1994), 178.

35. See ibid. 178–9, 270. 'By the time the main lines of my work are drawn and the frames filled in,' he wrote, 'I shall be forty-five. I shall no longer be young—at least not physically' (quoted, 270).

36. 15 Apr. 1835. Quoted in Martin Kanes, *Père Goriot: Anatomy of a Troubled World* (New York: Twayne, 1993), 14.

37. Alex Woloch provides a detailed account of this disparity between the internality accorded to Rastignac and the externality with which Goriot is viewed, linking it to economics (the 'effacement, and the destruction, of the human personality' by commodification). He also compares Goriot at length with Lear, seeing an important historical and literary difference between Lear's centrality to Shakespeare's play and Goriot's marginalization within Balzac's 'tragedy'. *The One vs. the Many: Minor Characters and the Space of the Protagonist in the Novel* (Princeton, NJ: Princeton University Press, 2003), ch. 4. Surprisingly, Woloch makes almost no mention of age, though it is a major distinction between those characters given interiority and those depicted merely externally.

CHAPTER 6

1. *Metaphysik: Begriff und Probleme* (Frankfurt am Main: Suhrkamp, 1998), ed. Rolf Tiedemann; *Metaphysics: Concepts and Problems*, 'Editor's Afterword' by Rolf Tiedemann, tr. Edmund Jephcott (Stanford, Calif.: Stanford University Press, 2000), 15.

2. *Rückläufig* implies a process operating or flowing in reverse.

3. Theodor W. Adorno, 'On Dickens' *The Old Curiosity Shop*: A Lecture', in Adorno, *Notes to Literature*, ed. Rolf Tiedemann, tr. Shierry Weber Nicholsen, 2 vols. (New York: Columbia University Press, 1991–2), i. 171–7.

4. 'Trying to Understand Endgame', in Adorno, *Notes to Literature*, i. 241–75.

5. Not surprisingly, 'Meditations on Metaphysics' is the chapter that gives Fredric Jameson greatest trouble in his influential defence of Adorno, *Late Marxism: Adorno, or, The Persistence of the Dialectic* (London: Verso, 1990): 'this final, logical stage in "negative dialectics" seems to me the only moment in which Habermas's fear—that this profound critique of reason and rationality might end up in the cul de sac of irrationalism—seems potentially justifiable' (112).

6. Simon Jarvis, *Adorno: A Critical Introduction* (Cambridge: Polity, 1998), 37–8.

7. *Negative Dialectics*, tr. E. B. Ashton (London: Routledge, 1973), 314; quoted in Jarvis, *Adorno*, 38.

8. 'Thoughts on Late Style', *London Review of Books* 26/15 (5 Aug. 2004), <http://www.lrb. co.uk/v26/n15/said01_.html>, last accessed 15 Feb. 2007; 'Untimely Meditations', *The Nation*, 14 Aug. 2003, <http://www.thenation. com/doc/20030901/said>, accessed 15 Feb. 2007; and 'Adorno as Lateness Itself', in *Adorno: A Critical Reader*, ed. Nigel Gibson and Andrew Rubin, Blackwell Critical Reader (Oxford: Blackwell, 2001), 193–208. These and Said's other writings on late style are collected in Edward Said, *On Late Style* (London: Bloomsbury, 2006). See also Kathleen Woodward, 'Late Theory, Late Style: Loss and Renewal in Freud and Barthes', in *Aging and Gender in Literature: Studies in Creativity,* ed. Anne Wyatt-Brown and Janice Rossen (Charlottesville: University of Virginia Press, 1993), 82–101.

9. Thomas Mann had access to a copy of it in 1934 when he was writing ch. 8 of *Doctor Faustus*. See Editor's Notes to Adorno, *Beethoven: The Philosophy of Music*, ed. Rolf Tiedemann, tr. Edmund Jephcott (Cambridge: Polity, 1998), 233.

10. See James Knowlson, *Damned to Fame: The Life of Samuel Beckett* (London: Bloomsbury, 1996), 124 (n. 231).

11. In *Moments Musicaux: Neu gedruckte Aufsätze 1928–1962* (Frankfurt am Main: Suhrkamp, 1964); repr. as 'Text 3: Beethoven's Late Style', in Adorno, *Beethoven*, 123–6; see also Fragments 362–6 on late style as 'leavetaking' (174–5).

12. 'Thoughts on Late Style'.

13. 'Beethoven's Late Style', 126.

14. 'Thoughts on Late Style'. See esp. the paragraph beginning 'But in what sense are they late ...' where he raises but quickly abandons the question of what lateness means.

15. Ibid.

16. He also came very close to giving it another name: theology. This is implicit in the *Aesthetic Theory*, more evident in *Negative Dialectics*, but closest to being explicit in the letters to Walter Benjamin. The late writings are deeply preoccupied with the relationship between *transience* and *transcendence*, seeing the latter, rather than revolution, as the means to redemption.

17. The lectures on metaphysics were delivered in conjunction with the writing of the final section of *Negative Dialectics*, 'Meditations on Metaphysics' (tr. E. B. Ashton (New York: Continuum, 1973)). Unlike other lectures closely related to the composition of that book, this series differs substantially. Most obviously, *Negative Dialectics* excludes Adorno's extended argument for seeing Aristotle as the founding figure of metaphysics by virtue of his treatment of the distinction between concept and form. The book also shows very little trace of the lectures' preoccupation with old age.

18. The 'immeasurabl[e] sad[ness]' associated with old age is not a general diagnosis of the culture but something approaching a personal confession: 'as far as my experience extends, there is [...] something immeasurably sad in the fact' (135).

19. Adorno, *Philosophische Terminologie* (1974), quoted by Tiedemannie, 'Editor's Afterword' to Adorno, *Metaphysics*, 196.

20. Tiedemann, 'Editor's Afterword' to Adorno, *Metaphysics*, 196.

21. Jarvis, *Adorno*, 216.

22. The original German reads 'Es ist die Gruppe des alten Titelholzschnittes: Nell und ihr Grossvater.' ('Rede über den Raritätenlanden von Charles Dickens', *Frankfurter Zeitung und Handelsblatt*, 18 Apr. 1931, 1–2 (1b).) The reference is puzzling. The first English editions of *The Old Curiosity Shop* were indeed illustrated by woodcuts, rather than the more usual steel engravings, but there was no title-page image. It is possible that Adorno was referring to George Cattermole's frontispiece for vol. i of *Master Humphrey's Clock* (London: Chapman & Hall, 1840), which contains two framing images of Nell and her grandfather, but the frontispiece is very rarely reproduced in editions of *The Old Curiosity Shop*. It is more likely that whichever edition of the novel Adorno was using (he doesn't say) included one of the original woodcuts from the main text by way of title-page decoration. The image that comes closest to his description is the one at the end of ch. 12, showing Nell and her grandfather leaving the old curiosity shop arm in arm. The accent on 'oldness' is interestingly superfluous, in tune with Adorno's particular attentiveness here to age.

23. Charles Dickens, *The Old Curiosity Shop*, ed. Elizabeth M. Brennan (Oxford: Clarendon, 1997), 103 (ch. 12), quoted by Adorno, *Notes to Literature*, 175.

24. William Shakespeare, *King Lear* (First Folio text), in *King Lear: A Parallel Text Edition*, ed. René Weis (London: Longman, 1993), 271, 273. Jon Sturgis argues that Nell is represented at a remove from her own allegorization—conscious of it, and actively accepting ('orchestrating', is Sturgis's stronger claim) her own martyrdom. 'Little Nell: The Monster with Two Heads', *Victorian Literature and Culture* 19 (1991), 293–314 (300). Sturgis concentrates almost entirely on the dark doubling of Nell and Quilp (he does not discuss Quilp's age), and on Dickens's failure to bring them to a final dramatic confrontation, which could not but contaminate Nell. I am more inclined to see Quilp as a grotesque externalization and displacement of the more intimate threat posed to Nell's happiness, and ultimately her existence, by her grandfather.

25. Cf. *King Lear* 3. 4. 26–32; and see Adrian Poole, 'The Shadow of Lear's "Houseless" in Dickens', *Shakespeare Survey* 52 (2000), 103–13.

26. Adorno argued that the dated form of Dickens's novel means that 'there is no psychology in it, or rather, that it absorbs psychological approaches into the objective meanings the novels depict' (172).

27. Clarendon edn., Appendix A. On the revision at proof stage see *The Letters of Charles Dickens*, Pilgrim edition, ed. Madeline House, Graham Storey et al., 12 vols. (Oxford: Clarendon, 1965–2002), ii. 131.

28. Alexander Welsh, 'King Lear, Père Goriot, and Nell's Grandfather', in Joseph P. Strelka (ed.), *Literary Theory and Criticism: Festschrift Presented to René Wellek in Honor of His Eightieth Birthday*, 2 vols. (Frankfurt am Main: Peter Lang, 1984), ii. 1405–25 (1405).

29. Adorno, 'On Dickens' *The Old Curiosity Shop*', 173.

30. But see ch. 54 for the nearest approximation.

31. See John Bowen, *Other Dickens: Pickwick to Chuzzlewit* (Oxford: Oxford University Press, 2000), 133 n.

32. Ibid. 15–51.

33. Dickens, *Letters*, ii. 270 n.

34. Ibid. 181–2.

35. The term 'allegory' was a late addition. Dickens took it from Thomas Hood's enthusiastic review of the serialized version of *The Old Curiosity Shop* and introduced it into the text of ch. 1 ('she seemed to exist in a kind of allegory') at the point where he detached the story from *Master Humphrey's Clock*. See *Letters*, ii. 221 n.

36. Bowen, *Other Dickens*, 142, 153–6.

37. Ibid. 142.

38. See also Tony Weller's account of his very robust grandson in one of the magazine pieces written by Dickens to accompany *The Old Curiosity Shop* when it started serialization. Charles Dickens, *Master Humphrey's Clock and Other Stories*, ed. Peter Mudford (London: J. M. Dent, 1997), 103–4. Discussed in an earlier and slightly longer version of this reading of Adorno and Dickens, without the Beckett material, published in *Victorian Literature and Culture* 32/2 (2004), 547–63 (558).

39. Adorno, *Notes to Literature*, ii. 248, 250.

40. 'Adorno Now', *Victorian Studies* 44/1 (2001), 33–9 (34).

41. 'Adorno, Benjamin and *The Old Curiosity Shop*', *Dickens Quarterly* 6/3 (1989), 89–95 (90).

42. *Letters*, ii. 180.

43. *The Theatrical Notebooks of Samuel Beckett*, ii. *Endgame, with a revised text*, ed. with Intro. and notes by S. E. Gontarski (London: Faber & Faber, 1992), 21. All references hereafter to the text of *Endgame* are to this edition, the revised and reduced text of the play, approved by Beckett, that resulted from his directing the play at the Schiller Theatre in Berlin in 1967, and again for the San Quentin Drama Workshop in 1980. It differs at numerous points from the more widely available text first published by Faber & Faber in 1958. Text in square brackets was added by Beckett for this 1992 edition.

44. Textual Notes to *Theatrical Notebooks*, 52.

45. See Introduction, ibid. pp. xx–xxi.

46. Beckett, *Berlin Diary*, quoted in Textual Notes to the *Theatrical Notebooks*, 65.
47. *Berlin Diary*, quoted ibid.
48. *Berlin Diary*, quoted ibid.
49. Quoted ibid. 52.
50. *Berlin Diary*, quoted ibid. 53.
51. Knowlson, *Damned to Fame*, 478–9. Adorno acknowledged that Beckett refused to interpret his own work, but defended the role of interpretation: 'Certainly this does not mean that interpretation can be dispensed with.' *Aesthetic Theory*, 27.
52. The same interpretation is repeated in the *Aesthetic Theory*, 133: 'as occurs in such exemplary fashion in Beckett's *Endgame*, art must either eliminate from itself the nature with which it is concerned, or attack it. The only *parti pris* left to it, that of death, is at once critical and metaphysical.'
53. Oddly, not something Adorno makes much of, despite his interest in World War II as the definitive historical moment behind *Endgame*.
54. *Berlin Diary*, quoted in Textual Notes to the *Theatrical Notebooks*, 63.
55. McGee interview, quoted ibid. 56–7.
56. Knowlson, *Damned to Fame*, 124 (n. 231).
57. For details of changes made, see *Theatrical Notebooks*, 43–71 (56).
58. Rick Cluchey (the actor who played Hamm at the Riverside Studios), quoted in Textual Notes, ibid. 61.
59. There is another of Beckett's analogies here: a structural reprise of Hamm's speech to Clov at p. 20: 'one day you'll know what it is, you'll be like me, except that you won't have anyone with you, because you won't have had pity on anyone and because there won't be anyone left to have pity on'.

CHAPTER 7

1. *Problems of the Self: Philosophical Papers 1956–1972* (Cambridge: Cambridge University Press, 1973), 82–100 (82).
2. Lucretius, *De Rerum Natura*, with an English translation by W. H. D. Rouse, rev. Martin Ferguson Smith, Loeb Classical Library (1975; rev. Cambridge, Mass.: Harvard University Press, 1992), 3. 830–1097 (pp. 253–75).
3. *The View from Nowhere* (New York: Oxford University Press, 1986), 224.
4. *How to Live Forever: Science Fiction and Philosophy* (London: Routledge, 1995), 14.
5. Indeed, Nagel explicitly deems our age pretty much beside the point, with respect to how we contemplate non-existence: death 'is a loss no matter how long [a person] has lived'; the expectation of nothingness is 'startling and frightening, and very different from the familiar recognition that your life will go on for only a limited time—that you probably have less than thirty years and certainly less than a hundred' (*View from Nowhere*, 225–6).

6. Other circumstances are imaginable: depression, for example; or believing that something will be achieved by one's death which is more important to oneself than going on living.

7. See e.g. Sherwin B. Nuland, *How We Die: Reflections on Life's Final Chapter* (New York: Vintage, 1995), chs. 3 and 4; Norman Daniels, *Am I My Parents' Keeper? An Essay on Justice Between the Young and the Old* (Oxford: Oxford University Press, 1988), p. viii; Julia Neuberger, *The Moral State We're In: A Manifesto for a Twenty-First Century Society* (London: HarperCollins, 2005), i–59 (esp. xiv, 29, 56–7). Neuberger is (rightly) as much concerned by the growing support for euthanasia of the old.

8. How they then deal with that change in self-perception is a matter of character, and of the novelists' concerns as expressed through the rendition of character.

9. J. M. Coetzee, *Disgrace* (1999; New York: Penguin, 2000), 4.

10. Adam Mars Jones, 'Stands to Reason: *Disgrace* by J. M. Coetzee', *The Observer*, 18 July 1999, <http://books.guardian.co.uk/reviews/generalfiction/0,6121,96805,00.html>, last accessed 15 Feb. 2007. The phrase was almost ubiquitous in the reviews.

11. See Jacqueline Rose, 'Apathy and Accountability: The Challenge of South Africa's Truth and Reconciliation Commission to the Intellectual in the Modern World', in Helen Small (ed.), *The Public Intellectual* (Oxford: Blackwell, 2002), 159–78 (173).

12. See J. M. Coetzee, 'The Novel Today', *Upstream* 6/1 (1988), 2–5.

13. 'Coetzee's *Disgrace*: A Few Skeptical Thoughts', *The Irresponsible Self: On Laughter and the Novel* (New York: Farrar, Straus & Giroux, 2004), 246–57 (248). Wood sees *Disgrace* as 'Almost too good a novel. It knows its limits, and lives within a wary self-governance.'

14. *Jude the Obscure* (1895), Wessex edn. (London: Macmillan, 1912), 405: Jude's child Little Father Time kills his half siblings and himself, leaving the explanatory note, 'Done because we are too menny.'

15. See Aziza Seedat, *Crippling a Nation: Health in Apartheid South Africa* (London: International Defence & Aid Fund, 1984), 9, citing L. G. Wells, *Health, Healing and Society* (Johannesburg: Ravan, 1974), 3. I am grateful to Colin Bundy for this information. Demographic data for South Africa in the mid-twentieth century are, of course, less than totally robust.

16. *White Writing: On the Culture of Letters in South Africa* (New Haven: Yale University Press, 1988), 15; and see Richard Begam, 'Interview with J. M. Coetzee', *Contemporary Literature* 33/3 (1992), 419–31 (423–4).

17. *New York Times*, 26 Oct. 1999; quoted in Peter McDonald, 'Disgrace Effects', *Interventions* 4/3 (2002), 321 30 (321).

18. SAHRC, *Investigation into Racism in the Media: Interim Report* (1999), quoted in McDonald, 'Disgrace Effects', 323.

19. McDonald, 'Disgrace Effects', 326.

20. This will not always be the case. For a young person on Death Row, acceptance of the necessity of dying might be less likely to express itself in this way.
21. 'Apathy and Accountability'.
22. See McDonald, 'Disgrace Effects', 329, for a subtle reading along these lines.
23. J. M. Coetzee, *The Master of Petersburg* (London: Secker & Warburg, 1994), 83.
24. Ibid. 208. In *Age of Iron* (London: Penguin, 1990), the dog represents our animal condition (pain 'hurling itself upon me like a dog, sinking its teeth in my back'; it is also given a kind of sixth sense for good and evil, in the same novel, 'sniff[ing] out what is good, what evil' (117). On our metaphorical use and abuse of animals more generally, and their right to dignity, see esp. *The Lives of Animals* (1999) and *Elizabeth Costello* (2003). McDonald also notes an intertextual link to the final sentence of Kafka's *The Trial*: K is executed ' "Like a dog!" [his killer] said: it was as if he meant the shame [or disgrace] of it to outlive him.' 'Disgrace Effects', 329.
25. Philip Roth, *The Dying Animal* (Boston: Houghton Mifflin, 2001), 16−17.
26. See esp. *Deception: A Novel* (London: Cape, 1990).
27. Zoë Heller, 'The Ghost Rutter', *The New Republic* 224/21 (21 May 2001), 39−42 (41). 'Seigneurial' is her apt description of Kepesh (ibid).
28. (London: Jonathan Cape, 2000), 339.

CHAPTER 8

1. 'Evolution, Ethics, and the Representation Problem', in Bernard Williams, *Making Sense of Humanity, and Other Philosophical Papers* (Cambridge: Cambridge University Press, 1995), 100−10 (109).
2. But see David W. McShea, 'Complexity and Evolution: What Everybody Knows', in David L. Hull and Michael Ruse (eds.), *The Philosophy of Biology* (Oxford: Oxford University Press, 1998), 625−49, for a caveat on the standard assumption that evolution works from simple to more complex structures.
3. *Human Nature after Darwin: A Philosophical Introduction* (2000; London: Routledge, 2004).
4. 'The Case against Evolutionary Ethics Today', in Jane Maierschein and Michael Ruse (eds.), *Biology and the Foundation of Ethics* (Cambridge: Cambridge University Press, 1999), 276−306.
5. See Williams, 'Evolution, Ethics, and the Representation Problem', and 'Nietzsche's Minimalist Moral Psychology' (1993), in *Making Sense of Humanity*, 65−76.
6. See esp. Ruse, *Taking Darwin Seriously: A Naturalistic Approach to Philosophy* (Oxford: Basil Blackwell, 1986), and *Evolutionary Naturalism* (London: Routledge, 1995); Michael Ruse and E. O. Wilson, 'Moral Philosophy as Applied Science', in Elliott Sober (ed.), *Conceptual Issues in Evolutionary Biology*

(Cambridge, Mass.: London: MIT Press, 1994), 421–38; John L. Mackie, 'The Law of the Jungle: Moral Alternatives and Principles of Evolution', *Philosophy* 53 (1978), 455–64. A concise overview of ethical non-realism can be found in Ruse's review of William D. Casebeer, *Natural Ethical Facts: Evolution, Connectivism, and Moral Cognition* (Cambridge, Mass.: MIT Press, 2003), *Evolutionary Psychology* 2 (2004), 89–91.

7. Woolcock, 'The Case against Evolutionary Ethics Today', 303.

8. It certainly does not license an evolutionary naturalist approach to old age of the 'let the weak go to the wall' kind that might be extrapolated from Darwin's own squeamish glance towards Spencerian social Darwinism in *The Descent of Man*: 'With savages, the weak in body and mind are soon eliminated; and those that survive commonly exhibit a vigorous state of health. We civilised men, on the other hand, do our utmost to check the process of elimination; [...] our medical men exert their utmost skill to *save the life of every one to the last moment*' (my emphasis). *The Descent of Man, and Selection in Relation to Sex*, A Facsimile of the 1871 First Issue, 2 vols. in 1, with an Introduction by John Tyler Bonner and Robert M. May (Princeton, NJ: Princeton University Press, 1981), i. 168. A pure, though not extreme, social Darwinism can be imagined as saying the following about old age: 'life is a struggle for existence, and we must not stand in the way of the forces of natural selection. We do wrongly if we seek to prolong life any further than, by dint of domestication, we have already done. Old age is prey to many infirmities and diseases which are not selected against in nature, and which must, by the laws of evolution, continue to accumulate in our aged populations. Without claiming that we should actively kill off the old (meaning, those past the age of reproduction, which we should define generously to include the care of offspring), we should certainly not be intervening medically to preserve their lives. Nature has deemed that the old are no longer of use to the furtherance of the species; moreover, in many respects they are competing for resources that should properly go to those who are young and still capable of reproduction now or in the future.' A sceptical-realist version of evolutionary ethics of the kind I am assuming has no truck with such an argument.

9. Thomas B. L. Kirkwood, 'Understanding the Odd Science of Aging', review article, *Cell* 120 (25 Feb. 2005), 437–47 (443).

10. See my essay ' "The Unquiet Limit": Old Age and Memory in Victorian Narrative', in Sally Shuttleworth, Jackie Labbe, and Matt Campbell (eds.), *Memory, 1789–1914* (London: Routledge, 2000), 60–79.

11. 'Freud's Theory of Metaphor: *Beyond the Pleasure Principle*, Nineteenth-Century Science and Figurative Language', in Helen Small and Trudi Tate (eds.), *Literature, Science, Psychoanalysis, 1830–1970: Essays in Honour of Gillian Beer* (Cambridge: Cambridge University Press, 2003).

12. Greg Bear, *Vitals* (New York: Ballantine, 2002), 287, 322–3.

13. Cf. Fredric Jameson's reading of Shaw's *Back to Methuselah* (1921). Jameson argues that 'the longevity plot is always a figure and a disguise for that rather different one which is historical change, radical mutations in society, and collective life itself'. 'Longevity as Class Struggle', in George Slusser, Gary Westfahl, and Eric S. Rubkin (eds.), *Immortal Engines: Life Extension and Immortality in Science Fiction and Fantasy* (Athens, Ga.: University of Georgia Press, 1996), 24–42 (32).

14. J. Leeds Barroll, 'Gulliver and the Struldbruggs', *PMLA* 73 (1958), 43–50; Paul Gabriel Bouce, 'Death in Gulliver's Travels: The Struldbruggs Revisited', in Rudolf Freiburg, Arno Löffler, and Wolfgang Zach (eds.), *Swift: The Enigmatic Dean. Festschrift for Hermann Josef Real* (Tübingen: Stauffenburg, 1998), 1–13; Marjorie Nicolson and Nora M. Mohler, 'The Scientific Background of Swift's "Voyage to Laputa" ', *Annals of Science* 11 (1937), repr. in A. Norman Jeffares (ed.), *Fair Liberty Was All His Cry* (New York: St Martin's Press, 1967), 231–3.

15. Clark's analysis of science fiction (much wider-ranging than mine here) shows that this is true of anti-immortality narratives such as *She* or *After Many a Summer* (*Vitals* postdates Clark's book). *How to Live Forever*, 12–15. It is also true of science fiction novels that use the fantasy of age-postponement or age-prevention to allow continuity of dramatis personae over centuries or millennia (e.g. Poul Anderson's *The Boat of a Million Years: Science Fiction and Philosophy* (London: Routledge, 1995), James Blish's *Cities in Flight* series), Kim Stanley Robinson's *Mars* series) and of those which imagine emortality: freedom from illness or ageing by means either of cyborgization or virtual existence (e.g. Iain M. Banks's 'the Culture' series, Greg Egan's *Diaspora* (London: Orion/Millennium, 1997), Richard Morgan's *Altered Carbon* (London: Victor Gollancz, 2002), and Brian Stapleford's 'emortality' series). In the latter case, a more strictly reductionist equation comes into operation between the person and the mind, now imagined as technologically independent of the soma (up-loadable, for example, into a computer then downloadable into another body). I am grateful to John Christie and Andy Sawyer for guiding my reading here.

16. Clark, *How to Live Forever*, 13.

17. 'Evolution, Ethics, and the Representation Problem', 102.

18. There are several good overviews of the current state of evolutionary science of ageing. See esp. Michael Rose, *Evolutionary Biology of Aging* (New York: Oxford University Press, 1991); Tom Kirkwood, *Time of Our Lives: The Science of Human Aging* (New York: Oxford: Oxford University Press, 1999), and Kirkwood, 'Understanding the Odd Science'. And for a succinct overview of all the main scientific theories of ageing, Brian T. Weinert and Poala S. Timiras, 'Physiology of Aging: Invited Review: Theories of Aging', *Journal of Applied Physiology* 95 (2003), 1706–16.

19. This does not rule out the possibility that they also have environmental causes or prompts.

20. *Modern Quarterly* 1 (1946), 30−56 (esp. 43). And see Rose, *Evolutionary Biology of Aging*, 11.

21. Medawar refers to G. G. Simpson, *Tempo and Mode in Evolution* (New York: Columbia University Press, 1944), 183, as one of his sources for this crucial insight into the evolution of senescence. George Williams gives a slightly earlier source in G. P. Bidder, 'Senescence', *British Medical Journal* 2 (1932), 583−5; cited in Williams, 'Pleiotropy, Natural Selection, and the Evolution of Senescence', *Evolution* 11 (1957), 398−411.

22. P. B. Medawar, *An Unsolved Problem in Biology* (London: H. K. Lewis, 1952), 23.

23. Medawar, 'Old Age and Natural Death', 46.

24. 'Pleiotropy, Natural Selection, and the Evolution of Senescence', 406.

25. Ibid. 402.

26. The most extensive experimental studies to date are collected in Michael R. Rose, Hardip B. Passananti, and Margarida Matos (eds.), *Methuselah Flies: A Case Study in the Evolution of Aging* (Singapore: World Scientific, 2004). See also A. R. Templeton and M. A. Rankin, 'Genetic Revolutions and Control of Insect Populations', in R. H. Richardson (ed.), *The Screwworm Problem* (Austin, Tex.: University of Texas Press, 1978), 81−111, and Alan R. Templeton, Teresa J. Crease, and Faith Shah, 'The Molecular through Ecological Genetics of Abnormal Abdomen in *Drosophila Mercatorum*. I. Basic Genetics', *Genetics*, 111 (1985), 805−18.

27. Rose, *Evolutionary Biology of Aging*, 68, referring to Roger L. Albin, 'The Pleiotropic Gene Theory of Senescence: Supportive Evidence from Human Genetic Disease', *Ethology and Sociobiology* 9/6 (1988), 371−82. See also R. L. Albin, 'Antagonistic Pleiotropy, Mutation Accumulation, and Human Genetic Disease', *Genetica* 91 (1993), 279−86. Bruce Charlton's coinage of the term 'endogenous parasitism' offers an interestingly different slant on the idea that '[a]s your life plays out, there is inevitably selective survival of those cell lines that are good at surviving, which unavoidably includes those cell lines that are good at surviving at the expense of the body as a whole'—leading Matt Ridley to conclude that 'Ageing does not need explaining; staying so young does.' See Ridley, *The Origins of Virtue* (London: Penguin, 1996), 30.

28. I am persuaded by George Williams's view that 'the idea that menopause is just a part of human senescence is wrong. It is too predictable and standardized a phenomenon.' (Personal communication.) Cf. the view summarized by Austad, below. Nevertheless, it has played a significant role in debates to date about the processes of senescence, so it is included here.

29. Steven A. Austad, *Why We Age: What Science is Discovering about the Body's Journey through Life* (New York: John Wiley & Sons, 1997), 153−6.

30. See C. E. Finch, *Longevity, Senescence, and the Genome* (Chicago: University of Chicago Press, 1990).

31. Austad, *Why We Age*, 151.

32. Ibid. 152.

33. See Williams, 'Pleiotropy', 407–8; and, for recent support from anthropology, K. Hawkes, J. F. O'Connell, N. G. Blurton Jones, H. Alvarez, and E. L. Charnov, 'Grandmothering, Menopause, and the Evolution of Human Life Histories', *Proceedings of the National Academy of Sciences, USA* 95 (1998), 1336–9.

34. Kim Hill and A. Magdalena Hurtado, 'The Evolution of Premature Reproductive Senescence and Menopause in Human Females: An Evaluation of the "Grandmother Hypothesis"', *Human Nature* 2 (1991), 313–50; C. Packer, M. Tatar, and A. Collins, 'A Reproductive Cessation in Female Animals', *Nature* 392 (1998), 807–11. Recent support for Williams's theory includes Alan R. Rogers, 'Why Menopause?', *Evolutionary Ecology* 7 (1993), 406–20, and James W. Wood, Kathleen A. O'Connor, Darryl J. Holman, Eleanor Brindle, Susannah H. Barsom, Michael A. Grimes, 'The Evolution of Menopause by Antagonistic Pleiotropy', Working Paper 01–4, 2001, <http://www.csde.washington.edu/pubs/wps/01–04.pdf>, last accessed 13 Aug. 2004.

35. For a lucid critical review, see Jocelyn Scott Finch, 'Menopause: Adaptation or Epiphenomenon', *Evolutionary Anthropology* 10 (2001), 43–57.

36. See 'The Tithonus Error in Modern Gerontology', The 1999 Crafoord Prize Lectures, *The Quarterly Review of Biology* 74/4 (1999), 405–15.

37. Kirkwood, 'Understanding the Odd Science', 438–9.

38. T. B. L. Kirkwood, 'Evolution of Aging', *Nature* 270 (1977), 301–4. Revised in subsequent papers, and summarized, for non-specialist readers, in *Time of Our Lives*, 63–80, and in his 2001 Reith Lectures, *The End of Age: Why Everything About Aging Is Changing* (London: Profile, 2001).

39. Kirkwood, *Time of Our Lives*, 68.

40. Michael Rose gives a detailed account in *Evolutionary Biology of Aging*, 127–35.

41. L. Hayflick and P. S. Moorhead, 'The Social Cultivation of Human Diploid Cell Strains', *Experimental Cellular Research* 25 (1961), 585–621; and L. Hayflick, 'The Limited In Vitro Lifetime of Human Diploid Cell Strains', *Experimental Cellular Research* 37 (1965), 614–36. For early criticisms, see E. Bell et al., 'Loss of Division Potential in Vitro: Aging or Differentiation?', *Science* 202 (1978), 1158–63; and Rose, *Evolutionary Biology of Aging*, 134.

42. See e.g. Judith Campisi, 'Cancer and Ageing: Rival Demons?', *Nature*, Review sect. 3 (2003), 339–49; 'Aging, Tumor Suppression and Cancer: High Wire-Act!', *Mechanisms of Ageing and Development* 126/1 (Jan. 2005), 51–8 (51), and 'Senescent Cells, Tumor Suppression, and Organismal Aging: Good Citizens, Bad Neighbors', *Cell* 120 (25 Feb. 2005), 513–22. Also, for a particularly bold (and premature) attempt to marry the cancer control mechanisms and senescence at the level of evolutionary theory, Bret S. Weinstein and Deborah Ciszek, 'The Reserve-Capacity Hypothesis: Evolutionary Origins

and Modern Implications of the Trade-off between Tumor-Suppression and Tissue-Repair', *Experimental Gerontology* 37 (2002), 615–27.

43. The account that follows draws closely on a review paper by Casandra L. Rauser, Laurence D. Mueller, and Michael R. Rose: 'The Evolution of Late Life', *Ageing Research Reviews* 5/1 (2005), 14–32. See also Michael R. Rose, Casandra L. Rauser, and Laurence D. Mueller, 'Late Life: A New Frontier for Physiology', *Physiological and Biochemical Zoology* 78 (2005), 869–78; Casandra L. Rauser, Laurence D. Mueller, and Michael R. Rose, 'Aging Fertility, and Immortality', *Experiential Gerontology* 38 (2003), 27–33; Scott D. Pletcher and James W. Curtsinger, 'Mortality Plateaus and the Evolution of Senescence: Why are Old-Age Mortality Rates So Low?', *Evolution* 52/2 (1998), 454–64; Brian Charlesworth and Linda Partridge, 'Ageing: Levelling of the Grim Reaper', *Current Biology* 7/7 (1997), R440–R442.

44. See Rose, *Evolutionary Biology of Aging*, 170–1, for a fuller description.

45. E. Lew and L. Garfinkel, 'Mortality at Ages 75 and Older in the Cancer Prevention Study. (CPSI)', *Cancer Journal for Clinicians* 40/4 (1990), 210–24.

46. B. Charlesworth, 'Patterns of Age-Specific Means and Genetic Variances of Mortality Rates Predicted by the Mutation-Accumulation Theory of Ageing', *Journal of Theoretical Biology* 210 (2001), 47–65; and Rauser, Mueller, and Rose, 'Evolution of Late Life'.

47. For an attempt at an explanation from within cognitive psychology, but drawing on autobiographical writings and literary materials, see Douwe Draaisma, *Why Life Speeds Up as You Get Older: How Memory Shapes Our Past*, tr. Arnold and Erica Pomerans (Cambridge: Cambridge University Press, 2004).

48. But see pp. 54–6 above on Aristotle and teleology.

49. *On the Origin of Species*, A Facsimile of the First Edition, with an Introduction by Ernst Mayr (Cambridge, Mass.: Harvard University Press, 1964), 188.

50. Michael R. Rose, personal communication, 21 Sept. 2005.

51. S. Jay Olshansky and Bruce A. Carnes, *The Quest for Immortality: Science at the Frontiers of Aging* (New York: W. W. Norton, 2001), 60.

52. I have remarked on the potentially misleading use of 'ageing' and 'senescence' to describe not only the general deterioration of the body or specific organs or systems within it over time, but the loss of replicative potential and associated functional changes within cells. (Campisi, 'Cancer and Ageing', 340.) The two processes may be causally linked, but that remains to be proved, and the use of the same words to describe macro and micro processes is in danger of encouraging a strongly pre-emptive answer to an open question. There are occasional caveats in scientific papers against that happening (Hayflick's is one), but many more cases where it goes unnoticed.

53. See M. R. Rose and B. Charlesworth, 'Genetics of Life-History in *Drosophila melanogaster*. I: Sib Analysis of Adult Females' and 'II. Exploratory Selection Experiments', *Genetics* 97 (1981), 173–85, 187–96; and in greater

historical, theoretical, and mathematical detail, Rose, 'Antagonistic Pleiotropy, Dominance, and Genetic Variation', *Heredity* 48 (1982), 63–78, and Rose, 'Life-History Evolution with Antagonistic Pleiotropy and Overlapping Generations', *Theoretical Population Biology* 28 (1985), 342–58. Rose summarizes: the concept of antagonistic pleiotropy, though not the term, 'is fairly old...It is vaguely in Darwin's *Origin*, and then resurfaces in more genetic form in the writings of Sewall Wright, [B.] Wallace, [E.] Caspari, etc.' (personal communication, 3 May 2005).

54. I have not been able to trace its first usage in evolutionary biology, though the concept is vaguely there in Darwin. The *OED* locates the first usage in any context as coming from hydraulic engineering in 1961, and only subsequently from economics in 1968—though this is surely too late. (Indeed, the citation given refers to 'the old argument of the "trade-off" between inflation and unemployment'.) No biological application is cited before 1976, and then the reference is to wheat farming, not evolution. *OED*, 2nd edn. (Oxford: Oxford University Press, 1989).

55. In later work he too uses the now standard language of adaptive trade-offs, while also continuing to use the language of price and expense. See George C. Williams, *Plan and Purpose in Nature* (1996; New York: Phoenix/HarperCollins, 1997), 1740.

56. The partial exception is prudentialism, where the term 'trade-off' does arise as a description of the kind of reasoning a prudential chooser adopts in distributing scarce resources across a lifetime; e.g. Daniels, 'The Prudential Life-Span Account', 261: 'I should pretend that I do not know how old I am and will have to live through all the trade-offs I impose at each stage of my life. For example, I know that if I give myself too much acute health care when I am dying, I do so at the expense of other services, e.g., long-term care services'. This is, however, obviously not an explanation of why old age happens or what its value is to us or what effect it has on a life, but a second-order description of how we provide for old age.

57. 'Understanding the Odd Science', 445.

58. Weinstein and Ciszek, 'The Reserve-Capacity Hypothesis', 615–27 615, 624.

59. 'Aging, Tumor Suppression and Cancer', 51. See also Campisi, 'Senescent Cells', 513–22.

60. First published in *Areté* 2 (Spring/Summer 2000), 53–61; repr. in *The Lemon Table* (London: Jonathan Cape, 2004).

61. This summary draws on the factsheets produced by the Alzheimer's Society, <www.alzheimers.org.uk>, last accessed 17 Apr. 2005.

62. Recent evidence suggests that some people maintain a very high level of cognitive and reasoning function despite advanced age-related disease of the brain. The *New Scientist* recently reported the case of a retired lecturer and chess player who had all the physical signs of Alzheimer's on autopsy but had shown no signs of dementia when tested by a neurologist, and was still playing high-level chess

two years before his death. (He himself noticed signs of impairment, however.) Lisa Melton, 'How Brainpower Can Help You Cheat Old Age', 17 Dec. 2005, <http://www.newscientist.com/channel/health/mg18825301.300.html>, last accessed 15 Feb. 2007.

63. See, *inter alia*, Norman Daniels, *Am 1 My Parents' Keeper? An Essay on Justice between the Young and the old* (New York: Oxford University Press, 1988), 5–6; Betty Friedan, *The Fountain of Age* (London: Jonathan Cape, 1993), 32.

64. (1992; London: Vintage, 1993), 5–6.

65. Recollections of the Bette Davis line differ. The most common is 'Old age is no place for sissies.' 'Bette Davis: The Official Website', <http://www.bettedavis.com>, last accessed 15 Feb. 2007.

66. This criticism seems to me slightly misexpressed given the sensitivity of the scientist in question. Ignatieff's concern is surely rather with the contrast between the scientific method and the philosophic method—but Vendler is right that the danger of schematization is there.

67. 'Death of a Soul', *New York Review of Books*, 20 Oct. 1994, 9–13 (13).

CONCLUSION

1. 'Replies', *World, Mind and Ethics: Essays on the Ethical Philosophy of Bernard Williams*, ed. J. E. J. Altham and Ross Harrison (Cambridge: Cambridge University Press, 1995), 185–224 (186).

Index